CROSSING MORE KARMA ZONES: THE FAMILY ODYSSEY

"George Douvris is a dear friend and neighbor here on the Island of Hawaii, also known as the Big Island. If one were to read Crossing More Karma Zones without knowing George and his family, I am sure that he/she would agree that the book is a fascinating adventure story. George and Stephanie not only lived this adventure but decided to raise their children in the midst of the adventure with them. The narrative of the adventure is articulated with humor, irony, and insight into a new paradigm. To know George, Stephanie and their children however, tells another story that continues into the present. In his books, George and Stephanie divulge what they learned about utopian communities, utopian food preparation and consumption, utopian music, and now have devoted themselves to applying what they have learned to create a model of the best they experienced in their countless adventures. To experience the community the Douvris family are presently creating underlines the narrative in his books. George Douvris' books are investigations into alternative, sustainable, and ultimately blissful expressions of this thing we call life and human culture. Importantly, he has inspired his children to embrace the wonderful diversity gleaned from a life far removed from ordinary conventions and motivated John and Ariel, Nicolette, and Sophia to join with he and Stephanie in creating a community that offers the best of technological innovation without impacting nature and integrates a lifetime of very special experiences into their vision of what can be done in the real world. The power of a book is to me the motivation that comes from learning new things. Learning new things is important. Manifesting new social and political models from what we learn however, completes the cycle. I strongly recommend George Douvris' books to anyone looking for an insider's view of the richness that exists outside the square, narrow box that so many exist in. Having seen firsthand what George and his family are creating, I strongly recommend that you purchase his books. To create utopian models requires financial resources. Buying this book will provide the Douvris family with the means required to manifest this amazing vision gleaned from a lifetime of serious inquiry. So, buy and enjoy this amazing journey as I have and support the ongoing efforts of creators of future utopia." Harvey 'Marty' Martin

HARVEY MARTY MARTIN is a prolific writer, world renowned holistic health practitioner, musician, alternative consciousness researcher and hands on director of a sustainable farm on the island of Hawaii.

∽∾

"CROSSING MORE KARMA ZONES is the incredible story of a Greek odyssey, but it is one that Homer would never have been able to write. George Douvris keeps his readers enthralled as he takes them along to visit historical and mythological sites, and to experience the highs and lows of modern travel. There is sacred euphoria here, but also violence, poverty, theft, and death. Yet above everything else, this is a remarkable family drama and how a family grew closer together while each member embarked on his or her personal journey."

STANLEY KRIPPNER is an American psychologist, parapsychologist, and an executive faculty member and Professor of Psychology at Saybrook University in Oakland, California. Formerly, Krippner was director of the Kent State University Child Study Center and director of the Maimonides Medical Center Dream Research Laboratory, Co-author PERSONAL MYTHOLOGY, Co-editor VARIETIES OF ANOMALOUS EXPERIENCE

∽∾

"A worthy successor to the well-received first volume of George Douvris' autobiography. Wonderfully readable, and a noteworthy document of the Sixties generation, which once aspired to be forever young and is now passing into old age."

CARL FREEDMAN is the Russell B. Long Professor of English at Louisiana State University and the author of many articles and books, including THE AGE OF NIXON.

∽∾

"CROSSING MORE KARMA ZONES" "THE FAMILY ODYSSEY" is an account of a family's entertaining, exciting, and at times bizarre adventure tirelessly wondering across the globe searching for their paradise. The author is reflective, always objective, and is consistently sincere in his conclusions of the people and places he and his family encounter.

The pace of their "odyssey" is stunning itself, they travel and intimately explore many corners of the world in an amazingly short time, experiencing ideologies and cultures that reflect some of the oldest traditions and religious practices as well as the "new age hippie" culture and all of its various cults, gurus, and spiritual/religious practices.

The author treats all of these experiences with the same steady hand, never shrinking from his purely objective truth so we are blessed with a reliable account of where, how and when he has encountered the pure spiritual vitality that he relentlessly pursued or the more predictable ugly raw disillusion of false piety that has always infested our world.

While the ODYSSEY details the family's perpetual wonderings, the reader is gifted with a nonfiction, in depth, exploration of culture, religion, traditional, contemporary and new age spiritual practices.

The author, intentionally or not, exposes them all to be hopelessly flawed and human while he finds beauty and purity inadvertently in mostly places he wasn't expecting it."

ED THIELK is the owner of MANA FOODS, the best and longest operated health food store in Paia, Hawaii. He also is a deep thinker and world traveler.

"Born into a traditional Greek family and raised in Raleigh, North Carolina, George Douvris became a world traveler early on. With his wife Stephanie and their three children, he explored his Greek homeland first, then ventured into wider domains — Fiji, Maui, Holland, the Czech Republic, Austria, Thailand, Bali and elsewhere. He explored not only the geographical world, but his own mind as well — marijuana, LSD, Ayahuasca, mushrooms, DMT and other substances. Outwardly and inwardly, George and Stephanie indeed became geographical and psycho-spiritual Odyssian travelers, ultimately settling in an alternative community on the Big Island of Hawaii. Crossing More Karma Zones is a fascinating biography appropriately subtitled The Family Odyssey. Exciting, informative, and adventurous — highly recommended."

LEE UNDERWOOD is a well-known musician, author and poet. His most recent book of poems is entitled DIAMONDFIRE. Underwood became an internationally well-known music journalist. He contributed interviews, essays, and record reviews to various notable periodicals such as DOWN BEAT, ROLLING STONE MAGAZINE, and the LOS ANGELES TIMES. He served as the west coast editor of DOWN BEAT from 1975 to 1981.

❧⁓❧

"The Douvris family's trek across a global canvas is filled with strokes of fun, adventure and surprises. If you want to read a highly entertaining, engaging and thoughtful story of family life, take a ride through the pages of this well written map of stories that everyone will enjoy."

CHRIS DYER, world famous visionary artist and author of POSITIVE CREATIONS.

❧⁓❧

"An epic hippie styled Swiss family Robinson travelling family, looking for that illusive homeland, which ends up being where you are from anyways. A very good read."

PETER TERRY, NAMBASSA founder and events coordinator of a series of hippie-conceived festivals held between 1976 and 1981 in New Zealand.

❧⁓❧

"What George Douvris has done in writing an autobiography is such an inspiration to me! I think we should all do this! I think of all the stories that died with the passing of my parents, and how much I wish I could go back and document every possible detail.

I hope to join George in this wonderful effort and write my own story one day. I hope you'll do this too, for our own memory's sake and for the future generations who will wonder 'how did we get here!'"

RUSSELL RUDERMAN is a state senator representing the Puna district of Hawaii. He is also a successful businessman operating several health food stores as well as lead guitarist in several bands including Terrapin Station which covers many Grateful Dead songs.

"It is hard to pinpoint exactly why I like this book so much. Perhaps it is because George and his family so easily join with other people in different countries on different continents at different times in their lives with goodwill, appreciating the happy times and taking the often difficult times in stride.

Perhaps it is because they are truly world citizens and thus feel that they are members of whatever group they are with. Whatever life lessons there are in this book and, there are many, none are moralistic. All come from examples of how things actually can be made, if not better, at least understandable. What I came away with is an awareness what it is like to have lived a life fully and actively yet kindly. George did and still does oppose the stupidity, the cruelty, and the injustice that prevent the world from being a better place, but he never makes the other into the enemy. That maybe is the deepest reason I so enjoyed this book."

JAMES FADIMAN is an American psychologist and author of THE PSYCHEDELIC EXPLORER'S GUIDE. He is acknowledged for his extensive work in the field of psychedelic research. He co-founded the Institute of Transpersonal Psychology which later became Sofia University.

"Almost no one who lived through the transformations of post WWII America, including the psychedelic era and beyond, has taken the time to accurately chronicle that entire period of history as it was actually lived and felt by them. In this second volume of his autobiography, George Douvris has once again done an impressive job of recounting his adventurous life in extravagant detail. It seems unlikely, now that corporations have supplanted humans as citizens and their subservient historians hold center stage, that the human race will ever recover the boundless optimism, compassion, personal empowerment, material wealth, and naïveté of that era, which now seems a million billion miles from where we are today. Yet it will be gratefully recognized by those who shared similar journeys, and will provide a valuable record for future historians wondering about the bygone Age of Humanity. If you are able to take time out from the busyness of life, this book offers companionship on the quiet road favored by lovers of delightfulness."

SCOTT TEITSWORTH, Author of LIBERATING OURSELVES,THE PATH TO THE GURU, and KRISHNA IN THE SKY WITH DIAMONDS

"The 1960's have taken on mythic status, for very good reason. The decade was a time of extraordinary cultural revolution, changing music, art, dress, language, politics, and generally busting loose from the constraints of the Eisenhower era. In his first book Crossing Karma Zones, George Douvris captures the broad sweeps and the nuances of this revolutionary period in US history, from the vantage point of a hippie, war protestor, and savvy observer of people and their behaviors. In this sequel Crossing More Karma Zones we are taken from George's upbringing as a Greek American, to his travels with his wife and children throughout the Pacific Isles, Greece, Europe, and various parts of India in search of a "new homeland". His always wide perspectives evolve through the spiritual landscape, Woodstock, psychoactive drugs, and the many diverse expressions of a decade busting loose. Both books Crossing Karma Zones and Crossing More Karma Zones cover more than the 60's, but that decade serves as a hub, connected to all the other spokes of events and people. With a keen observer's eye and an intact conscience, Douvris makes Crossing Karma Zones a fun and insightful account."

CHRIS KILHAM, author of MEDICINE HUNTER, international facilitator of natural healing workshops.

CROSSING MORE KARMA ZONES

THE FAMILY ODYSSEY

George Douvris

ISBN: 152392313X
ISBN 13: 9781523923137

PREFACE

In case you haven't read the first book of this autobiographical narrative, CROSSING KARMA ZONES- THE JOURNEY BEGINS, I would encourage you to do so. The book is a fun and reflective romp across time and space which covered my formative years growing up in North Carolina during the 1950's and 60's, and then my eventual move to San Francisco as well as hints of more travels and epic experiences ahead. The adventure included growing up in a Greek-American family, dealing with racism, becoming an anti-war activist, the psychedelic revolution (including of course the fabled "drugs, sex and rock and roll" lifestyle), Woodstock, Haight-Ashbury, college life and more. As the first book ends, another part of my life starts where I fall in love with my significant other Stephanie with whom we are still enjoying a wonderful romance after nearly 40 years two-gether. Book one can be considered our BC years (before children) and now the journey continues around the world with our children in what we call a family odyssey.

Old age, as I am learning, often is bruised with faster moving time and diminishing memory. A situation that might be explained because us elders have a lot more information to remember and be stewards of. But even though I might have forgotten some facts and details and might not even remember what I ate yesterday, the stories are all true and the lessons still being processed. Stephanie, however, is making sure through her marvelous editing that all those details are in order and that my terrible spelling gets corrected.

And as in my first book, I dedicate this sequel to my beloved wife Stephanie and my three children John, Nicolette and Sophia. In covering such a large area of time and space, I also wish to apologize to dear friends that might not be mentioned in the stories. Remember that even though I might not remember the sequences, you are all very present in my heart and between the pages.

DEDICATION

This narrative is a chronicle of adventures and reflections of our family searching the world for a "new homeland". Many people around the world were part of the journey and mentioned in this book. And as to the many friends that I might have overlooked, I apologize as there were not enough pages to fill it all in. Yet none are overlooked or forgotten in the journal of my heart.

People have many reasons for writing their autobiographies. Certainly leaving a record for one's children, grandchildren, and anyone else that might have interest in reading it is reason enough to do so. In my case, I also found in writing this book a map of looking at my past as a key to better understanding who I am now. When we are caught in a particular moment, we sometimes lose the context of an overview that comes with a retrospective perspective. Not to succumb to revisionism of past experiences is an important factor to watch out for in such an analysis however.

My life has been challenged as well as enriched by the many opportunities that I have been presented. My relationships to friends and family have been an integral part of my landscape and if any way any comments in this book seem painful or embarrassing, I apologize. My context of interpretation has always been in flux depending on circumstances or personal awareness.

Of course, a special dedication goes to my parents who I had many struggles with but I would like to feel at some point I was accepted in their hearts and their perspective of my life-style appreciated or at least better understood.

Another loving dedication goes to our three wonderful children John, Nicolette and Sophia whose lives were in many ways influenced by where we lived around the world. They are forever travelers together in my heart and soul.

And my deepest dedication goes to my wife Stephanie who has put up with my excesses and with whom I have been on a honeymoon of bliss since we first met in the mid 1970's. She has been my beloved partner and best friend on this journey of one peak experience after another.

"I need a miracle every day" is not only a melodic line from a Grateful Dead song but also represents a very important and precious reality for me. Yes, I do have a miracle every day, and that is my relationship with my wonderful, beautiful and loving wife Stephanie. Besides being my lover and best friend for over 40 years, she is also the main reason for the successful journey of life for our family. No matter where we would be in the world and foreign the languages around us, she always provided us with a feeling of comfort and security. Whenever something would go wrong our kids would always say with confidence that "mommy fix." Whenever a home or car repair is needed, she is the multi-talented gem that understands the problem as well as the solution. Her well grounded personality keeps my hot headed idealism from flying off the handle as well as providing the consistent energy in supporting all the family projects. Even though I am on the internet every day, it is my wife who provides order to any display of digital madness that frustrates me and proves that no high tech machine can outwit her innate talents of comprehending owner's manuals and repairing unruly machines. Whenever anyone in our life has been sick, it has been her healing touch which has brought back the smiles. My feeble memories for numbers has been compensated by my wife's impeccable memory and precise accounting skills. Even this book would not have been possible without her adding the beautiful pictures she took of our global meanderings, as well as her patient editing skills. With total devotion, I proudly declare my unending love for my radiant goddess Stephanie.

ACKNOWLEDGEMENTS

With so much movement between time and place, this book has taken quite a few years to complete. Although life still goes on, I would like to say that I have reached a solid space of grounding to be able to write about my life from my birth in 1951 to now in 2014.

My fondest acknowledgement is to my wife, best friend and ultimate goddess Stephanie who has been helping me with the book editing and technological needs that my left-brain has problems in being able to navigate. She also has been a clear reminder of specific dates to my chronicles that my own memory has been foggy about.

I also want to acknowledge our son John and our daughters Nicolette and Sophia. Our crisscrossing continents and "karma zones" were at times quite unsettling but hopefully there were residual benefits from the scenery and experiences along the way. Our correspondence school was one long field trip across the world and a homeopathic dose of different cultural traditions, beliefs and behavior. Wisdom often needs experience to compliment knowledge and for that I feel they benefited. Still not having a place to call "home" and having to nervously come up with an answer when asked "where are you from" was not easy for them. Hopefully they learned the lesson that home is where the heart is and wherever they were, they were always very much loved and at Home.

The beautiful family odyssey portrait photo on the cover and our family photos were provided by our daughter Nicolette. You can see more of her photography on her Facebook page:
www.facebook.com/wilddragonphotography

INTRODUCTION

As a sequel to his first book Crossing Karma Zones, the Journey Begins, George continues his very interesting and engaging travels to even more places around the world. Along with his wife and three children they embark on a family odyssey in search of a new homeland. Leaving their home in Hawaii, they take George's 92 year old mother back to her ancestral home in Greece where they stay for eight years in a small and very traditional village. Their experiences and reflections are at times happy, sad, comical, horrible but always exciting. After many years of living in Europe, India, Thailand, Fiji, Bali, Australia and New Zealand their quest eventually brings them back to Hawaii where they finally call home.

George John Douvris is an author, journalist, social media activist, educator and story teller who is happy to live a simple off grid life along with his wife and family. His adventures in alternative places and dimensions of consciousness also have enriched his vision of a compassionate and environmentally sustainable world.

The only son of Greek immigrants, he grew up in Raleigh, North Carolina, where he witnessed racial injustice firsthand. He graduated from the University of North Carolina, Chapel Hill, with degrees in psychology and political science. He met his wife, Stephanie, in San Francisco in 1975 and were married in 1978. Along with their 3 children John, Nicolette, and Sophia, they have traveled the world together and have lived in such widespread locations as the Hawaiian island of Maui, the mountains of Montana, and a village in Greece.

Douvris has been a holistic health educator and a radio presenter. In his newsletter Links by George, which reaches over eighty-five hundred people, he shares his views on shamanism, spirituality, environmental causes, political conspiracies, health, and music. He and Stephanie currently live on an organic farm on the Big Island of Hawaii.

CONTENTS

CHAPTER THREE: NEW TRAVELS ACROSS AMERICA

CHAPTER FOUR: HAWAII PART ONE

CHAPTER FIVE: FIJI

CHAPTER SIX: BALI

CHAPTER TEN: BEYOND GREECE

CHAPTER ELEVEN: HOLLAND

CHAPTER TWELVE: THAILAND AND BALI REVISITED

CHAPTER THIRTEEN: RETURNING TO GREECE

CHAPTER FOURTEEN: HAWAII ONCE AGAIN

CHAPTER FIFTEEN: GREECE FINAL CHAPTER

CHAPTER SIXTEEN: CONTINENTAL DRIFT

CHAPTER SEVENTEEN: INDIA

CHAPTER EIGHTEEN: NORTH THAILAND

CHAPTER NINETEEN: THE BALI VILLA

CHAPTER TWENTY: AUSTRALIA AND NEW ZEALAND

CHAPTER TWENTY-ONE: AUSTRALIA, FIJI, NEW ZEALAND
AND AUSTRALIA AGAIN

CHAPTER TWENTY-TWO: ENDINGS AND NEW BEGINNINGS

CHAPTER ONE

GREECE 1991

Early in the year, we decided to spend some of the money we earned from selling our house in Hawaii into organizing a three month summer trip to Greece. I purchased several of the budget travel guides to the country and started intense study to organize the "perfect itinerary" with intention of providing a wonderful experience for everyone in the family. Eventually I condensed all the pertinent information into one travel notebook and proceeded to plan a day by day guide including the color coding of places to travel, where to eat, sites to visit, transportation information and so forth.

Considering the possibility of a long stay, I also felt it was important to also apply for Greek passports and thus expand our options. Even though both my parents were born in Greece, the procedure for obtaining dual-citizenship was quite a chore. I needed to obtain ours as well as my parents birth certificates, marriage in a Greek church certificates, baptismal and much more. With perseverance, I managed to obtain all that was requested but in order to complete the application, I needed to personally go from Montana to the nearest Greek Embassy which for us was 2000 miles away in San Francisco.

Not leaving any room for error, I bought my Greyhound bus tickets and off I was to the west coast. The trip itself was quite an unforgettable witnessing of Americana's cultural shadow-land. The derelicts, drunks and mumbling psychos on the bus were not especially menacing. But when one of the rednecks pulled a knife on a young black man, I made sure to keep my eyes wide open. The incident was taken care of by the driver calling ahead to the highway patrol who flagged down the bus and arrested both of the loud mouthed antagonists. After a few hours of drowsy rest time, I was startled by a scream that broke out from a woman in the back of the bus who was yelling for help as a very obese looking guy was trying to fondle her breasts. Apparently they did not know each other, so it became necessary for the driver to call cops and have the guy taken away at the next bus stop up the road. After both these exciting incidents, it felt a bit boring for the rest of the ride until we pulled into Portland, Oregon.

For several hours since the last rest pause, I needed to go take a pee. Arriving in the big city bus station meant relief at last. However, stall door after door that I opened found me looking at a homeless person's camp adjacent to every toilet. Not discouraged but definitely in need to find a bathroom fast, I ran outside the station but no necessary facilities were in sight. Thus an empty lot had to suffice and before the bus departed I was back on again and on the way to San Francisco.

It had been a few years since I had been back in the City and I wasn't quite prepared for the changes in people's attitudes that I noticed upon arrival. I had rented a small room in a downtown hostel and in my walk towards the Greek Embassy, not one person that I smiled at returned it back. And the few times I said hello, people looked at me with mild terror and suspicion of my motives. I reflected on to my memories of a friendlier San Francisco in 1969 and glad that I had been living in more pleasant social milieu of Hawaii and Montana ever since.

My reception at the Greek Embassy was in itself another weird experience. Assuming that since I had all their required papers notarized and in order, I would be finished within the hour and on my way back on a (hopefully different) bus ride to Montana the next day, it was frustrating to now be set back again. The agent in charge was a typical macho, irritating bureaucrat with no reason to hurry to expedite my trip back to my family. Not relying on computers, every line on every page that I handed him was cross examined with long pauses for his cigarette and coffee breaks. After four hours of waiting in his office while he wasted my time, he finally announced that my paperwork was appropriate except for one detail. My mother's birth certificate had her name listed as Despino while her marriage certificate stated Despina. In Greece, both spellings are considered appropriate but because of this insignificant point, the consulate agent told me that our passports could not be finalized. At that moment, the nightmare and fury of his announcement left me speechless and totally disoriented. But being a Greek bureaucracy, I also believed there had to be a solution. Greeks in such positions usually point out a terrible fact but go through some classically heroic stretch that comes up with a way around the problem and for which they expect great appreciation (and often monetary reward) for their brilliance. In my case, he told me what I had to do was to find an old person in Greece to verify that they knew that my mother was indeed the same person by that name and to have the affidavit signed and sent to the Embassy. So with faith that he would be able to pull it through, I left him the copies of all the paperwork we had completed and returned back to Montana. A lot of time for me to reflect, worry and even sleep on was welcomed relief, as on this ride back, no rapes, assaults, fights or even flat tires presented themselves. And I made sure to use the bathroom whenever I had a chance along the way.

The weeks passed and with a smile of appreciation, our Greek passports showed up in the mail one day. And by researching Greek travel agencies in New York, I had found some very low priced tickets to Greece whose journey would start by taking us to Raleigh where we could pick up my mother, then to New York and on to Athens. I felt a little nervous about the tickets as the travel agent didn't send them as fast as he promised and with only a few days before departure, I contacted an attorney in New York that called the travel agency to make sure the tickets would be sent. Even though we ordered them two months earlier, they showed up in our hand by courier just three days before we were to leave. A close call to a blunder that would have been too difficult to rebound from. So again the usual goodbyes to friends and neighbors, my mother blessing the house and off we went.

New York was the next step of craziness. The airline carrier we were traveling on was TWA which by then had been reduced to one step from bankruptcy and was offering cheap seats on charter flights in its struggle to survive. Remembering the bankruptcy of the charter flight we once took from Hawaii, I prayed that it wouldn't happen again. By the looks of the passengers waiting with us, it was obvious that we weren't a very high end group and so all expendable possibilities were in my mind. Looking in the street outside our terminal, I could see a family from India leaving their luggage in front of a taxi stand and a moment later a car of teenagers zipping by and grabbing their belongings off the curb before they even had a chance to react. Welcome to America as we were about to depart to our own unknown future soon.

The flight itself was long and what made it both interesting as well as a nuisance occurred when on board came twenty young men who had been working in the US and were now on their way to their home in Turkey. All during the trip they kept going to the bathroom area to smoke cigarettes and then would try to pinch many young ladies and boys that walked by them in the aisle. At one point one of these guys asked for the pretty stewardess to come over to where he was sitting and lay in his lap while he showed her his big wad of twenty dollar bills that he wanted to buy her with. I'm not sure what her plans were in Istanbul, but for now she politely shrugged him off with a smile.

Once we landed in the Athens airport we weren't hearing English being spoken, but our Greek lessons had proved rewarding as the kids were delighted to be understanding the basics of what was being said. And having been familiar with my mother and other Greek families in the US, they felt quite at home with the new mannerisms and the more emotional intonations of this new land.

YIASAS ~WELCOME TO ATHENS

Waiting to meet us at the airport was our long time family friend Spiro, whom I had a wild time once before in Athens on my 1970 trip and who a few years afterwards had come to stay with us for a summer in Raleigh. He now was much more sedate and "mature" than the time we visited cabarets and brothels together, but still he was very positive and fun to see again. Common sense seemed clear that it would be impossible for the six of us as well as all our suitcases to fit into his small automobile that looked like it had just enough room for four passengers and a couple of shopping bags. Yet Spiro would not hear any of our offers to pay for a taxi to carry what he could not fit. With quick motions he tied the suitcases on the roof and as seat belts were not yet mandatory, we were able to fit snugly inside. It also was a preview of the determination, self confidence, and at times hardheadedness of the many people we would be meeting in the next few months. In about half an hour we arrived at his house where we met his wife and daughter and enjoyed the hospitality they provided while we were in Athens.

As most of the people we would meet on our trip, they were very impressed on how my kids, unlike most other Greek-Americans, were

4

able to speak the language and even have the idea that one day we might want to come with my mother along to live long term in the country. Being a spoiler, every time we suggested our plans, my mother would cut in and say that we should drop such stupid ideas and be eager to get back to the US to make money and be more respectful citizens. And in every such case, people would be totally confused with her opinion as the dream of most people that left Greece was to one day come back to retire close to their ancestral roots.

During our stay in Athens, we also visited several other family members who all knew me but none of them seemed very familiar. One cousin was a young teenager that I had climbed the mountain behind our house in the village on my earlier trip. He now was married with a couple of children and was a borderline alcoholic but very hospitable.

On a couple of the days that my mother stayed at Spiros house talking with his wife, Stephanie, I and the kids went on our explorations of the city. The Acropolis and the ancient sites of the area provided an awesome feeling of the depth of western civilization while all the smells of food coming from the restaurants was also expansive in gastro-consciousness. The sprawling flea market was a never ending source of treasures and the National Museum was the real deal of even more impressive art and statues of antiquate. Not to mention the first easy access bathroom with a flusher that we found in the city. The first pitfall of our trip unfortunately happened that evening when my mother had her hand smashed when Spiro accidentally slammed the front door of his car on it. A painful memento that she would have to carry for the rest of her life.

At the time we arrived in Greece, there was a war going on between the US and Iraq, and the Greek government was not allowing US warships to use its port in Athens as a staging ground to what seemed like an unfair invasion of a harmless country. Among the ways that the US countered the Greek decision was to promote stories in the media that Greece was "unsafe for American travelers" thus hurting the local tourist economy. For us, it was a beneficial situation because prices for rooms, food and services were lower and thus our money could go further on our trip.

When we entered the country, we were quickly informed by the US Embassy that we register our contact information so we could be "evacuated if need be." Since Greece was the friendliest and safest places we had ever been to, not only was the idea of leaving ludicrous but when we looked at the fine print of the warning, it stated that it would cost us $5000 each for the evacuation service. Such extortion diplomacy is not even worth laughing at its fear based lies, so we happily tore up the embassy's offer and went on with our glorious journey.

ON TO THE VILLAGE

One particular sight in Athens that we visited required riding a small train to the top of a high hill that had a 360 degree panoramic view of the whole city. As soon as we got off on the top, a short shifty eyed man with a camera came up to us and started taking our pictures. Right afterwards he gave us a sales pitch that if we paid the price, he could mail the photos to us anywhere in the world. My retort in Greek of saying we weren't interested was a surprise to him, and then when my wife told him that apparently he didn't have any film in his camera, the shocking expose led to his quick disappearance act before we called the tourist police.

On her previous trips to Greece, my mother had always arranged for a taxi driver whose roots where in the village and serviced most of the returning natives back to Xirokambi. This time around, we changed the routine and took the public bus which gave us a chance to not only enjoy the lovely scenery, but to also listen in on people's conversations so as to get a better reference point on what to expect ahead.

The Isthmus of Corinth provided an impressive rest stop which gave us a chance to walk out on the bridge that divided the country. We also had a firsthand experience of having to pay a nickel to a lady sitting outside the bathroom in exchange for her handing us a few sheets of toilet paper. I'm not sure if she had a career job, but it did serve a necessary function in society. And as our stomach also wanted to discover new experiences, we were happy to go the bus station restaurant and eat fresh cut potatoes fried in olive oil and seasoned with sea salt and oregano. Such would be one of our regular inexpensive meal choices over the next few months which, along with other fine tasting food, could be eaten not just at restaurants. Even gas stations would often have a little old lady in the back room slicing potatoes and cooking pots of pungent smelling delicacies which along with homemade wine would be served at a table in front of the shop. What a wonderful new culture we were experiencing in this foundation landmark of western civilization.

As the bus ride was taking us into high mountain valleys, out the window we saw ancient ruins, castles, monasteries and shepherds with their flock of sheep. But inside the bus, the gabbing of gossip and listening to monotonous Greek pop music was not as pleasing to the senses. Finally we came to the hub city of Ancient Sparta which also served to tie my own family roots and provide clues to their associated attitudes. Ahead, lots of pleasant looking shops and tavernas that we would soon be visiting, but for now, our most important need was to use the bathroom. The facilities at the Corinth bus station however were far more plush than the ones here. We were directed to a closet size room with a hole in the ground that looked literally "Spartan" and as if it hadn't been cleaned since Alexander the Great's time. Instant constipation saved us from any major distress, so we moved on to our next need which was to get on a local bus that would bring us to Xirokambi. The twenty minute ride took us through several small villages and past lots of churches which brought on a competition among most of the old ladies on the bus as to who could make the most signs of the cross in five seconds. My mom was feeling quite at home in doing this ritual but for me, I found my attention going to the exotic looking young ladies getting on the bus with high heels and short tight dresses. The look was seductively Gothic but still all black in compliance with the favorite color of the region which to the older crowd signified suffering and death from previous wars and for mortality in general.

Just like I remembered it, the family house still looked the same but was missing my grandmother who used to sit on the front porch eager to greet any of us in the family arriving back from America. We were, however, warmly received by the family that had been renting the house for a number of years from my mother. Although we weren't going to be staying here on this trip, we were greeted with lots of hugs, kisses and food from the husband, wife and two kids as if we were all long time friends. I'm sure the sentiment was genuine, but over time when I learned that they were only paying fifty dollars a month rent for a two story house, I sensed that they also were nice to us as being landlords whom they didn't want to have their rent raised to a more appropriate and contemporary fair price. But all in all, we felt the house was in good hands and Taki, the husband, invited us out later for a wood fired pizza at the town square. Perks are meant to be enjoyed, so we took him up on it and enjoyed one more fine meal that night. But then again, on our whole three month stay in Greece, not one meal was less than wonderful.

Our home base for the next few months was in a small village next to ours called Kaminia. My mother, just as her brothers, were born there and we were set up in an empty house that belonged to another relative that happened to be living in Canada at the time. The kids were already having a wonderful time in the country and now the experience of riding a donkey which our cousin brought to the house along with a bicycle for the kids to use while here. But as I had a trip planned that would cover about 3000 miles of the mainland and over twenty five islands in the next few months, we were happy that my mother had a comfortable niche here while we planned to do a lot more than just relaxing in one spot.

PANAYIOTIS

One of the few people in the village that I considered a long time friend was Panayiotis. We had met and played together on my first trip to Greece with my parents when I was about seven and again on my 1969 visit, we had shared some nice times together. He was an excellent musician and enjoyed playing and singing folk and Rembetika music that expressed the sounds of freedom. Also he had liked 1960's rock and roll, so over the years I would send him cassette tapes of Santana, Hendrix, Rolling Stones, Doors and other such groups. Besides playing music at local festivals, he would usually pick up his guitar or clarinet and play late night at the local taverns. We attended a few situations where the food and wine would keep coming and our friend would play until either he passed out close to three in the morning or stumbled his way home.

Panayiotis was also a professional house painter and handy man. Once the long term rental contract of the tenants upstairs in our house was to be over, he wanted to move in and promised to not only pay a higher rent but also would do improvements on the house on his own. Since we were planning to come back to Greece in a few years as permanent residents, we were happy with his offer as we knew the house would be in good hands and that when we returned,

8

he would move on to stay elsewhere. A few years later when we were again in the US and started organizing for our move, my plans for Panayiotis to stay in the house were sabotaged. My mother and her brother Chris did not want us to come back to Greece and concluded that if we didn't have a house available, we would be blocked from such plans. Along with Panayiotis mother, they had the bizarre notion that our friend would turn the house into a brothel and a den of drugs and wild music. So without asking us, they found another family to move into the house and pay only $85 a month rent with a long term lease that they thought would keep us out. What happened afterwards is another story which I will save for later when I talk about our follow up trip to Greece.

I would like to make a comment though about the irony of their worries that our house would fall into a state of depravity. In talking to some of the old timers in the neighborhood, they told me that in the 1920's and 30's, the bottom floor of our house was a Rembetiko music cafe where men would come to smoke hashish in water pipes, be seduced by young belly dancers and listen to the sounds of bands and my grandfather's enchanting clarinet playing. So basically our intention had traditional roots and would have been given the blessings of my dearly departed and fun loving grandfather Leonidas.

FUNERALS

Funerals are always major events in the villages. Everyone sitting in the town square is invited to at least a drink of cognac, coffee and a cookie and most are also expected to come to the free meal provided at a local restaurant. A system both civilized, affordable and unlike how in the US lots of money has to be paid for various state health law requirements. Not costing the thousands of dollars as it does in America, village funeral costs were here just a few hundred dollars which goes to not only feeding everyone in the village but also some of the money is set aside for the church and the gravediggers. With so many old people in our area, I suppose some folks have funeral calendars so they can plan when to go for the free food feasts that are in loving memory of the departed soul.

One day we were driving through a nearby village and paused for a coffee break. Once we realized we were in a funeral situation, it would have been rude on our part if we didn't partake in the meals

9

what was freely being given us. The host family was insistent in fact that even though we never had met the dead person, it was still right for us to stay and eat. But when I went up through the greeting line to offer my condolences to the surviving family members, I was nearly thrown out for not saying the proper words to them. Since I was not familiar with the appropriate phrase which means "May God forgive his sins" and because I did not thus say it correctly, I was looked at as a dumb tourist who should just eat fast and leave the devotees to their rituals.

SHROOMS

Sitting on our outdoor veranda would mean not only swatting flies but also it was a chance for us to catch up on gossip from relatives and friends coming down the road. Among the regular passersby's was a friendly man and his wife that would wave and smile as they would ride by on their tractor on their way to work as well as back home again from their fields. We hadn't seen them for a few days when we learned the sad news of their bizarre death. Every year around this time, their family would pick wild mushrooms from the same spot as they always had and after cooking them up with garlic and onions, would enjoy the tasty meal. This time around however, after eating their seasonal feast, the man, wife and three of their children all died that night from a painful death caused by their food. Anti-mushroom talk spread throughout the village and people were pronouncing how they would never eat fungi again. But upon my reflecting and learning more about the situation, I found out that the particular field where they picked their mushrooms had been recently sprayed with the Monsanto pesticide Roundup. Up till then all the farms in our area had been organic and pesticide free. But now because farmers were promised a higher yield if they used modern agricultural methods that included the use of pesticides, this man had earlier covered the whole area with this poison. Mushrooms have a remarkable power of pulling toxins from the soil and in this case they had absorbed the pesticides which wound up in the fatal family meal. The witch hunt should not have been against the mushrooms but against the Monsanto chemicals that the farmers were all now starting to use and killing themselves slowly and, like for this unfortunate family, sometimes more quickly.

About the same time that these deaths occurred, we learned of another strange and horrifying death to a lady that was a close friend of my mother's. It seems that one morning while her husband was away taking care of their fields, she went to use their primitive outhouse and while sitting on the toilet, the floor collapsed and she fell into the sewage pit where she eventually drowned to death. One more terrible reminder that "shit happens". (My apologies to her departed soul for the joke.)

SOCCER

On most Sunday afternoons, we would be able to watch the local soccer games in the big field right next to our house. Teams from the region would show up not only with their friends, family and fans, but also with their own village priest for support. During the tense moments of the game when tempers flared, pushes were exchanged and obscenities came out of player's mouths, the priests would run out in the field to restore some sort of moral order. But there were those occasional moments when priests from both teams would run up to each other and accuse each other's teams of cheating. I'm sure in another culture they would be opposing shamans exchanging curses instead. But as they were still Greeks, once the games were over, the players would hug each other and start sharing their wine and invitations to dinner. Such would be a fine example for the rest of the world to make peace together by and breaking bread not heads and bodies. The only person that was not that interested in the soccer games was my mother who would be reading her holy books and yelling at the players to keep away from her water hose when they wanted a drink to refresh themselves. She also would yell at the players to make sure they didn't kick any balls into our garden. Perhaps she had a better view of the game than we did.

ROCK THROWING

As was common in traditional societies around the world, people that are not as fully mentally competent as the norm are not be put away in institutions like they do in the US, but can be cared for as regular members of the community. Behind the soccer field was a small hut that was built for one such person named Christopher. Christopher was about sixty years old and had no immediate family

11

still alive to take care of him. Some people would offer him some light work to do in exchange for food and other necessities. As long as he took his medication he seemed to be okay. One day we heard him screaming in the road in front of our house at every passing car that came by. Perhaps he wasn't crazy at all and could see the menace to society of these noisy fossil fuel guzzling vehicles. When we saw him actually hitting a few of the cars with rocks as they swerved to avoid running into him, we decided to call the cops.

Our village had a one room police station but we hardly ever saw the two officers outside of its premises. Once we noticed one of the cops trying to give a ticket to a bus driver who drove his bus the wrong way on the one way street leading into town. The driver looked at the ticket and then threw it back at the cop. On this occasion, as we called for help with Christopher, cops reply was that they could not leave the police station unattended. They further told us that they were not psychologists and that we should either tell him to take his medicine or to call a priest to have a talk with him.

As it turned out, there actually was a divine intervention of sorts. On the second floor balcony of the house in front of where Christopher stood trying to smash passing cars, the mentally ill big bearded priest of the neighborhood was sitting on his deck wearing nothing but his underwear and priest hat while holding a holy book and chanting vespers. Upon seeing Christopher's antics, the priest yelled at him with a deep voice telling him that he was sinning by being a nuisance to the priest's chants. Hearing a voice from up high, he must have thought God was yelling at him from the sky and so he proceeded to run all the way home. Instead of the blind leading the blind, this situation was a case of the mentally ill helping the other mentally challenged.

MY FATHER'S VILLAGE

High up on the Parnon Mountain range east of Sparta was the ancestral village of my father called Zarafona. It used to be a major all day production to get to the village, but with the building of modern roads, it now was closer to four hours driving time from Xirokambi. My dad's sister was still alive and lived with her husband, daughter, son-in-law and three kids in a village about half way there and one of the family members had driven down early one morning to take us up there for a visit. Being the family that my father's mother had said pushed her down the stairs and crippled her, I was a bit tentative for our going there, but I knew as she was my aunt, an obligatory need to visit her was warranted. And besides that, they had promised to take us up the mountain to Zarafona as well.

Anticipating us to be regular Americans, they had prepared a meat based lunch in order to make us happy. When we told them we were vegetarians and preferred "peasant food" a peculiar break-through surprised us. The younger part of the family went to the kitchen to eat the meat dishes while we sat with my aunt and uncle in another room who were extremely delighted that our diet was closer to what they usually ate. So we feasted on delicious fried potatoes, salad, wild greens, and their home made wine, olive oil, olives, wood fired baked bread and cheese. Once we had our coffee and dessert we loaded up on the rear trailer of their son-in-law's tractor and headed up the rest of the way to Zarafona. One more town remained to be passed and as five of us riding in the back of a tractor was illegal, once we entered the city limits, we got out of the trailer and walked the few blocks across the village and where picked up again on the other side of town to continue our ride.

The village of Zarafona was in a picturesque high mountain for-est setting. The air felt cleaner and crisper than where we were staying in Xirokambi which was down in an agricultural valley. My childhood memories of having stayed here before were not as impressive as how much I enjoyed exploring my family roots now. Our first stop in the village was to my father's ancestral home. In this small two room stone house there lived ten people at one time. My grandparents, my father, three brothers and four sisters. My dad used to tell me how the kids would look through the crack when their father, even though with one arm, would regularly make love to his wife. The legend was that the town spring had certain properties which helped enhance longevity as well as masculine virility.

Right after my aunt started crying over nostalgic memories, she mumbled that I should deed over this house to her as a nice family gesture. My confusion was magnified when out of a small stone home next door, a very short old lady came out and dragged me over to tell me that she was a friend of my family and not to listen to anything my aunt said. Her story was that my aunt was a thief as well as a liar and that my father had given her a lot of money as a wedding gift as well as

13

the family land of about ten acres up the hill. With this secret of hers making sense, I decided to be evasive on anything else my aunt asked of me.

While my aunt and her family where visiting some old friends in the village, Stephanie, the kids and I strolled to the town square. The street appeared abandoned but a door opened to a small cafe where the proprietor served us some coffee and sodas. Since my mother had told me many times that I would never find any more relatives here, I took a chance and asked if he knew of any Douvris family still around. Quite startled at my question, he asked me who I was and who was my father. He then disappeared for a few minutes and not much later, about twenty people showed up from all directions to come talk to me. Not only were there a lot of Douvris cousins that I never knew still living in the village, but also quite a few people came over to kiss me out of deep respect for my father. When he had emigrated out of Greece, not only was he mailing regular cash each month to his mother and sisters, but also to many of the poorer people of the village as well. Hearing these stories brought tears to my eyes as well and taught me one more higher level of respect for my father.

With the hour getting late and another four hours to get back home, we caught up with my aunt and back down the mountain we went. Before leaving I made many promises that I would return. But since the village priest came over to meet me, we agreed to first have a look at the village Byzantine church which they said was built nearly 1000 years before. The icons on the wall still had some color on them and the images were amazing, including dragons and half human half animal figures. Much more intrigue into the village of my roots and reason to come back again soon.

Realizing that driving in Greece could be a hazardous endeavor, our intentions were to only ride on public transportation or by local taxi. But once we saw that at least traffic in the small village areas like where we were staying were no more risky than taking a left turn on a busy San Francisco street, we rented a car one day in Sparta so we could take a ride back to Zarafona again by ourselves. This time around we had more chance to talk to people that knew my father as well as to even meet a few cousins I never even knew before. One of my first cousins Thomas was an all around handy man that liked to help people and also to get drunk on his wine and go singing in the streets. Another first cousin who lived most of the time in Chicago invited us up to his very nice new home with a panoramic view where we enjoyed his hospitality. He also showed his workshop where he built guitars and a local musical stringed instrument called a bouzouki. A delight for us to meet a family member who also used to be in a Rembetika band with his brother, which was the style of blues music popular at one time in Greece.

Besides the cousins, I heard a dramatic follow up story about one of my father's brothers Elias who had died at an early age. As a young man he and a young lady in the village were very much in love. The girl's father decided to arrange a marriage between her and an older man who was the village priest. During the wedding, Elias charged into the church, grabbed the girl and together they fled and hid in the mountains. Eventually the police found him and forced the girl to come back and marry the old man. Elias fell into depression and died soon after. I found out that the girl was now an old lady and was living alone in the village. She rarely came out and the story was that she too was miserable after that incident. Excited by what sounded like an epic movie plot with perhaps Johnny Depp playing the part of my uncle, I picked some flowers and took some chocolates we had to her house. But I suppose she realized what had passed could never be as she chose not to come out to meet us. We left the flowers and candy at her door in any case as a message from a past memory whose love together was eternal.

ISLAND BOUND

As nice as our village and the landscape around was, we only had three months for our trip and to experience the thousands of miles of sights that still laid ahead in our travel plans of where to go and what to see. Our six months of travel preparations had given us a good step by step plan of how to go about maximizing the experiences. First we were going to start with the islands south of the mainland and then up the Aegean Sea on the east and after returning back to the village, proceed to visit the western Ionian islands and finishing with a tour of the northern mainland mountain region. The trip would understandably be a rush with at times less than a day to explore some of the islands along the way. But the plan was for maximizing our exposure and with the economy in our favor, now was a perfect time to travel as much as possible.

About twenty miles south of our village was the port town of Gythion where twice a week a ferry boat would make an eight hour trip to the large island of Crete. Half way there was an island called Kithera where we could stop over for the day and then catch another boat for Crete the day after.

Once we arrived at the Kithera harbor, we asked at the first cafe that we came to about any recommended taxi drivers that could give us a tour of the local sights. Such was a working procedure for many places on our trip and we were soon to be quite satisfied. Besides beaches and ancient sites, our driver was eager to showcase many other beautiful places as well. When we told him the only thing we missed in Greece was an island with a waterfall, he pleasantly shocked us by taking us to a nice waterfall where we all enjoyed a refreshing dip. When we told him that we were interested in churches with old icons, he took us up high on a hill to a monastery that had beautiful 800 year old sacred paintings. And when I told him my surname was Douvris, he took me to a family who had a beachfront home and whose name was Douvris. It turned into quite a wonderful homecoming as the husband turned out to be another cousin on the family tree and who knew my father's side of the family very well. This particular man had emigrated to Australia where he and his wife had a flower nursery and had now retired to grow flowers here at their home in Kithera. Without much of an argument, we stayed the night at their house and after a nice breakfast the next morning caught the boat to Crete.

CRETE

Crete is the largest island in Greece and in some ways can be considered a separate country. People there have a different way of talking, mannerisms and feisty independent spirit. When we disembarked in the harbor, we took a few photos and found a comfortable room in a nearby pension. After enjoying a sunset of pink and violet colors in the sky, we took a walk back to the same harbor area later where we couldn't believe that our eyes were looking at the same place that we had been earlier in the afternoon. As we would learn over the next few months, Greece comes alive at night with colored lights and festive spirit. To this day, that view of the port of Hania is one of the most beautiful bays we have ever seen, and would hope to return again in some other lifetime.

Because of its large size, we separated the ten days of our visit on Crete into three different sections of the island. If we had more time, I would have liked to have seen the famous caves on the far side where in the mid to late 60's, hippies from all over Europe, including the folk singer Donovan, had come and lived there in a tribal paradise. But even so, there was plenty to see and never a dull moment.

Our first destination was the Samarian Gorge which is thirteen kilometers long and would require a few hours for us to hike to the end of the trail and then spend the night and return the next day with a boat ride back to Hania. To get to the start of the trail required a two hour bus ride across some hairpin mountain turns. The driver seemed quite skilled at navigating through the narrow one lane village roads but we did worry at one point when he got into a macho game of "chicken" with a motorcyclist. After being passed by the motorcycle, our driver took a long drag of his cigarette, flicked it out the window tough guy style, then stomped on the accelerator and not only passed the motorcycle on a blind curve but also forced it to spin off the road as well. Such was our first taste of Cretan mindset. At least the bus driver made a call at the next pay phone he found to tell the police to come help the motorcyclist who had a bad accident.

At about the halfway point, we were driving through a typical mountain village, but were forced to stop by a smiling elderly man standing and waving at us in the middle of the road. Once the driver opened the door to ask what he wanted, he nonchalantly came aboard with a large tray of glasses that he proceeded to fill from his bottle of homemade liquor called raki. Since it was his 95th birthday and as was the tradition, everyone that came through his village that day was to be treated to a drink. On the bus was a couple of German tourists that were panicked by the notion of this unexpected pause and demanded that the bus had to be on schedule. They kept pointing to their travel brochures which did not mention a stop in this village. But the old man kept insisting that they have a drink as well, which they liked so much that they asked for seconds. The bus driver too was getting tipsy and put on a Greek dance music tape on his stereo. In a few minutes, most of the passengers were dancing in the aisles and listened to the old man say that he had outlived two wives already and was ready for a new one. He didn't care about age or looks just as long as she had a few teeth left. So now that the bus ride had been transformed into a party, the remaining journey was even more magical, as we all waved at the birthday boy and promised to look for a mail order wife for him. I'm sure if he could have waited a few more years, the internet could have hooked him up with the perfect match.

The gorge itself looked straight out of an award winning photo in National Geographic magazine. The narrow trail went straight along a river bed with tall peaks on both sides and reminders of how some tourists had drowned when heavy rains brought flash floods that trapped them in the turbulence. We looked to the skies and as we saw no clouds and historically no measurable rain had ever fallen in this area during June, we felt safe to proceed. Stephanie and John carried the backpacks while Nicolette was riding comfortably on a high quality kid's pack on my back. We were walking briskly enough with occasional stops to take photos when in back of us I heard some loud mumbling demanding we get out of the way. A group of German tourists with their big hats, short pants and expensive looking hiking shoes put me in a precarious position of almost falling down a hill which would have been a bad accident for Nicolette as well. In my anger, I yelled back at them the Nazi expression "Sieg Heil" in reference to their aggressive marching. The air then felt thick as they came to a halt, turned around and loudly shouted "What did you say?" Not holding back my temper, I launched my own explanation of how their movements almost caused my daughter and myself a serious injury and that they should be a little more courteous. A few huffs and puffs later, they got back into their fast stride to get to somewhere without even looking at the beauty of where they were.

After staying the night at a party oriented beach campground, we caught the small boat and by early afternoon we arrived back in Hania and left early the next day for the big city of Heraklion which was located in the middle part of the island. Walking to the bus station, Stephanie was carrying a small bag of trash in search of a container to dispose of it. Not having found one, as we were getting on the bus the driver reached out his hand to politely take her bag, we felt that he was going to place it in the trash can next to his legs. Instead he tossed it out the window and showed us yet another example of Cretan disposition.

The main attraction near this city named after Hercules was the cave where Zeus was supposedly born and also the Palace of King

Knossos. The cave would have required a rugged hike, so we settled for just touring the impressive palace that still had part of the original paint on the columns 3000 years after it was built. Quite a testament to the architects of that time as well as the natural dye paint they used.

The last part of Crete we visited was the tropical eastern side that was referred to as "little Hawaii". Although it lacked the waterfalls and lush mountains of its Pacific Ocean sister city, the beach was beautiful and the coconut palms all along the perimeter did give it an exotic appearance. Tropical fruit such as pineapple was also evidenced as were very thin bikini bottoms and tanned upper body parts wearing nothing except gorgeous views of nature. Before leaving this village of Agios Nikolas, we visited the church which was the namesake of Nicolette and in fact most of the people we met here were named either Nikos or Nikoletta. There was also a nice night market where I purchased a leather belt for my pants which still works well 24 years later at the time of this journal entry. As was our mission to keep moving on, we next caught a boat that left from this easterly port to the island of Rhodes later that night.

ISLAND HOPPING

Rhodes was as impressive in beauty as when I had previously visited the island on my 1969 trip. The main change I observed was that the hippies and backpacking youth element was now replaced by casinos, expensive cars and people dressed in formal clothes and opulent jewelry. There were reasons enough for us to consider moving here such as access to culture, beaches, forests and modern medical facilities, but the attitude of elitism would be a nuisance. Before leaving the day after we arrived, we did enjoy the hike to the "valley of butterflies" where we experienced these magnificent angels and also a few waterfalls along the way as well.

The next island we visited, Samos which was situated between Rhodes and the shores of Turkey, was lush and had a nice mix of Greek and Middle Eastern influence in architecture, food and art. Our taxi driver took us to all sorts of scenic spots including a very nice waterfall and the impressive temple of Hera. Perhaps it was the presence of the divine feminine or the influence of the coiled snake skin we found on its mosaic floor, but that was the night we calculated that our next child was conceived. For us at 40 years of age, this unexpected surprise and for that gift into our lives we would name her Sophia. Not exactly a name calling that would make my mother happy after not having our first daughter named after her, we decided in order to keep peace in the family to name her officially Despina-Sophia and gain illumination from both sacred namesakes.

The enchantment of the temple and the wonderful local wine which we drank with our dinner had us in especially high feelings that night. Maybe we could also attribute some of the conceptual alchemy coming from making love under the ecstatic Dionysian energies as well.

Nearby Kos was another surprise in many different ways. Not being as heavily touristed as the other Dodekanisan Islands in this region of the Aegean, here we were able to enjoy a slower rhythm of life which was also expressed in the relaxed and content energetics of the local people. We enjoyed our sightseeing and coming to admire the island's main attraction which was the tree where the famous Hippocrates once taught natural medicine over 2500 years ago. Today's physician's take the Hippocratic Oath which means to never prescribe anything that can harm another and to not care about personal gain as much as healing. Although it still sounds like the correct path, I tend to believe that what happens today is more of a "hypocrite oath" than the idealized intention in the wording.

While sitting in the town square meditating on this great man and his influence where something totally unexpected happened. I went to get an item out of my backpack and found the zipper open and my precious travel notebook missing. Having taken six months to organize travel notes that were like the perfect guide to our Greek expedition, I was devastated and went frantic. Now how would we find the right places to visit, cheap hotels to stay at, where to eat, bus connections, etc.. Almost on the verge of tears from this blow, I dramatically perked up and started laughing. The wise healer Hippocrates could well have snatched the book so that I would be free to enjoy a more spontaneous trip without having to rely on such prescribed directions. In some way I was now healed and confident without the need of my book crutches. One more hug of the ancient tree in gratitude and off we went on our brand new and freer journey.

Sailing away from the Turkish currents and slightly north, we now came to the island of Naxos. Very few tourists, nice beaches, extensive forests and lots of marble. In fact, at one time, most of the statues and temples of antiquity, such as a large statue of Apollo greeting ships in the harbor, were chiseled from marble coming from the many quarries located here. Besides the history and scenery, we also enjoyed the deep hearted friendliness of the people we met as well as their delicious food and wine.

Next stop was the island of Santorini. Although it was an island of much tourism, we still found unspoiled beaches with hardly anyone on them and magnificent views of the landscape carved by the volcanic eruption thousands of years ago which gave the island its unique beauty. Instead of staying in a room and since we were carrying a tent that we intended to use at some point anyway, we checked into a private campground located in a woodsy area right next to a nice beach.

All was pleasant enough until we learned how camping in Greece was different in some ways to what we had been used to in our previous experiences. First of all, Greek families don't believe in camping without what they consider "proper appearance". Along with their mandatory loud generators to power a television, stereo and bright lights, the wives keep sweeping the front of their tent areas while staring at the other wives to see who has a cleaner looking habitat. When it's time to eat, it's not sandwiches and chips, but full course meals on fine china and wearing fancy clothes. It was humorous to observe the Greek style but later that night we were to see that the Germans were even more of a nuisance. All during the night we would be hearing them chug beers, talk loudly and play un-tuned guitars. Adding to the makings of a sleepless night, there was even a disco on the campground where young tourists and local guys wanting to pick up tourist girls would also be stomping till nearly dawn. However, before we left Santorini, we were able to enjoy our hike up to the ancient city of Thira which encompassed several acres of remnants of an ancient civilization which some scholars consider to have been the mythic Atlantis.

Our next stop was the famous island of Mikonos. It's signature windmills looked just like the postcards but for the rest of it, we were eager to leave on the next boat heading to Athens later the same day from seeing some of the worse aspects of Greek tourism. Obnoxious rich people floating on their yachts, loud young couples making out in the town squares and drunks in front of bars from the night before still puking. No signs of intelligent life forms anywhere.

Pretty close to Mikonos we got off the boat for a two hour tour of Delos before the next boat stopped en route to the mainland. This whole island is like an open air museum with long stretches of statues and temples from thousands of years ago. Feeling culturally enriched after our exposure to Mikonos, we left with a smile and lots of photos.

THE IONIAN

Just after a quick stopover in Athens, we were riding a bus that would take us four hours due east to Patra. Seated behind us was a young guy who kept mumbling that the people who drew the maps of Greece were all part of a conspiracy to make people think it was a smaller country than what it really was. With a little more volume in his voice he went on with his monologue explaining if it takes 15 hours to drive on a highway from the farthest north to the lowest southern part, why is the map so disproportionately smaller. Most people at this point were laughing at him, but after listening to his analysis, I felt that he had a point and should have been listened to more seriously.

Patra is not only the biggest city in the southern part of the country referred to as the Peloponnese, but also a major harbor for boats heading for Italy and to the emerald islands of the Ionian Sea.

We first did a quick walking tour of the sprawling downtown section of the city which took us past the many fancy shops, nice smelling restaurants, busy cafes, historic castle, and even one of the largest churches in the country, Saint Andrew's Greek Orthodox Cathedral. The mural on the ceiling that portrayed the story of creation was quite fascinating as was also our standing in line to kiss the top of a glass case that housed the skull of the saint himself. I made sure to kiss it twice for good luck for the rest of our travels. Too bad I hadn't been here to kiss it twenty years earlier when my Aunt Stamata passed away and left her house on top of the hill to her boyfriend instead of anyone in our family.

A short ferry boat ride from Patra took us to the island of Cephalonia. Although it was one of the largest Greek islands, it did not have much of a tourist infrastructure thus leaving large tracts of forest relatively undeveloped. We enjoyed taking a small boat tour of a large cave that opened to a turquoise lake and afterwards a bus tour to a monastery reputed to have another famous saint's head to kiss. While John and I were looking to find free opportunities for the conventional monastic hospitality of bitter coffee and stale cookies, one of the older nuns directed us down a cellar where she said we would see the site where the saint had died. While walking through the narrow dark room, we didn't see any remnants of the saint but we did notice enough live rats to prompt our climbing out of the underworld. To our shock, someone had closed the trap door that we had come down through and we were essentially locked in. Our banging on the door and screaming didn't do any good, but a few minutes later someone came and opened the door and let us out. When the rest of the bus tour had boarded and the driver was about to take off, Stephanie kept insisting in broken Greek to wait because her husband and son were missing. A bit of investigative work came up with the fact that the senile nun had forgotten we were still down in the dismal basement and had locked the door for the day. Breathing the clear air of relief again, we made sure to run to the relic box of whatever body part of the saint it held and gave it a kiss of thanks for the miracle of our escape. I suppose if we had been left there till we died, future tourists could have assumed we were the saints and given us the kisses instead.

As the enchantment of the islands was encouraging us to consider an eventual permanent move, we would sometimes mention to locals our interest in buying land. In the case of this island, a realtor came to meet us and besides giving us a tour of the area which he had land for sale on, invited us to be his guests for the night at his house and also treated us to dinner at a nice restaurant owned by his brother-in-law.

The next Ionian island that we hopped off on was Zakinthos or as it was known to posh European travelers, Zante. As we were coming into the port, we were impressed by the high green peaks of the mountains which reminded us a little of Hawaii. But unlike the US, as soon as we got off the boat we were met by lots of people trying to talk us into renting a cheap room in their house and also the delicious smells of eating establishments in all directions.

Our plan was for a one day scenic tour and then back to the mainland the next day. But while we were sitting in a cafe going over our maps, our attention was drawn to an eccentric artsy hippie sort of young local guy who was wearing bright yellow sun glasses held together by a candy lollipop stick. He was eager to meet us and after his paying for our drinks encouraged us to ride with him in his open roofed Volkswagen car called "The Thing" to pick up some friends of his in the harbor and afterwards go back to his beach house for a party. Figuring it would be fun, we agreed and soon we were riding with a few more hippies from Athens that had come to visit our new friend. Obviously this guy was living in multiple realities as when we came to a stop sign, he refused to drive any further because it didn't say he could do so. After a few minutes of being stuck in this glitch, one of the other kids jumped out of the car with a magic marker pen and wrote the word GO underneath the STOP letters and thus the car was mobile again.

As it turned out, our friend's family owned a large amount of land on a beach and he was eager to share. He invited everyone for a party at his house and for whoever wanted free land, he was glad to sign papers giving away ownership. Not wanting to be left out, we had our deed signed as well and felt the miracle of kissing dead saints heads at the various monasteries must have been working. Too bad a few weeks later when we called the phone number he had placed on our deed, we were told by one of his family members that yes, his family did own all that land but our friend was crazy and did not have the right to give it away. A bit dejected, we weren't quite sure if we should stop putting our hopes in dead saints heads or keep on doing so until we found one that specialized in manifesting free real estate.

Back on the mainland, we planned our return to Xirokambi by heading first to the ancient town of Olympia. It was here that the Olympic Games were first held and also a place where lots of thefts would happen from the museum that housed many beautiful statues of antiquity in a poorly guarded outside meadow which was also the site where the games used to take place. The town itself had a prosperous look and the cafes were busy with both Greek and foreign tourists. While going over our map and anticipated plan to take buses across the country for the next few weeks, our conversation was overheard by a young taxi driver who politely introduced himself and offered us an option which was too good not to accept. His proposal was that since even he himself had never visited all those places in the northern part of the country that we were talking about seeing, if we just paid for his gas, cheap room and occasional meal, instead of taking buses, he would drive us in his comfortable Mercedes taxi. Not only

24

would that save us time but it would not even cost as much in the long run and also take us to sights that a bus wouldn't. Not having to twist our arm too much, he agreed with the extra request that we take my mother along as well. Since she herself had never seen these scenic spots of Greece, we felt it would enhance her own appreciation of her homeland.

Throughout our trip we would sometimes pull into a village and a few of the old timers would come up to chat with us about their travels and working in the US and other places abroad. Once a guy told us if we ever go to New York City to ask around about his cousin Vasili and tell him hello from the village. In their minds, America was about the size of Sparta. A more common conversation would revolve around people asking us where we were from. If we said Hawaii, they would think we were saying Ohio. And usually when we said we were from America, they would ask if we lived in New York, Chicago or Toronto. These being the three most common places that Greeks had emigrated to besides the ones that went to Australia, Canada or Germany.

TAXI RIDE ACROSS THE COUNTRY

True to his word, Triantis Triantofilos (which means three flowers) showed up in front of our house one day with his freshly cleaned Mercedes taxi ready to take us on a two week ride across Greece. My mother was being her usual stoic and stubborn self refusing to come along. We all pleaded with her that it would make us feel happy that we could give her this gift of a scenic experience of her country. Even her cousin and neighbors were just as stubborn telling her that she shouldn't even think twice about it and get in the cab. And as she let it be known that she wasn't going to pay a penny for this trip, Triantis opened the front door for her and we gave her a pair of sunglasses to wear and off we went on our multi thousand mile expedition of varied experiences.

The first place to explore was the Byzantine castle town of Monomvasia hovering over the southern coast about an hour's drive away. The Templar Knights that had gone on the Crusades during the Middle Ages decided that instead of taking the wealth they stole from the Ottoman Turks back for the Pope's treasure chest in Italy, they would be better off staying here, building a fort and creating their own mini-feudal kingdoms. Examples of which we would find all over Greece. The castle that we visited was still in excellent shape and much of it had been converted to apartments for German owners that wanted to live in castles and feel as if they were kings themselves. To accommodate these folks, there were many cafes, shops, restaurants and musical events taking place in the various levels of the building. The only part missing was the moat and armored soldiers.

This part of the country is referred to as Mani and I believe the word maniacs has its origins here as well. My mother's family was from these parts and now I could understand her genetic temperament better. The landscape was dotted with stone homes that looked like mini-fortresses with narrow windows. I assumed that from here the residents could shoot at invaders such as pirates and Turks, but what was explained to me later was that the shooting did happen, but not at whom I thought. These villages were notorious for family feuds of mainly neighbors shooting at their own neighbors and sometimes even relatives. Thus, I concluded a historic connection to the Mafia of southern Italy as well as to an old legend that the original vampires lived here before they were chased away to Romania. In fact, many family names were Drakos which translates to Dracula. One gas station even had the name Drakos on it, so we made sure that we didn't buy our gas after sunset and that it was black and oily instead of bloody red.

Nearby was the famous caves of Dorou which required going on a guided boat through the subterranean lake to see the natural formations up close. The 45 minute ride took us through much natural beauty but the fact that besides these eight miles of the caves that had been opened to the public, another twenty remained which was still not open where archaeologists had found evidences of humans as well as remnants of temples. As a final note, many geologists had traced the caves to the top of Mount Taygetos about fifty miles away and at a 7000 foot level. Much unknown and amazing history remains that we can never be sure of and can only guess.

As the windy road east took us past the rocky terrain and into greener fields and healthy looking olive tree patches, we also saw one white sand beach after another with hardly anyone on them. We also were impressed when we stopped in Aeropolis and saw a castle that had been converted into a hotel which was called Pirgos (castle) Kapetanakos. That being my mother's maiden name, she explained that this fortress belonged once to her great grandfather. On our tour of the facilities, we mentioned this fact to the reservations desk in case they could offer a free room for such an honored family representative as my mother, but they declined, so off we went to find a cheap room for the night elsewhere.

Getting closer to Ancient Olympia which was where our taxi driver was from, he was proud not only to point out to us beautiful beaches on the coastline but also lush mountain scenery to encourage us not to get stuck buying land on a remote island when we could have a better situation by purchasing some land here instead. But as we had our mind set on finding a picturesque island setting for our future holiday home, the sensibility of what he said did not dawn on us at the time.

Back for a meal in Patra and an overnight stay gave Stephanie and me a chance to wander through its many side streets where we found a variety of live music playing along with a festive nightlife. As hectic as most big cities in Greece presented themselves in the day, by evening time frustrations would transform into a social atmosphere of passion and laughter. By now however, Triantis was getting a little more frustrated with my mother's nagging and complaining (mostly about us and her misconceptions about our lifestyle) which was not showing signs of relief either in day or night. Overall though, no signs of mutiny on our crew yet, so we crossed the bridge that divided the two halves of the country and continued north.

One of the most important surprises of our expedition was Lefkada. Unlike the rest of the Greek islands, it was connected to the mainland by a simple drawbridge and thus was not dependent totally on summer tourism as desperately as other places. There was always an ongoing flow of people which included more mature travelers in contrast to the party animal teenagers looking for the all night club scene of nightly barfing and daily drinking again. Lefkada had white sand beaches, traditional arts and crafts, sturdy mountains, and delicious smelling restaurants and thus became the top choice in our mind for a place to one day perhaps be living on.

Crossing back to the mainland, we proceeded north towards the Albanian border. On a high mountain pass we stopped to enjoy the refreshing springs and clean air of the village of Metsova. Then down the valley to the large but very attractive city of Ioanena which was nestled between the mountains and an adjacent beautiful lake. Because of its university, many intelligent looking young students were in the town squares and lots of night clubs were provided for their entertainment. One of the specialty foods of the city was baked fresh frog which was caught in the lake and considered a delicacy. As much as Triantis tried to make us eat a bite, we held our vegetarian ground and even my mother refused to eat any either.

Afterwards, we rode on a boat to the middle of the lake where we visited an old fortress which belonged to one of the ruling Turkish governors who eventually was beheaded by orders of his own emperor for embezzlement. He must have lived a happy life until then though as we saw paintings depicting him with a hookah hash pipe in the midst of his very large and gorgeous harem.

One more sight before leaving was the wax museum which was built in a large underground cave a few miles out of town. Walking behind us on the tour were two obnoxious teenage boys that kept making fun of all the statues of the heroes of the Greek War of Independence from the Turks in 1821. Not being able to restrain myself any longer, I finally turned around and told them that they should be more respectful of these men and women who sacrificed their lives for their freedom. My sentiments were also shared in a more aggressive tone by another person in line which totally silenced these kids from yapping any more.

What most tourists don't realize is that Greece is a very mountainous country and that each of its regions has its own unique historic and cultural essence. As we traveled east into the central part of the country, we felt that we were on sacred ground. The town of Meteora can easily be included as one of the remaining wonders of the world. About eight giant meteor shaped mini mountains stand in proud and mysterious display with monasteries located on the top of each. At one time, hermits and monks moved here to get away from the material world. The only way to get up these cliffs was by one of the monks above throwing down a rope and then being pulled up in a bucket. Today, the buckets and pulleys are just there for display as roads and trails have been carved for the monks to chose between temptation, isolation or various blends of both.

In our many monastery visits, I would often get into discussions with the monks or nuns about the corruption of materialism and the lack of spiritual values in contemporary society. That would be the key topic that would lead to my being offered fresher cookies with my coffee and a bonus iced glass of water and at times free icons and blessed trinkets. There would also be a switch in their usual scripted conversation with visitors and talk to me in private about how the 666 mentioned in the Bible was a prophecy of the present condition in the world. I heard that this number which is referred to as the "mark of the beast" in the book of Revelations is represented by credit cards and eventually the "chip" which would be implanted in people and will mean total control by Satan of the human race. Constant prayer to Jesus and following the dogma of the Greek Orthodox Church while resisting seductions of the flesh and mind control of the government was the solution. They would go on to explain that the sinister allies of the Antichrist in this plan included masons, Illuminati, the pope and the Zionist Jews. Curiously I wondered if anyone of these contemplative holy people suggested that the mark of the beast might also have referred to ex president Ronald Wilson Reagan whose profile could be considered as nasty as the Antichrist's and whose name added up to the 666 prophecy.

THE SACRED MOUNTAIN

After the visit to this important location of Greek Orthodoxy (where of course we kissed a few more encased saintly skulls and fingers), we then went to the Temple of Delphi where in ancient times the oracle would determine the fate of kingdoms and rulers. The setting was majestic on a high mountain valley, but I didn't find any special resonance calling through the ether. I found relief however from the 103 degree temperatures at a roadside bar that materialized an ice cold beer for me.

Our next destination was to the most prestigious and sacred site in present day Greece. Agion Oros (also known as Mount Athos) is an island on the northeastern coast near Thessaloniki where at one time over 2000 monasteries and thousands of hermits lived in caves. Now only about twelve such active monasteries remain and a handful of men living in caves. No women are allowed on the island and at one time not even female cats. The rat epidemic forced a slight change in that part of the dogma however. The land itself is wild and many mountain lions still roam through the terrain. To be able to visit the island, one needs a signed and notarized letter from one's village priest saying that you are a good person and believes in Christ before you can be given permission to go there. Having brought such official paperwork with me, John, Triantis and myself took the boat over while Stephanie, Nicolette and my mother stayed at a hotel room for a couple of days.

We arrived on the wild and beautiful island and viewed many impressive looking Orthodox monasteries. The Russian one especially had an assortment of relics and icons that promised miraculous healing. John and I were totally into the expected protocol of waking up at four am for prayers, then a vegetarian breakfast which like the rest of the monks we ate in silence, followed by help in the kitchen. Triantis however was more of an opportunist and encouraged us to leave right after breakfast before we would be stuck working and head to a few of the other monasteries for more hospitality treats.

Before leaving Agion Oros we saw a few of the hermits and heard that one among them that was telepathic and performed miracles. A couple of men also visiting the island said that they met an ascetic living in a cave who asked what airplanes were, as since he never had seen one or even a car or train. For most Greek men, coming here is a pilgrimage to do at least once in a lifetime. However, as we noticed in the dorm room we had spent the night in, most of these guys don't come here to reflect on their soul or spiritual issues, but as a social obligation. Overall, John and I had a thrilling two days and had the intention to come in the future and stay longer. Even if we did have to peel potatoes in the kitchen.

The second largest city in Greece is Thessaloniki which has not only a deep and wide connection to history but also looks quite modern and cosmopolitan. We enjoyed visiting the ancient towers and Roman archways as well as the head shops and health food stores. Posters announced a variety of interesting film and concert events and after we sampled some of the more wonderful restaurant aromas, we continued on our long drive back to Xirokambi. Our trip was a mixed bag of wonderful experiences compromised by a nagging mother, yet we were all glad we went. I'm not sure if Triantis said good by to my mother as he was probably happy to not hear our dramas any more, but he was pleased for our connection and for possible future voyages together.

A HOLY TRIP ENDS

Just about the time that we arrived back in the village, our church lady neighbor was busy organizing seats for a charter bus and then continuing with a ferry boat ride to a sacred monastery on the island of Lesvos (also known as Mitilini). Departure would be in a couple of days hence and since we were intrigued by the possibility of more special saint skulls to kiss as well as the opportunity to see an island that we had heard was very artistic both in beauty and in its hosting an international art community, we made sure to reserve our tickets. Sensing that my mother wanted to come along with such a devout group of neighbors that had signed up for this pilgrimage, we talked her into joining us along for the blessings waiting for us ahead.

Every August 8th, the monastery would have a church celebration for Saint Raphael and, for the devotees that were pure of heart, even a chance to see the saint himself make an appearance. From the top of the bell tower he would read the names of the Christians that would be joining him in heaven. With such a sales pitch, our neighbor had no problem filling all the seats and then passing out church song books that had appropriate hymns for us to chant on the bus.

All the way to Athens, our group sang, smiled and wore the look of calm purity. At the port in Piraeus, we soon climbed aboard the ferry boat ride which six hours later would bring us to the island. One song book after another was exchanged by our joyful group, so the energy was continuing to build in anticipation of the main event ahead. Being early afternoon when we arrived on Lesvos, we left my mother at the monastery while Stephanie, John, Nicolette and I hired a taxi to take us on a short tour of the area. Being one of the larger islands of Greece, we didn't have time to see the famous bay where artists congregated, but we did see enough to encourage us to come back for even more exploration at another time.

Our group had by now become part of an even larger assembly of mostly old people from all over the country that go on the circuit of feast days in search of the miraculous. Not wanting to be so absorbed in praying all night, once our kids went to sleep, Stephanie and I went on a walk around the area. The sky was shining with a brilliant display of sparkling stars. As we were about to reenter the monastic grounds around midnight, we witnessed an incredible slow moving shooting star that accented the night with its brilliance. Could this well have been signs of the saint arriving for his appearance party? We met our token commitment and listened to the monotonic vespers for about an hour then came back, said good night and went on to our designated non-coed sleeping arrangements.

Shortly after dawn, both Stephanie and I were awoken by the sounds of screaming women's shrill voices coming from the room where our village ladies were staying. Almost at the point of pulling each other's hair, the argument started when a couple of the women claimed they witnessed the saint at dawn floating in space and calling out names. Of course these women's names were on the list but because the other ladies were not there to experience the apparition, theirs were not mentioned. The lucky two were so engrossed in the miraculous appearance that they forgot to wake the other women up and so the fight began. All the way back, on both the boat and the bus, no one was smiling nor reading holy books any more. Angry glances were being exchanged and the masks of piety were replaced by the more human expressions of anger, malice, and revenge. With such a thickness and loud silence in the air, the bus driver did not even dare turn on the radio.

A memorable interlude on our boat ride however did channel some of the festive energy of Greeks at their happiest. Being as my 40th birthday, Stephanie asked one of the coffee bar stewards if they could help create a little party for me. Not wanting to waste an opportunity themselves for creating the venue for maybe meeting some of the younger ladies on the boat, we soon had a Greek disco going on. The deck was filled with dancing and the coffee was replaced by wine and whiskey which appeared close enough to be a miraculous transformation enough. But right about the peak moment of the appearance of pagan god of ecstasy and pleasure Dionysus, through the deck door popped in our church lady neighbor to tell us we were slightly sinning and needed to stop having fun. As always this time of year, it seemed that the old farts of our village did not consider the first two weeks of August as allowable under the church code for anyone to celebrate birthdays. Before the party broke up, I did receive a few hugs and kisses while the boat guys managed to score a few phone numbers from our village ladies that they had been dancing with. And even my mother was happy to see me getting busted for promoting happiness instead of sorrow and persecution. In retrospect perhaps I should have announced that Saint Raphael had appeared to me on the auspicious moment to announce that I was on the heavenly guest list and thus I was celebrating the news.

TINOS

Arriving in Athens, we decided to let the rest of the village "fun club" continue back to Xirokambi while we took a different ferry boat to Tinos for another holy picnic. Similar to its famous Catholic counterpart Lourdes, Tinos had a monastery that honored the Virgin Mary and on this day of her commemoration August 15th, thousands of mostly sick and old people flocked here in order to be healed. Discarded crutches and eyeglasses filled huge boxes in back of the church as proof that they would not be needed anymore after the anticipated miracles took place. For days some people had been fasting while others would be doing penitent feats such as crawling on their knees up steep roads leading to the church.

Waiting to see another holy magic show, we stood in the huge line which eventually led us to the rear of the large cathedral. The main bishop was saying all the proper prayers and then the moment everyone was waiting for arrived. The communion he and the other five priests standing next to him were about to dispense to the masses was the one with the high octane juice that would bring health and happiness to whoever swallowed it. But as Greeks like to express their passionate nature in different ways, several fights were breaking out in the front of the lines. In one case, one old person started hitting another even older person with a cane over which of them would get to go up before the other. One claimed that he had been standing in the outside line longer and the other guy retorted that he was sicker and thus was higher in the que. In another fight, an old lady was yelling to a priest that she did not want to receive the communion he was giving her as she wanted to get the dose from the bishop whose brew she thought had more healing power because he wore a larger hat and carried a gold cross. With the pushing escalating, the bishop grabbed the microphone and announced that with this sort of behavior, everyone was going to go to hell and that he was not going to give out any communion at all. At that point "all hell broke loose" with people yelling threats at the priests and punching anyone in their way from getting to the front lines. As this sort of reaction might well have been common, the bishop had a change of tone and in a deep authoritative voice asked everyone to make the sign of the cross in forgiveness and that he would stay to pass the holy communion bread and wine to everyone. That of course included us too who not only savored this food for the soul but as this moment marked the end of the fasting period, we could go out to a restaurant and enjoy my late birthday dinner.

With August just about over, our long distance trips were ended and soon enough we were packed for our return back to America. And as a surprise for the village's suspicions, Stephanie formerly announced that she was pregnant and that the baby was happily conceived in Greece. After a very fulfilling three months, we left with satisfied memories. My mother back to Raleigh and we back to Montana. And as one famous US general once said, "We shall return."

CHAPTER TWO: MISSOULA

GREECE SOLO TRIP

Before winter approached, I made plans for my solo trip to Greece. As I explained in my first book, we had made a profit from selling our house in Hawaii and we needed to use up that sum in purchasing other properties or else we would have to pay a hefty income tax. Thus we agreed to spend twelve thousand dollars on land in Greece as an excellent investment opportunity as well as a back door option in case we ever wanted to move from the US. The country had not officially entered the European Union yet, which also meant prices would be much lower now than waiting later.

As the colder weather would have made my search for land even more challenging. November and December were actually prime months to be in Greece because the main part of the tourist season was over and so prices were lowered accordingly. As I was on a specific mission with no time or money to spare, I did not tell anyone that we knew in Greece of my arrival. And as soon as I landed in Athens, I took the first bus available to Lefkada.

This time around, not only was I able to enjoy much more of the beauty of the island but also I felt very well received from the local people. From the first day I arrived and rented a room in the port-side Byzantium Hotel, my intentions to return to live in the homeland of my ancestral roots was considered wonderful. Thus many local people wanted to be of help both in hospitality and in suggestions. The lady that owned the hotel was a bit spooky in her conversations of Satan's growing influence on society, but the price for the room was low and she often treated me to coffee and made sure I had enough blankets for the cold nights ahead.

I soon made good friends with some of the town's bus drivers who would often treat me to beers and wine at the end of their work day. In the next few weeks I would also be taken care of by a cafe owner in one of the villages that I would be based at who would provide me with free breakfast every morning of fresh baked bread, cheese and olive oil. Also in the main town I made friends with a man who had a restaurant and would treat me to wine and dessert every time I ate there. Furthermore, they would all be providing me with helpful advice in regards to the island as well as to my real estate goals.

The warmth of all these folks towards me was well appreciated, but I didn't have much time for extra socializing as my days were pretty busy from dawn to night. Being in good physical shape at the time, I literally walked around the whole twenty miles of the western side of the island over the course of the next week and asked at each village cafe if anyone knew of any good real estate deals in the area. Usually within ten minutes there would always appear people with land for sale and eager to talk me into buying it. As I wanted to have a look at all the options, I kept on walking from place to place and staying at cheap rooms in the evenings.

The one lot that was perfect with a large track of cleared land with ocean view and a spring was a bit out of our price range and in retrospect it feels a mistake not to have made an offer of long term payment arrangements towards buying it. Another prime spot in a lush mountain setting with a panoramic view had a low enough price but when I came to close the deal, I found out that the land didn't even belong to the person claiming it was his and I feared that he could scam me into giving him my money.

Another frustrating situation made me feel like I was playing poker instead of negotiating on buying land. I was interested in a nice lot and had agreed to the price that the owner was asking. The next day when I came to sort out the details, he told me that he had consulted with other members of his family and since they had some financial stake in it as well, thus now warranting a higher asking price. Again I agreed and told him that I would meet him the next day to write up a contract. This time around, he said that the selling price was even higher. When I told him that I wouldn't be able to buy it at that price, he laughed at me and said that in a few weeks since Greece would be joining the EU, there would be lots of rich Germans eager to purchase it instead for the cash price that he was now asking.

Eventually however on one of my walks, I came across a woman who said she had the perfect place for me to see. Nicely situated and close enough to the main town and with a wonderful view of the ocean,

I agreed to the purchase and found an attorney in town to set up the paperwork. Nikos was a very pleasant young man who has helped me in many legal matters over the years and prepared a contract of sale and my leaving him the power of attorney for any follow up matters after I left the country. As I would find out later, perhaps I did not chose the ideal property.

Even though the land was found to be okay by the attorney as being free and clear, a short while after the purchase I received a message from the Greek Department of Natural Resources informing me that the land I bought had been designated as "wilderness" because of an endangered bush found growing there. But for me on the trip, I felt I had done my best and after saying goodbye to all my new friends I set off to search for land on the islands located on the other side of the country.

SPORADES

Skyros was located in the Sporades island chain. My having been given the title from a Canadian magic mushroom association of "Sporades minister of Montana", it seemed fitting that there might be some interest in a closer look on these islands for our next bargain basket land purchase. They were all fairly green and Skyros had the bonus of a European holistic consciousness center that could always be a place of social interaction for our family in the future.

The ferry boat ride was about three hours from a port north of Athens and on the trip over I made friends with an interesting French man who told me he lived half a year in Sri Lanka and then would sail his boat to Skyros where he chose to live the other six months. Being enthusiastic about my checking out the tavern that he stayed at, I agreed to set up my base there as well.

The village of Aspous was located about six miles from the main town and had a fine beach frontage. My friend's tavern suggestion provided good food and every night dancing that got wilder after the wine would start pouring freely from the owner. Knowing that I was looking for land, he introduced me to his uncle who took me up to his hillside property that he agreed to sell at a very low price. A year later after the final papers were signed, the old man sent complaints to my attorney that we had underpaid him and the land was worth much more. Even though I respected him and his wife and knew that he needed the extra cash, I felt a little sad that I was not in a position to have paid any extra bonus to him.

In retrospect, I feel okay in having secured the two places I did. If I only had a little extra money at the time, I would have been able to have come up with more satisfying choices. But at least the family has two more options of places to go if ever the need in the fast and unpredictable way the world keeps changing.

Before coming back to the US, one more unexpected adventure laid ahead. The cheapest air flight I could find was with Yugoslavian Airlines which had a brief scheduled stopover in the civil war torn city of Belgrade before heading across Europe and eventually the US. I had no problem with the uncomfortable rips on my seat or that my reading light did not work since I was saving a significant amount of money by not flying with another carrier and besides, I figured the on board meals would have a more ethnic taste. After a few minutes of refueling, the plane proceeded to move onto the runway so as to take off. Just as I was relaxing in my seat, a convoy of military vehicles pulled up in front of the plane and about twenty soldiers running on board and started pointing their assault rifles on each passenger as one by one we were asked to open our carry-ons for inspection. Meanwhile, outside another large group of serious looking soldiers were examining everyone's baggage which had to be unloaded from the plane. Since I was not smuggling anything out of the country, I did not feel terribly concerned of being arrested but just the fact of having a gun pointed at me as I showed my passport and belongings to these guys was a very nervous experience. As the slow moving hour finally passed and we were cleared again for takeoff, I made an intention to never fly through a war zone again even if the airline offered better food.

Upon my arrival back home, Stephanie updated me on news from the home front while I was gone. Most of it fairly mundane, but when she told me of our house fire I was quite shaken. Apparently the chimney cleaner we had hired for maintenance on the fireplace did not do a thorough job. During one day while John was at school a fire ignited in our chimney which could well of burned down the house and trapped Nicolette and Stephanie in its blazes. Luckily she detected it in time to contact the volunteer fire department who actually showed up quickly enough to put out the fire and prevent a catastrophe. I promptly changed my opinion of this group which I previously felt its members were more interested in starting forest fires to make money than actually helping put out fires and for which now I was extremely grateful for their prompt service.

SOPHIA ARRIVES

With Stephanie's smoothly expanding belly reminding us that we had a new child on the way, we did our research and were referred to a midwife in Missoula who worked closely with a naturopathic physician that allowed the upstairs of her clinic to be available for home births. Although midwifery was not as openly supported by the local medical establishment, it was still a borderline legal option in Montana. Heavy media and lobbyist campaigns started the year before to not allow home births, but the key chairman of the legislative committee considering the issue changed his opinion at the last minute and agreed that certified midwives could indeed keep delivering babies. Coincidentally, I had received a handwritten letter from this senator explaining that my letter to him that expressed reasons for legalizing the status of midwives helped in changing his decision. One of my lifetime's most important good deeds.

As March came and the birth imminent, we started accelerating our organization of what would be needed. The invitation to our Greek friends in town of Hamilton, Fotini and Dino to be the godparents was accepted, the naturopath said her birthing room was available and the midwife affirmed she would be prepared but encouraged us to perhaps be located closer to Missoula in case of an emergency or because of possible stormy weather. To maximize comfort and security, we rented a studio apartment that was connected to a motel located within walking distance to downtown Missoula. Not to mention that we now had a happy holiday setting for all our family to enjoy. For a relatively inexpensive weekly rate, we had a nice room with wood paneling, heat, cable television, kitchen and access to the motel's indoor heated pool. And during the two weeks we stayed there we had opportunities to explore Missoula for more reference points for our possible relocation.

Not forgetting that our purpose of renting this room was more than our fun vacation, the moment came when we had to call the midwife and help Stephanie to the car for us to quickly get to the clinic. We also called Fotini who was able to leave her restaurant and come as well to be part of the wonderful miracle of life. It seemed as if each time Stephanie gave birth, the labor was a little less intense and of shorter duration. True to form, a new daughter came into our lives and the whole room shared in the enchantment. Stephanie smiled, our beautiful baby with a full head of silky hair cried, Fotini was amazed, Nicolette was elated in having a sister, I kept filming in a state of bliss and John was an active helper by cutting the umbilical cord. Truly an extended family event.

LIVING IN THE CITY

Spring was a happy reemergence for all of us. Our new baby daughter Sophia, the snow melting and a new move for us to Missoula were all epic events. Our rental property manager Jeff was aware of our intention to find a comfortable home in town to move to and among the several places we financed to buy included a house for my mother, as we assumed she would want to live close to us. Both these places were also lucrative rental units which meant that until our family moved in, they would still be bringing us income.

The place we picked for my mother was an older but attractive two bedroom Victorian style house with a winding wood staircase to a second floor and even a large chandelier in the living room with an ample garden space in back and a lawn in front. We thought it would be perfect for her as on the corner were two bus lines, downtown was only about a twenty minute walk, a large park across the street, a supermarket and the Greek Church were just two blocks away And conveniently right around the corner was a drug store and a Greek restaurant. The street itself had many large old trees that created a beautiful canopy with lots of bird songs. But when dealing with my mother, her hard headed stubbornness would often prevail over logic, so the possible reality of her moving to Missoula turned out to be only a sweet unfulfilled pipe dream.

The house that Jeff had encouraged us to buy for ourselves was a modern two bedroom home with an extra office space and with a full basement where I could finally showcase my thousands of interesting books, records and posters. And with a few changes, we were considering creating a play room in it as well and some seating area for friends to come over and party with us. The fenced yard was large and the neighborhood fairly quiet. Within a short walk were a couple of shopping centers, the school that John would be attending, a whole wheat bakery that made great pizza and a Greek restaurant that served the best vegetarian gyros we had ever ate. Downtown was about a half hour walk that would take us through a couple of nice parks along the way. During the summer, the sprinklers would stay on for kids to play under them or get in a small swimming pool where they could wade as well.

Missoula itself was a happy choice for us to live all the way around. After dealing with racist rednecks for too many years in the small provincial enclave of Darbarians, we welcomed the relief to be in a progressive social base that often was called the "Berkeley of the Northwest" because of its many environmental groups and open minded residents. The University had about 12,000 students and its emphasis was on liberal arts. The school hosted lots of great concerts and its campus was adjacent a tall mountain with many trails to the panoramic views waiting for anyone who made it to the top. Around the school were many fine eateries, cafes, health food stores and interesting shops. Bike trails extended not only through town but connected to other trails that went into the forest and state land reserve. The town was divided by a large river with several bridges across it. Walking paths lined both sides of the river that included benches along the way and street lamps for evening strolls. On weekends there were regular enjoyable music festivals in the area and a large farmers market downtown. The many bars and clubs usually had fine rock and roll bands with no cover charges which for us meant going out for entertainment was affordable. One of our more memorable outings was to the Top Hat Club where we got to see a Bo Didley concert. We had John along with us and as part of Bo's encore, he brought our son on stage and put a guitar in his hand while singing his classic tune "I'm a Man" together.

Another special event was the "Day of the Dead Parade" which was more significant than the Halloween festivities later that night. Many indigenous and even our own Greek heritage consider that day to be special in that one's ancestors are closest to contact to our dimensional reality.

Being Montana, it did mean winters would eventually bring in a chill, but as we had an efficient heating system in the house, we could easily hibernate or dress warmly and take brisk walks.

The Greek Orthodox community was happy to see us now having become active members of their congregation and were always inviting us to events at church as well as taking part in their cultural outreaches such as the yearly Greek Festival and also their part in the International Food Festival. The major influx of Greek immigrants to this part of Montana came originally to work for the train company and lumber industry. The current profile of local Greek-Americans included many restaurant owners, attorneys and real estate company owners as well. Our son John was recruited to be a regular altar boy and my voice was added to the choir on Sundays as well. When Sophia was baptized in September of 1992, the church was filled with happy smiles to welcome one more member to the fold with well wishes and a nice pot luck lunch we provided afterwards.

My mother had flown from Raleigh for the event as well and even though she was proud of having one more gorgeous granddaughter, she was suspicious as to why we attached the middle name "Sophia" to her formal naming of Despina. After my mother felt betrayed for our not naming our first daughter after her, she thought that we had personal animosity to her instead of understanding that we felt the name Despina did not translate well into English and that our daughters would have had social challenges because of it. Similarly if we had given our kids hippie names like Rainbow Blossom or Daisy Leap, etc., there would have been the same sort of problem.

Besides her lingering bitterness from our "name callings", my mother also had a feeling of being ripped off by us when we persuaded her to donate $100 to the church for a project of ordering new seating pews. The deal was that they would have a small sign on the pew that we purchased with the wording "In Loving Memory of my Husband John Douvris". Even though the pew was delivered, the name placard was never placed on it. Mom was intuitively correct again in her distrust of people.

In the couple of months that she stayed with us, we took her to all the Greek restaurants in the area where she made many friends and seemed to enjoy their company. She became good friends with Despina Sophia's godparents Fotini and Dino and enjoyed Missoula in general. But as much as we tried to persuade her to move into the house we felt that she would enjoy, she refused to accept it and kept insisting that her home was in Raleigh. Thus we were sad to see her leave instead of being part of our extended family here in Missoula.

Our children, on the other hand, unlike my mother, were pleased for our move to this big city. Nicolette was happy to be going to Avalon Preschool which was fairly progressive especially in encouraging an arts and crafts curriculum. She liked the fun projects as well as the other kids and her teacher Suzie. After school I would have fun taking Nicolette to various cafes that would make her hot chocolate drinks with plenty of whipped cream on top. We enjoyed exploring various shops and places in the downtown area together as well. Being a private school, we were required to pay tuition but most of the cost was deducted because Stephanie and I would clean up the classroom after school hours which also meant scrubbing the cages of the various pet rabbits.

John started fourth grade at the public school that was only about five blocks away from our house. Just like his sister, he now was able to expand into other extracurricular activities including roles in various plays. An excellent dramatic organization called The Missoula Children's Theater would even travel throughout the country and put on plays that would create roles and scripts for all the children that wanted to participate. Although John never went on any of their tours, he did have a few major parts and even had his picture on the front cover of the nationally syndicated Parade Magazine which had an article on the organization.

By now John was starting to play guitar and was quickly learning songs and even crafting his own melodies. I was also helping him write lyrics to the music and one of our joint efforts resulted in his winning first place in some sort of school competition in the area. Because of its award, John was invited to play live on the local college radio station one Saturday morning. The children's program was called "The Pea Green Boat" and the song of this very first broadcast of his music was called "Tick-Tock". The radio hostess was not used to having to talk to intelligent children like John on the show, so she was very impressed as to how he was able to explain the environmental meaning of the song which was a lament and warning as to how the clock was running out on the world unless people took better care of nature.

Besides our cultural activities, we also did a lot of hiking throughout the area and on one winter day, took our kids to a frozen lake which was set up for ice skating. None of us were able to stay up on the ice too well and were happy that our friend Dave had come along with us. He was much better at pulling Nicolette around the ice in a sled with baby Sophia in her lap while John was exploring other edges of the lake. Stephanie and I were happy enough just watching while drinking our complimentary hot chocolate around the bon fire.

With more socializing going on, all of us were having friends coming over for various parties and other activities. For Nicolette's birthday one year we organized a festive gathering at our house but in the process we all also learned a lesson in what could go wrong if too many people that you don't know also show up to such gatherings. In this case a lady that Dave had met at a Rainbow Gathering and whom he was trying to get romantic with came to our party with her daughter Maya who turned out to be one of the youngest psycho people we ever met. We knew we would have some problems from the moment we went to pick her and her mom up to bring to our house and all the way over she kept hitting our windows with a heavy stick. When the party started, she then started kicking all the other kids and crying over not getting her way. Finally Dave took her aside and after lecturing her and her mother, he was responsible enough to take them both away and save some pleasant moments for the kids at the party without having a crazy girl kicking and hitting them.

Right across the street from where we lived was a family that had a daughter about the same age as Nicolette called Missy. They became good friends and Nicolette would often go to their house and play as they had more toys and a bigger playroom than us. On one particular Halloween night, both of them went trick or treating around our neighborhood and were able to fill their bags with lots of candy. Somehow they were able to smuggle a lot of this sweet loot which we had told them to throw away into a hiding spot that our eyes had not detected. About a week later, when they went to their stash in a bush in front of our house, they were both attacked and bit by a nest of wasps which had taken over the candy that the girls had left there. After all the crying from the bites, there was no reason to add any additional punishment or lecture like "we told you so" as I think the instant karma of the situation was a sufficient lesson.

Every few weeks our friend Dave would ride up on his motorcycle from Hamilton and we would have fun times getting high then eating pizza, ice cream and watching interesting movies that we would rent from the nearby DVD store. One of our favorite double features was selected by Nicolette which were the memorable "Killer Clowns from Space" and "The Stuff".

Dave has continued being a good friend for several decades and he has always been part of our extended family. Even my mother, who usually had harsh impressions of our friends, liked him and kept warning him to not let sweet talking ladies rip off his meager financial savings as he was prone to have happen. Over and over he would meet women whose eyes shined like angels but soon would turn into what he would call "psychic vampires".

Another popular activity for us in Missoula would be to go to parties where people would bring drums and have a wonderful musical jam together. A local family called The Drum Brothers would make high quality drums for an affordable price and would be happy to come to these events and teach people some rhythms as well. One of the brothers was also a guitar teacher and taught John some of the basics of that musical instrument. Once we set up our house with enough pillows for a lot of people to sit on, we also hosted several such fun drumming parties. And always a fine pot luck would make for a wonderful evening.

One of the larger venues for drum gatherings was the Unity Church where at times up to several hundred people would participate. It was also a focal point for interesting classes that would be offered there at other times. For instance, Stephanie received her first level Reiki training here besides our attending many other wonderful lectures in the areas of spirituality and natural health.

As in all non-mainstream gatherings, a few people were a bit more non conventional than "normal". One day at the church we met a lady hugging a tree and wearing a children's' birthday party hat on top of her head. She explained that the cone shaped design of the hat allowed her to communicate with all forms of life such as trees and extra dimensional beings. Although her ideas seemed a little too unbelievable for me, I did put on a birthday party hat one time when I had a severe headache and it brought relief. As far as I know however, I was not aware of having been abducted at the same time by extraterrestrial visitors. Perhaps that was the historic reason relatively stupid children were forced to wear "dunce hats" to improve their cognitive capabilities.

Not quite extra dimensional, but curious enough a system to draw my interest in, Unity hosted regular classes in a consciousness expanding program based in Indonesia called Subud. One of their overviews was that by going into a room with other members blindfolded, you can become spiritually healthier by screaming and bouncing off the walls. Stephanie and I had gone to a similar exercise class when we used to live in San Francisco at the Rajneesh/Osho center called "chaotic meditation", so she was not too interested in going to this one. However our son John had a curious nature, so the two of us went for this very dramatic experience. If done correctly and regularly, their guidebook suggested that you could clear up not only your own personal karma but also that of seven generations of ancestors. As I was well aware that most of my family and relatives screamed at each other anyway, there wouldn't be much need to come back for another session that might result in getting knocked down by someone in the room that was wrestling with their burdensome demons.

Having learned about psychic healing in Brazil and the Philippines and when I heard one of the more respected such healers was coming to give a presentation in Missoula, I was excited to go but at the same time, knowing how easily for me to get involved in areas that otherwise I would later regret, I told Stephanie to not let me sign up for any such therapy that might be getting scheduled afterwards. But when I heard the Filipino man's lecture, I was impressed enough to not only sign myself up for a "tune up" treatment but Stephanie as well.

When I showed up to my appointment, I made sure that John came along with me so he could be a witness to what would take place. As instructed, I laid down on a table and after a few prayers, the psychic surgeon placed his fingers on my stomach areas where I felt a tickling sensation inside of me. A couple of minutes later I was told that I could open my eyes and was shown something that looked like strands of black tar that the man told me was inside of me and could have well resulted in cancer in the future. When I asked John afterwards what he saw during the experience, he confirmed that yes, he did see the surgeon's hands go inside my body after a small hole seemed to have opened for about ten seconds and that John could see my internal organs before the hole closed again after the hands came out. He also affirmed that he observed the black tar like material that was then taken out. Even though I did not feel any better or worse after the treatment,

I was glad that I went. Stephanie also had a similar experience but she did not feel any need for John to have come be her witness.

Another highly attended event that we went to was a presentation from one of the top members of a popular "new age" psychic channeling group called Church of Miracles. Having heard very positive reports about this group, I came with open mind but left early after I felt totally disgusted. The idea of personal responsibility in karma sounded interesting but when the speaker said that the Jews chose to come together to get gassed in the Nazi prison camps, I realized that I was listening to gibberish. Likewise I was angered when the answer to the question I asked about shouldn't we help someone on the street if they were getting mugged was that in many cases, it was their karma to get mugged and that we shouldn't interfere in the "divine plan". I realized that it wasn't my karma to listen to this nonsense anymore and perhaps these so called spiritual "new age" groups could well have been funded by other agencies that want people to feel it is okay not to care about how governments and corporations might be abusing others and the planet. But then again it could well have been the presenter's interpretation and another reading might have expressed the material differently.

There was also a Rajneesh/Osho center that we went to several times and later John attended to learn the fundamentals of Aikido which was a much more gentler martial art than the Tae Kwon Do training he received from an ex-marine drill sergeant in Hamilton.

THE REIKI SYNDICATE

During one of our visits to a holistic health fair, I had a tremendous experience from a practitioner demonstrating the benefits of the Oriental healing art of Reiki. By simply placing her hands on my head and my then going into a meditative space, I felt a general lightening of pressure and a feeling of transcendental bliss. Later while living in Montana, Stephanie went on to take the workshops necessary to become certified in this practice so as to be able to provide these benefits to her loved ones as well as to augment the rest of the healing modalities she was learning which would help in her own consciousness expansion and soul growth.

The first level of Reiki taught her the basics of the process and then the second level taught her other aspects including distant healing. This initial certification cost $100 and the second $250 which were a reasonable amount of exchange for such a vital training. However for her to take the final level step three, also known as "becoming a master", the price tag jumped to $10,000 for a three day class. I was not only totally shocked by this ridiculous cost but also aggravated by the response I received from the International Reiki Board where I had addressed my concerns. Their official justification was that for their training to have value, people needed to have an intention serious enough to be able to commit to such a high payment.

Not wanting to go into a head on confrontation with such an esteemed group of healers, I went instead on a thorough search in new age and holistic healing magazines and soon found a classified advertisement from a Reiki master with all the proper certificates and pedigree who shared similar feelings as mine as to the over inflated price tag. Her offer was that if we could organize five other people that would be willing to take the Reiki level three training, she would be happy to fly to Missoula from her home in Wisconsin and teach it for $1000, a very significant difference in cost.

Finding five people to take the class was not a problem. One lady was even about to mortgage her house to pay the standard ten grand and was excited for this wonderful opportunity that Spirit (with my help) had brought her. All went well and after the three days, all the participants beamed in high health and smiled with deep appreciation for their certificates of mastery in Reiki.

About a month later when I received a personal letter from the International Reiki Board with extremely caustic and aggressive wording not very characteristic of a new age healing group. Basically they told me that the universe was abundant and if someone wanted to take Reiki three with pure intentions, the money for the class would manifest. (As would the hefty check to the Reiki trainer.) They even went on to say that I was on a demonic path of encouraging limitation instead of expansion and abundance in the universe. Not to leave such a perfect opportunity of timely retort, I went on to ask them how much did Jesus Christ charge in laying of the hands and raising even dead people. With all due respect, I asked them to explain to me how their system was any better or more valuable than His. I also went on to say that they were not only expounding a system of elitism but that they were precipitating limitation in healing on the planet by only allowing the few people who could afford the $10,000 fee to become Reiki masters (and mistresses). I never heard back from them but I am happy to see nowadays that Reiki three is being taught around the world for around $1000 or so. Viva the power of the pen and common sense.

DR. SYNN

Several times a day on our local television channel there would be an advertisement for an acupuncturist named Doctor Synn. His presentation would stress that he had been trained in the best medical school in Hong Kong and that all his treatments were guaranteed to remedy the health problem that was diagnosed. From the time he was a baby, our son John had a difficult time breathing and would snore a lot as well as often having a runny noise. Both sides of our family were demanding that we take him to a doctor who could surgically remove his tonsils and drain his adenoids. Being equally adamant that time and natural healing would eventually normalize his problem, I was happy to give Doctor Synn a chance to cure our son.

Wanting to be empathetic and supportive of the procedure, after we signed up John for ten treatments, I made an appointment for a few tune ups as well. Laying in side by side beds, the doctor would stick the many pins in our bodies, darken the room and come back forty five minutes later to tell us we could go home. And of course he would take the pins out first. Stephanie came into the room one day and took a great picture of both of us looking like pin cushions. Our resolve to persist the treatment for the ten sessions came to an abrupt end early however. While watching the local televised news one night, a picture of our good doctor Synn was flashed on the screen with the story of how he was just arrested for being a fraud. Not only did he not have any medical training but he had also been hiding from Chinese authorities for other crimes. I can't say if my health improved or not from the needles, but not too much time later, it was clear that John's nasal problems resolved and now he sleeps well without snoring. Thank you Doctor Synn irregardless of which country's jail you might be in.

THE INDEPENDENT

Being a fairly hip college town, Missoula also had an excellent alternative newspaper called the Independent. Local news, commentary and events were well covered and after I had several of my letters to the editor printed in it, I applied and was hired as a delivery person for the paper. Most of the time we enjoyed a pleasure to drive around discovering new areas of town but when the icy roads of winter made it tough to drive safely and people's dogs started attacking me when trying to place the newspaper on their porch, I changed my home delivery route to the downtown delivery of stacks of papers to various stores and vending machines. The new routes also meant I had a chance to talk to some of the shop owners who often would treat me to cups of coffee on chilly nights and random slices of pizza and even gourmet popcorn which I would bring home to share with the family.

CREDIT CARDS

Like so many other people in the early 1990's, our original credit card debts kept escalating as our payments could not keep up with the compounding interest. It had even reached the point where we were taking cash advances from one credit card to pay the minimum amount due on another card. A situation that is not a very healthy financial posture to be in.

When I heard of an agency called Consumer Credit Counseling that offered a mediation plan between the banks and ourselves, we promptly set up a meeting and were soon following a designated plan to end this growing financial nightmare. Essentially we signed an agreement that we would no longer use any of our credit cards and the banks in return would not add any more interest to our debt. Their philosophy was that since we could just as easily have quit paying any more on these cards, it was better for them to at least be making some money off our principal payments to Consumer Credit Council than nothing at all. Over the years we have been sent many offers for obtaining new credit cards but we are happier without them in our life. Since tearing up our credit cards over twenty five years ago, we have felt more empowered and free of the noose around our neck and have felt better ever after.

OUT OF TOWN

Besides enjoying activities in Missoula, we would often take excursions to other places in the region such as Glacier National Park, Big Fork and once to the interesting town of Hot Springs. At one time this place was a famous spa and resort but over the years fewer and fewer tourists were coming and the hotels and other buildings were looking decrepit. The smell of sulfur still emanated from steam vents but most of the town looked abandoned. Before we left I had a passing thought that possibly a group of hippies could buy all the town and have a wonderful community with year round hydroponic farming and healthy soaking in the pools. Oh well, there's always future potentials.

HOLIDAY

During one Thanksgiving weekend when Stephanie and our daughters were visiting her family in San Francisco, John and I were able to masterfully organize quite a delightful holiday ourselves. First we went to Fotini and Dino's house for a traditional meal of turkey and all the fixings including several of their tasty homemade Greek specialties. As their family settled into watching the Dallas Cowboys playing against the Miami Dolphins football game, John and I made our excuses that we had to leave and went straight to a celebration at a Tibetan Buddhist Center on the other side of town. The vegetarian feast was not quite ready, so since we were still on a plan to go to one more event afterwards, John went into their kitchen and helped speed up the cooking process. A few mantras, Hindu Namaste greetings and fast feast food later, we were out the door and off to another part of Missoula. Our friend Linda had also organized a wonderful vegetarian gathering that included karaoke and older people dancing to calypso music. A fun day for us in a variety of places.

MOVING ON

But as much as we felt family roots growing nicely, there came a moment of realization that it might be time for us to move. My mother was needing our help in some ways, but even more importantly we were concerned in regards to the health hazards of living in Missoula any longer. Before the Westerners settled into the valley, the indigenous Native Americans warned them not to do so because of the limited elements of wind. With industry, cars and fireplaces filling the air with pollution, the surrounding mountains blocked a healthy air flow which brought the city one of the worst ratings in the country for such inversion. One day when we climbed one of the adjacent mountains and could see a dark rusty cloud of pollution blanketing the city, we realized that we would be committing child abuse to our family if we stayed any longer and subsequently made the affirmation of our need to leave.

CHAPTER THREE: NEW TRAVELS ACROSS AMERICA

ON THE ROAD AGAIN

In the summer of 1993, we drove across the country to go live again with my mother in Raleigh. There was an emphasis of checking out festivals along the way as a theme to our journey. We attended several neo-pagan gatherings, and we also were interested in visiting various alternative communities in case we would consider living in one someday. So even though our intention was to eventually reach North Carolina, our itinerary took us first to the west coast to visit Stephanie's parents in San Francisco.

Visiting the family was okay, but our focus was to get on with our travel plans, so we only stayed with them a few days. It was fun to take the kids on a tour of the city and show them some of the places we used to enjoy going to and how they related to our memories and experiences. On our last night, we went along with Stephanie's parents to a fancy restaurant which left much to be desired. Besides the fact that the food and service were awful, price tag high and the atmosphere uncomfortably stuffy, the family dynamics were not at all smooth. Our kids were looking forward to the opportunity to express themselves but their grandparents made it clear that "children should be seen and not heard". A totally opposite manner than our own lifestyle and freedom of communication but as sad as the kids felt, they were also happy to realize how lucky to have us as parents instead of a stunted upbringing as the sort we had.

The first pause of our journey was the Church of All Worlds gathering located a couple of hours north of San Francisco. Lots of colorfully dressed people swirling in a mix of pagan, Celtic, and hippie celebration of nature and life. There was not much emphasis on dogma but more of an embrace of the varied expressions of spirituality. Seeing our friend Ralph Metzner was a nice surprise and getting our alignment grounded by such a happy social tune-up was a road side empowerment after our family dramas in San Francisco.

Not too far away was a place popularized in new age magazines called Harbin Hot Springs. Our first intuition of incompatibility came in the parking lot when we were aggressively warned by the attendant that if we stayed longer than one hour he would have our car towed away. Noticing his Krishna hair style, I replied with a hearty "Hare Krishna" greeting which by the looks of his smile left me at ease that we could probably stay a little longer than the complimentary hour.

In walking around the various crystal shops, Indian boutiques and massage rooms on the premises, I was impressed with how healthy and vibrant everyone looked. With possible future long term stay images in my mind, I went to talk to the director of this center as to possible residential options. Not beating around the spiritual bush, he explained to me that the focus of this place was in being a new age resort for singles wanting to enjoy themselves and mingle in a relaxing environment. Old people, children and even less than physically attractive visitors were not desired as it would distract from its beauty. Enough was said from his explanation for this center not to pass our audition and we were happy to leave even sooner than our allocated one hour visitors pass. I did however say one more thankful Hare Krishna greeting to my new "friend" working in the parking lot.

Not too far away was one of the largest intentional communities in the country which was called the Ananda Center. Back in the late 1960's, I had heard the charismatic Kriyananda give a lecture in which he invited people of spiritual interest to move to this community that he was forming in the beautiful area of Nevada City located in the foothills of the Sierra Mountains. At the time I heard his talk in San Francisco he clearly postulated his vision as an open door mix of any spiritual path that would suit the individual's growth. So in order to verify if the situation was the same now, I asked the lady who was giving us a tour of the facilities of any problem if, as members of this community, we brought in our eclectic interests such as Tantra, Sufi and psychedelics all of which had been mentioned by their founder as legitimate. However, with a startled look, our tour guide replied something to the effect that the "master" had refined the teachings so as to not leave any confusion on the path to higher consciousness. Only the books he had written were now allowed for study and practice here. Stephanie and I gave each other startled looks as well and telepathically agreed this community did not meet our needs of freedom of expression. Over the years, however, we have met many wonderful people that were part of this community and still continue in the direction of the original teachings. Different strokes for different folks.

Near the coastal town of Mendocino, Stephanie and I went to a health spa where we were buried in special healing sand for 45 minutes. The flower garden around us was peaceful as were the wind chimes, but even though I felt rejuvenated afterwards, most of the time I was uncomfortable with an itchy nose that I could not scratch because only my head was situated out of the sand mound and my hands unavailable to use to scratch or encourage flies not to land on my face.

When we camped at Panther Meadows high up on Mount Shasta, we were aware of being in a sacred area that many spiritual teachers considered a power spot. Although we did not observe any UFO activity nor the sounds below the earth that also were mentioned as common, we did feel very energetic during the day and our night's sleep was deep and full of dreams.

On the border of California and Oregon, we stayed a few hours at a small but functioning community of nature worshipers whose metaphysical conversations did not impress us much however. But when John and I took a small walk around the land, we saw two huge deer with stately looking antlers hop through the forest and then disappear in front of our eyes. Obviously the totem energy of the Native Americans that once lived on this land was still affirming higher realities.

About half way up the Oregon coast, we dropped in on the Alpha Center, a long established community that seemed to be functioning well. Unlike many of the other ones we would visit, they still retained their original ideals. Yet they were also active in their nearby town where they operated a health food store and book shop.

In many cases, intentional communities fail because by purposely removing themselves from the mainstream, suspicions arise as to their cultish or strange peculiarities. By remaining active in their social interactions, these folks removed any such misconceptions and were less open to harassment.

Also in Oregon, we visited Breitenbush Hot Springs which impressed us as an all around good choice for living at. Ongoing spiritual and holistic health seminars held here were interesting, the residents were all open minded and tolerant, the ambiance was funky freedom and the hot springs were wonderful. Unlike Harbin, even fat, not fashionable, older adults and lots of young children and babies lived here thus creating a more fulfilling reality base. But there were still problems of harassment from the nearby townspeople. Because of the environmentalist activism and belief system of the community, the predominantly redneck loggers were making life difficult. Community members were having their car tires slashed and their children beat up at school. Another sad example of the stunted mindset and heartless behavior of mainstream Americana.

During the two days we camped at Breitenbush, we met a large group of Sufi practitioners attending meditation and dance workshops. Being inquisitive, John had managed to enter their conference hall without anyone seeing him. When we asked if we could go inside and take him back out, the person at the desk said that because it being a private class, we would need to wait two hours before the workshop had finished. At the end time, John came out wearing a bright smile as did the facilitator who informed us that our son was performing a dervish dance and many of the advanced students felt that he was a reincarnated Sufi master teacher.

The Olympic peninsula was lush and gorgeous. We took a walk on a trail which started near our campground which was full of animism and natural rhythms. Not being able to see far through the fog was not a problem as we were presented with views that kept appearing and then disappearing of ancient trees, wild bird sounds and eventually, a dip in a relaxing hot spring.

Evergreen College, which would one day be a possible choice for our children to attend, was a few miles away from the progressively attractive town of Olympia and had a healthy feeling in being nestled in a verdant forest. Our purpose for coming here was to examine a book in the rare book section called "Mushrooms, Russia and Religion" written by Gordon Wasson. The author was not only one of the first known westerners to have witnessed and partook of a magic mushroom ceremony in Mexico but also was a wealthy banker who wanted the world to be aware of the connection between sacred plants and spiritual consciousness. This particular book was a treasure chest of paintings which were exquisite exhibits of his premise. In order for them to be preserved for posterity, he had presented these limited editions to several libraries around the world along with a large donation of money to each library in exchange for making sure they would be protected for the future.

After an hour or two of strolling through downtown Olympia and its many interesting shops, we found our way to the next pagan gathering site. For a few days, Stephanie, Sophia and I slept in a small dorm room while John and Nicolette joined the other kids in another building just a short distance away. The activities here were a bit more dogmatic and Wiccan than the Church of All Worlds but still a worthwhile experience for us. On the last day, there was a ceremony which was to be a reenactment of the ancient Greek Eleusian Mysteries. Being both a masquerade and adults-only activity, I encouraged Stephanie to represent us while I volunteered to stay with our family as well as to be a babysitter for the seven to twelve year old kids in the dorm.

Taking the stance of why should just their parents be able to get dressed up and have fun, I put my energy into creating exciting games for us to play in the dorm room as well. We invented our own rules and props in organizing ancient Olympic games such as tossing socks into a basket and kicking around various balls into designated target areas. Several times during our sports activities, a 15 year old girl that was taking care of the smaller children in the floor below would come up and tell us that we had to quit playing because we were keeping the babies awake. She then went on to boast that she was being paid $20 from each of the parents and wanted to make sure that none of the babies would start crying. But as we refused to stop our fun to accommodate her selfish interests, we kept on playing. Wanting to punish me for our insubordination to her demands, the girl went and found the mean looking muscular security guard with the satanic tattoos on his arms and was bringing him back to the dorm to probably kick my ass for some presupposed child abuse that she might have accused me of.

Feeling the stomping footsteps of this ogre coming up the stairs, I quickly asked the kids to join me in creating a magic circle of protection. Figuring that here was not only a way to keep myself from getting hurt but also a chance to educate these kids on magic rituals, I asked the four oldest looking ones to position themselves in each direction while I grabbed a book of fairy tales and started reading them in a very calm manner. Suddenly the door was flung open and the guard barked out "What's going on here?" The kids and I looked at each other and politely replied that we were just reading some bedside stories. Satisfied with our explanation he then looked at the girl who brought him here with disgust and scampered back down the stairs. The girl then gave us a dirty look before going back to her babysitting project and thereupon we tossed the fairy tale book away and went back to our loud and lively fun activities.

Relentlessly seeking revenge, the teenage girl must have been spreading all sorts of stories of my awful behavior. So at the closing presentation the next morning, with the adults still looking splendid in their mythic costumes, an announcement was made that I had been reported to have been abusive to the children that I had been taking care of. In terrifying unison, everyone turned around to stare at me and I could even see fists being raised and my crucifixion imminent. At this tense moment, all the kids that I was playing with the night before ran to me and held hands and made a circle around me. They exclaimed that not only did I not abuse them but they had more fun with me than with their own self glamorizing parents. The stares transformed into a moment of confusion then to recalculation and finally into looking very angry at the girl who started the trouble. As the noose of my lynching was now possibly being made smaller to fit the young girl's proverbial neck instead, I hugged my young friends and smiled in the comfort of feeling that many times I enjoy the company of children more than closed minded adults. Even if they are wearing childish outfits. And also pleased in the kids having learned to be able to cast magic circles of protection effectively.

Somewhere in Wisconsin, our next pagan gathering weekend was more oriented towards feminine spirituality. The setting was among meadows and hills with lots of tribal dancing, music and natural delights. The workshops were educational and I especially liked Morning Glory Zeler explaining how in the days before recorded history, goddess societies were predominant but the men were not treated as being subservient but as equals to the women. When the Aryan invasion came, the men stood on the front lines and were willing to be slaughtered to protect the women and children.

Towards the third day, Stephanie, myself and even our family were feeling comfortable like most of the other people at the gathering in being at total peace with tribal respect of nature. When we were leaving, it even felt a little odd to have to put on our "normal" clothes again to wear in what we sadly called "reentering the Kmart world".

SWAMI SATCHIDANANDA AND YOGAVILLE

One of the most influential spiritual teachers in our lives was Swami Satchidananda. I was first aware of him when I saw him on stage inaugurating the Woodstock Festival in 1969 showing our huge crowd how do yogic breathing. Beyond his saintly look and physical appearance as an Indian guru, he had a very comforting presence that incorporated yoga, humor and relevant interpretation of spiritual truths that can be applied to daily life.

Coincidentally, Stephanie had also been impressed by a lecture he had given in San Francisco around the same time, so we both felt happy to take regular yoga and meditation classes at one of his centers after our work day was finished at the Cliff House. Besides the wonderful benefits in health and calm energy that his programs offered, it was also a nice relief to be able to share time with spiritually conscious people in a beautiful round dome temple building in the attractive setting of Mission Dolores Park where we would also at times take walks and have a picnic.

Since Swami Satchidananda's Yogaville ashram in Virginia was only about a five hour drive from Raleigh, we made arrangements to go visit. With summertime approaching, I contacted the center and applied for a free tuition option for our kids attending a two week summer camp program there in exchange for Stephanie and I working as "camp counselors". Not long after mailing our applications we received the happy news of acceptance and plans were organized for our being there for a two week session in July. John, Nicolette and Sophia would all be able to stay and enjoy the healthy meals, yoga and recreational activities as Stephanie's job was to stay at nights in the cabin with the girls group while I stayed with the young boys.

The setting of the ashram that Satchidananda had selected was a beautiful expanse of acres in the foothills of the Appalachian Mountains. There was a lake to cool off from the sweltering summer heat, a river, organic gardens, meditation hall, cabins and a spectacular temple dedicated to all religions and spiritual paths. He always stressed universality in his philosophy that there is one truth but there can be many possible paths towards reaching it. During the next two weeks our daily routines included eating delicious vegetarian meals, doing yoga, taking hikes, swimming and listening to Swami's discourses with question and answer sessions afterwards. But even more important for us, Satchidananda would come by the children's camps every morning before breakfast to not only talk with the children but also to play with all of us as well.

Joining us along with his entourage of robed devotees, Satchidananda saintly erect figure, clear eyes, wide smile, long white hair and beard, was a joy to look forward to every day. One day a boy asked him if drugs such as marijuana were bad. Swami illustrated a reply by explaining that a knife can both kill someone but it also could cut a watermelon for several people to eat. A very impressive answer indicating that most objects are tools and the intention of how they are used can determine their worth or not.

One morning I told him that I had seen him on stage at Woodstock and mistook him for a rock and roll musician. Without missing a beat, Swami replied that he was indeed a rock and roll musician which he demonstrated by picking up two rocks to bang together in percussive harmony while rolling on the ground and joining the kids and myself in laughter at his performance. However, by noticing an embarrassed look in his upper elite devotees that were following him, I could sense that they did not approve of such open hearted expressions. Certainly after he would be leaving his body, the politics of Yogaville would not allow as much uninhibited laughter and childlike play. A reminder of how Jesus would enjoy a similar perspective and said if people did not act childlike, they would not have an easy time getting into heaven either.

Even though I missed sleeping with my sweetheart Stephanie, being a night counselor had its own share of interesting experiences. One of the 10 year olds in my group started crying on his first night with an obvious preference to be back at home with his parents instead of "roughing it" like the rest of us. Seeking a pleasing solution to his misery, I invited him to join a few of our adventurous cabin mates in sneaking into the kitchen after midnight with our goal of "liberating" a few quarts of the tasty Ben and Jerry's ice cream that was exclusively reserved for the adult meditation group staying in the more plush accommodations. All of us, including the no longer distressed kid were happy with our hunt and with gusto gobbled down all the various flavors of usually unaffordable gourmet ice cream.

Obviously from the start of camp the kids in my cabin were going to have a different experience with me as their supervisor. One of their main complaints about previous stayovers was that they had to be asleep and quiet by 10 pm and could not use any "inappropriate language". Being a child at heart and feeling their anguish of how that on their only summer vacation time each year they had to feel oppressed instead of happy, I made some immediate changes. Bed time was now going to be midnight and slightly dirty jokes were to be encouraged. To further having adventures worth remembering, we started organizing our own event of special interest. With John knowing the basics chords to the Jimi Hendrix rendition of "Wild Thing", our plan was to sneak over to the girls cabin late one night and make a racket whereupon as soon as one of them woke up our chorus of boys would sing the song lyrics of "Wild thing You make my heart sing....". With great anticipation, we carried out our prankish mission with grand precision. At 2 am on the designated night, we threw several rocks at their cabin door which a sleepy eyed girl opened and on queue we sang our very loud and festive song. All of the boys were laughing with great glee at our heroics but the reaction of the girls was not quite as festive. Most of them were actually quiet confused. Nicolette was furious at seeing her father and brother acting like "immature idiots" but I would like to think that at least a few of the girls had felt their fancies tickled and might even have been a little jealous a bit over our approach to summer camp. And as to the idea of "breaking the meditative rules", I'm sure that Satchidananda would have chuckled over our youthful antics and might have even been part of our band banging rocks to a rock and roll rhythm. Especially with his Woodstock experience.

As the camp came to a close, we were elated to find that Swami Satchidananda would allow our family a 15 minute private audience with him. Probably unlike most people that would focus on spiritual discourses, his interest was to ask us about life in Hawaii and then encourage five year old Sophia to demonstrate a hula dance which he tried to imitate as well. All of us shared jolly laughter with the wise old sage and were honored by his giving our kids their spiritual names of initiation.

And as a final bonus before leaving, all the boys made sure to tell me that I was the best counselor they ever had and to please come back again and share more fun and pranks with them again.

GEORGE AND JOHN DO NEW ENGLAND

While visiting Thea and Frans, I picked up a brochure at the Kripalu Yoga Institute about a summer program for kids that would teach camping skills and moderate wilderness training. Figuring that John was of age for such a possible initiatory experience, I wrote their organization explaining a bit about us, which also included a request for one of the few scholarships being offered. To our delight, we received a quick reply that included a full tuition credit for John. And to even make the situation sweeter, it meant an opportunity for me to come along on another trip back to New England.

Our bonding experience started well as we made swift time up the various freeways from Raleigh to our destination up north. Pulling into the rugged beauty of Maine, we stopped for a touristy view of where the Mayflower first landed with the Pilgrims from England and then on to visit my long time friend from high school and college, Richard. Our reliable Isuzu Trooper which had been a steady mode of family transport across thousands of miles and several years decided to break down about two blocks from Richard's doorsteps. Not to be dismayed, he joined us in pushing our vehicle to his house where he tinkered a bit with the engine and had it working soon thereafter. He then proceeded to cook us some memorable whole grain waffles with fresh picked organic strawberries which we enjoyed with a nice conversation before making our goodbyes.

Our next stop was Burlington, Vermont where we had been invited to stay a few days with a neo-pagan pen pal I had been in touch with for a few years. It was another exciting sleep over for John and me which was sort of an initiatory experience in itself. Crowded into a very small downtown apartment lived my friend, her Native American boyfriend and seven children from various partners of theirs over the years. Besides the lively mix of domestic arguments and kids screams, the neighborhood itself had an interesting variety of ongoing dramas. The usual big city presentations of lonely people finding fellowship in talking to themselves, pimps and prostitutes, drifting scents of cannabis, barking dogs and even louder barking couples screaming at each other. We did observe one unusual experience of watching a bearded fat guy with long balding hair wearing some sort of ladies negligee and strolling a doll in a baby carriage.

Rounding the corner from our human merry go round, John and I took a quick stroll through the very picturesque downtown. Touched by the beauty of Lake Champlain, the city had an appealing blend of a fine university, diverse ethnic accents, interesting shops and an outdoors pedestrian mall protected from the noise and fury of automobile traffic. We had an even more intense tour of downtown later that evening with our friend, who showed us not only many funky cafes, eateries and hang out zones, but she also put us in the somewhat uncomforting loop of her own sort of survivalist urban foraging. With many of the upper crust restaurants lined up on the side streets of the mall, she whisked through and started picking up leftover slices of pizzas and other food items with negligible notice and hearty appetite. Not sharing the same confidence, John and I opted to keep a reasonable distance of association away from her but still be able to enjoy her handy talent and some of the bounty of her efforts of hospitality.

Later on the same evening as we felt it better to leave our friend and her boyfriend to scream at each other without us being around for their warpath ritual, John and I walked downtown as well eager for checking out even more "action." Not wanting to grab food off of tables as our friend had earlier demonstrated, we chose instead to go eat at a meager rice and beans meal at a nice smelling Caribbean restaurant. Although the food was tasty enough, the spicy sauce we added had us both tearing profusely. We asked the waiter for a glass of water but he tormented us even further by saying that there wasn't any more bottles left and that the sink water was not very healthy. Not being in a position to argue over the validity of his possible practical joke on us, we raced out of the store and found a small mini-market where we bought a big bottle of water to quickly chug all of.

On another occasion we had a less than pleasurable dining experience at an Indian restaurant. Being quite hungry we partook of the "all you can eat" with gusto and filled ourselves a few plates of the fine food. The owner however interrupted us on our third plate to tell us that we had eaten more than enough and that we had to leave.

Again not wanting to argue the point, we took another stroll into the nightlife of Burlington.

Feeling well fed, we then found our way to a wall where a young black man was playing a guitar and hoping people would toss in some spare change in his empty hat. Understanding our appreciation of his music, he chatted with us and even offered John a chance to play his guitar and have a turn busking for awhile. Within about ten minutes, John's talent brought about two dollars worth of happiness from passerbys. When the guy who owned the guitar came back he was delighted that we split the loot with him. We gave him a dollar for use of his instrument while keeping the other dollar for ourselves to buy and split a lemonade which we needed for the still reoccurring throat burning from our earlier meal.

On our last morning stroll of Burlington, we took notice of a poster announcing Ben and Jerry's ice cream company's annual celebration/stock holder's meeting coming up that same day. Without further ado we boarded one of the ongoing shuttle of hippie style painted buses that were taking anyone interested to the free event just a few miles out of town. What a thrilling surprise to be able to experience several stages of excellent music, vibes and food provided to the community. And even more appetizing bonus was in observing an opportunity on how we could partake of free food goodies as well. In a big circus size tent was the actual "stockholders meeting" which seemed like just a party of folks wearing tie dyed t-shirts listening to Grateful Dead music. On one of the table was a box full of tags with the word "stockholder" that allowed members the perks of fresh brewed organic coffee, homemade bagels and cream cheese and even as much Ben and Jerry's ice cream as one could eat. Not missing our chance, John and I put on the badges and kept on eating as much as we could. We even were able to sample flavors of ice cream that weren't even available to the public yet. Having purchased lots of quarts of Ben and Jerry's in the past, we felt ethically entitled to rub shoulders and fill tummies with the rest of the faithful.

With our week of extracurricular activity over, we drove a few hours to the Kripalu Institute in Massachusetts where John registered for his one week outdoor wilderness program. Conveniently, our friends Thea and Frans only lived a few miles from the center and provided me with a place to stay and hang out with them and their sweet hospitality. Our fun get together turned into a mild panic when we received a message that John had been injured while camping and needed medical attention. While slicing a watermelon, the knife he was holding had decided to take a slice of his hand and so he was taken to the hospital for stitches. The program itself was not too far into the "wilderness" (being less than a mile from downtown), so thus he was still able to catch up with the rest of the group before the camp session finished.

Joining me at Thea and Frans's house for a relaxing day and sleep over, we exchanged our last hugs in the morning and set out for our return back south again. Being still early enough to do so, we plotted our course not always on the freeway, so we could enjoy the back road scenery. Since the date was Independence Day, July 4th, John and I decided that an all American start of the trip would be to go to an authentic roadside diner for breakfast. We had no trouble finding one just out of town on a rural road where we stacked up on home fried potatoes and coffee for our carbohydrate and caffeine body fuel needs and filled our car with super octane for the few hundred miles ahead.

The ride was going smoothly along until we encountered an unexpected thunderstorm in western Pennsylvania. Even though we were on the freeway at this point, the rain was so heavy that the highway surface was becoming dangerously slippery as cars began sliding from side to side. Checking the map for alternate routes to at least pull off on was not easy, as the exit ramps as well as the rural roads leading off of them were becoming small lakes. Flash flooding warnings were announced on all the radio stations and the sight of floating cars made us even more nervous. Eventually we found a still driveable exit lane that we pulled off of and decided to stay safely parked in a shopping mall for a couple of hours until the thunder, lightning and rain calmed.

With the weather taking a turn for the better, our own nervous exhaustion perked up again as we approached Washington DC at the very auspicious moment of an epic fireworks display that was commemorating across the sky. But with the "rockets red glare" was not such a happy moment as now our car started making a terrible rumbling sound that only quieted down when we slowed our speed to under 40 miles per hour. Not only were we instantly back in a state of panic but now the added stress of having to drive with our emergency blinkers on for what would be another six hours back to our home base in Raleigh. Being a holiday weekend and not having the money that it might have taken for a major car repair, our slow pace was the only viable alternative.

RALEIGH

Our road trip eventually came to an end in Raleigh. My mother greeted us warmly but in the same breath complained, as usual, that I needed a haircut. The house still looked the same and being early September, we enrolled John in my old Junior High School, Daniels, while Nicolette started first grade at nearby Wiley Grade School. Sophia was still our "baby" and could now be the full time focus of our attention as the other two had fresh social interactions of their own to manage.

Cafes and visiting old friends felt a boring waste of time, so mostly Stephanie and I would stay at home and help my mother on projects as well as John and Nicolette with their school work. Sophia was also a gem to hang out with and at nights we slowly integrated back into watching movies on television. Our VHS player had a timer and with careful study of the television guide book of the month, we could program recording all sorts of classic films along with MTV and other entertainment to enjoy and archive. Not to mention that by fast forwarding the tape we would be saving valuable hours by not having to watch the commercials.

Since John was now old enough to appreciate other cultural pursuits, I bought him and myself two tickets to go see a real live World Wrestling Federation event. Dorton Arena at the fairgrounds was the venue that I had once seen Jimi Hendrix and Led Zeppelin concerts. Now, over twenty years later, I would be in a totally different world. All around us were sub-intellect rednecks yelling and screaming at the various athletes going through a variety of theatrics to bring them enjoyment and stress relief. The wrestling moves were silly enough as even without any actual contact, these guys would act as if the objects they were smashing each other with were bringing nearly fatal blows. But as ridiculous as this poor acting was, more terrifying was hearing the comments of the audience all around us who were totally mesmerized by what they felt was totally real. After this evening, John and I lost our taste for watching any more wrestling on television. But

I must admit that if ever Hulk Hogan is mentioned on the internet, we do rekindle our old fan excitement in checking out the details of the story.

One Sunday morning, John and I took a drive to a park where we wanted to shoot a few basketball hoops. Several black kids were playing on another court and invited us to join them. About an hour later after a satisfying period of sweat and exercise, our new friends pointed to a church not too far away and invited us to join them in the congregation. Even though we were the only non black people, we were treated with respect and hospitality and definitely enjoyed the high energy choir songs and the open hearted passion of the church service. Many people greeted us afterwards and kept asking us to come back again.

John didn't have to wait too long to replace his interests in wrestling or basketball, On his birthday, he was happy to be presented with a guitar case that he expected to open and find the inexpensive acoustic guitar we had looked at together a few weeks before. But in the interim my friend Tony was able to get us a nice deal on a more expensive Jeff Beck signature series electric Fender Stratocaster guitar instead. Not only did his eyes almost pop out of his head with delight, but he has been enhancing the world ever since with the sounds of wonderful electric rhythms.

Our daughters were also having adventures in their own realm. By now they were not only just sisters but best friends as well. Unlike John who would not show much interest in interacting with his older sister, Nicolette was happy to be a playmate as well as teacher and protector of her little sister. During school hours, Sophia would be getting attention and pampering from relatives and when Nicolette came home, they would promptly disappear into their own lovely world. Besides dolls, dressing up and drawing imaginative art projects together, Nicolette had a pink Barbie car that Sophia would snuggle next to her and together they would peddle around my mother's back yard.

STATE FAIR

Autumn was a nice time to be back in North Carolina as the leaves on the trees where changing into an array of brilliant colors and the temperature was very comfortable. The State Fair came to town in September and Stephanie, John, Nicolette, baby Sophia and I joined the other thousands of folks that piled in to get on the rides, see exhibits, eat foot long hot dogs, try to win prizes and get silly with friends. Teenage romantic rendezvous was another obvious observation as were the kids finding private spots to get drunk, stoned or both. By far the most enjoyable event for us before we went home was seeing Ray Charles that evening in the same indoor arena where I had once seen Jimi Hendrix, Led Zeppelin, The Harlem Globetrotters and more recently Championship Wrestling. (The latter being a memory that our son can still remember as well.) Perhaps Nicolette might one day have a recollection of her own in paying a quarter to see the world's largest pig as well as the lady with two heads. My own earlier memories were of haunted houses, strip shows and the ridiculous Ku Klux Klan hate booth.

With such a pleasant time of year, we tried to convince my parents to join us on a few picnics. But with my father's continual health deterioration, it was evident that it could not be. But still the memories were real of a similar time of year when they were both in better shape. A few years previously we had access to a mini motor home that we were eager to impress them with the full benefits of our "home on wheels". I had persisted in nagging them enough until they agreed to go with us for a two day trip to Carolina Beach. To maximize their pleasure, we filled our small refrigerator with food and played non-stop Greek music on the stereo for the three hour drive to the coast. Ironically, as fun as it was to hear my parents laughing and enjoying the ride, my anticipation of reentering the comforting nostalgia of when we used to come to this redneck family resort of my youth, was nowhere near as pleasant this time around.

Instead of the cute vacation cottages, we now saw tacky apartment buildings. And in place of parents and grandparents vacationing with kids, the boardwalk was packed with drunk and loud teenagers. Even the beach itself looked dark and murky unlike the white sand and clear blue ocean that we remembered. Trying to salvage at least some pleasure from the trip, we drove along the coast and stopped at what looked like a nice place for a picnic. Within a moment of opening the car door, we were attacked by squads of blood thirsty mosquitoes eager to make our life miserable. I can still remember my father loudly muttering "God damned Carolina Beach" over and over while spitting in the wind. With all the considerations of our visit, we decided to have lunch and drive back to Raleigh. At least our stove still allowed Stephanie to make a nice meal and even Greek coffee afterwards. So with the Greek music still playing, we cheered up and headed back.

As the end of October brought in the first gusts of cooler air and took away the bright leaves on the trees, our kids were excited about another Halloween. On his own, John had made the rounds on my parents street and was familiar with neighbors we never had met ourselves which was helpful that night in his knowing which houses would give him the most goodies. After last year's Halloween in Lahaina though, he was slightly disappointed that all he got was lots of candy and no money in the bag. Although Raleigh did not have a fabulous parade like in Lahaina, there were still lots of entertaining activities around town that night. Spending a lot of money to buy John a costume was not possible, so Stephanie used her skills in transforming an old gray blanket that we had bought when we camped in Oregon into a perfect little monk's outfit. And by adding ghostly white makeup and bloody red lips, John looked perfectly ghoulish. At a fraction of what other parents were buying for their kids, his outfit was cool enough to not only win first prize in a costume contest at nearby Pullen Park, but he also was able to win a few more similar contests in the years ahead. It even was a hand me down for Nicolette who won a giant pumpkin a few years later in another similar contest. That thrift store blanket along with Stephanie's talents were a wonderful match for displaying fashionably trendy trick or treat wear.

Even though we were happy to be discovering fun activities for our son and meeting a few interesting people as well, staying again with my parents was not at all pleasant, especially with my mother's continual complaints. We were amazed on how she could act so nice to the local rednecks yet hiss at us as if we were the lowest dregs of the world. And if ever anyone showed appreciation towards us, my mother would consider them as suspiciously part of whatever cult or negative profiling she had of us. Her lack of understanding our life style or intentions was sad and part of it seemed to be from her not speaking English too well. For example, one day she was watching a talk show on television in which two young men who were convicted of being pedophiles were on television explaining how by becoming born again Christians, their lives were now more righteous. As she stared at these clean cut guys with suits on, she started aggressively mumbling how she wished I was more like these images that she was watching. When I graphically explained to her what kind of sordid activity they had been engaged in, she started yelling at me in disbelief and demanded that I leave the room for saying such terrible lies about these boys who kept mentioning the word "God" in their interview.

MORE FAMILY EXCURSIONS

That December, Sophia experienced a traumatic incident which affected the whole family. Because John and Nicolette needed immunizations for public school, we were satisfied with their having been given homeopathic remedies from a naturopathic physician in Montana which left us feeling as if their health was protected as well as it satisfying the school's admission requirements. When we had been living in Montana, since Sophia was not then of school age, she had not taken them as the other two had. But it turned into a terrible day for all of us when Sophia came down with whooping cough. Since neither John nor Nicolette were infected, we felt somewhat secure that the homeopathic remedies had worked. But as we were not sure of how Sophia had caught it, we were never clear on its origins into our family nightmare. That Christmas season of 1993, we were all quarantined for two weeks at home and couldn't come out until Stephanie's birthday on the twenty ninth of December. Worse than the damper on the holidays, whenever Sophia would have a coughing bout that sounded as if she was chocking and her face would turn blue, the rest of us would feel helpless and terrified in worry. I personally would beg every god and goddess I knew for divine intervention to heal her or else I would be pounding my fists on the floor in anger at the same astral beings for bringing her and the family such cruel punishment.

A few months afterwards, another sad incident occurred one day which also left a traumatic imprint on Nicolette. While Stephanie and I had gone out for a couple of hours, some of Nicolette's new friends in the neighborhood came over and asked her to go across the street with them and play. But as she was running on the sidewalk, her foot went inside a hole that was from an uncovered water line pipe resulting in a large gash and shower of gushing blood. When we came home to the crying chaos of the injury, Stephanie almost fainted when she saw Nicolette's leg but managed to stay conscious enough for us to rush to the nearest hospital where she needed an agonizing fifty stitches.

Even if we had been at home, the outcome of the situation would still have been just as painful for her. Adding insult to injury, we hired an attorney who even after several years of pursuing our law suit on the city of Raleigh for obvious negligence, she only was awarded a small settlement. In retrospect we wondered if we picked the right attorney to represent us instead of someone who had his hands laundered at city hall.

Feeling in need of a road trip to make up for some of our recent injuries and health problems, we organized a couple of satisfying excursions that everyone in the household enjoyed. I reminded my mother of fond memories of an earlier trip to the mountains we had taken my father and her and surprisingly I was able to convince her to join us on a weekend trip to the same area again. Asheville and the Blue Ridge Parkway were scenic sidesteps to one of my favorite mountain towns, Boone where we went to see the famous play "Unto These Hills" at a drizzly evening performance in the town's amphitheater. Even with the wet setting, it was a moving depiction of how the Cherokee Indians were driven from their homes in this area on the infamous Trail of Tears. This information roused up the freedom fires of my mom who came out sad at seeing what the indigenous people had to endure. All the way back to Raleigh we kept hammering at the lousy American conquerors' cruelty. A historic reference to how she felt Greece had been similarly betrayed by the English and French in their political dealings during the Balkan wars leading her to "distrust" of such imperialism.

On a nicer note, on the way back we first stopped at the town of Blowing Rock. Of my mother's own accord, because she felt Nicolette was neglected when we bought John his electric guitar, she bought her granddaughter a musical instrument that was similar to a dulcimer and had a baby angel drawn on it. For the many months we would still be living in Raleigh, my mom would take delight in hearing the angelic sounds that Nicolette would play for her.

A couple of days after we dropped my mother off back in Raleigh, we were driving through more lovely destinations again. Stephanie had signed up for a weekend seminar on cranial-sacral therapy in Charlottesville, Virginia located in the Shenandoah Valley area along the foothills of the Appalachian Mountains. I had fun with the kids exploring some of the local colonial and civil war history ripely located in the area. Also, I dropped in at a nearby seminar on psychedelic mushrooms from the invitation of the host and by now fond pen pal, the illustrious fungal wizard Terence McKenna. Here we also met our now long time friend Lisa Amani and my introduction to the wonders of the internet. Terence kept referring to "emails" which sounded more like a hallucinatory flashback from the future, but as he would personally demonstrate for me, it was indeed a very present reality. As I now often stay on line researching and communicating through the internet, I can clearly state that it was Terence who literally talked me through my first web search as proof that information can be download out of seemingly empty space. I was surprised that as I was leaving the class I didn't hear him say "beam me up Scotty" and disappear into another cosmic dimensional star warp. But it was with real time understanding that I now relate to his message that the internet will be an important source of connection for the tribal hive brain of the alternative consciousness movement ahead.

Not too far away was Washington DC where we made a quick visit to the fabulous Smithsonian Museum and out of it in time before the two hour parking meter expired. We skipped the idea of meeting with our congressmen and settled for checking out some of the statues and monuments instead.

With still time for another side trip, we drove the long stretch from Virginia to Massachusetts to go visit our friend Thea and her husband Frans for high vibes, warm hugs and a pleasant stay in their world a few days. For me one of the highlights was in buying Stephanie an ankle bracelet from one of the many cute shops in town and with Thea's help, convincing her that we needed to head back again to Hawaii soon where obviously we could thrive better among mutual minded friends, nicer weather and further away from family traps.

With school still about five days from starting again, we took a side trip to another pagan gathering on the rural border separating New York from Ohio. Several thousand people were camping in the area and by the looks of the various venues and service stalls, it was one of the better organized and grander events that we had been to. Also we noticed from the many black cloaks and jewelry worn by the attendees, the philosophical theme was very Wiccan.

What a nice surprise to see that our friend Terence McKenna was one of the scheduled lecturers, so we promptly ran over to the particular stage he would be speaking as to not miss hearing any of his mind expanding words. As Terence was quite direct in expressing his views, after his statement that once someone ate a psychedelic mushroom, there would not be need for plastic Jesus dolls or Aleister Crowley black magic amulets anymore, a numb silence spread and even some light hissing in the room. Seeing me in the audience, he felt happy to be hanging around supportive company and so for the next couple of hours, he and I had a fine time walking around the various booths and talking very casually. The last memory I had of Terence was after a conversation together was interrupted by two beautiful and scantily clad nymphets who came up to take his hand and invite him to join them in the Temple of Aphrodite. Even within the same deeply intellectual sentence that he was telling me, he paused to give me a smile attached to a telepathic wink with the fading words "Later dude" as he scampered off with the beautiful young ladies.

The rest of the event was a mixed bag of interesting music including John's highly applauded solo in front of hundreds of people singing the very pensive environmental anthem I wrote for him called Tick Tock which was a reminder that if all the trees of the planet were logged at the present rate, the earth would be made desolate. Later during the night, someone, either psychotic, on drugs or wishing to make a pagan fashion statement of his own, decided to jump into a large bonfire and wind up with severe burns. An ambulance had to be called in and the police came along to investigate. I made sure we disappeared early before the cops started to make sense of the situation after seeing several thousand people gathered together with black cloaks and one of the members possibly sacrificed in the fire. Time for us to switch reality channels and re-embark for the mainstream Raleigh zone.

LEAVING AGAIN

With our travel bug and visions of distant horizons reignited, we made plans to drive cross country once school was over and move back to Hawaii again. Organizing our ideas and needs was simple enough but once our Isuzu was crippled by a bad mechanical servicing at a Shell station, we faced a hurdle of how to transport ourselves. A few telephone calls was all it took however to find a car rental company with a special discount on a two week van rental and also the option of driving it from Raleigh to San Diego and then dropping it off at the airport there before boarding our flight back to the Aloha state.

As always, we made our promises of returning again one day and waved our goodbyes before down the road we scampered in our shiny red rental van. By now, Stephanie and I were pretty familiar with the terrain ahead of us, but as our children were seeing this scenery for the first time, the excitement was as potent as ever.

By the time Interstate 40 brought us to Texas, our minds were both on getting through the never ending desolation of the state as well as watching out for strange occurrences such as those shown in the many zombie movies which were usually filmed in this part of the country. But on a more pleasant thought, Stephanie and I also remembered the fantastic Mexican food we had previously eaten at Leo's restaurant, so even though it would be a detour of several hours, we changed our course of direction and headed down to El Paso to fulfill our gastro-fantasies. Leo's restaurant was no longer in the same downtown location but not to despair, we asked around and were directed to its new location in a shopping mall on the other side of town. Even before we went inside the restaurant, we knew we were at our kind of place as one of the kitchen employees standing outside the back door gave us a few avocados to take home with us. I wound up ordering the el grande plate that included perfectly prepared enchiladas with three different sauces and wonderful taste. Needless to say, all of us left the restaurant feeling rewarded by the food gods and early enough to not have to deal with the full moon over El Paso nightmare that Stephanie and I had experienced after eating at Leo's on our first trip here about ten years before.

Taking such long detours was actually a pleasurable choice since living in Hawaii does have limitations as to how far one can drive around in circles. We thus ventured to check out some very artistic self sustainable futuristic community models, as well as traditional Native American cave dwellings in Arizona. Also in the area were our long time friends at the Peyote Way of God Church. This time we didn't stay for any ceremonies but did purchase some of their visionary inspired peyote plates before leaving. When we reached San Diego, we visited our friends David and Briana and went out for one last delicious authentic enchilada dinner at a very casual looking fast food place before we dropped off the van at the airport. As we prepared to board the plane, we had a farewell look at the mainland and then made sure that in our carry-on baggage we had room for our short pants, flip flop sandals and t-shirts that we would be putting on once we arrived back in Hawaii.

CHAPTER FOUR: HAWAII PART ONE

ALOHA

In the summer of 1994 our incarnation of living again in Hawaii found us in Kihei staying in the one bedroom apartment that originally we had purchased for my parents when we had hoped they would have found it suitable for living near us at the time. The beach was only a couple of blocks away and also within a short walk were shopping malls and other services. But as they refused to move from their home in Raleigh, we had been using the apartment for several years for rental income.

The neighborhood at that time was one of the more exciting blocks to be living with ongoing police cars driving by every night. As we would take our evening walk to the beach, we would often hear sounds of domestic abuse and associated fighting going on as well as loud television sets and clouds of cannabis smoke scenting the air. The building our unit was located in only had eleven apartments of which about half were going through such incidents regularly as well. Having five of us living in an apartment intended for two at the most meant being a little loud as well, but with so many other screaming matches going on, we were definitely one of the most quiet apartments in the area.

Although our living situation was not ideal, it was a nice base camp for us until we could come up with another option. Schools, beaches, shops and parks were close by and we didn't need to buy a car to get around. If we wanted to take longer excursions, we could rent a vehicle from a nearby agency. But even with all such amenities, the tourist and residential mainstream society on this side of the island was not where our tribe or social activities were centered. The call of the jungle was appealing and we knew that our apartment life in Kihei would only be a temporary crash pad until opportunity showed us a way out. But until then, we took advantage of being close to the ocean and every day we made sure that "life's a beach."

Being John's twelfth birthday, we ventured to go out and celebrate over dinner. We had first considered a picnic but the health food store nearest us was exploitively expensive. Dominoes Pizza was our second suggestion but we reminded ourselves on how we had felt sick in the stomach on our last two feedings there. And as all restaurants in the area were also high in price and low in quality, we chose our budget approach of taking a forty five minute family stroll along the beach road to Taco Bell. And with discount coupons we had collected from a tourist value advertisements magazine, we were set to dine in fine style.

An unexpected turn of events however made the rest of the evening somewhat challenging. One of the reasons that Kihei had developed into such a popular beach resort was that during the year there would usually be only a total of two or three days of rain. But when we were about to start our walk back home, the skies opened up and a heavy downpour started falling. The heavens must have been celebrating John's birthday as well and even provided a backdrop of thunder and lightning. Facing the concern of getting soaked, Stephanie came up with the perfect solution. The staff at Taco Bell were happy to provide us with four large garbage bags as well as loaned us a pair of scissors for her making the family our own customized set of raincoats. I'm sure John would have been okay with just wearing his birthday suit, but we were all happy that Taco Bell not only provided us with an affordable party venue but gave us free rain jackets to take home with us as presents. The cutest member of our family was Sophia who was being pushed on her stroller and now had a plastic bag covering the top of her head as well on our expression of functional fashion. And to finish our evening when we got home we had cake, ice cream and played our portable stereo a little louder than usual.

Changing residences regularly also meant that our children were exposed to a variety of schools and class mates. John was at that point in sixth grade while Nicolette in second at the local Kihei elementary school. Her first week of school was an orientation to becoming aware of important information such as avoiding thugs in the bathrooms looking for fights and sticking weird chemicals in their orifices. On her first day of class they even sent home some students for sniffing spray paint canisters. Surprisingly, the drug of choice at the time was not pot or alcohol but rather sniffing glue. This new craze had even reached the point of hardware stores on the island having signs next to the registers saying anyone buying spray paint would have to show an identification proving they were over eighteen years of age. Stephanie and I were startled one day when we went to the local ACE hardware store to buy a can of spray paint for our car when we were actually carded as well because of the law. As we left the store, I looked around the entrance and parking lot to see if any strung out kids would be waiting to offer us lots of money to go back to the store and buy them a can of paint for their fix. No such luck. And at the first "meet the teachers" event, the principal made an announcement that they needed parents to volunteer riding around the campus in a golf cart trying to bust kids for using drugs, fighting or destroying school property. At this point we were assured that we would not be having our kids in public school too much longer and besides, no reason for us to consider busting kids or even risk getting terrorized in the process.

Because of our continuous need to be economically frugal, our meal plans were based on sale items, discount coupons and on a few occasions, free-food kitchens. One such access was a church within a short walk that provided free lunches several days a week. Our venture to take part on the opportunity was okay as the food was concerned but the social factor had much to be desired. Making small talk with one of the ladies who was also there feeding her family, led to her clinging to our family afterwards and then insisting that we come along to her apartment. As much as we tried to be comfortable, we felt trapped by cigarette smoke, cheap beer, dogs and worse yet, her alcoholic husband wanting John to join them in their Christian rock and roll band that he maintained would soon have a gig in Las Vegas. Bearing the responsibility and the angry looks from my family, once we reached the safety of our condo, I promised I would never take them to any more free food kitchens.

LTAR

With most of our friends living on the other side of the island, we would occasionally rent a car to go visit people and also to attend events and enjoy scenic activities outside of Kihei. The cheapest deal on rentals was from a guy that advertised his business as LTAR, "long term auto rentals." His fleet consisted of mostly older big American gas guzzlers but even worse, their working status was very temperamental. He and his wife were an older Jewish couple that had moved to Hawaii after leaving Miami and didn't even have much of a knowledge about cars or how to maintain them. Our first outing with one of his vehicles took us about a couple of miles before the engine light came on and the radiator hose burst. His replacement car lasted about an hour before it too broke down. By now our family wanted to erase his LTAR advertisements we had noticed in town and change the T into an I and call his business LIAR. But instead of putting up an argument when we went back to his office, he met us wearing his robe and gold chain and took the defensive posture of saying: "you're good people, I'm good people, no problem, we'll come up with a car that will make you happy". And soon afterwards he explained that we should be satisfied with a vehicle that could just take us around the five mile length of Kihei and why would we need to drive anywhere else on Maui. Quite a ludicrous statement, but as we were elated to finally have a car that could take us out of town without breaking down, there was no reason to waste energy on looking back to our previous frustrations with LTAR.

THE KITE
With the consistent trade wind breezes, kite flying was an excellent and popular activity in the many beach front parks in the area. Wanting to provide John with the right tools to be able to enjoy this sport as well, we went to a well stocked hobby shop in town and purchased him a $100 kite with lots of pictures on the box showing happy people delighting in the joys of flying. To make it a full family fun day, we all went along for a picnic, swim and took a camera to film the golden moment of aviation. But even though the winds were steady that day, our kite flying experiences were not very impressive. In fact in the hour or so that we were running across the meadow trying to get our kite to fly, I don't think it stayed up more than a few minutes each time before crashing to the ground. Stephanie and Sophia eventually got tired of watching Nicolette, John and myself trying every sort of way for a successful flight and listening to our bickering and arguing as to whose fault that just about all our efforts failed. Eventually we gave up and while we were eating our sandwiches, Stephanie took out the instruction booklet from the box which explained the need for another part that we hadn't bought for it to fly properly. Just our looking at the

box was obviously not enough to fully understanding the process. And as we were leaving, Stephanie did take several photos of other kids flying kites so it wasn't a total loss for the picture collection. Ironically most of the kites in the sky were simple ones that only cost a fraction of the high tech one we had purchased at the specialty shop. But John kept insisting all the way home that it was our fault for having bought a "cheap kite" with missing parts.

WALAKA STREET

Walaka Street was notorious for being an area having one of the most domestic abuse problem on the island. Screams and slammed doors was a normal background soundtrack and looking at angry people pushing each other was common. Our own apartment building was in on the action as well as one day one guy pushed his girlfriend out the window and another time someone tried to commit suicide but the bullet he fired missed his head and went through the wall where it almost hit another tenant.

Our own involvement in the weirdness was initiated innocently enough when Stephanie took the garbage out to the dumpster one morning. In so doing she met and had a friendly talk with the building's one armed handy man who also turned out to be our next door neighbor. Later that night we started hearing a loud fight in their unit as he had locked his wife in the bedroom while she kept screaming at him that he was "in love and wanted to screw that whore Stephanie." Needless to say, we all had our ears peeled to the wall that night worrying that perhaps someone else might be shooting through the walls and even in our direction. Nothing more was ever heard from the man nor his woman who wound up moving a few days later. When the unit was being prepared for the next tenants, we looked inside at the many broken items and also saw a lot of empty bottles of prescription drugs tossed. This incident was another wake-up call to not talk much to our neighbors and to keep our intention clear about moving out of "Ki-hell" soon.

BUGS

Living in a socially diverse and volatile neighborhood can also offer lots of fun in watching the living theater of humanity unfolding in many ways. One day we heard some screams and then doors slamming at the apartment unit across the street. Expecting to enjoy another episode of relationship issues and body slams, we were treated instead to an incident closer to being a wildlife documentary. Two vans of the "Suck-em-up" septic cleaning company had been working on a septic line problem when all of a sudden they must have opened up the portal to the cockroach mother lode. Consequently the three Hawaiian septic technicians were showered by millions of bugs and as they ran out of the unit they were working on, we could see the cockroach armies spreading their dark shadow all over the parking lot. The comedy then turned into a threat of a horror movie if the bugs came across the street to move into our apartment building. With such level of excitement, why settle for mundane normal entertainment such as watching television or playing tennis. Maui had so much more to offer when you consider the reality shows on Walaka Street including now even our own wildlife safari in the empire of the cockroaches.

With so many other people enjoying "being naughty" in our neighborhood, I didn't want us to be party poopers and miss out on the fun. So with magic markers in hand and my three children along for the art lesson, we took turns drawing funny faces on some of the more obnoxious looking real estate sales signs. We didn't slow down the high momentum of development in Kihei but as urban graffiti artists, we did have satisfaction of leaving the signboard faces with horns and mean looks as expression of what we felt these greedy real estate agents were doing in destroying infrastructure and quality of life by selling ever inch of land that they could.

CRUISING WITH SUZY

With more and more activities of interest, we developed a pressing desire to buy our own car but on a pauper budget. When Stephanie took Sophia back to the mainland to visit her parents, Nicolette, John and myself caught a ride with a friend to Kula where we checked out and then bought a very funky island style small, economic Suzuki Samurai four wheel drive convertible jeep. It had plenty of rust holes and dents, but for the price of $400 and the mechanical check up saying it was in good shape, we were elated in having found our "perfect vehicle". Our proud maiden voyage down the highway was a reminder though that we needed to find a new canvas top as the present one had enough rips that the rain we encountered drenched all of us. But no complaints as we just felt it to be a baptism or champagne celebration of our new hot rod which we soon decorated with several bumper stickers and a small window decal that christened the car as "Little Wing" (though we mostly called it by its nickname Suzy). And not too many days later we found someone that sold us a replacement top so we were relieved that Stephanie wouldn't come back from her trip and have any complaints about our new vehicle.

FLAT ROCKS

Our intention to move to the jungle side of the island was perked up one day when we saw an advertisement for a large seventeen acre block of land for sale near Twin Falls called Flat Rocks. Usually these sorts of estates cost many millions of dollars but the proposition we saw was advertising two acre portions of the land for $50,000. The video of the property was also a lovely glimpse of paradise with waterfalls, ocean views, fruit trees and several structures that seemed to be calling to us to enter their magic kingdom. Katrina who was selling the property, explained that she needed to come up with $450,000 to pay off the bank's threat of foreclosure. She also told us that many friends of hers were already sending her their share of the money and that we needed to act fast if we wanted to be part of this enchanting opportunity.

In the next couple of days we connected with a private money lender to whom we mortgaged our condo at a high interest rate, but nevertheless, we still felt as if we were on the right stairway to heaven. Even though an attorney we consulted told us to be cautious of joint ownership with others, the land title company told us however that our contract with the owner looked legitimate and so we preceded to pay Katrina the money she wanted with confidence that we were soon going to be moving to Flat Rocks.

FLOOD

As much as we adjusted to living in what we were now referring as Ki-hell, the pressure of not feeling totally "in our element" was building. My determination to move to the jungle side of the island was bringing me on the verge of temper tantrums as the ladies of the family were just as insistent that we couldn't move anywhere that wasn't "comfortable and hygienic".

One day as we returned back from the beach, we were horrified to find that a water pipe had burst and our apartment was flooded.

Wanting to look at the situation in a positive way, I was able to convince the family that divine intervention was encouraging us to move out. So without much argument, we took whatever stuff was salvageable to a storage unit we rented and trusted faith that now was the time to move to our portion of land at Flat Rocks.

The only decision we thought was left was where on the land we wanted to move to. The bamboo forest on top of a hill had beautiful ocean views and a sweet breeze all day long. Along the river the spaces near the waterfall were appealing as were so many other building sites on this magnificent land. Ultimately, whichever area was picked, the waterfall and pools were available to all the residents for swimming in the refreshing pools below. And to add spiritual help in our property claim, we asked the Greek Orthodox priest on his next visit from Oahu to come bless the land for us.

Around this time as part of our preparation of possible camping opportunities on the island, we had purchased a mini motor home that included a sleeping loft upstairs and a red decorated bed area in the back. A sort of Elvis in Las Vegas with a bubble space ship appearance which had previously been rented to newlyweds visiting Maui. The car itself had mechanical issues but the rest of us found it perfect to bring it as our new home in the Flat Rocks bamboo forest.

At this point we were determined to make this land our home. We had both a Greek priest and a Hawaiian Kahuna bless it and every time I swam under the waterfall I made a special prayer that the waters baptize me as a new resident. In fact, we made prayers to all the elements to help us manifest our intention. Camping with us in the bamboo forest was our friend Dave, who was very much part of our tribe and together we would enjoy the evening breeze and sunset. Our friend Jason came over a few times and showed John how to play "Hey Joe" and often we would have friends come stay late enough to share meals and music jams afterwards. Either by ourselves or with friends, we would swim not only in the magnificent waterfall but also hike along the river to many of the other delightful pools too.

But alas, as much as our heart and soul wanted to believe that we were part of the land, the legal system foreclosed the property and we were served eviction papers. Katrina's land offer had swallowed our money and our hopes. She also had borrowed money from many other friends that she had to pay from any money that she would make from the bank sale of the property. With so many millions of dollars that she owed, our share was in last place and came out to only about a fifth of the money we had given her. When the inevitable final day of moving came, at least the higher spirits of this area that we had befriended did not leave us homeless. Just a few minutes away was a tract of land owned by a Krishna devotee named Makunda who allowed us to rent a space for our motor home. And as a bonus, it too had a waterfall just a short way to go swim at.

EASTER PLAY

During those challenging moments of trying to protect being expelled from our heavenly homestead, we still were socializing and attending parties and other community events. One Sunday at a Unity Church service, Rolando, who was the musical director, asked me if I would like to play the part of Jesus in an Easter play that he was producing for the church. Since we were already friends with most of the twenty or so members of the congregation and since I had the most biblical looking appearance of long hair and beard, I agreed to take on the part. Being Jesus for an hour was nowhere as intimidating as if I were asked to play a shopping mall Santa Claus where kids sitting on my lap could pull my beard, urinate in my lap or complain afterwards that their Christmas gifts were lame or broken.

Nonetheless, I agreed to play the part of JC and even to help co-write the script which was basically a contemporary drama of how a troubled teenager is in a hopeless situation until the Lord appears and helps him out of his misery. And since I was in charge of writing the story, I even recruited our son John to play the "troubled child" role. Thus by being given full freedom to create the story and dialog, I chose a real life situation in which when Jesus appears to the crying child and asks him why he is crying, John would reply "My family and I gave a woman we trusted $50,000 for land that she was selling but we lost our money and now we are all out on the street". By talking about our own story, I felt that we would be not only clearing out our frustration but also making it clear to at least the Unity Church congregation that someone that had a recognized profile in the community as Katrina was not exactly ethical.

A few days before Easter weekend Rolando broke the news that the play was going to be performed at the grand opening of the Maui

Arts and Cultural Center. No longer was it my concern of being nervous talking in front of twenty people but more like 2000. Understandably for the remaining days before the play I was a nervous wreck and in a state of panic. There was some comfort in that the play was only one small part of Rolando's presentation, so even if I screwed up my role, there was plenty of professional music, entertainment and an Easter sermon from our Unity church minister.

The big moment finally arrived and just like the oncoming peak of a psychedelic trip, there was no turning back. Mumbling the lines over and over in my head, one of the backstage crew members seeing my predicament came over and told me what I needed to do was to speak fast and not look at anyone in the audience. Trying to plant his advice in my head, I was then approached by someone else who told me that I needed to speak my words slowly while looking closely at the people sitting in the front row. Such was my confusion and just before the curtain went up, I did what Jesus had done before the soldiers arrived to arrest him. I turned my head upwards and asked God what should I do next. Just then a transformation occurred and I felt I was Charlton Heston playing Moses in the Ten Commandments movie. And as I entered the stage I felt very comfortable and both John and I acted as professionals in telling our real life story. The most poignant moment came when I was telling the troubled youth that he needed to toss aside the stone blocking his heart and be forgiving. With an inspired flow I turned to the audience where I recognized Katrina sitting in the middle section and then with open arms and a beatific smile, I looked directly at her and said with all sincerity that she was forgiven. At that moment, the whole venue was taking part in a living theater as Katrina got up in embarrassed tears and ran out of the building while just about everyone stared at her. Before the whispering and gossip became too epidemic, I made one more statement to the audience about the power of love which then brought on a standing ovation and a perfect ending to the drama.

We never saw Katrina again that year but learned afterwards that she had fallen into personal and financial problems. Even though the pain of losing our money and what we felt as our land, I felt sorrow for Katrina as she was a victim of the situation. Again I sent out a blessing and wished her well. As for me, I kind of stayed high in my Jesus trip thinking I could walk around town and tear up unfortunate people's parking tickets and other such appreciated miracles, but the excitement wore off after the play and my role was over. Not everyone can be as blessed as Charlton Heston who could convince my mother every year when she would watch reruns of the Ten Commandments movie during the holiday seasons that he was the real and full time Moses.

CHAPTER FIVE: FIJI

FIJI

While over at our friend Tina's for dinner one night, my browsing through her travel books enticed a desire for travel to the exotic countries of Bali, Thailand and Fiji. As I have a tough time picking from multiple choice options, I decided that now was our chance to visit all three of these beautiful places. Off season travel seemed relatively affordable and as we were clearly not going to be able to have any ownership potential in the Flat Rock's property, we needed to have our spirits rejuvenated. And since the court awarded us enough settlement money to purchase the tickets, we felt it was not only the karmicly correct decision but also a chance for our children to experience these exquisite cultures before time altered them into homogeneity.

To maximize the value of such an expedition, focused research and organization were vital. From the local public library I checked out as many relevant travel books as I could while also constantly comparing airline ticket prices for the best deal. As for schooling, we promptly started our kids in a correspondence school program as soon as their public school terms finished in June, so we could get an affirmation that they would be able to handle it comfortably. We examined about twenty different programs and finally settled on Oak Meadow as it had no religious agenda and offered the most appealing curriculum. Their holistic approach was influenced by Rudolph Steiner's Waldorf school system which was popular in many other places around the world and was also very flexible in allowing us as parents to substitute text material if we felt it to be more appropriate than their lesson suggestions. The specific weekly lessons and student support system also looked beneficial to our travel plans which would make our journey an educational hands-on field trip. The goal was thus set for leaving in September as that would give us a couple months first to evaluate satisfaction with the school program besides giving me time to study the travel books for designing a pleasing itinerary. Although all three countries were in the same general area of the world, they were not easily connected with the airline destination maps, so the idea was to go to Fiji on a round trip ticket and then soon after fly to Bali and from there to Thailand before returning home to Hawaii. Being assured by Makunda that we always had our jungle campsite available upon our return, we left a few of our belongings with our friend Dave, and found a place to park our jeep and motor home (which we eventually sold).

BULA

Secure in knowing our children's satisfaction with Oak Meadow's school program and with our detailed plans of touring several islands in Fiji, we followed the time lines across the Pacific leading us to Fiji.

Looking around at our fellow passengers decked out with fancy polyester casual wear, dazzling jewelry and sun tan salon skin coatings, I was feeling a bit concerned that Fiji might be an uncomfortable experience of expensive tourist resorts full of loud mouthed fools and their arrogant attitudes. Their shiny pale skin seemed as if they could find an easier time blending on the advertised white sand beach resorts than with the darker toned indigenous people of the country. We smiled with deep satisfaction that within ten minutes after our plane landed we saw all of these folks disappear into long lines of fancy vans that whisked them and their tennis rackets away to private fantasy island vacation resorts. Happily, for the next month we would hardly see another tourist on our trip without having our time interacting with the local people contaminated.

Immediately we could sense that life moved at a slower pace here than even Hawaii and that the foliage and fauna of nature were bright and healthy. Suva was once a colonial capital of the British Crown which still retained a charming architectural style and was well laid out with green belts and public parks. Following the suggestions in our travel book, we rented a couple of large clean and inexpensive rooms in a local hotel which was located just a small walk from downtown and away from most traffic noise. Eager to start exploring the surroundings, we soon visited the local museum, arboretum and harbor. But our motivating priorities were for our eyes and noses to evaluate the local eateries first. The price and menu choices were reasonable but even more so were the many other food options at the downtown outdoor public market place.

Strolling along the long tables of fresh fruit and vegetable selections, I noticed that the women were mostly the ones selling while the men sat on the ground with their kava bowls drinking the brew and playing ukuleles. Everyone smiled and looked extremely content which is one of the healthy benefits in partaking of this nation's most popular beverage. I felt it a great pleasure as when many of these men invited Stephanie and I to sit down and drink a few bowls with them. Any jagged edges in our mind and body from our long air flight were soon calmed and we also soon found ourselves smiling from an enhanced sense of well-being.

Over a century earlier when the British tried to force the indigenous Fijians to work in the sugar fields, the locals made it clear that they preferred the simpler life of drinking kava, singing and dancing with their family more than entering the rat race of toiling for unnecessary money. Thus the British brought workers from India to do the sweaty work and thus developing the present situation in the country where that most of the businesses are operated by Indians while the Fijians prefer to live simply and to simply live.

When the first missionaries landed on these islands, they were quickly eaten by the locals and thus the name Cannibal Islands was given to this part of the world. By such a dietary practice, the natives were spared what had happened to other Polynesian islands of having their land ripped off by these black robed predators. In one of the downtown museums hung a painting of a local chief who, even though was a short skinny man, he had managed to eat fourteen Christian missionaries. Eventually, even though these men were eaten, they did leave behind bibles which brought the indigenous people out of practicing cannibalism and tribal warfare to a more compassionate and peaceful life style.

Besides delighting in drinking kava in the market, many vendors were also selling a variety of fresh fruit juice for about twenty cents a glass. Stephanie and the girls were reluctant to drink the water, but John and I gulped about five glasses each which satisfied our thirst and kept our smiles and health glowing. The only problem we found in the marketplace was that, being tourists, several pushy younger guys kept pestering us to buy generic souvenir trinkets whose proceeds they claimed would be going to needy people in their village.

Within our first couple of days in Suva we were acclimating nicely to both the land and its people. On a whole, Fijians were the friendliest people we had ever met and when they passed on their greetings of "Bula", it seemed as if the sound was coming with sincere emotion from a deep well in their heart.

Back at Tina's house where we first entertained the idea of coming here for a visit, we had watched a short video sent to her by a friend that had moved to Fiji from Maui. Our possibly following a similar plan seemed affordable, so just in case we might decide to make a similar move, I had contacted the two real estate agents mentioned in her video and made plans to visit them when we arrived.

David Miller was a real estate agent who had moved to Fiji with his wife and daughter many years previously from Australia. We first checked out his credentials with the local title company before taking the elevator up to meet him in his top floor office overlooking the beautiful Suva skyline. His big teddy bear appearance and gentle personality quickly put us at ease and we accepted his gracious offer to take us out to lunch. Afterwards we returned to his office where he gave us a map of several land developments on the island that he was offering and then an invitation to come to his house for dinner one night and let him know if we were interested in any of his listings. During the course of our two week stay here on the main island of Viti Levu we did take a look at his places, but for one reason or another we weren't totally satisfied enough with any to consider living at. But even with our feedback, David and his wife were very hospitable and assured me that if he ever had a listing in the future that sounded more appropriate to our criteria, he would let us know.

Touring the other parts of the island was quite a pleasurable experience of riding on the public bus through lush scenery and listening to the giggly conversations of happy Fijians. Stopping in the town of Nandi, the jolly Indian man who was driving the bus we were on, walked back to the rear where we were sitting and said he liked us and wanted us to come to his house the next day to join his family for the Indian new year's celebration of Diwali. Appreciating but not taking his very hospitable greeting as nothing more than his being happy that a rare family of American tourists were content in riding on the local public transport system instead of air conditioned taxis, we went on with our exploring more of the exotic culture in this predominantly

Indian section of the island. The scent of fragrant curry spices, Hindu temple architecture, and the faster pace of commerce and entrepreneurship was a delightful immersion into yet another colorful side of Fijian society.

Feeling happy with our walking tour of Nandi, we returned to our hotel with anticipation of going out to a yummy smelling pizzeria down the street afterwards. Upon walking into our room and finding all our suitcases gone, our joy vanished as panic of having been robbed took over all our senses. We ran down the stairs to express our emergency to the lady at the front desk but in a calm attitude, she smiled and simply pointed to the street outside. Turning our heads in that direction, we were surprised to see a pickup truck parked in front of the hotel with a young Indian man waving and all our suitcases stacked nicely in the back. A moment later, it all started making sense, as out of the front seat of the truck jumped out our Indian bus driver friend who had not only come to take us to his house, he even had paid our hotel bill.

No longer feeling as if we were just tourists without any local roots anymore, we delighted in our festive weekend of eating lots of delicious homemade Indian food that various family members prepared, setting off firecrackers and drinking several cases of Fiji Bitter beer together. We even went for a picnic at a nearby waterfall and stream but were a little disturbed as to how our hosts tossed several large bags of garbage into the otherwise clean water. As we would find out in the course of travels, people all over the world unfortunately have the same insensitivity to such polluting habits. But on a nicer note, as we parted ways and shared our last hugs, the Indian family expressed how much they enjoyed our company and invited us to one day come live in a small apartment they offered to build for us next to their house. Our new roots kept growing.

Before leaving Nandi we had a very photogenic visit to a magnificent Hindu temple but afterwards had a related dose of an impending reality that was disquieting. On one of the street corners downtown stood a very white Caucasian man, wife and small child, all dressed in bright suits, bow ties and looked as if they just came from Kansas. In the adults hands were not tennis rackets but small bibles which they passed along to Fijians that were being ushered into a large meeting room. The young boy had a box of candy from which he was likewise encouraging local kids to take and to come inside to hear the presentation as well. From the looks of a poster they had taped on the doorway showing the Hindu deity Krishna wearing horns and having a long tail, it was clearly an intention to incite Fijians to hate their Indian neighbors and eventually lead to a dissonance in the otherwise harmonious relationship between these two ethnic groups. It smirked of one more "divide and conquer" power play from the Christian missionaries eager to burn down other peoples temples, enslave their souls, and follow the same formula of stealing their land as they did so well in Hawaii.

Fiji's topography was an impressive blend of clear blue ocean, lush mountains, many waterfalls and wide swift flowing rivers. Our next visit was to a large botanical nature reserve where we went on a one hour hike giving us a chance to walk through the scenery and even a possible dip in a waterfall pool. About half way on the trail, a tall, skinny Fijian man with a machete in his hand jumped out of the bushes, showed us some sort of identification card while mumbling a story about how he was a police officer trying to catch an escaped murderer supposedly hiding in the area. He asked us to keep walking on the trail while he would be near us and if the suspect attacked us, the "cop" would immediately apprehend him. Somehow the idea of being bait did not feel comfortable to us and even worse was the idea that maybe this new friend was not a policeman at all but instead was a thug himself who planned to find the right moment to rob us. So far we had been the only tourists on the path but when we heard the voices of what sounded like young Americans ahead of us, we quickened our pace to catch up with them and distance ourselves from any potential threats. We never did have a chance for a swim, but reaching the exit gate not harmed or robbed was satisfying enough.

That night we stayed in a nearby hotel but did not get any sleep. Not because we were scared of being stalked by the phony cop or because of too much partying, but because once we turned the lights off in our rooms, the walls would be covered with huge cockroaches. Turning the bathroom light on gave us some comfort but there were still so many flocks of these creatures that, although probably do no harm, still make me nervous and in a state of alarm. Possibly it was because of the many science fiction movies I had seen when I was a kid in which giant bugs start terrorizing humanity. Now I feel humanity with its giant ego is terrorizing all of life in general.

With one more day left for us on the main island, we decided to take a river cruise on a boat navigated by a friendly guy who invited us to come to his house afterwards for some kava and socializing with his family. His house was fairly modern in style, but like the traditional village home, sparse in furniture or decoration. He did have a small black and white television which he turned on and placed in front of us. Since we were Americans, he assumed that we would want to bury our intention in the canned laughter of an "I Love Lucy" rerun and wanted to please us. A reflection on the idiocracy of modern western culture that uses the couch potato as its new archetype but also a warning to how this infectious slime will one day mean that he and his friends might well give up the traditional kava bowl ceremony and might be chugging beers and watching Fijian soap operas instead. But once again, since his intention was to be hospitable, we showed respect by watching Lucy and Ricky Ricardo squabbling over some glamour issue on the world wide matrix channel of oz.

The next island we visited was called Taveuni and locally referred to as "the garden island" because of the many varieties of flowers that graced its landscape. Getting off the ferry boat we enjoyed watching lots of young children having fun sliding down a natural water slide that gave us also a glimpse of a nice waterfall to perhaps take a dip in at some point as well. At the harbor we were met by a young man who took us in his car to the beach side campground not too far away where we had reserved a couple of traditional style bure huts to stay in for a few nights. For us it was a regal experience of relaxation, swimming, hiking and enjoying some wonderful local food prepared by the very personable owner himself.

Not far up the road was our first actual local village that we came to visit and maybe stay at. Besides its beautiful ocean front setting, it was also the village where our friend on Maui, Mercury, had asked us to go visit. Several years beforehand, he had lived there for several weeks and because of the nice impression he had made with the residents, one of the families had a baby which they named Mercury in his honor. Following the prescribed custom of bringing a bundle of kava to the chief before being given permission to stay in his village, our audience and kava ceremony went well and were directed to a family whose home we would be staying at for the night. We also were introduced to the family that named their baby after our friend who were delighted with the small presents we had been given by Mercury to give them.

That night in the traditional home bure, we learned a few more lessons on Fijian customs. No chairs were noticed in the rooms and seating for meals and other activities was on large weaved family mat called a tapa. For me it was a pleasure eating cross legged and also not having to use any silverware. Food always tasted better when eaten directly from hand to mouth. The family kept bringing us more and more delicacies which, even though we were getting filled on many of the more starchier items, we did not want to offend our hosts hospitality, so we still kept eating. But what we realized afterwards was that the Fijian custom was to feed the guests first and then eat what was left over. In our case, we must have eaten most of their dinner and only left them a few morsels of rice. Even worse, the beds they gave us to sleep on were their own and thus they wound up sleeping on mats outside all night. But we didn't have much of a chance to experience guilt as their blankets were full of fleas and kept us up all night scratching all parts of our bodies.

The next morning, we were greeted by several young children of the village who wanted to help us hike to a nearby waterfall where the romantic scene of the famous movie Blue Lagoon was filmed. The walk itself was not too difficult except for the times when we had to cross the river on slippery rocks. Seeing our predicament, two of the older girls put our daughters on their backs and were able to help us get to the pristine corner of paradise where we swam and relaxed for over an hour.

On our way back to the village, we passed a spot that was even more like out of a page in a dream. On one side of the road was a gorgeous white sand beach and on the other a lush green mountain with several tall waterfalls dipping into a stream that rippled along the edge of a village. Seeing us walking on the road, the chief who looked very much like an indigenous Yul Bryner playing the role of the Pharaoh in the classic Ten Commandments movie, came out of his hut wearing several honorific emblems. In a clear Oxford English accent, he greeted us saying "Good afternoon and welcome to my village where I would like to invite you to come into my home for hospitality".

No reason to argue with a chief, so we followed him into his large bure where after we shared kava together, the slightly telepathic nature of the brew convinced him we were good guests. He then clapped his hands and several giggly women brought us a large feast of fruit, vegetarian food items and more kava. As evening approached and we were once more heading back down the road, we pondered the chief's last words of saying we were welcomed to live in his village and his friends would build us our own bure near the beautiful waterfall. It was bittersweet to know that a key to heaven was offered to us but for whatever reason, we needed to leave and go back to a different social jungle in America.

Among the standard instructions when you are an airline passenger is mainly to explain the importance of keeping your seat belt on during designated times as well as what to do during other emergencies such as plane crashes, etc.. While waiting at the one room airport for our twelve seat inter-island flight to the second largest island of the country, Vanua Levu, a whole other sort of crisis occurred that I had no clue on how to deal with. While Stephanie and the kids were already starting to board the plane, I went to the rest room for an assumed under a minute visit. But when I tried to leave, the door knob was stuck and my shouts and door pounding were not being heard. Finally after delaying the flight until they could find out what happened to me, Stephanie remembered that I had gone to the bathroom and was able to get a maintenance man to push open the door. Luckily they did not find me either dead or constipated and as this was laid back Fiji, we all had a good laugh about the situation and all's well that ends well. And besides, in just twenty minutes we would be landing on one more beautiful island paradise.

Savusavu has one of the more picturesque boat harbors in the Pacific. The bay is surrounded by hills and gentle breezes while the laid back ambiance flows well with the locals drinking kava and the boat captains sipping their cold beers. Of course, the sad curse of development had already drawn up plans for shopping malls, hotels, fancy shops and all the other prides of Babylon that would eventually squeeze out the natural beauty and usher in more tourist congestion. But for now, the streets were fairly empty as we took a stroll to the hotel that we had reserved staying the night at. By now cockroaches crawling across the walls was an expected part of our travels and we managed to actually feel comfortable sleeping with them in the same room. Next to the hotel was a natural hot spring that for some reason was not being used for people to soak their bodies in but only for washing clothes and steaming food. Around the corner were some nice smelling restaurants to pick eating our dinner at and also making contact with the other realtor we wanted to see on this trip, Bob Morton. Bob was quite a bit different than our real estate friend in Suva, David. His personality was more rigid and lacked a sense of humor. Also upsetting was his constant racist remarks about both the Fijians and Indians and expressed a very colonial attitude. Still, he was able to show us some very nice properties including one stunning five acre parcel on top of a hill with a complete 360 degree view of ocean, mountains and the nice waterfall below. Of course the property was out of our price range but Morton eventually did find a nice buyer who was a famous under sea film maker instead of a land exploiting elitist.

From Savusavu, we took the local bus that would take us to the predominantly Indian town of Lambasa located on the other side of the island. The three hour ride itself was a like a magical mystery tour through one magnificent view after another. Mountains, streams, waterfalls and fresh breezes blowing through the windowless sides of the bus. About half way to our destination we reached an impasse on the road. The bridge across the river had cracked and there was no other way to get over to the other side. A team of men from the nearby village soon showed up with lots of tools and intentions to make repairs in a speedy fashion. Meanwhile, as if all on cue, most of the passengers ran out of the bus and jumped in the river with their clothes on. Even the elderly folks took dips and splashed each other while many of the other ladies danced and sang. Within an hour the bridge was repaired and everyone brought their wet bodies back on the bus. Perhaps we were being too cautious, but instead of testing the structural quality of the bridge, we chose to walk across and then get on the bus when it reached the other side. All refreshed from our rest stop and the bus and bridge still in one piece, we rode on for another hour to the sound of passengers singing.

As we were approaching an Indian enclave, the sight of more plywood houses instead of bures appeared along the way. The end of the road brought us to the noise and bustle of Lambasa where busy merchants and shoppers were scampering in all directions. Incense and background sounds of chants and arguments filled the air as did the stares of people who were not used to seeing Western tourists. After checking into a nearby hotel off a side street, we set out for an evening stroll around town. There were plenty of fine looking (and smelling) Indian restaurants to chose eating at, but instead we decided to go to a Chinese eatery called Joe's which was recommended in our travel book. Perhaps a bad choice as during the night, all of us felt sickly. Even worse, the next day we read a local newspaper that had an article on how Joe's restaurant had been cited by the government health department for using dog meat in their meals. At that time we still ate chicken and as that was one of our menu choices, we felt a little concerned that there might be some other meat item in the mix that only tasted like chicken.

For our return trip back to Savusavu the next day, we hired an Indian taxi driver who gave us a less expensive price than if we had taken the bus. The bridge we crossed the day before was still standing and the ride was smooth while we listened to contemporary Indian pop music on his tape deck instead of the Fijian songs of the day before.

Along the way we stopped at some nice scenery and felt satisfaction from our visit, dog or not. And at the island airport, I made sure not to close the door all the way when I went to the bathroom. With just a few more days remaining on our trip to Fiji, we stayed once again in the first hotel we had stayed in Suva. With the bus, we made a visit to a couple more ocean front places that our realtor friend had suggested we look at. Even though none of them were particularly interesting to us, we did enjoy walking on the beach and an occasional swim. The ocean was perfectly clean, but difficult to swim on most beaches because of the coral reefs. Sometimes you would need to walk out about fifty yards into the ocean before you could find a place that wasn't overly shallow. Still it was a refreshing exercise and also fun watching Fijian adults and children who would be likewise splashing around but with all their clothes on.

Our final visit before leaving the country was to one more nearby village that was discussed in our tour guidebook. As mentioned, it was very scenic and the children that greeted us as we got off the bus were happy with the rubber balloons we passed out to them as gifts. For the chief, we presented him with both a bundle of kava roots as well as a big bag of sugar which made him doubly happy with our arrival and subsequent insistence that we stay the night as his guests. Our conversation with the chief was cordial as well as informative. He explained how in Fiji, the land rights of each village are under the supervision of its chief. The Indian population, which now comprised over half the total, could only lease land from the chiefs so as to maintain control from what they considered harmful exploitation. The fear being that if Indians could purchase land, then foreign corporations could become land partners with them and thereby bring in sneaky corporate plans for a takeover of land and resources.

While we were conversing with the chief about these issues, we noticed two police cars pulling up the driveway. After hearing a knock on the door and several policemen come in only to hear a lecture from the chief as to their inappropriate interruption of our kava ceremony. With downcast faces and their hats in their hand, they explained how a young teenager from this village had gotten drunk the night before in Suva and had caused harm to someone he had been in a fight with as well as some damage to the bar he was drinking at. Besides being in charge of land distribution, the local chief is also responsible for arbitrating justice in his village. In this case, the police brought in the sad and hung over looking young man and presented him to the chief before they left to return to their headquarters in Suva. As for the "criminal", the chief, even though he only had one arm, without a comment, grabbed the kid and gave him five sharp kicks and numerous slaps. To add even more humiliation for his behavior the night before, he told him that for the next two weeks, he had to clean out the pig shit around the elderly people's homes. Somehow there seemed to be much more wisdom in such an approach than in the US where prisoners are thrown into cells with other criminals to be brutalized into becoming either psychos or more hardened criminals. A very front row educational workshop for us to experience before setting off back to Hawaii. And with heartfelt intention as we said our last "Bula" we added "We shall return".

CHAPTER SIX: BALI

BALI

Just a few days after we returned to Maui, we repacked our travel bags and were soon flying back across the Pacific to the enchanting island of Bali. The flight itself was not too comfortable. Not because of yuppie tourists as when we went to Fiji, but because at that time Indonesian air flights still allowed passengers to smoke in the cabin. Both Greece and Indonesia were ranked high among per-capita tobacco use, and it seemed that on this flight, they wanted to keep practicing for the top place in the honor as well as probably climbing in the global lung cancer rankings. Consequently once we landed my first steps were to run into the bathroom and barf up all the clouds of smoke that had infested my lungs for six hours. This pause was probably helpful in other ways as we bypassed the first wave of clinging locals waiting to grab tourists once they passed customs in hopes of convincing them why they should stay in their overpriced and far out of the way guest homes.

With so many exotic images of Bali, the city of Denpasar was quite a letdown. Between the scattered statues and temples there was also excessive traffic, motorcycle noise, pollution and shady looking people. Our taxi driver took us to our hotel where at least we felt our room to be adequate for us to relax during the night and get oriented better. My travel book was full of ideas of where to go not only in Bali but even to other parts of the country, so I was confident that once we got out of the metropolitan chaos, we would be enjoying the rest of our itinerary. Quite obviously we realized to expect a more congested visit here where five million people were crowded in a small island instead of how in Fiji less than a million people lived on several islands the same size. And besides, instead of the relaxing effects of kava root brew as in Fiji, Indonesians were pumped on caffeine, nicotine, betel nut juice, and nonstop religious ceremonies.

Not very interested in watching the caged monkey which was the showpiece of the hotel lobby, we took a long walk the next morning to visit some of the more interesting tourist sites in the area. At one of the more popular temples we visited we were approached by a friendly man who offered to take us on a scenic drive for a very reasonable price. Having made arrangements to be picked up the next morning from our hotel and with our giving him a few suggestions of where we would like him to take us to, we felt relieved that we would thus be able to start seeing more of the Balinese world than just a big city. When we came back from one of our first exploratory walks, Nicolette wanted to have a closer look at the caged monkey. But instead of it showing an affectionate response back to her, it reached out and scratched her arm instead. Even though we were assured by the proprietor that it did not have rabies or any other dangerous disease, we were feeling that the Balinese omens were telling us to be making plans soon to explore other parts of the island.

By now we had yet to see evidence of those colorful outfits that the glamorous new agers on Maui would prance around in and call "Bali clothes". All we could notice so far were mostly jeans and normal clothes that you would find at Kmart. Were such outfits reserved only for expensive workshops in Hawaii or would we actually see them worn elsewhere on the island? The mystery quest was just beginning.

Of all the places in the world we have been to, Bali was one of the most dogmatic in following rituals and ceremonial details. The rate of repressed feelings and neurotic disorders has been correspondingly documented high as well. A Balinese person is discouraged from ever leaving the island because of duty to say specific prayers for not only ancestors but for the land as well. One day I even heard an older lady crying over what was explained to me was their failure to light incense under a certain tree. Gongs and parades are non-stop and as extended families live in one home compounds, there is always need of such expressions.

The taxi driver that we had met and who came to pick us up at the hotel was named Wayan. Only five male names such as his are predominant in the local cultural vernacular. Along with him was another person who he also introduced as Wayan and would be the driver of the van. What our new friend had not explained clearly the day before was that we would not only be paying for him to be our guide but would also have had to pay his partner for being the driver. Being affordable enough to hire both of them, we agreed and set out on a drive to the artistic town of Ubud that we planned to have as our base for the next week.

The combination of having the two Wayans actually was beneficial as the guide would point out scenery and interesting information, while the driver kept smiling and playing a Bob Marley tape on his car stereo. After the tenth time we heard it, however, we made him happy by buying him a "Best of the Rolling Stones" cassette which added another musical perspective to the panoramic landscape floating past our car window.

Leaving the urban high rises and impressive historic statues of Denpasar, our eyes feasted on lush mountains, tropical farms, people of all sorts working in their rice paddies, women carrying heavy objects on their heads, motorcycles with up to five members of the family snugly riding together, kids and old people taking baths in the irrigation ditches, and random parades and even cremation ceremonies. Temples popped out from all directions and the feeling of time extended to include hundreds of years of living history in the passing scenery.

For the most part, we were satisfied with our guide and driver, but we also had moments of uneasiness when they would stop to take us to places to look at overpriced souvenir treasures and trinkets that they would obviously be making commissions from our purchasing. Likewise, whenever they suggested we stop to eat, instead of the simple roadside eateries, they would always find the expensive tourist places to take us with white table cloths and credit card accepted signs. Somehow they could not understand that we were not the usual high rolling tourists that they were used to pleasing but simple travelers that were happier in "local style" experiences.

Ubud was about a ninety minute drive from the big city and we could tell that our Balinese experience would soon take a leap into more delightful realms. Although we still could not see the fabled Balinese costumes that our Maui friends wore, we also could not see any more high rise buildings or fast food restaurants. Art was overflowing not only in galleries but also in the temples and natural beauty of the social and physical environment all around us. We had asked the Wayans to take us to a simple hostel to stay at, but as was their style, they took us to an elegant hotel with fountains, pools and maids eager to carry our bags and bring us an exquisitely designed pot of herbal tea. The price for such luxury was not that over the top, so we agreed to stay here for at least a few days. We also treated our two friends to lunch at one of the finer restaurants in town and after we paid them for their services, Wayan the driver invited us to come to his wedding which was to take place on the coming weekend.

For the next few days we took walks in all directions soaking in the exotic (and sometimes annoying) sights and sounds of this enchanting island and its 5000 year old cultural history. We certainly were in a brand new world where it seemed as if every square inch of the town was a never finished art canvas filled with decorations and religious offerings. Flowers were beautifully arranged as temple offerings while incense mixed with the smell of mosquito coils drifted from every doorstep. Men and women were dressed colorfully (but we still saw no trace of the elusive Bali clothes that the trendy upscale hippies wore on Maui). Motorcycles screeched and blew their horns while roosters crowed. Taxi drivers would drive by us, pause, make turning their steering wheel motions and say "Transport?" as if we looked that we needed to ride instead of walk another block or two. (After learning some Balinese phrases), I would confuse them by saying the equivalent of "No, I prefer to walk with my two feet instead".

The shops and marketplace were filled with beautiful objects of art and functionality at low prices, but it was an impossible mission to buy so much more than we could take back to the US. The prices they asked were inexpensive enough but as the merchants expected the customers to argue for even cheaper prices, just about everywhere we went seemed a bargain. We never put a limit on eating out at the many restaurants in town where, even though they would take a long time to be prepared, meals were remarkably priced at about a dollar. On every street corner downtown there would stand ticket vendors encouraging us to attend the traditional dance and music performances. And on many days, torrential rains would wash away all traces of humanity for about ten minutes until the sun would reappear and business would go on as usual. After awhile of all this sensory onslaught, flocks of people in your face asking you to buy stuff and as every record playing in the stores sounding like the same song, the diversity of repetition was becoming overwhelming. To find a nearby retreat sanctuary of nature, we walked quickly past all the merchandising and entered the very lush and refreshingly cool Monkey Forest natural park preserve on the far side of town.

On every tree in the park, monkeys would be happily swinging on the branches and making faces at the tourists walking the trails. Although these primates did not look scary, they did show bothersome tendencies which were not very well brought to light in Walt Disney family movies. In some instances they would try to pee and even throw shit at people and often be seen masturbating themselves to the stares of young kids asking their embarrassed parents for explanation of what they just saw. But where we felt the line was crossed into what could be perceived as criminal behavior was when we would see trained monkeys leap down from the trees, snatch someone's purse or sunglasses and then disappear. Their master would soon show up and offer to get these personal belongings back to the tourists in exchange for a financial reward for doing so which made me wonder if any monkeys were ever arrested for robbery and their masters as accessories in crime. Such thoughts did not last long enough for an answer as in trying to leave the park, we still faced the need to walk past other even better trained monkeys that would try to stick their hands into your pockets in a quick attempt to grab your wallet. So between the never ending wave of both pestering monkeys and humans, we felt it better too move out of our hotel and go a couple of miles out of town where the home stays were in rural areas far from such activities. The fast and inexpensive internet cafes would not be missed however as the tourist savvy Balinese made sure these services were always available nearby.

The weekend came and with it a chance to enjoy quite a variety of events. First came Wayan's wedding which felt like an honor for us to be allowed to be there as well as, it seemed, for his family to see him having brought tourists to their humble home. Everyone looked wonderfully ornate and had the patience to sit there for two long hours of hearing monotone readings by the Balinese priest as was part of the tradition. At least food was being passed around during the waiting time of which we made sure to avoid the meat based items. Also the village toilet facilities looked very primitive, so we made sure to wait for our hotel before having to use any.

The next day we finally agreed to buy tickets from one of the more persistent vendors to a traditional dance performance which turned out to be another very pleasant immersion for us into Balinese culture. There was not much room for improvisation in these classical music and dance selections, but nonetheless they were very engaging and brilliant. I especially enjoyed the percussion sounds of the gamelan as well as the group trance dances.

On our final day at the hotel, we were treated to a major cremation event right next to where we were staying. Hindu families all have to save money for the burning of the dead bodies of their relatives, and the more wealthy the family, the more expensive and elaborate the cremation. Unlike western rituals, instead of crying and sadness, the cremation is like a full scale party with everyone laughing while the funeral pyre soars its flames. They want to make sure that through the banging of gongs and loud levity, the departed soul does not find its way back to haunt people which is another reason the Balinese like to hit stray dogs which they feel are discarnate spirits seeking revenge. Even food vendors meandered through the crowd and perhaps even t-shirt salesmen. Besides the excitement of this new approach to funerals for us, we also had the pleasure of meeting a tall bearded Italian man named Pius who invited us to come see him at a yoga center where he was staying at on the northern side of the island.

So with all these cultural events finely integrated into our memories, we also were able to encourage our kids to treat them as field trips to be able to describe for their home schooling needs. All of which were projects that they worked on the following week in what would be a home stay in a Balinese family's compound near a rice paddy. A change now from the sound of pestering town noises and monkey thievery to a more relaxed base listening to the ducks following their masters and fertilizing the irrigation paddies. One more example of a sustainable way of living for thousands of years that would inevitably be facing challenges from the changing world outside to this one time island camouflaged from global interference.

Of all the various accommodation options, for us the best choice was to actually stay in rooms rented in a local person's house or on their land whether they be called pensions, couch surfing, or as here in Southeast Asia, home stays. The price is only a fraction of the cost of what it would be in a hotel chain and the money goes directly to the owner which is usually a great help to their financial needs. You no longer feel like a stranger but instead are treated personally and can learn more about the area from someone that actually lives there. When guides or other services are needed, you will have better access to reliability and trust. And usually you will be offered meals direct from the family's kitchen and even invited to attend cultural and social events with them. Last but not least, I always preferred the smells of waking up to the fresh scent of food being cooked in a nearby kitchen instead of the synthetic Lysol disinfectant embalming that corporate chains make sure is poured over every inch of their rooms. What a pleasure to see birds flying across a sky with so many shades of beauty and hear the distant chimes of bells and laughing people working in the rice paddies.

The Balinese system of agriculture has been mainly labor intensive and the integrative relationship to the environment including the use of oxen, simple tools and the importance of prayer and ritual. Men would usually be doing the work required by staying in one place while the women would bring them supplies which they would carry artfully balanced on their heads. The work pace would be steady but there would often be pauses to share stories and make prayer offerings to the gods, ancestors and even their crops. Cooperation on a village level was a vital link in success as every member was responsible to maintain their part of the irrigation system for it to be accessed by all the other farmers down the line.

As times were changing, diversification of the Balinese economy meant that some members of the family would not be working fully on the family farm but would also be finding other jobs in town as merchants, taxi drivers and other such tourist related services. Local art had a high worldwide reputation and art galleries and schools were even located in rural settings next to the farms. It was amazing to see how even very young children would be sitting in front of their doorsteps carving beautiful statues and tools while still having time to finish their school work, go to traditional dance classes, help on the farm, and still be able to go to the temple with their families. We made our own prayer that the insidious toxins of the television and video games world would not tear up such a beautiful texture of society as it had already done to most other parts of the world.

Besides the wide assortment of cultural and artistic activities, we found Bali to be a magnificent assortment of interactive scenic panoramas to enjoy. Conveniently for our explorations many trails that started in the rice paddies next to our guest house would lead us into many exotic places of interest. On one particular hike, a heavy downpour forced us to look for protective cover. In a nearby field we saw a small temple that we rushed to stay dry in, but to our shock, a local farmer with a stick jumped out of the bushes and tried to hit us for having the audacity to want to enter his particular place of worship. Again it proved the nonsense of religious ritual as what sort of righteous deity would allow people to get soaked instead of finding sanctuary in their temple. But with the rain pouring on us, we took it as divine inspiration to grab the large leaves of a elephant ear plant and use them as umbrellas. We even managed to place a few over Sophia's baby stroller and then continued walking in the rain until about ten minutes later, the sun reappeared in all its drying glory to restore comfort into our excursion. I suppose the farmer was likewise happy that he chased the "white demons" away from the temple which brought some sort of prosperity and better karma to his life. One man's religion is another man's wet misery while reminding me that the religion of love might be the only true path to continue on.

On another one of our hiking excursions, we walked past an art gallery with some sacred looking paintings drawn by a very gifted man who was both an artist and member of a priestly class. One of his influences was the compassionate Sri Chimnoy who also used to teach classes around the world on the use of art as a sacred tool. We visited Gusti a few more times and eventually he asked us to be his guests and go with him to meditate at a special high mountain temple.

With proper respect and humble anticipation, we rode along with Gusti as he drove us in his small car up the windy road of the holy mountain. The high altitude changed the scenery from tropical to a different sort of forested realm which eventually vanished between the fog and clouds. About the time that the thickness of the enfolding elements only left us about ten feet of visibility, the car stalled. Gusti went outside into the cold mist and raised the hood of the car for examination of the situation. Stephanie, who has always been, among other talents, the designated car mechanic in our family, suggested that perhaps the spark plugs were wet and if we dried them with a rag, the car might resume its motion again. But with a very peaceful smile, Gusti informed us that after meditating, his awareness revealed that we were not dressed in suitable colors for the gods to allow us to be able to drive up any further. The same gods prescribed lighting incense and by our collective meditation, the car would work again. Amazingly after we lit the incense and meditated the car did start up. It drove about another couple of miles and, even though it died again, Gusti was excited as we had almost reached our destination which was only about a ten minute walk ahead. Hardly able to see our footsteps in the thick fog, we finally came to a giant gate which was the entrance to what we were told was the Mother Temple of Bali. A profound moment which we cherished and were elated not only with the magnificence of the view, but also in that we did not have to do any human sacrifices for our car to work. On our return drive down the mountain, no more mechanical problems presented themselves which indicated that the gods were happy with our visit to their sacred temple.

DEAL OF THE CENTURY

Back in Ubud, every time we walked down the main streets, the annoying and persistent sounds of hawkers trying to sell us dance tickets was only outmatched by the taxi drivers who would pull up next to us and insist we hire them. By now I had hoped that they had the good sense to recognize us and that we did not need a taxi for the few short blocks that we were walking. But outside one of the restaurants, we took notice of one particular driver who would stand outside his van and mention each time we walked by that he would give us the "deal of a century". Attracted by his comical stance and his obvious ability to speak conversational English, we finally did ask him to explain what his proposition was. For about twenty dollars, he offered to take us on full day individualized tours and would also be available to take us on a one week excursion around the island if we wanted.

Picking Nyoman to be our driver turned out to be the right decision. He was able to speak English, had a nice sense of humor, was witty, had a comfortable van, and we would no longer have to listen to the best of Bob Marley tape ten times a day as we had to endure with the last drivers we had hired in Denpasar. He never took us to any rip off souvenir stands or over priced restaurants as he respected our intentions and had a sincere desire to make us happy. The only lie he would ever tell us was that he had a very ugly wife. I'm sure he would say that because he didn't want too many men to know how beautiful she actually was. A realization for us when one day he brought us to his house for dinner.

Nyoman also had the social skills to understand that we were somewhat different in what we wanted to see and experience on Bali than most generic tourists. In the next few days on his tour we saw the beautiful vistas of mountains, temples, villages, waterfalls, wild animal parks and beaches. Knowing how much I looked forward to swimming in both fresh spring water pools and hot springs, he took us to some fantastic ones that were very ornate with decorations and palatial statues and carvings. Every evening of the trip he would find us inexpensive and hospitable accommodations and every time we went to eat he made sure we were at places that he had eaten before. The night markets that he would take us to were where local people went for deals, good food and also a chance to socialize. And as for our interest in traditional healing, Nyoman was happy to take us to some very interesting village natural healing practitioners.

The first healer he took us to was someone that he explained was a chiropractor. After dealing with a very frightening dog that growled and brought his huge teeth near enough to my legs to feel the heat of his angry bark that guarded the doctor's doorway, I was then taken to a room and prepared for my adjustment. Unlike any chiropractic treatment that I ever had or would have again, the doctor brought out a stick with which he hit various parts of my body as a method of health evaluation. He then proceeded to stretch my toes in some sort of reflexological way that brought tears to my eyes as I almost started begging he stop inflicting on me the intolerable pain any longer. His final move was to do an adjustment on my forehead which when he did so, I heard a loud crack and all of a sudden all previous tension was relieved, my eyes became wide open and then all head pressures were gone. Feeling a fresh flow of healing bliss, I immediately went to my family in the waiting room and encouraged them to experience one of these outstanding adjustments as well. With Stephanie and Nicolette not looking too brave to enter the healing realm I had just been in, I grabbed John and pushed him for a head adjustment turn. As with me, there was a loud crack on the forehead and he too looked much more alert and open eyed when he came out of the room. During that night it was also gratifying to not hear him having his snoring or shortness of breath episodes.

A few days later, Nyoman took us to another one of a kind healing experiences. The belief that people can put curses on you and use magical means to bring ill health and bad luck was still quite common in Bali. In most villages there would be a practitioner skilled in sending out curses to people you didn't like and, for keeping balance in the community, there would be someone likewise gifted in removing such inflicted black magic spells. Feeling that I needed some help from my recurring headaches, I followed the procedure Nyoman instructed me of bringing an offering to this lady whom he had told me was a very powerful healer. He had neglected, however, to tell me that she might have been at least somewhat psychotic as well. With Stephanie and the daughters being served tea by the healer's housekeeper and with John who instead of hanging out with me as promised was now watching some Indian vampires versus kung fu heroes movie, I was all by myself when the time came to meet the healer. Her appearance was quite dramatic. A tall elderly woman with long hair stretched out in all directions, big eyes that shot out piercing stares and no teeth in her wide open mouth. Nyoman's last words were to take off my clothes and sit in a meditative position with eyes closed for the healing that would take about twenty minutes.

With my eyes shut and apprehension mounting, I felt it to be a good start as I could hear her making prayers to the gods while I could smell the aroma of incense all around me. In this relaxing moment I was startled by this woman screaming like a wild banshee while hitting me with a stick. After some long moments of confusion, I then heard a cracking sound and felt warm liquid on my head and running over my shoulders and down the rest of my naked body. Calming my now frantic state of anxiety as to what was going on, I heard the voice of John telling me not to worry as what I was feeling was the juice of a young coconut that she had poured over my head and that I could now open my eyes again. With Nyoman asking me how did I now feel, I should have paused to reconsider that I was about to say that I still had my headache. Immediately upon hearing Nyoman explaining to this woman what I just said, she again started a new round of screams and pounding of her fists on my arms and legs. Apparently she felt that demonic curses were still remaining in my body which she was making sure to kick out of me. Maybe literally. So after a few more minutes of abuse, I gained enough clarity of mind to tell Nyoman the next time he asked me if I was feeling better, to emphatically say thank you to the lady for helping me feel better. Giving her a smile of gratitude and seeing her smile of satisfaction in return for getting rid of one more demon out of someone's body, I wondered if the kung fu kicks that were playing still on the television screen were likewise not just for entertainment but could have been some sort of training program on the kicking techniques the healer was using on me. In Bali such mysteries could well be more than meets the eye.

The next healer that Nyoman took me to worked also as a high level politician and the walls of his outdoor salon had many photos of famous people that had come to see him for therapy. After our own photo session together he went right to work. He entered his meditation chamber and then came out to tell us that our problems revolved around curses that were in our life from family feuds among ancestors from previous centuries and only by following certain prescribed steps could we have our long history of this karma cleared. From the brightness of this tall man's outfit, the self assured gait of his legs and pontificating mannerisms, it was obvious that he was a self assured bureaucrat and not to be argued with. Since it was only drinking young coconut juice and sprinkling incense around our doorways that he told us to do and not having to perform anything more drastic such as cutting off the head of a chicken, we felt no reason to feel compromised in our agreement. And from learning a few years later that we too had our photos attached on his wall, it gave us a feeling of not only now having better health but also visually documented importance.

Irregardless of the at times aggressive persistence of local solicitors trying to convince us to buy souvenir and art objects that we did not need, Balinese society was mostly warm and peaceful. We never felt ourselves in danger of being victims of violence or major crime. Only once were we involved in an incident with a gang of thugs which caused concern for the safety of our family. Actually this gang was not human but monkeys. On one of the windy mountain roads which Nyoman drove us on, we took a pause for a pee break that only brought us more trouble instead of relief. As we were getting ready to get back into the van, a group of about eight monkeys actually encircled John. Apparently he had made some sort of gesture of teasing them which resulted in their ready to teach this little human a lesson of true "manhood". Well actually more a lesson on crowd violence as they were showing signs of doing him some harm until I showed up in his defense with a large stick and my own growls of ready to get into the fight. Luckily Nyoman was able to drive the car next to us which dispersed the monkeys and gave us a chance to save face from being pummeled by these distant cousins of our family tree.

On the last day of our trip, Nyoman wanted to take us to the house of a very prominent member of the priestly caste. He was proud to be able to showcase to such an important dignitary that he was bringing to his house friends that were from the western empire abroad. The house and gardens were quite impressive as was the lavish decor and the attractive arrangement of antique furniture. Several maids and gardeners also hospitably smiled as tea was brought to us for what seemed to be a cordial visit. Having learned enough Balinese words to be able to at least chat on basic subjects, I sensed something was wrong as the more I kept complimenting this noble man, the more frustrated and angry were his glances to both Nyoman and myself. After a few minutes of my tortuous attempts to make conversation, Nyoman came over and whispered in my ear that I was being insulting. Even though I thought I was speaking Balinese clearly, people of higher class would be lowering themselves if they responded to the dialect that was spoken only among workers and merchants. So since I did not know any such higher caste vocabulary, I switched to a combination of Indonesian and English which became a saving grace for all parties concerned. In leaving, we witnessed one more verification that the language of the heart and soul can be spoken without need of special mantras, definitions, badges or ego gimmicks.

Having enjoyed Nyoman's company which had developed into friendship, we invited him and his family out to dinner. By now we thought we had a fair idea of the inexpensive prices at the many restaurants in Ubud, but on the night we went out with Nyoman, his wife and children, we were happily surprised to find out how much better both the prices and the food was when going to a place mainly frequented by local people and off the tourist trail. His choice of places was a restaurant that specialized in fresh fish which was at that time still part of our diet. No chairs were used and we soon were sharing a few smiles with the other cross legged customers surprised to see westerners coming to eat at a non tourist place while sitting on woven mats just like them.

There was a noticeable absence of silverware on the tables because we would be eating with our hands and afterwards washing them off with a big bowl of warm water and several towels that were provided. Since no one seemed to speak English, we relied on Nyoman to do the ordering with our only request being that we be spared from eating any shellfish or eels. We avoided the first course of soup but were happy enough when a big plate of fresh caught small fish were brought to the table along with several large bowls of rice and iced tea. Feeling well fed with what we thought was the meal, Nyoman explained that it was only the appetizer. A moment later, the waiter brought even bigger plates of a different type barbecued fresh fish that was almost too much for us to finish. Very satisfied with the food, service and traditional setting, we asked for our bill. When our eyes saw that the price for everything for all of us was around ten dollars, we were even happier with our dining experience.

On one of our walks about town, we met an Afro-American Viet Nam veteran who had been living in Bali since the end of the war. His smile carried the tone of a satisfied man as he eloquently explained his reasons for having expatriated to this far away island. He said that if he had gone back to the US, he would have received no respect for his military service and his pension would only be enough to pay part of the rent in a terrible big city ghetto neighborhood. But here the amount of his income was such that gave him the right to be married to two beautiful women and also having a very fancy home with orchards and extended family support to his health and happiness. Real world examples like this that encouraged our thinking of perhaps relocating as well to an exotic "third world" country like Bali. Not because we wanted multiple spouses but for the ability to live affordably in a civilized society.

Our original travel plans were to visit several other nearby islands and maybe even a more expansive trip across Indonesia. But with so many beautiful places, cultural activities and healers to kick the devils out of me, our two month visa was coming to an end. For our final excursion, we made reservations to stay a few nights at the Pacific

Center that our Italian friend had told us about which was located on the northern side of the island about an hour and a half from Ubud.

To get there, we hired Nyoman who made a few stops along the way for us to enjoy the high country scenery of the volcano and the adjacent large lake as well as a visit and swim at a waterfall and afterwards a hot spring near a Buddhist monastery. We also visited Singaraja which was the second largest city in Bali and at one time was the Dutch colonial capital. Still influenced from that time period, many of the main roads, parks and architecture resembled a Western designed provincial capital. I suppose with all the money the Dutch made from the spice trade, they were thoughtful enough to invest at least some of it in appreciated infrastructure development. In our short visit we noticed that prices for merchandise were significantly lower here than in other parts of the island which implied that it was still a regional trading center. Quite a few Chinese businessmen were seen around the city but very few English speaking tourists.

The Pacific Center was in a lush beach front setting and featured a large community hall for seminars and yoga classes, an ocean front covered dining area and lounge, spring fed pool and many cute Balinese style cabins for guests. A friendly looking Balinese staff was bringing towels and meals to people and the scents from the kitchen were exciting to our senses. Satya, the Swiss manager was a very personable man our age who had been on many hippie trails in his life and had been closely aligned with the spiritual teachings of the Indian guru Rajneesh also called Osho. He showed us the many facilities and then pointed out the various homes along the ocean front that were leased by the center to people around the world who wanted to come stay in this peaceful, beautiful environment.

It was the right way to end our visit to Bali by integrating our variety of experiences in a comfortable place of relaxation, walks and friendly conversation with other travelers from many parts of the world. Nyoman as well decided to stay a few days and enjoyed the opportunity to flirt with the pretty maids. An activity which his wife found out about afterwards and punished him by making him work and sleep in their filthy stinky pig shed for two weeks instead of getting to ride around his taxi having fun social networking.

During the days of our stay at the center, a Tantra sacred sexuality workshop was being held by a group of middle aged guests from

Germany who had each paid about $5000 for their two week spiritual pleasuring. Sitting in the cafe after a refreshing swim in the pool, I suggested to one of these folks that it would be a nice gesture to leave a few extra dollars for the staff which had done a lot of work and only were paid about seven dollars a day wage. His very cool rational reply was that if they gave money to these workers, the rest of the people in town would be jealous and would cause disharmony. Maybe the excuse was plausible but somehow the words still did not settle well in my heart. The justification of greed is its own language. But on a better note, most of the guests that were prancing around the center where wearing those bright outfits that I had seen on Maui called "Bali clothes" worn by the more glamorous new agers and their copy cat entourages. Finally we got to see where and who wore them here as well.

CHAPTER SEVEN: THAILAND

THAI TIME

    Towards the end of our travels in Bali, we went to a budget travel agency and bought inexpensive tickets for a two week round trip visit to Thailand. At this point we were happy that we were able to change our return tickets back to Hawaii to allow for this new destination which would not interfere with our expired tourist visas since when we arrived back from Thailand we would not leave the airport before continuing home.

    By flying to Southeast Asia on a different carrier than Indonesian Air, we were relieved in not having to deal with clouds of nauseating tobacco smoke as on our previous flight. As we were descending to land at the airport, we looked outside our windows and could see that Bangkok was a huge city which would require patience and good maps to navigate through its streets and dimensions. After getting clearance through customs, we avoided the anticipated army of loud and pestering local touts of rooms, tours and other services, made our way to the taxi stand and followed the directions in our Lonely Planet's guide book to the budget backpacking hub of the city nicknamed Banglamphu.

    Through our taxi window we could see an interesting mix of palaces and gated communities for the rich located right next to shacks and tall skyscrapers. Humanity likewise unfolded in just as many hues of appearance. The Buddhist views of tolerance and non-attachment gave a feeling of ragged parts fitting together in such a social matrix where a large number of people wore masks over their mouths to avoid the bronze clouds of car pollution. Even when we arrived in the wild and dilapidated area which would be our base for a few days, the opulent king's palace and many impressive statues of Buddha were only about a ten minute walk across a flowery landscaped park.

    Banglamphu was not the sort of place I would recommend for the typical American tourist family to stay at. The long main street of the district looked like a shanty town hosting a permanent parade with an onslaught of a wall of noise generated by the pumping techno music beat from the crowded bars and cafes. And as we would soon find out, it turned into a never ending 24/7 experience that for some was exciting while for others a horrid nightmare of unstable bardos.

Ko Sahn Road and its many side streets and alleys feeding off of it was a backpackers and bargain hunters utopia. Cheap clothes, cheap room and cheap women. It was pleasing that the cost of the rooms we rented were under three dollars but the loud music made if very difficult to sleep. Counting cockroaches on the wall was more realistic than counting sheep. And speaking of bugs, we observed that rowdy drunk Australians loved eating the barbecued scorpions and roaches from the street vendors that would show up selling late night munchies. In front of the police station was a booth displaying a variety of counterfeit passports and identification cards that for fifty dollars each, they could be custom made for you with an official stamp from the cops themselves. Illegal DVD copies could be bought for a dollar, full massages for ten dollars and if you wanted an erotic bonus, about thirty dollars. Although we were fascinated by experiencing such a fringe global reality outpost, on the second day of our stay in Bangkok, we decided to move to another room about five blocks away from the center of this district where which we found much quieter and closer to an authentic Thai reality. Even if it meant doubling our rent to six dollars a room.

One of the main highlights that brings many tourists to Thailand is the sex trade. Within every block there are wonderful studios where someone can experience a very healing and pleasurable Thai massage for under ten dollars. Even more prevalent, for about double that price are prostitutes and escorts advertising their own style of deep pleasure healing strokes. Because of the culture, economic needs and wide variety of the "sex trade", I don't feel it to be a topic that one can make a general judgment about. On the worst end, I felt both anger and sadness when I saw young girls and boys under twelve years old with gaudy makeup, suggestive outfits and parents pushing them to the street to proposition elderly western men who find such pedophile interests fulfilling. But there are also lots of lonely men and women who can hire someone to be an intimate friend and travel companion for a number of days, weeks and even for a long term marriage. Such arrangements might indeed be beneficial to willing parties. Especially if they are both adults. Not as acceptable, however, was witnessing in our travels around the country, young women who were hired by men to travel together. Paying their way to places and fine restaurants that the girls could never have afforded was pleasing just as the sexy clothes that were bought for them to appear even more appealing. Yet in most cases, all these trinkets were for glamorizing the males to bloat their ego as feeling other men would be envious of their borrowed prize. Too often, the women were told to sit at the end of the table and not interfere with the conversations that the men would have with other western tourists. The girls were painted and waxed like furniture and given minimal respect as humans. But again, perhaps a more satisfying life for these women than what they would otherwise face trying to survive in the squalor of Bangkok's ghettos.

Except for intermittent relief from sudden bursts of rain showers, Bangkok was hot, humid and sticky. The air conditioner in our room did not work but the noisy fan was well appreciated. Our windows overlooked the river that was a blend of mud and garbage but still a major artery of commerce and travel. One day we took a ride from one end of the city to the other on a small ferry boat which was an affordable way for most people to get around. Besides the inexpensive tour of getting off the boat and seeing interesting sights, it also was an opportunity for us to mingle with the local culture and how people were able to live in shanty structures along the river banks. Yet just past many of these shanty neighborhoods, we were able to observe traditional dance performances in the parks and visit beautiful Buddhist temples and statues built for the many rulers of this very long and interesting civilization. The present king's image was always displayed and on certain times of the week, everyone in the country was expected to stand as a quiet moment of respect for him. Interestingly enough, besides being considered relatively divine, we found out he was a jazz saxophonists who had once jammed with many of the great musicians of the 1940's and 50's. An even more reason for me to stand in respect for this noble and jamming personality that ruled the country.

One more attraction remained for us to see before leaving the city. Found on an internet web search of "bizarre interests in Thailand", we read an article about a listing for a museum next to a medical university that featured strange biological specimens. Some of the examples mentioned included the mummies of cannibals and two headed babies suspended in a large jar of embalming fluid. Stephanie did not even want to bother going with the rest of us and by the time we visited only one of six floors of many such exhibits, John and Sophia also lost interest and chose to go to a nearby music shop. Nicolette and I remained ever so fascinated by this educational opportunity usually reserved either for medical students or perverts.

Three days in Bangkok was enough for acclimating to the country and now it was time to explore some of the other sights before we had to leave in a couple of weeks. The cheap travel agents offered all sorts of specials to areas including many of the gorgeous islands. For about twenty dollars a ticket, we picked going to the island of Ko Samui which would be about an eight hour bus ride to get to.

The bus to Ko Samui left late at night in order to bypass most of the city traffic, but it still took almost two hours to get past the never ending city limits of Bangkok. Once on the open highway, our underage bus driver popped a few amphetamine pills, turned on the television for us to watch intermittent kung fu and Indian Bollywood movies and then zipped at super fast speed into the darkness of the highway. Out the window we took notice of the many night markets, temples and people working in preparing their products to sell the next day. At one point the bus stopped for us to have a complimentary meal, but by the looks of the ants crawling on our rice and the general lack of sanitation in the kitchen, we decided to buy a bag of sealed potato chips instead.

After four days of scrambling for delights between the noise, pollution and big city compression of Bangkok, we now enjoyed the pleasurable relief to be on a very lush and beautiful island with white sand beaches, turquoise colored ocean and clear streams of water flowing from the hills and mountains. Ko Samui was an island popular for tourists but without the five star glamour resorts nor the wild rave soundtrack for the full time party set. Its beautiful scenery had the most appeal for us but also many Buddhist temples and other cultural attractions provided us with places to explore and experience.

The island had one large town where most services could be found, but all through both the coast and inland were small pockets of cheap rooms for rent in locations where internet cafes, local eateries and massages were provided. These structures, for the most part were simple, functional and blended well with the natural surroundings. Plus, unlike other tourist resorts, the money spent went directly to the local people that lived here.

The first place we stayed at was a Yoga Center operated by a soft spoken American expatriate that had been living here for over forty years. Every morning we enjoyed the group yoga class in the meadow and then invigorated ourselves with a complimentary fresh fruit smoothie. Between the two cabins we had rented was a row of coconut trees where a crew of local men would come every few days and harvest a fresh crop. The actual work was not exactly done by these men with their own hands nor with any mechanical devices. Each time they came they would bring a couple of monkeys on ropes that would climb the trees and skillfully drop the coconuts into the open bed of the pickup truck. While the monkeys worked, the men would relax drinking tea and then afterwards reward the monkeys by paying them several bananas for their work. Somehow it did not feel like any exploitation was involved as all the parties looked satisfied and the environment was not harmed nor was there need for extra fossil fuel wastage. I wondered what it would be like if we could bring a few of these animals back to Hawaii and teach them the same sort of work. Besides the probable complaints from the local coconut pickers that didn't want any more competition, there might be some sort of labor laws or animal rights provisions that wouldn't allow it. Perhaps an easier option might have been to take a few to Greece which had no restrictions on bringing aliens into the country. We could baptize these pets into the Greek Orthodox Church. And then if we were to dress them in human work clothes, perhaps most people wouldn't mind. The elderly could use them as friends, protection and as service animals. Perhaps they weren't too different from us after all as each time they would be brought to do work, one of the males would keep staring at Sophia and make all sorts of romantic winks and constant lip puckering gestures at her. Thus maybe even there would be opportunities for lonely people in the Greek villages to find more intimate friendship as well. At least Sophia did not find much interest in the chimp that liked her, so no chance for me to have become a "monkey's uncle".

Like the rest of the more "undeveloped" islands which we would visit in Thailand, many paths through the forest led to picturesque beach settings where small huts could be rented and usually with a cantina serving delicious meals. At just such a place we also had the bonus of a library of DVDs provided to chose watching on a big screen television. Since we had not seen any movies in several months, we were enjoying the opportunity undisturbed until a German tourist who was also staying in the compound told us that we Americans are all addicted to television. The irony of how we had given up commercial television decades before and how we also lived in harmony with nature in the Hawaiian rain forest was not comprehensible to our new neighbor's profiling. We were relieved that he chose to leave us alone. For us it was a holiday to be able to watch movies as well since we did not have such options to be addicted to back home. Proudly we were reminded by this man's criticism that we were not your usual American tourists.

Before leaving Ko Samui, we had fun riding elephants (all the family except me as I'm scared of heights), hiking and swimming in waterfalls and staying a night at another yoga center that was managed by a young Greek holistic health entrepreneur. We also made friends with a sweet lady named Jana who operated a small internet cafe next to her house. She liked us a lot and we have been friends ever since. Throughout Southeast Asia and later in travels to India, we found that people enjoyed meeting us as we were not the usual bombastic tourists from the west. And unlike most other tourists, we were very close with our children which we always traveled together with. In such respect, we found ourselves more comfortable in traveling through traditional societies where extended family is respected instead of the US where old people and young children are often ignored.

CHAPTER EIGHT: RETURN TO HAWAII

BACK HOME AGAIN

Returning back to Maui in the fall of 1996 felt like a continuation of our same journey which we were experiencing across exotic places of the Pacific. No longer interested in the trappings of tourism or mainstream American life, we found our living place again in the same rain forest jungle neighborhood as when we left many months before. We rented a space on Makunda's land close to the waterfall and with enough room to eventually build a couple of shelters and a natural earth wall that gave us privacy from the rest of the world.

The park like setting was blessed with many colored plants, tropical trees and a feeling of sacredness. Our friend Dave lived in a small bamboo hut within shouting distance down the hill and not too far from him was another hut occupied by a guy named Andre who was also the caretaker responsible for keeping the landscape looking nice.

"Suzy", our small four wheel drive jeep was still driving okay and was the perfect car to take us back and forth to places on the island that we couldn't otherwise get to. And for the times we had to drive to nearby Paia town, if we had the convertible top down, we could easily fit several hitchhikers in the back seat. We met many interesting people that way but would always be cautious enough to let them out right before we reached town so as not to get busted by cops for having too many passengers in the car.

Our first shelter on the land was a large camping tent which was soon to be our base while we slowly developed a more permanent and comfortable living situation. Some remnants of a tarp covered our kitchen area on the carved side of the adjacent hill which we improved with thrift store tools, pots, pans, shelves and other such cooking and dining equipment. For water we would carry our five gallon bottles down a trail from the parking area about 100 yards up the hill. One bottle would be purified water from the health food store and the other from the faucet of the Haiku Community Center for general cleaning needs. From a power pole near the landlady's house about 500 feet away, we ran a very long extension cord that gave us access to electricity for some of our simple needs which included a few lights and our lap top computer. We even hooked up a telephone line (which became a popular item of interest to our jungle community neighbors that wanted to make emergency calls) and high speed internet service. For bathroom needs beyond the call of the bush, our landlady had built a small bathhouse with a flushing toilet and hot showers to service our mini-community of seven residents.

A few weeks after we established our presence in the jungle, the tenant in our Kihei apartment moved out and with my mother agreeing to come visit us, we made a decision to let someone else rent the land space until we returned after our planned move to Kihei.

SOCIALIZING

By now our children had found a satisfying balance between home schooling and socializing with friends and other activities. As a wild shot, I asked Stephanie to call several restaurants in the area and ask them if they had any free meal coupons for students that were achieving high grades in their class. I had been aware of Pizza Hut, Taco Bell and Burger King providing such incentives to public schools, so I figured what did we have to lose. Surprisingly all these places were happy to supply us with such award coupons. When they asked Stephanie how many students were in our class, she turned to me for a reply. Twelve seemed like a suitable number and in a few days, care packets of free food coupons showed up in our mailbox. Of the three restaurants, only Burger King was the problem. When our "students" showed up at the Kahului store for their free meals, they would not allow them to have free cheese burgers without the meat. Our expectation of coming out with cheese sandwiches did not match the bureaucracy of inventory needs that the store manager used as an excuse to not provide us sandwiches without meat. But rather than argue with the strange logic of these rules or take the meat off the bread ourselves, we decided that we didn't want to be part of Burger King's animal killing karma after all. Plus it would have felt weird scraping the meat particles off of the bread.

Family hikes and waterfall swims were a few of our more satisfying ways of enjoying the beauties of nature around us as well as staying fit. I had planned for John and me to play basketball up at the Kula gym where I used to be active at many years earlier. But alas, some idiot had set fire to the place and it had to rest in peace as part of our memories. To come up with a happy adventure, the two of us decided to organize taking the seven mile hike across the Haleakala Crater. Knowing that there would be challenges, we came up with the right motivating incentive to help us complete the long walk up and then back down the zigzag trail. The night before we set out, we went to the health food store and purchased a bag of gourmet snacks that otherwise we could not afford. Our program was to stop every half hour for a five minute pause to enjoy the delicious treats as a reward for each stretch of the hike. With such a brilliant plan, the hike went well and we felt prepared to take the same approach for every similar venture in the future.

Not too much later, John, Nicolette and I organized another crater hike on the full moon with a crew of eight other friends. All went well for the descent down and as the cannabis and energy of the volcano enchanted our senses, we decided to take a pause and light a fire. The ambience was very dreamy as we felt we were on another planet. But the energy changed after one of our friends started having a bit of a temper tantrum because he felt no one was paying attention to him. Right as we were dealing with our own shame for not having been fully conscious of our friend, we noticed in the distance about twenty people marching swiftly and holding torches. Our drug enhanced paranoia convinced us that they must be some sort of federal rangers coming down to bust us for lighting an unpermitted fire.

Feeling the dire threat of being busted and the need to protect my children, I quickly kicked the fire pit to destroy the evidence while telling John and Nicolette to act as if we were Greek tourists and did not understand the rules of the park. Our group psychosis however was soon dissipated as we observed that the people with the torches were not heading in our direction. As we later learned, they were a boy scout troupe that was also hiking across the crater that night. Fear turned into laughter and even an apology to our friend for not having paid attention to him earlier was expressed. Our ascent up was likewise mystical in tone as the full moon reflected radiantly over the blooming silver-sword cactus. The otherwise lunar landscape was now lit with thousands of these glimmering lights that helped us clearly see our footsteps even though the hour of the night was quite late.

Besides the socializing with friends, John became involved in another dramatic production with a small part in the Tennessee Williams play Cat on a Hot Tin Roof. Although not as brilliant as the film in which Paul Newman's performance had left a blazing impression on our family movie nights, the Maui production was enjoyable and gave John another dose of appreciation of his talent from the many people that attended the play and then writing very positive media reviews.

By this time in his life, John was also showing interest and talent in playing guitar. He never learned how to read music, but he could learn how to play songs of all genres by simply listening to the tunes. Thus he was able to expand his personal repertoire as well as he and I writing a few songs together. We had many friends on Maui that played a variety of music, so he was able to learn many different techniques ranging from Hawaiian slack key to rock and roll and blues. Two different amazing musicians, our friends Jason Matsui and Scott Huckabay were especially instrumental in showing him the basics to several Jimi Hendrix songs that he learned to cover quite well.

An unexpected development however would put a damper on John's enthusiasm for a couple of months. After returning from the beach one day, he kept complaining of sand in his hair that wouldn't stop itching. On closer inspection, Stephanie found the suspected sand particles to be moving and alive because in actuality they were head lice or as commonly called in Hawaii, "ookoos". Even past the preliminary blame on the source point, the outbreak reached all of us in the household and became a problem that lingered for months and across several continents. Neither colder weather nor various remedies seemed to work very well but in time we all became scratch free and proud not to ever have to deal again with these tiny "nitpicking" varmints.

MOM VISITS MAUI

Even though we weren't able to get my parents to move to the condo when we first bought it, we were now able to convince my mother to come stay with us for the winter rather than spend a cold winter in Raleigh by herself. Since she had been to Maui before, we didn't stress the idea of touring too much with her and hoped that on this trip she might enjoy and find familiarity with Kihei and that she might change her mind and even decide to relocate.

Living with four of us was a tight enough squeeze for our one bedroom apartment, but now with my mother staying with us as well, we felt like even more of a traditional extended family. With so many televisions blasting full volume sounds in the building and the various loud arguments and parties in the neighborhood, we managed to conceal our expanding family size while being okay with our cozy living arrangements.

My mother's usual routine each morning was to take her beach chair and church book on the short walk to the beach overlook where she would sit a few hours reading and enjoying the warm weather. She even managed to meet a Greek guy there who would come by every few days and converse with her. And on a couple of occasions when the Greek priest came over from Honolulu, we would take her with us to the church that the congregation would rent for such gatherings.

Having our own car again was nice as we could take occasional excursions to scenic spots and for other fun activities. One holiday we made reservations at a fancy Sunday brunch restaurant in the tourist resort of Kaanapali. The parking lot attendant was all confused when we pulled up and after giving him the keys to park our car told him to be sure to handle it with care. Our car was the only old Maui cruiser that had ever made it to this line up of expensive vehicles and probably the most fun of all of them to drive. What a happy feeling to be able to ride around in a convertible and be able to impress my mom as well. Especially as we made it without the radiator overheating or dead battery problems. My mother had grim enough memories of the time we took her from Montana to Canada in a car that often did break down and that also needed us to add a quart of engine oil each hour.

Our friend Cave Dave whom she had also remembered from Montana was now living on Maui and would drop by now and then. We also had connected with a neighbor named Mercury who would often come over with his electric organ to talk of high consciousness and jam musically with John. So on some evenings, we would have the seven of us eating dinner and then Dave would join in with John and

Mercury and play music till late. We always seemed to have enough room, food and fun in life with no need for a television to distract our attention.

John was also playing music with a lounge band in a nearby hotel. Understandably, he did not want us to come listen to his lame play list, but Nicolette and I did sneak a few peeks during some of his shows. Ironically, he never did get paid for any of the gigs as the band leader, Junior, figured out a way to have the rest of the band mates pay him to buy sound equipment that he wound up keeping himself. After a few weekends, it dawned on John and the rest of the band that Junior was basically an opportunist that was using people, thereby no reason was left to keep playing any longer. But during the time they played together, at least John didn't have to wear some silly outfit at the performances and he did get free appetizers to eat.

THE MEN'S HIKE

Going on hikes and swimming in waterfalls was one of our favorite activities on Maui. One day we learned that one of the more active members of the alternative and spiritual community of Maui had organized a "men's gathering". The idea was to hike together as a group and then reach a clearing where we would beat drums, exchange stories, sing and bond. Since John and I were looking for a chance to connect with a hiking group, we agreed to be part of this expedition which was planned on a full moon date which would add even more enchantment to our ceremony when we reached our destination.

Our start was full of good energies with about twenty of us males mustered up at the top of the crater hike trailhead with our drums, sleeping bags, all sorts of healthy power snacks, jovial fraternal feelings, handshakes and hugs. The total distance to our destination, the parking lot on the other side of the crater, was a total of twelve miles with much climbing and descending switch backs. But the day was sunny with a cool enough breeze to get our early morning momentum off to a good start.

About a quarter of the way down the trail an awkward step resulted in my twisting my ankle and thus painfully had to slow down significantly. John was way ahead of me when it happened and had no clue of my accident. But as I took the posture that real men don't cry or ask for help, I hobbled along and was at least content that I had such a notion to bring up for discussion that could ultimately lead to everyone offering retrospective support and sympathetic tears as part of releasing such a manly stereotype. Arriving at our designated campsite for the night about an hour late was a relief for the group that had expressed concern at my absence. And yes, then the ongoing offers from everyone on helping me feel more comfortable as well as assuring me that someone else would carry by backpack out in the morning. John also was made aware of my situation and promised to stay with me on the climb out of the crater in case I needed his help as well.

Night at our 10,000 foot elevation was majestic. Stars sparkled and shooting stars darted across the sky. Moon rays were also activating their reflective glow on the rare Silversword cacti giving the crater an even more other worldly veneer. With enough wood gathered, the fire was lit, hands were held in a circle and then we all moved back a few feet to set up our bedding in sitting postures ready to express our emotions and stories of our lives. But instead of poetics and reassurances of companionship, the mood took a very sour turn. Some of the men were interested in either complaining about their wives or saying how much they missed them which in turn triggered a couple of the homosexual men to complain of the subject matter. The group leader asked us all to breath and to listen to the drumbeats being played but instead of settling anyone's attitude, the arguments kept engaging more and more of us and finally reaching the yelling level. In due time, guys started filtering out of the campsite and went off to do their own thing. One man that had eaten a handful of magic mushrooms started crying because of the fracas but hardly anyone showed any interest in soothing his strained consciousness. But through all the excess of emotional out letting, the steady drum beat kept going on and at least about half of us still remained in the circle. Perhaps it was too much to expect a changed collective persona from our men's' group but it did show the rapid reflexes of conditioning and false egos. Sadly we never organized a follow up meeting but my foot was well enough for me to make it up to the top of the trail-head the next day. With a little help from my friends.

MAUI JUICE FESTIVAL

The annual community festival held every spring by the now defunct Maui Juice Company in the now burned downed remnants of the Makawao High School was a wonderful hippie gathering where for the price of free admission one could dance to the swirling psychedelic musical light shows, enjoy the voluptuous belly dancing and of course the high point of being able to drink as much fresh pressed delicious Maui juice as you would want.

John and I were only too eager to volunteer our services for this beautiful event in handling the counter where we would be pouring juice all night to the long lines of thirsty folks that kept coming for more. One guy had even turned red in the face from proudly proclaiming he was on his tenth glass of the spicy Ginger Rush. Ever happy to follow the Biblical dictum of "take freely what's freely given", we kept filling the many empty cups at a fast enough pace to bring smiles and quench the thirst of the masses. But just as the momentum was in a pleasant motion of speed and smiling appreciation, a short lady with a sour facial expression came up to complain that John and I were not wearing sanitary gloves and so our vibrations were infesting the juices. Her need to make herself known by now had thus slowed the line up enough to create dissatisfied throngs waiting for their juice. So with a flash I told her to move along and that not only was she making people upset in causing delays but also that John and I were spiritual adepts accenting each cup we poured with love vibrations.

BIRTHDAY PARTY

March is the astrological sign of Pisces, which meant organizing a joint birthday party for my mother, Nicolette and Sophia. We were able to book the Haiku Community Center for what turned out to be a wonderful event. Lots of friends, fine food, presents and debut of an all star band that featured our friends Mercury, Dave, Roy, and our son John. One of the best "unknown" guitarist friends on the island, Jason also came out to add his Hendrix riffs to the jam session. Even though Jason grew up on Maui, he hardly left the 20 mile radius of his home in Kahului, so we were greatly honored and enjoyed his presence. What mattered the most was that everyone had a good time. Our birthday girls enjoyed playing with friends, opening gifts and gazing at the rainbows in the sky. Watching my mother laughing and even nodding to the rhythm of the music was a special gift for me to behold. Moments like these are especially precious in retrospect as we look at the flow of time and space. The daughters have all now grown up into adulthood, our friend Mercury soon passed away from a rare heart condition that he never told us about. Dave is still high in the hills and Jason continues to play amazing music by himself in his room. And as for my mother and us, it was time again to fly back to Greece.

CHAPTER NINE: GREECE

COLD ARRIVAL

We arrived in Greece during the month of March, 1997 and stayed for four years before leaving again in January of 2001. Many roads, travels, passing sketches have gone by and many were the moments I wanted to catch a thought, poem or road sign for future recollection and reflection of our life in Greece. Although starting this project a few decades late, each present and future moment is a unique and fresh eternity; so better late than never. As in many such other spots of the memory wheel, some semblance of orderly thinking will be apparent, but there could also be journalistic excess which hopefully would garnish rather than distract from our experiences. A historic parameter will not be inflicted on these entries not to encourage even further anarchy, but rather to underline a free rambling trek across space and time. And in so doing, if previous memories and destinations are triggered, they too will be allowed entry across the border of these pages without a passport.

One of the nicest times of the year to visit Greece is Spring. The mountains are highlighted by wild flowers and herbs of brilliant hues and enchanting scents. But we did not realize that Spring here starts in late April instead of our present arrival in March. The winds were blowing cold and harsh in Athens as we scampered from the airport to our hotel near Syntagma Square. My mother of course wasted no time in complaining of our stupidity in our choice of timing and thus was not much emotional support in our dealing with the weather. But as we knew that in a few more weeks warmer rays of the sun would be more apparent, we focused the next couple of days in enjoying the big city without the usual throngs of tourists and high prices. Being March 25th, Greek Independence Day, the atmosphere was festive and patriotic. My mother's attitude cheered up as she watched the military marches and took pride with the loud jets that flew across the sky. Somehow the lure of men in uniform is deep rooted.

Beyond the usual shocks and polite agreement in local conversations about its horrors, we found Athens always a many layered treasure feast. The cup of coffee in Plaka Square was eventually beyond our budget and the dark shadows of humanity around nearby Omonia Square would leave us holding our breath when scampering through at night.

As in other cities, when traveling alone through Athens, I feel a detached loneliness. Not so much however from being alienated or distant, but rather from smelling the passion of humanity and wishing to share bonding, a "parea" with the substance of its life beat rhythm. Before leaving I did map out many places in the city that I would have liked to return and discover better.

Driving south to Xirokambi did not at all mean the temperatures were any more comforting. In fact the high mountain ranges still showed snow caps and attracted more chilly humidity. The situation at home was not much easier to live with either. While in Hawaii, I had contacted my long time friend Panayiotis who had agreed to rent the downstairs part of my mother's ancestral stone house. Being a carpenter, he would have made it more comfortable and painted over its drab moldy green medieval dungeon ambience. But as I mentioned earlier, my mother and her brother decided to keep him out as they felt he would turn her family home into a party house of "drugs, sex and wild music." For them an embalmed funeral parlor would be more to their preference. Furthermore, they felt if they made it challenging enough, we would drop our own notions of moving here. By renting the house long term to a local family for about seventy five dollars a month, they were certain that no way we would want to live in such adverse circumstances.

But determinism ranks high in my personal history, so we met the challenge and went about turning our gloomy warehouse of a room into a livable situation. The room was divided in two by a paper thin wall separating where we would be staying from my mother's side of the partition. There in this dark cold room, we bought a small reading light and set up our tiny home schooling office. Stephanie and I slept in an old partially broken bed, the girls paired up on a better mattress next to us while John became my mother's roommate and slept on another small moldy old bed. For warmth, we relied on my grandmother's thick woolen blankets which were helpful, but we still had to turn on an electric portable heater at times. With the high cost of electricity and the poor wiring of the house, we only did it when our bones would be shivering more than resting. For more privacy, we hung up two long sheets in front of our beds, but typical village style was still that people would drop into our lives unannounced. Worse yet, they would be reluctant to leave and would want to pester us with nosy questions which we had to be on guard to give appropriate answers or else risk our statements being circulated as local gossip.

Not fitting the typical American profile which meant driving brand new cars, bragging about our chain of pizzerias we owned and having kids wearing bright Kmart clothes with gold chains meant we were an oddity that could be analyzed and discussed fully.

Staying in the village taught me many lessons such as to live your dreams or be starved pursuing your nightmares. Xirokambi, is made up of two year round groups of people: old retired farmers and young farmers wishing they were retired and living a lazier life with a pension. In the summer, the population swells from the homecoming of US, Canadian and Australian relatives who had migrated "over the hill and ocean" to the wealthy, fertile fields of their dreams. Now was the season they return to brag about the riches they have collected in their life and to show off their opulence. Bright new polyester shorts, baseball hats and disconnected looks on their kids trying to fit into their gold necklaces, while putting up with the discomfort of being dragged by their parents away from the familiarity of indoor shopping malls and now being stuck out here in the "sticks". Disturbed looking and stuffily dressed wives complaining of their lack of the necessary material comforts, appliances and services that they have been used to. Puffy looking husbands not sure if they should identify and relax with their old friends in the platea/town square or hurry home to take care of "business." As props in a summer play, these figures are not toxic by nature, but the scripts allowed for their psychodramas to enter our home without notice to ask the same predictable questions for which we can never deliver a satisfying enough answer so that they can quit asking, "Do you like it here?" "What do you do?" "Are your children in school?" A relentless barrage of oppression that led me to feel that I was soon following the same path of the rest of the town residents in practicing the yoga of Crucifixion instead of my preferred yoga of Resurrection.

The most important time of celebration in Greece is Easter. Coinciding with the advent of Spring and the return of a fully restored sun, many days of church activities culminate in a day of feasting with the family. A few days beforehand, the preparations include the slaughter of goats for the dinner table while watching their carcasses hanging in front of the homes with growing swarms of flies and dogs barking for first bite. For vegetarians like ourselves, the plan was to stay home all day and not be exposed to the horror or death stench. Priding our success of avoidance, around 10 pm as we prepared to go to bed when a knock was heard on the door. To my surprise my Uncle Tasos had made a special trip to come by and greet me. With his son-in-law eager to drive back to their village located nearly an hour away, he beamed a smile while saying "for my beloved nephew George, I bring you this present". He then proceeded to hand me a large section of a dead goat in a blood stained sheet and then gave me a kiss and left. Standing there in my pajamas totally startled by the cosmic joke the universe played on me, I could hear my family sounding disgusted as much as I was while my mother was laughing at me from her room. Solemnly I took the dead animal body to her, laid its carcass in her lap, and wished her a happy Easter before going back to my own dreams filled with life instead of death.

As a follow up story, the next Easter, one of the village priests came to our house and insisted I follow him to his nearby farm where he would show me the proper way to cut the throat of a goat as was the correct action to take in the village at this time of the year. However, I was just as adamant in insisting that I was not at all going to do so. Eventually I won this psychic tug of war by explaining that in my stay at a holy monastery on Mount Athos, I was instructed by the monks to love life which included not killing or eating animals. Thus by pulling higher religious rank on him, the priest politely left me alone.

On a future visit by another Greek priest to our house, I was questioned about why we named our youngest daughter Sophia. His inquiry was probably because in the Gnostic tradition which the early Christian Church considered a heresy, Sophia represented the archaic sacred feminine archetype which was the antithesis to their male dominated patriarchal religious institution. Again knowing my church literature, I replied that she was named after the main cathedral of the Byzantine Orthodox Church, Saint Sophia which was the holy wisdom of Jesus Christ. Again, I won the debate and the priest left our house satisfied.

On still another occasion, a priest came by for a nosy visit and kept staring at the wall where we had painted a rainbow. When we assured him that our art job had nothing to do with the "heathen hippie rainbow gathering" emblem but rather it was our expression honoring the biblical Noah who was graced with a rainbow from the hands of God for his good faith, he left politely without the need of an inquisition.

The final example of my interplay with the various village priests came when another one came by one day to introduce himself and within a few minutes left a suggestion that I cut my beard to a shorter length than his own. His reasoning was that only the priest in the village can have the longest beard. For me it seemed similar to men wanting to be the most well-hung studs having the largest penis. Sacred sex and the resonance of the polymorphous ancient god Zeus seemed like the message of the moment.

In regards to my mother, I felt it was the right choice to bring her back to her roots. She wasn't able to communicate with most people in the US with her limited English vocabulary and with my father now passed away, she was not capable of even paying bills and other such necessities of contemporary life. Here in the village she was embraced by culture, relatives, respect and a simple, affordable life style she could understand. Yet, in her mind she felt dedicated to be living in her home back in Raleigh where she had made a relative success of herself and which housed the many memories of youth and love that she shared with my father. There certainly where painful memories and ghosts of her past, but I was looking at it from the present and future reference points. Being sensitive to all these factors, my intention was that she live in Greece half the year and then go back to the US the other six months. With the money she had in the bank she could have shipped a container of household stuff to the village and created a more comfortable setting for herself. Her social security check was more than enough for her simple needs and thus she could be happy in having the best of both worlds. But being the stubborn woman that she always was, she did not want to make life happy. When we bought her a new bed, she refused to get up out of her mother's broken bed and kept saying her bed was in Raleigh. When we bought her a television she refused to turn it on claiming her television was in Raleigh. We tried taking her to the town square for a coffee or ice cream and she refused to go saying only prostitutes and lazy people go to town. With such attitudes there was indeed conversation being spread about our household which centered mostly on confusion as to my mother's reality basing.

The hometown village was the place that Greeks who had emigrated abroad planned all their lives to return back to. My mother's attitude was totally baffling while we were looked upon as heroes for trying to bring her back to her roots while dealing with the adverse living conditions of our house that her and her brother had challenged us with. But there was always hope and we felt that eventually she would appreciate our bringing her back to her family roots and be part of our extended family. But to make sure she wouldn't leave Greece, we hid her passport. But even with her demands that we return it to her I managed to overcome my guilt and her anger and kept it away from her.

UPSTAIRS

Living in relatively primitive conditions on the ground floor while upstairs the tenants were enjoying the comforts of a nice house for a measly seventy five dollar a month rent was not emotionally soothing. But since the tenant law in Greece was such that the renters could stay for as long as they wanted of their remaining three year contract, there was no way we could tell them to leave their sweetheart deal and for us to move upstairs. A situation that my mother enjoyed watching us struggle through in her determination to break our resolve to live in this country.

The family upstairs was understandably not showing any interest in moving either. Taki would leave early in the morning to go work on his farm land up in the mountains while Maria would stay home taking care of their baby son George. As was typical in the village, the husband goes to work and the woman stays home cleaning house, taking care of kids and then prepares a full course dinner. Maria would only be seen in town once a week on market day or at church. On both such occasions she would be dressed up with a sexy short dress, high heels and lots of makeup. After work, Taki would join his friends in town, get drunk and watch the soccer game on the big screen television at the village town square cafe. A couple of nights in the week he would grab his wife for about five minutes of erotic bed play. The walls and flooring were very thin and just as we could hear their personal dramas, they could certainly hear my mother and I screaming at each other pretty often. The few times we had to go upstairs to tell Maria anything, we noticed that instead of just cleaning and cooking, she would be dressed up in her sexy outfits while watching fashion shows on television. Village men with young wives would normally treat their woman as their prized livestock and keep them locked up in the corral but on the right occasions would bring them out in public to show off to each other their attractive possessions. Eventually Maria found reason to escape the cage and had an affair with the mailman. One more scandal that would be the talk of the village for several weeks.

ARGUMENTS

Arguing with my mother was becoming a very regular occurrence. In her eyes and from the statements coming out of her mouth, my family and I appeared as total scum of the earth. Her loosely based reasoning revolved around how we did not show total allegiance to authorities (especially the church), we never made it as financial successes or had a 9-5 career, and that we often had the audacity to laugh and show that we were happy instead of acting that life was all about comparing who was "suffering" the most. Ironically it was usually when she was reading her church literature and Bible that she would insult and try to shame us the most. On one such instance, she was holding one of her holy books in one hand and with the other was blessing the house with incense while mumbling how bad we were and telling us to more or less to "go to hell". Not wanting to sound disrespectful of her ritual, I mentioned my doubt that such a curse which she was directing at us was anywhere on the page that she had been meditating on. Her emotional trigger point now activated, she began screaming at me that I was too much of a heathen to dare quote or interpret sacred text. She then put down the incense holder and grabbed her cane to shake at us as she continued her harangue at our blasphemy. Not wanting to back out of a good argument, John took up my point and kept asking her to show him where in her holy books does any righteous saint or messiah tell other children of God to "go to hell". But by the time John was explaining that the message of God is that people should love each other, my mom was already hitting him with her cane. Her thrusts were so powerfully fueled by righteous spite, that her cane broke which gave her not only proof of how evil we were but also that we now owed her a new cane.

Our loud fights by now had reached the gossip news of the neighborhood and in some ways were adding reason enough for the upstairs tenants to leave the nuisance of having to listen to us even if it did mean they might have to pay a higher rent elsewhere. My mother's insults would even lure me into making fists and hurting my hands from punching the stone wall in frustration. Another time I punched her paper thin interior wall and wound up putting a hole in it. Not only did she demand that we pay to have it fixed again but also she asserted that I must be "on dope" for acting so violently. Having a happier relationship with my mother was a daily meditation for me in the never ending war drama that we were stuck in.

THE PAINS OF LOVE

One night when my ninety year old mother was already in bed and the late hour was leading the rest of us to day's end as well, after a heavy knock the front door was pushed open and in our house stomped a fast paced visitor. An elderly lady but with an appearance of a domesticated grizzly bear, sniffed out my mother's location and with stretched arms yelled: "Despino! Despino!" Within a whip of a second she yanked my mother out of bed and with a levitating hug squeezed her in air saying "Despino, Despino I Love You, I Love You" while my frail framed mom was feebly screeching: "Stop it, stop it, you're killing me." In a snap she put my mother back down in her shaking bed, slurped some more kisses on her, then jogged out the door exclaiming: "My children are waiting to drive me to the airport." Meanwhile, my stunned mother, in lots of pain, explained how she used to pick olives together with this brute over forty years ago and that she had just been passing through on the return part of a quick village visit from New York. In the other woman's mind, she will always remember the hugs and kisses. But as we found out the next day, her hugs had cracked two of my mother's ribs and for her part, my mother would have to carry this love pain for about four months.

BLESSING OF THE BROTHEL

Behind our house was a large soccer field that would be both a place for weekend sports as well as for families to bring their kids to play. As a stone plaque in front of the entrance explained, the land was donated by a number of land owners whose names were clearly listed for the community to use for such activity in perpetuity. As politics and greed would have it, the present mayor of the village decided to sell the land to the military to construct several apartment buildings for high ranking officials to have as holiday homes. Being a government agency, the military was able to bypass any safeguards the original owners had placed on the land usage and the town council was also eager to make a lot of loot from the sale. The excuse given was that there was a better area to build a more modern playing field and by encouraging higher quality people to come stay in the village, more money would be spent on local goods and services.

Over the next few months, we sadly watched the field where we not only enjoyed playing with our kids, having occasional picnics and nightly star gazing, now fenced off and modern apartment buildings blocking our clear view of the mountain scenery behind it. Instead we would notice taxis bringing over prostitutes to spend the night with the important military officials enjoying their hide-away.

After the buildings were fully finished, the village planned a grand welcoming event. There was a public school chorus singing patriotic songs, church choir and many dignitaries including the regional bishop who led the parade of people inspecting the facilities while he blessed each of the rooms. Not wishing to be left out, I joined the visitation and wondered how the holy spirit felt about the blessings bestowed on what was essentially a brothel. Moreover, the people that were being screwed the most were the people of the village who lost their kids playground but were too mesmerized by the glamour of the priestly robes, incense and sparkling top brass medals to question the purchase.

MOVING UPSTAIRS

With our relentless and loud arguments downstairs, the upstairs tenants agreed to end their rental contract and finally move. By now the neighborhood was convinced we were heroes for being able to withstand the primitive conditions of living downstairs and were

138

pressuring Takis to be ethical and let us move upstairs to the more modern part of the house which my father had renovated in 1960 as part of a plan for our family to move from the US back to Greece.

Over the many years of various renters, the house had taken some beating and definitely needed an overhaul which we were only too eager to actively organize and participate in. Besides the restoration of the furnishings and adding a few kitchen appliances, the kids chose to paint their rooms in varieties of colors that enhanced the otherwise white walls of traditional home interiors. Stephanie continued washing clothes by hand as we still could not afford a washing machine which again brought some sort of respect from the older women of the village who also washed their own laundry. But it drew confused stares at us from the younger women who felt that they were more glamorous and progressive in owning modern appliances such as washing machines.

An important upgrade for the house was the need for better electrical wires and fuse boxes. We made an appointment for the town electrician to come rewire the house but from the moment he came upstairs and looked at our works in progress, we knew that there would be a problem. By the bright orange room that John had painted and the now burgundy hallway, the electrician accused us of being "communists" and as he was of right wing political persuasion like most of the villagers, he suggested that we find a communist electrician to do the job. White walls were the only ones he accepted jobs on and absolutely no reds. However, after our assurances that we were not at all politically inclined, he reluctantly finished the job and hissed off after we paid him. Since Greek money had tinges of red in it, we wondered why he accepted such colored denominations with regards to his right wing beliefs. Apparently the civil war between Communists and Royalists was still not over.

Even with the pitfalls of too much color in a village used to drab black and white, it felt wonderful to have a comfortable living space again. And to celebrate our new life we purchased a wide screen television which we hooked up to our stereo speakers so as to enjoy our much missed movie nights. The only person that did not seem so happy with our home improvements was unfortunately my mother. The few times we were able to persuade her to join us for a meal upstairs she was full of complaints on how we ruined her house by changing the decor instead of leaving it exactly as she had left it many decades before. Another domestic civil war that she wouldn't end with me.

TOWN SQUARE

The village square was the main gathering place in town. In older times families and young ladies in pairs promenaded around its perimeter. Anyone looking to leave messages for other residents could always find someone that they could pass it on to. Times had changed social conduct and telephones had now brought quicker communications. Yet many habits and rituals still remain the same. The open aired seats of the square seemed to have designated sections of interest where you would always find the same people. Communists would sit with their friends on one end, while right wing and Christian fundamentalists sat elsewhere. Because anyone coming or going through town needed to walk or drive by, it often felt like a courtroom as the people sitting would stare then whisper gossip and judgments about the passer byes.

Stephanie and I would always be a center of attention and certainly would be talked about. Most men did not walk with their wives to town and the idea of our being a regular couple having coffee together seemed strange especially after the summer months. Men liked to be with other men to discuss politics, the weather, sports, sheep and women. It was only when I came to town on my own one day and accepted the invitation to drink several glasses of the homemade "moonshine" raki drink called tsipero, did I finally feel acceptance as a "real man". The heavy dose of alcohol did not dull my senses and actually uplifted my spirits. That sensation only lasted until I tried standing up and then found my legs to be made of wobbly rubber.

Over time, I made another observation of the layout of the town square which fit quite well with the nature of the village. By picturing the square from one end to the other, the first cafe was the one where mostly young kids went to drink sodas and play arcade games. The next cafe on the block was mainly frequented by teenagers smoking cigarettes, listening to techno music and making comments while staring at the young ladies smiling by. On the third side was the place where middle aged folks would gather to talk about their health and business. And on the last side was the cafe where the elderly would gather to talk mainly about their pensions and who was sick or dying.

Right behind it was the drug store, church and cemetery. A layout that was quite a visual metaphor of our village.

XIROKAMBI

Every summer they come. The pilgrimage of people who left their native villages to emigrate to Canada and the US. They come to reminisce about the "good old days" and complain how the present day Greeks here are not as good as the Greeks of before. They make plans to one day build big villas on their family land and retire. Some actually do. The ones that can't come send their children. Born usually in New Yorkie, Toronto or "Seekago", they come during the summer to visit the relatives in the villages: the grandparents, uncles, aunts and cousins. All smiles and kisses, they enjoy being pampered as the pampering itself must bring pleasure to the village relatives obviously so proud of their family who have "become so successful." I have asked many of these young people what they do when they come here. Do they go on their own independent travels to exotic islands they have never seen, meet interesting new people; fellow travelers with views from the other side? Somehow this question scares away these visitors. It spreads an awkward distancing between us; a polite retreat from further conversation. They tell me that they go nowhere except the ancestral village with perhaps a day or two in Athens and always taken there by the same relatives. The same food every visit, the same conversation, the same faces growing older. Like visiting a graveyard because of duty, they are taken from relative to relative to hear the same old stories about their parents and how wonderful they look. They fill their bellies with mousaka and never empathize with the politics or social needs of their village-the living museum their parents left behind. Their faces filled with kisses, they go back to their new country like a postcard to report "it's all fine and everyone's doing the same as always". Disneyland could save these people time and money by adding "immigrant villages" to their theme parks. Animated manikins programmed to speaking various accents and serving familiar old world style home cooking without the spice.

Going back to my original feelings of this time in life here is a paragraph I wrote expressing my thoughts:

I waited patiently to live among the sounds of angels and waterfalls. Rainbows whispering and the hum of dragonflies. The sermon of the breeze and the dew drops singing. Even the harmony of drums and melody of guitars and laughter. Now I lie dizzily exhausted in this ancient bed. Prison walls close me off from life but don't stop the noise from torturing me. Rumbles of trucks and screaming motorcycles crashing through the torn road blocks of my brain tissue. Battered speed bumps helpless to the onrush of mechanical noise that pave their racetracks through my head and terrorizing any access to my memories. I light my candle as the darkness spreads. With pen in hand I sketch maps out of this hellhole but only find my manifestos written with invisible ink and fate blocking my every key out. My friends and family are distancing themselves away from me now as the noise and darkness embrace me on my new journey. The piercing sound of the potato salesman driving up and down the street shouting his megaphoned mantra interrupts the motorcycles pause and squeezes the nerves all the way down my spine. "Help, get me out of here" I pray to unknown gods as well as to my free fall destiny. The darkness mocks me with silent answers.

NITSA

One of the last places in Greece to enter the "modern age" are the numerous stone homes where grapevines with multi-generational roots, sprawling olive trees, and farm animals blend in the background of limping old men with canes and hunchbacked women dressed only in black and carrying branches along with their bags of vegetables and eggs. One such place is Xirokambi, the village in southern Lakonia where we lived at and one such little old lady was our neighbor and sweet friend Nitsa. Even though two of her three daughters had clicked into a contemporary lifestyle and the one left behind had only an old pickup truck to access the remaining cultural residue, Nitsa had pretty much bypassed the "modern ways." She would wake up at dawn, feeds the animals, milks her goats, prunes her trees, weed her garden and says her prayers. Lately though, contemporary society had managed to find an opening into her life. Every time I went to see "Yiayia Nitsa", even though she still honored me with the traditional hospitality befitting a guest of coffee and sweets, a new activity was preoccupying more and more of her time. On her little black and white TV, Nitsa now devoted her attention to watching sensationalism on the news and even the hyper excitement of game shows. Her compassionate nature considered the story lines as true and the actors as real as her other neighbors. Her eyes glued on the screen and her heart seeked eye contact with the TV unfortunates in back of the tube. The last time I visited her house when the soap operas were playing, she was explaining to another old lady who also glued her eyes on the TV phonies that one of the younger ladies down the street will be hosting a seminar in Nitsa's one room house. She didn't know how to explain any more than they would be demonstrating to her some "very useful products." With the sudden appearance of Amway labels in local neighbors' weekly garbage drop offs, more change was on its way.

SPARTA WITH THE YIAYIAS

The city of Sparta was about twenty miles away, and at times when we had need to go there, we would take along my mother and Nitsa to take care of their city needs as well. After finishing our business in Sparta one afternoon, my mother insisted we go to a restaurant for something to eat. Usually we ate at the downstairs taverna where the old timers and "wanabe" local culture seekers crowd in for homemade food and service. Since the last time we had eaten there she complained that the food was over salted, I followed up this invitation for her to try eating somewhere new by suggesting we walk into the fancy looking hotel restaurant next door. Although appearing a bit out of place to the local scene, the waiters looked more modern wearing bright wardrobes matching the pink and white decor of the establishment's walls and tablecloths. Crystal on the tables, fancy named dishes on the menu (though prices seemed surprisingly comparable to "village dives") and a comfortable air conditioned ambience. Besides my mother's company, along with us was the equally looking traditional old lady "yiayia" (grandmother) with her black peasant outfit on, our friend Nitsa. All the other fancy tables were vacant and when we sat down it was awkward seeing my mother looking restlessly out of place and Nitsa sinking swiftly into shock from finding herself in such an intimidating environment. Her eyeballs swelled up and I thought they would both pass out on the fine table china. She shyly mumbled that she only had a 1000 drachma note (about $3) to contribute and perhaps there was still a chance to escape before the waiter showed up.

The performance falling spontaneously into place, I instructed them to relax explaining that both the food and the bill would be comforting. And indeed it was. My mom enjoyed her lamb dish; Nitsa her chicken with okra and refreshing wine for all of us. Soon the place filled with chic dressed upscale tourists who certainly sat in contrast to the two very authentically traditional Greek ladies I was with. By this time the old ladies were eating with gusto, gulping down their wine, and if they were men, could be imagined easily pulling out cigars to finish off their dining experience. For me the peak moment occurred midway during our meal when the background muzak program switched from generic Greek disco music to Talking Heads satisfying my mind's soundtrack with "Once in a Lifetime" and with David Byrne singing the appropriate lines, "This is not my beautiful life; my God how did I get here?"

DINING OUT WITH YIAYIAS

Oh how times and people's attitudes can change with a fine meal in their bellies. Even a pauper can feel like a prince. On another occasion after deeds were finished in Sparta and my mother requested we go to lunch, I felt the appropriate eatery choice to be the cheap but good home cooking of the part time taverna up from the mountain town of Mistra. Besides the grandparent ambience, sweet breezes, delightful views, delicious spring water and homegrown food, the prices were very low and, since I might have had to pay the bill, coming here was a sensible choice. However, hardly had I headed up the hill before my mother put up a temper tantrum refusing to go any further. Sweet tempered Nitsa was with us and she too was at a loss for words on what to do. Having eaten twice already at the fancy downtown hotel restaurant, mom's taste buds have acquired dining in a place offering the sort of food that she likes but doesn't usually find at home. So as not to disappoint the old ladies, who I now decided would have to pay the bill, I drove them back to town and entered the by now familiar upper crust restaurant. The polyester tourist crowd and shiny glasses no longer intimidated the old ladies who together with my son and I behind them, found their way to their favorite corner table, and soon were ordering in a smooth and smiley fashion. The waiter's opening small talk concerned how especially nice was the fresh fish selection to which my mom replied that the reason it was so because today was Friday, a day on which the church prescribes a fish diet. The waiter found it a humorous concept and erred in ridiculing his mother-in-law who also follows the church diets religiously in vain attempts to mummify her body when she died and thus place her hopes in achieving sainthood. My mother chewed him out and even threw in a few jabs about the spreading power of the "Antichrist" while she scanned the menu for prices as well as Masonic 666 numbers. Another faulty move was the waiter telling us that he had spent nineteen years in New York and was eager to get out of this "backwater birthplace" again and get back to the American action spots. So I had to go for even more reliable connective attempt; appealing to his manhood by suggesting my son's disappearance from our table meant his perhaps rendezvousing with the young beauties parading along the sidewalk outside. Yes, yes, he agreed and with the key to harmony finally in place, he proceeded to return to our table with especially large portions of wonderful food and chilled wine. We all dined nicely and I was able to make my gracious exit to get the car in time before the bill arrived.

TRAY CARRYING

As the eternal torch came back to Greece for the 2004 Olympics, there could have been a consideration of fresh games to spice up this tournament of champions. A local entry which spawned from the same environment as the original games and could be just as competitive is the kafenio/cafe "coffee delivery motorcycles" challenge. It is amazing watching young men and ladies (and even older veterans of the sport) skillfully sliding through crowded streets dodging hectic pedestrians, beefy freight trucks and ancient road cracks with potholes in delivering the still steaming coffee cups to their customers workplaces without a drop spilt. In fact, as an official game, the number of drops in each cup ("flinzane") can be scientifically measured by the judges with high tech instruments to determine each team's ratio of coffee drops spilt or delivered intact. In this birthplace of democracy, the judges themselves can be customers who also will deliver possible complaints which could disqualify the contenders for "service without a smile" or "wisecracks" as well as hand out the winning trophies or coffee pots. These trophies can then be held and displayed by the delivery boys and girls with one hand as they similarly carry their coffee trays and parade around the same streets expressing their victory in this tournament.

HELPING NITSA

Even with her many kids, grand-kids and large extended family, Nitsa could rarely find any of them interested in helping her with errands. Not a problem for us to help out whenever we could as we appreciated the daily attention she brought to my mother, as well as listening to her bountiful story telling.

When she needed to replace her old vinyl flooring, Stephanie and I were glad to be able to buy the materials for her in Sparta and then go to her house to do the project. The first step was to move some furniture out of the way. But when we asked her twenty year old grandson to help us move a rather heavy table, his reply was that he did not want to over exert himself as that might lead to him sweating and then to catching a cold, so he politely declined. A screwed up family indeed.

An even more extreme situation with Nitsa occurred when she was having a serious heart problem and again no one in her household had the time to give her a ride to the cardiologist in Sparta that we had arranged an appointment with for her. On our return back to Xirokambi, I noticed a couple of police cars up the road with several policemen in brand new outfits happily pulling cars over and proceeding to give them tickets for not wearing seat belts. The law making their use mandatory was new and the police were eager to hand out as many expensive tickets as they could to pad their income bonuses. With five of us in the car the officer seemed especially elated as he added the numbers to the bill he was about to present us while my feelings were sinking from shock to depression at this costly situation we were facing. But once Nitsa understood the nature of our predicament, she leaped out of the car and had no fear going right up to the cop and unloading quite a barrage of insults and litanies at him. She reminded him of how she was an eighty year old woman who needed an emergency ride to town or else she would have died and then she pointing out that his job should have been to help people instead of being a highway robber. Then lifting her cane in an even more aggressive manner she told him that he should be ashamed of himself and then interrogating him as to why didn't the police help people in need like herself in such situations. She went on to say that instead of her family or the police taking her to the doctors, it was a good family like us that did and that here he was trying to rob us in return while possibly aggravating her heart with the stress for which she would have her death on his conscience. By now there were several other people starting to pay attention to this entrapment which eventually led to his tearing up what would have been a $600 ticket and telling us to be wearing our seat belts next time we were on the road. Now if all citizens in the world could be as clear and assertive as this little old lady was that afternoon!

TRADITIONAL HANDICRAFTS

As in most countries around the world Greek society was changing while efforts were being made by some organizations to remind people of various aspects of their heritage. Skills that used to be passed down from parents to their children were no longer commonplace. With the advent of readymade clothes and fabrics, family arts of weaving and heirloom making were rapidly disappearing. A cultural awareness program was organized one weekend in Sparta and as its director was aware of Stephanie's beautiful macramé designs, she was invited to come to the forested park behind the ancient amphitheater to be a participant in the educational outreach as well. The event was not only a showcasing of traditional art forms but also included training workshops for all ages. During the weekend Stephanie enjoyed even teaching young children how to make various knots and then macramé with them. Traditional music was also being played and all the food was organic and grown by various families that complemented the theme of emphasizing presentations sustainability.

On the Sunday session, we brought Nitsa and my mother who not only were impressed by the festival but also were treated with deep respect and honor. In fact during his closing speech, the organizer who was also a university professor in Athens, made mention and praised Nitsa, my mother and all the other grannies in the area who actually were the highest level of educators and vital stewards of such essential arts. With such an impressive highlighting, my mother was a little more reserved when nagging Stephanie about wasting her time making macramé decorations. Yet, it didn't limit her interest and purchasing of the sweat house made cheap clothes from China that were being sold in more and more places around town and thus replacing the handmade clothes whose tradition was now waning.

FREE MONEY

One morning we started chatting with a neighbor who walked by the house and stopped to tell us how there were free bags of rice being passed out in the county office building for people to take home. Leaving us a sample to try with our dinner, it was a disappointing taste experience which we attributed to its probable genetic modification. After Greece had entered the European Union, many traditions such as organic farming would soon be encouraged to change as to benefit global banking and marketing interests instead of growing healthy food.

Not too many days later while Stephanie and I were sitting in the town square one afternoon sipping our thick Greek coffee, we noticed that the people getting off the bus from Sparta looked especially elated as they proudly walked by carrying what looked like small religious prayer cards in their hands. Eager to explain the new treasure, one of these folks told us how the banks were giving away free money. What the general understanding was that the German government wanted to help the Greek people elevate themselves to Northern European financial standards by offering everyone credit cards which entitled them to spend up to 5000 euro with no need to ever pay it back. When I tried to tell them that not only was it not free money, and if they did not make payments back to the bank they would punish them, but they only kept admiring their new glossy credit cards and laughed at me.

My looking like a fool at the time for doubting such a gracious gift looked pretty accurate with the current economic crisis in Greece. The lure to cultures that do not understand the fish hook of such hit men as the bankers who gave out the credit cards, destabilizes a country's future by creating permanent debt from interest payments that can never be paid off. National treasures and land are sold by desperate citizens trying to survive in the maelstrom created which becomes quite a lucrative opportunity for foreign "investors" who can buy low priced land and exploit resources. Greece had been a stable cash only society but now times they were a changing for the worse. What German soldiers could not fully conquer during World War II was now completed by the German banks proving that at times that rich people's pens that sign contracts of debtors are stronger than the sword. Even more ironic that the lesson of the Trojan Horse was a story written in ancient Greece.

FRIENDS

Except for a few friendships, we felt somewhat isolated social-ly. We knew how to communicate the basics but did not have a full enough grasp of the language or the contemporary cultural reference points to develop necessary depth of expression. Over the years we were visited by friends from the US which always was a wonderful and fun opportunity to enjoy each other's company while showing them some of our favorite local sites and activities.

My long time friend from high school and college Richard and his daughter stayed a few days after his visit as a journalist to the Middle East. They both liked Greece and especially the mountain area be-hind our house enough that they considered a possible move as well. Richard remains as a friend and political comrade.

Our friend Lisa came and invited us to fly together to the island of Santorini where we had a fun time exploring ancient ruins and con-temporary culture. I had met Lisa at a Terrence McKenna workshop in Virginia and she has been an enchanting dear friend ever since. At one point we had even considered being land partners and neighbors in Hawaii.

Our friends Rick and Tina came from Hawaii and enjoyed the traditional village community activities. They were especially liked by my mother and Nitsa whom they shared lots of smiles and good emotions with. Tina being a midwife was perfect in compassionate understanding and providing emotional nurturance. And Rick with his handy building tools did some much appreciated repair on our old house.

JAMES AND PAM

Another long time friend from both Raleigh days and also as college roommates, James came with his wife Pam and had a wonder-ful visit with us. The timing of their trip coincided with Greek Easter which meant lots of traditional activities as well as being enchanted in their frequent walks through the blossoming wild flowers and herbs on the mountain trails.

Meetings James and Pam at the airport was not only the joy of reuniting with a friendship extending back over 30 years but also the pleasure in picking up the Fernandez travel guitar that they were de-livering for John. We had a delightful time reacquainting ourselves in

Athens and then took the bus to our favorite Greek island of Lefkada. The Hotel Byzantium was home base for most of our activities and we got a good deal on renting a car to tour around the island. Not having John and Nicolette along made it easier to fit in with just Sophia. James enjoyed sampling every single opportunity of drinking tsiporo and would have brought back a barrel or two of this local style fire water had not Pam and custom regulations not allowed it. One of our highlights was spending two days at Tzorello's beach and taverna where even though James did not catch any fish, he did catch up on a lot of fish stores and social philosophy with the waiters at the taverna. Just like every other restaurant we ate at, numerous photos of the excellent food were taken as a delicious memento of their travels in Greece.

Arriving in Xirokambi and meeting Nitsa was a delight for them, as was the whole traditional living scene in the village. They were able to connect with lots of folks and I wouldn't be surprised in their returning back to climb even more trails up Mount Taygetos as well as sampling more varieties of home brew tsiporo.

Pam enjoyed the many types of foliage and flowers whose images she etched in her notebook while sitting on our porch. Being Easter week, although we couldn't provide a roast goat on the spit setting, we did get an early start Holy Saturday evening to the monastery of Zerbitsa and afterwards hiked the hour down from the mountain singing together the traditional Easter chant "Christos Anesti" (Christ has risen). Hopefully we will be able to visit each other again sooner than our previous get-togethers have been.

ACTIVE KIDS

Since our Oak Meadow school program required including physical activities as part of the curriculum, we made sure that our children not only learned movement exercises such as yoga at home but also took part in organized extra-curricular classes in the community. The girls attended several traditional Greek dance classes while John studied playing various Greek musical instruments. All of them were also enrolled in bike clubs and an excellent hiking club called EOS which took various age groups on expeditions up tall mountains, cave exploration and taught them rock climbing and also skiing on the high mountain slopes. Stephanie and I even went on a few of the adult hikes but found them too strenuous for our out of shape bodies.

We even needed help being carried over some of the more rocky riverbed terrain which we couldn't manage too many hours of climbing over the big boulders. All our family experiences however were wonderful and well appreciated.

Besides EOS expeditions, our children often hiked with us from our village to the medieval ghost town of Komosta, then followed the newly restored gorge trail through the forest to the snow covered monastery of Gola. It wasn't as tiring as feared, and it felt wonderful walking through a mushroom and fern forest. We crossed a small Roman era bridge and walked a stretch in the snow. Afterwards the bus taking us back to Xirokambi got stuck in the mud and with many of us helping, we eventually pushed it out and continued our return journey.

Sometimes John would take it upon himself to go on full day hikes on his own. On one particular late afternoon winter day, we started worrying because he had not come home or called us on the cell phone we had given him for making contact in case of emergencies. Knowing that when the sun would set, the weather would be colder and the darkness too treacherous to walk in, we shared our concerns with a few neighbors who also felt concern and soon organized a large group of men to go on a search for our son. Besides the bone shaking mountain chill and not seeing where to place his footsteps, they were afraid that he might have fallen down a ravine or worse yet, met any of the packs of wild wolves that the government had let lose in the area because of their endangered status and need for a less threatened habitat. As word of the perceived emergency spread, because of John's possible danger and need of help, many men showed up with ropes, flashlights, medical kits, manic hunting dogs, holy icons and thermoses full of coffee to keep the search party awake during the night.

However, just as all options and back up plans were organized and the trucks ready to take the guys up the hill, John appeared on the back road strolling home nonchalantly as if nothing was amiss. Startled by all the active concern, he simply expressed his story of having hiked to a high mountain pass where he hung out in a friend's cabin where he shared some stories and wine before coming back home. Even though it was already past 10 pm and he never called back by 5 as was his promise, I was ecstatic to see my son well, happy and healthy. Stephanie and the daughters on the other hand were not as easy on him and scolded his lack of responsibility for not letting us know his situation. My mother who was all in tears and making prayers to various saints was not yelling at him for being so comfortable with all that was transpiring. But for the men who now did not have to spend their nights chasing shadows in the dark, it was a perfect opportunity to save John from the family tribunal and take him out to drink more wine in the village tavern and hear of his heroic exploits hiking through the mountains.

RAINBOWS

One of the most familiar customs of going to a Rainbow Gathering for us is the persistent driving around in circles on the first day looking for the setting until by magic, the little signposts verifying that indeed we were in the right place became clear. To our delight, even though the gathering spot was again on a beach near Pilos in the Patra region of the northwest Peloponnesus, there was a lot more woodsy forest area here so as not to be as oppressed by sun and dunes as the last gathering.

Over the next few days we enjoyed not only meeting new friends and swimming in a secluded stretch of ocean, but also were within a short walk from a thermal hot springs spa. The thick mineral fumes were enticing enough for several of us to sneak past the entrance gate to what appeared like an old factory warehouse in search of the right place to soak. Being Sunday, the entrance to the springs were closed which made it even more convenient for some of the braver members of our group to climb through an open window and soon find the pools waiting to enjoy the bliss of a rejuvenation soak. Our son John had even brought his guitar and small amp which he started playing and adding even one more dimension of perfection to the experience.

Being used to staying aware in these "perfect moments" of possible problems, I kept looking out the window and when I noticed a car pulling up in front of the building, I gave a quick warning of trouble ahead. Not wanting to find out if we were about to be busted or the car being just a random person checking out the facilities, we all managed to be out of the building and walking briskly and very refreshed on our way back to the camp. John however, had stayed in the building longer but climbed back outside before the manager of the spa drove by to check out what the activity was all about. Wanting to give John a chance to escape, I started a conversation with her that we had not seen evidence of any Albanians hiding inside. Luckily she didn't open the door to see John climbing out the window.

A few familiar faces and new contacts shared our life for a couple of days in this full moon cycle. Again we drifted away from any organized activity which this time seemed mostly yoga and tai chi groupings, but John did volunteer his time for kitchen duty. Kentauros looked bright as he was now paired up with an attractive young girlfriend as did Thomas who pulled up in his convertible with a new lady friend. Also happy to see us was Emmy who always beamed positive vibes and love. The drumming and singing was fine and John stayed up late with the happening while the rest of us walked back to our camping spot under the trees. The next day we were leaving for Lefkada early and taking with us a couple from the US, Ryan and Michelle who had dropped into the gathering. The ride was fun, giving us a chance to enjoy the music together and talk of Grateful Dead shows and other related topics.

In Patra we stopped for a traditional wood fired pizza since Yanni's Gyro Taverna was seemingly always closed when we came to town. Before leaving the city we had one more view of the ever impressive Agios Andreas Church. A few weeks afterwards we heard from them that our suggestion that they go next to Lefkada instead of another Greek island option was satisfying to them finding it to be beautiful as well as enjoyable. Ryan didn't care for the crepes too much, but the ill feeling must have passed soon enough as he and Michelle were thoroughly in lust with each other and certainly found pleasurable opportunities to express their passion.

PATRA

Lacking the extension, compression, and at times frenzied chaos of Athens, the large city of Patra is a many lustered jewel in the Peloponnesus peninsula. Besides being the gateway to the islands of the Ionian Sea, the city unveils a panoramic backdrop of towering mountains in its shadow. Patra has exquisite and affordable tavernas, movies, shops, plateas, bakeries and walkways.

Another important reason we came to Patra was to buy a car. Bus connections were ample and taxis affordable, but by having our own vehicle, we would be able to expand our panoramas and parameters of opportunities to explore, experience and enjoy more of the beauties of Greece. Unlike the United States, the procedure for buying a car here was much more complicated. A Greek citizen had to show how much income he was making before being licensed to purchase an automobile. The more money you earned, the more expensive vehicle you were allowed to buy. So because I was not making any money in the country, I did not have the right to buy a car as a citizen. However, foreign visitors had the right to purchase certain cars that were owned by the Customs Bureau of the government. These were vehicles that were either impounded or left behind by travelers from other countries who did not want to pay the registration costs in the car's country of origin and/or the shipping costs to have it transported back. The limitation was that the buyer would only have between three to six months use of the vehicle while in the country as that would be the usual limit for a tourist in Greece to be able to drive the car. At that point a customs agent would come to where the car would be parked and put a lock on the steering wheel and take away its special green license plates. The car could then be sold to another tourist with the same understanding and if it were not used for five years, the government would again take possession of it.

Being a major gateway port for Europeans coming into Greece by boat, Patra had several car lots full of such foreign registered vehicles from which we could choose from. The one we finally picked and felt to be perfect for us was a Mitsubishi four wheel drive van that had been converted in Germany into a camper with a sleeping loft, small stove, sink and refrigerator. Not only did our eyes and travel plans spark up but also the $2000 price was a satisfying deal for us to pay and soon be on the road without the need of bus, taxi or car rentals. The five speed transmission meant decent gas mileage, and the four wheel drive would give us a wider options of rough road destinations and security from being stuck in the mud. Stephanie and I would be sleeping in the bottom bed, John and Nicolette in the loft and at night we would lay out a small mat across the front seats for baby Sophia to dream on. And because of its very unique appearance, we would never lose sight of our van in large parking lots and could now go to Rainbow Gatherings in an appropriately unconventional vehicle.

Driving the van was easy enough for both of us, though when we came to larger cities, I always preferred Stephanie to take over the wheel because of my sensitivity to the neurotic pressure of pushy drivers on the road. Too many cars trying to squeeze into lanes that were once reserved mainly for donkeys did not leave much room for patience. Also typical of local over caffeinated drivers in a hurry would be for them to start flashing their headlights, blowing their horns and then passing us on the right side emergency lanes. Also challenging was trying to board our van unto a ferry boat by driving it backwards and following the hand signals of the parking crew wanting to squeeze cars into literally every inch of space available. They would shout mean and confusing sounding directions to drivers. But if it was a foreign woman like Stephanie at the wheel, they would have a completely different courteous and charming script without the yells that they would pound wimpy guys like me with.

TRAVELS IN NORTHWEST PELEPONESOS

With carefully planned anticipation, we turned past the village of Figalia to start our first hike from the "Trekking in Greece" book. (pg.99). The directions sounded simple enough; the duration suggested as around one hour; and the goal being to reach the inviting waterfall on the Nedhas River pictured nicely in the book.

We vaguely stumbled through a skeleton of a town as with a partially remaining hint of a once mighty kingdom that lived in ancient times behind huge stone structures. A German family whose motor home shared the same ethnic accent as our license plates asked us for directions to which we tried to reply in English. Through sporadic language retrieval, we got the impression of a narrow road and misleading trail markers. Trusting a sign which pointed down the hill to be our destination: "The Falls", we parked our car at an end of the road spot and then walked a steep trail down to the river for about forty five minutes. The waterfalls were interesting and the river nice, but we somehow felt we were at the wrong place because we didn't find the landmarks mentioned in the book such as bridges, churches, pools and the expected highlight of two rivers converging into a mystic stone vagina shaped cave opening which the ancients considered a gateway to Hades.

A bit disappointed, we climbed back up before the darkness of the hour reached us; avoided the growling dog that we had previously encountered; tried in vain talking to a possibly insane old woman and finally reached the security of our motor home. There were some people talking at the nearby house from whom I learned that we had indeed not gone to our anticipated destination and that the trail we wanted was at the other side of town. This sacred spot was honored by the village every August 23 when a pilgrimage goes down to the small rock church that had been built there. People nowadays throw rocks into the hole in place of the earlier traditional animal sacrifices to keep the demons from entering the world. Thanasis, the fellow who looked a lot like my uncle Ntalianis told us about these happenings and invited us to come back as his guest. If it wasn't for the usual "goat innards" feasting that inevitably occurs, I would have marked it in my August calendar of events.

We did stop at the correct trail head which John and I explored a bit of and verified its parallel to the travel book's description. We also found evidence of ancient structures as well as a very present huge live snake which slithered across the trail. A good luck omen I suppose. Stephanie prepared a Greek coffee in her initial use of our car stove to imprint the idea that our Mitsubishi camper was now our debt-free home. We intended to spend the night in the adjacent field and early the next morning to hike down the trail. The owner of the field happened to drive by and indeed invited us to camp on his land as well as to inform us that a new road had been built leading very close to the spot we were planning to hike to. Since Figalia had no food to offer us, he suggested we drive first to the next town Pervolia where the spring was located to procure some "light eats" and then return later to our campsite.

When we pulled into town we met a friendly man who was working at the church across from the town square water spring. He was one of only several remaining people still living in the village and had taken charge of instructing an elderly couple who were proprietors of what, in its heyday, would have been the "coffeehouse/meeting hall" to put together a meal for all of us. We conversed awhile together and found out that he (I think his name was Socrates) had left his village and moved to Long Beach, California for several years, training and working later as a master mechanic. He wasn't impressed much by the "American Dream" so he returned back to this village creating a small machine shop business and feeling much happier. He bought us a few beers and in a short while we were served an ample home cooked non carnivore dinner. Tasty potatoes cooked in home-grown olive oil, eggs, salad and lots of cold beers imported from Holland. Afterwards we were exchanging conversation with a group of elderly folks about my mother's legal situation of evicting her house tenants. We were persuaded to camp outside the cafe that night and spent a little more time talking, watching TV, and playing backgammon. (If you're collecting statistics on the matter-No the bathroom did not flush well).

The next morning we took the short drive to the trail head/ dirt road and even though we were not sure if the strong winds and darkening clouds would be dumping a storm on us, we slipped the car into four wheel drive and proceeded down the road cautiously. At times we argued whether to continue driving as the road conditions deteriorated. Often I jumped out of the car to toss large rocks out of our way and encourage Stephanie to keep driving with faith. The view as we descended down the river valley was magnificent. After about half an hour we eventually reached a short bridge with a marker designating the end point. A tiny church icon was on the other side of the bridge which was a pretty spot to visit and take a few pictures. Several yards back we followed a path leading through a small green gate with a faded warning sign of some sort. We continued our hike cautiously but eventually turned back after it led us down to a farm hanging off the canyon ledge. We retraced our steps to the gate and followed an even more overgrown path for fifteen minutes. At one point we jumped in fright after Nicolette screamed at the sight of a large snake near her steps. However we persisted onward, omen or not, eventually reaching the awesome site of the river leaping into a huge hole carved into the cliff. This surely being the very holy site of goddess worship, ancient sacrifices and certainly eternal moments of passion and kisses exchanged. Such being verified by several old condom packages and lacy underwear now composting ecstatic memories in the earth. There was the nice waterfall and pool we recognized from our hiking book's picture, but the water was too cold for even John to jump in. The actual sight of the water entering the primordial womb was too treacherous to climb to, but even viewing it from a distance was satisfying. There was a small church built along the adjacent cliff which we visited and rang its bell which echoed throughout the canyon. Pleased with our accomplishments, we then circled back up the road.

Several months later, John would hike down the same river valley with the EOS hiking club and actually did stare into the famous "hole" which he's encouraging us to visit together.

As on the day before, the drive up from the Perivolia junction past the Apollonian temple of Vasse and eventually to the mountain hamlet of Andritsena was rich in extending panoramas offering inspiration to the poetic eye of the soul. Andritsena was somewhat of a letdown except for the flushing toilet of relief. We just missed the arrival of a bus group of Japanese tourists who were all shuffled quite amazingly into a very small cafe. After buying a few groceries including corn meal biscuits from the bakery, we followed the ridge highway east.

ARKADIA

It was an especially noisy drive, arguing with the kids and the frustrating effort to wake up Stephanie during one of my rare moments of excitement. All of us were impressed of the profile cast by the majestic castle at Karitena which we hope to one day explore more closely. But the elusive concept of not enough time had other vistas for us to enjoy.

As we ascended up the mountain road, the most obvious view in the valley below was of Megalopolis appearing awfully disgusting in its grey gaseous appearance covered in fumes from the two nuclear power plant (though locals assured us that they were only steam driven and not radioactive). But as we followed the curving road to Dimitsiana, the scenery improved dramatically. En route we passed the picturesque "Greek Alps" appearance of the town of Stemnitsa which we added to our return plans. To a lesser degree, our route's end point of Dimitsiana was likewise pretty, but it also had the look of a town about to lose its character to the siege of tourism.

On the way back we took a dirt road with a placard pointing to the Monastery of Agion Filosophon and a peculiar sign for a hydroelectric plant museum. Several months afterwards we returned and were pleased in visiting this museum which was actually a reconstructed village using running water from a stream as part of its model of self sufficiency technology.

We took another turn at the dirt road to the monastery of Agios Ioanis Prodomos and set out for the site mentioned on pg.96 of our

"Trekking Greece" book, under the heading "River Gorges of Arkadia-Lusios River Valley." After a little confusion in picking the right road, we eventually came to the small church of Agios Ioanis very near the monastery. From the roadside the church looks adequately picturesque, but when you walk around its balcony facing the canyon, the view becomes breathtaking. Several monasteries appear tucked into the cliffs, and a string of villages dot a horizon of textured slopes. We drank refreshing cold water at the spring and had lunch on the deck which was a somewhat shaky experience for my scared of heights nerves.

Afterwards we took the path along the ridge of the monastery of Agios Ioanis Prodomos whose porches defy structural logic by standing up only from a few twig like beams. There was a nice small orchard outside and inside the resident monk gave us sweets, coffee and directions. Yes, we did see the well maintained trail to the river described in our Trekking book, but the monk suggested we drive instead five kilometers to the site of Ancient Gortys.

The setting was a beautiful combination of the roaring river Lusios, the sharp mountain cliffs, rolling hills, meadows, wildflowers and several small churches. The ancient Asklipon therapeutic center of Gortys lies in front of an old farmhouse and resonates its healing energy throughout the environment. We were so enchanted by the setting that we then left a couple of written messages on fence posts inquiring about land for sale in the area and made a mental memo to come back and camp as the several other German motor homes there had done so.

EXPLORING MOUNTAIN VILLAGES

They cling scattered on the sharp slopes of rocky mountains; these proud old stone villages in Greece. Clinging has become a common denominator of life here nowadays. Medieval churches which once swelled with large numbers of the faithful for services now cling mainly to the yearly pilgrimage of the villagers left behind by urban migrations. Memories of war victims which once dotted the national scenery through the black mourning outfits worn by the surviving widows are now being replaced by brighter skirts representing happier times. A few roadside name plaques and grave markers are now overrun by weeds. And on the drawing boards of land developers slowly erased are the commemoration of their exploits as respectful token enough to go on with more important construction projects. But the memories, traditions, names and villages cling together in a rhythm not quite camouflaged but still within a modern portrait of the Greek environment.

Arriving rather late, we settled into the tavern for a light meal of eggs, potatoes and salad. Afterwards we parked nearby at a flat space overlooking the distant mountains and nearby plains. The next morning we attempted once more to find the Rainbow crowd in the village. Down the road, we visited the famous church of Agia Theodora that proclaimed having seventeen "miraculous trees" growing from the roof and holy spring water flowing underneath the outside wall. Sophia did put her thumb which had earlier been stung by a bee into the water and the swelling and pain diminished. I wondered if someone suffering from syphilis could dip their afflicted body part in this miraculous water without being evicted as a pervert. Around the church was quite a large settlement of food, trinket and religious paraphernalia merchants. Also there were signs for more expensive tavernas with a view (of God perhaps?).

The road led us past green autumn colored foliage and plump chestnut trees (of which we later picked a bundle). In Likeo we drove up to the top of the mountain and walked into the chapel of Profitis Elias and enjoyed hearing ourselves chant within the stoney acoustics. We would have liked to return again to hike from this church to the Temple of Vasse. Afterwards our visit to the ancient ruins at Likousoura was not very pleasant as Nicolette, by possibly angering the local gods in arguing with her mother, fainted and fell from a pillar unto the cement flooring below. The site setting was ominous for any possibilities: a sacred place in which mystical sacrifice and rituals took place; the alter of Despoena, the most ancient and sacred city of the Arkadian empire. (Our daughter Sophia's baptismal name is Despina). Nicolette and Despina-Sophia had been fighting over who got to stand on the pillar for a picture. Suddenly Nicolette's eyes rolled up, her face paled, she fainted and fell straight on her head. The first minutes after the fall were hysterical for me, as I petitioned all the gods and goddesses to help Nicolette who eventually did recover enough for us to drive home. We considered a visit to a hospital emergency room but as she screamed even more at the mention of the idea, we quickly agreed that it might be more traumatic than our decision to go straight home.

Nicolette's fainting spells had been a fright to us on several other occasions as well. While at a festival at one of the mountain hamlets above Xirokambi, she fell backwards after standing near an open fire. Luckily her friends were there to help her and take her to the hospital for stitches.

Even earlier when she was about five years old, after a loud crying spell, her eyes rolled up and she passed out while I again felt helpless and cried and screamed at the gods in anger at the situation they tortured us with. Many years later she also passed out while catering a luncheon for older student alumni where she attended college in North Carolina. Most of these times she was on an empty stomach which was a reminder to all of us to never forget eating throughout the day whenever necessary.

After everyone felt rested and healthy we were soon on the road again. One of our most transcendental moments occurred at the small chapel of Profits Elias on a tall peak in Arkadia. It was soon apparent after our entry that the circular layout enhanced the depth and dynamic range of our voices. All five of us joined the vocal toning and harmonizing improvisations of the Amen. Alleluia and variety of other chants from Hindu, Native American and free floating inspirational sources. Even when I walked outside to the solitary beauty of the wide angle view, I continued my part of the chant which led me back soon to the remaining family in the chapel to join together in this consciousness raising experience.

The Greek countryside as well as urban neighborhoods are dotted with churches, large and small. Some are the obvious centers of busy plateas (town squares) while others in remote valleys and mountain tops are just a frail whisper away from crumbling apart. A few are built by donations from the whole village congregation while many of the smaller chapels are constructed by one person's offering in memory of a departed family member or from a previously occurred personal miracle that was promised to be paid back to a specific saint. Once a year there is a Panegeri festival whereby the saint the church was named after is honored by pilgrimages and church services. Afterwards the people engage in eating (usually goat meat) in a setting of music and dance. At the larger panegeria and famous miracle church and monastery locations there are year round pilgrimages as well as bus tours to them. Often a cottage industry develops at these holy sites with booths selling fast foods, t shirts (including heavy metal death and Satan images), loud bouzouki music and action toys (rubber guns and miniature tanks being quite popular). To someone sensitive to the various juxtapositions and clashes in the whole scene these variations can seem both humorous as well as horrific. The sight of people coming to pray can easily be overshadowed by the carnival atmosphere of gawking kids shooting at each other with their toy guns, their mothers eager to buy another superstitious charm bracelet to protect them from their fears while grabbing for plastic Jesus medallions; bored fathers buying cassettes of over hyped bouzouki singers moaning about the same themes of broken hearts and alcohol; and teenagers parading around with their new biker black "I buried Jesus t shirts". (Maybe they should be selling holy water for the water guns as well.)

The cacophony of new saints and sinners is a sobriety test to identify ones beliefs in the hodgepodge of dogma, practice and illusions. In any case, one must have an open mind and stay fairly detached so as to be able to enjoy the carnival as well as the sacred. Greece seems to have a historic ability with its deep cultural fabric to accommodate Pagan and Olympian gods along with stoic Christianity. In town kiosks which serve as a concentrated general store, on the same sale racks appear Christian saint biographies propped next to triple X porno. And, if I'm not mistaken, the voluptuously breasted women on the cover sometimes wear crosses while the priests faces on the holy books next to them are smiling, sharing a wink or perhaps even a friendly pinch instead of pulpit condemnations or holy war jihads.

The main road down from Vasta is narrow and fairly steep. As Stephanie was driving our car down it, she correctly pulled over to the edge to allow a carload of older folks a chance to drive up the road. No way would they budge however. A couple of times they tried to ascend but their old clunker car died. Not wanting to "lose face" to their vintage "chicks" in the back seat, the older of the two men in front honked his horn at us while, as if on cue, the women in the back all yelled at us to "back up!" as if it mattered. We calmly watched their car's inability to power its way up until they figured out that one of the men had to get out to relieve the weight load on the little car's engine to finally get them out of their predicament. Through the antics of their curses I sensed a similarity to 1950's American teenagers and "hot rods" facing off to see who is the toughest and bravest, I feel perhaps our non-involvement might have been the "superior act" as we stayed calm, laughed at a funny situation and actually went down the road without a problem as our "opponents" yelled and screamed for nothing as they still swallowed their pride in the embarrassment of having a helpless car until its body fat was removed.

On one of our extended detours, we took a drive to the northeast corner of the Peloponnese peninsula to visit an area which was devastated a few hundred years previously by a volcanic eruption and subsequent series of earthquakes. There among the rocky desolation we found a small village built entirely out of lava rocks. On a quick glance, the structures blended so well with the terrain that they were relatively camouflaged from perception. Even more astounding was that there were still a few inhabitants living there with no obvious gardens. And as even the smallest of villages anywhere else in the country had at least a small cafe, no such signs of civilization where obvious. As we got out of our car and started walking around the landscape, we were met by weird stares from the local people that had facial and body deformities that probably came from both their poor diet and also from many generations of inbreeding. Quick photos were taken and before we were in a position of having to interact with any of these very strange looking folks, we got back in our vehicle and started looking for another village to stop for a coffee and flushing toilet. Both hallmarks of contemporary Greek civilization.

FROM ZARAFONA TO THE COAST

With summer heat blowing into the valley and obligations to finish building my father's parental cottage long overdue, on Sunday, June 14th, we drove to the somewhat remote village of Zarafona to start our three day "next adventure." Most of the day we stayed at my cousin Mimi's house where we had lunch. Around noon, a couple of local musicians dropped in to admire Mimi's craftsmanship in making traditional stringed instruments such as guitars, violins and bouzoukis. They offered a couple of suggestions, ordered a violin and even demonstrated the emotional beauty of the instrument by playing on the deck alongside the panorama of Mount Parnon. And as John expressed interest in learning Greek style violin playing, Mimi promised to build him a bouzouki (possibly from a large squash shell) and later an even more exotic instrument the Ute.

Having finally finished our "family affairs", we followed the dirt road behind the house up for about 45 minutes, but as it didn't seem that it led to any conclusion, we circled back and set up camp in a field adjacent the road. It was very refreshing not to have the highway noise that we have been usually dealing with back in Xirokambi and enjoy instead a beautiful canopy of soothing stars over our eyes. There was a chill in the air but Stephanie and Nicolette did have a nice opportunity for star gazing. Afterwards we cooked a tasty dinner, even though I do not remember what it was.

The next morning we followed the dirt road through the pine forest to the awesome beauty of the village of Tzinzina where John and Nicolette had previously taken snow packed mountain bike trips with the EOS hiking club. A view like out of a picture book of the Alps, alpine forests and meadows circled the town in scenic embrace. An icy cold delicious tasting water spring greeted our entry into the village. Later we discovered another nearby spring that was an even colder one which poured out of a larger rock below a shady plane tree. Of course that spot was our choice for a picnic and we were soon admiring the cave church a few meters away.

Our dirt road choices led us through enjoyable mountain scenery even though we were jittery about running out of gas. From the town of Agios Vasilis we came to the familiar monastery of Elona. Then, after lighting the customary candles, the customary drinking of holy water and the customary discussions with the nuns about fighting the sinister 666 symbols, antichrists, mark of the apocalyptic beast, etc., we steered our landing in the nice sleepy beach resort town of Leonidion.

Just a typical day at the beach. Not happy with the first spot that we decided on camping at, John and I encouraged Stephanie to drive the van down the dirt road to the Plaka beach which she did so. Unfortunately even the low four wheel drive gear couldn't help get us out of the fine sand that we were soon sinking helplessly into. In mild panic, I ran down the beach to the village to ask for towing help. Like angels from heaven, a couple of guys appeared on the beach with their Toyota truck which they drove down the same road of our misfortune.

I feared their yelling at us for trespassing but was instead relieved to see that they had come to help us out of our jam. I managed to find a rope to attempt pulling our vehicle but was pleased to see that we could push our car out instead. Since they weren't receptive to my wanting to pay for their help, we agreed to come later to one of these guy's taverna, "Tou Psara" for dinner. We did; we ate; we enjoyed; and the next day, we had fun swimming in the clear waters of the sea. Besides the many minutes and phone card calls necessary for "business", we otherwise had a very pleasant day on the beach. Dinner had as a background, nice rock music classics on the local radio. "School's Out" by Alice Cooper, played several times in a row as it was the last week of school. Near sunset, we walked along the bay to the church of St. George. The coves were very pleasant (one of which we swam at), but the heat and bees were oppressive. Trying to get some tan on my pale butt was also unsuccessful as bees were stinging relentlessly.

KITHERA

A few days and miles later we were on the island of Kithera again. Our newest "discovery" was a spectacular beach a few kilometers past Paliopoli. The "K" word beach. The windy dirt road leads you after ten minutes to a flat spot overlooking a beautiful bay, coral caves and intriguing rock formations. The footpath down took about fifteen minutes to a dreamy setting reminiscent of some exotic pictures I've seen of beaches in Thailand. Nice snorkeling and an interesting cave were also a bonus. I would have considered camping here if it wasn't for the many boatloads of people being dropped off on the beach looking for remote "public privacy".

LEFKADA

After another day of turns and twists, our travel road brought us back to the island of Lefkada for fresh experiences. For instance, once you pass the port town and enter Nidri on the road to the right you go to Raki where the waterfalls are. This time we actually walked far enough to reach these delightful falls. First we enjoyed swimming in a small sized natural pool but after a few minutes further up a slippery trail, we reached an even larger pool and taller waterfall. The pool was very refreshing for all of us to swim in. Afterwards on our return to the parking area we met an interesting fellow "Tom" who was filling up large containers of fresh water from the spring. Tom told us that German scientists had examined this water's quality and found it to be among the world's healthiest.

In Sivota, the mini market offers homemade olive oil pressed by a traditional stone method. Nearby in the village of Poros we saw a very beautiful beach surrounded by green hills. Plans were made to one day return and snorkel as well as rent paddle boats. On the main beach area on the right, there was a sign leading to the rear of a restaurant with a sign for "free showers".

Porto Katsiki ("bay of goats") had one of the most exquisite beaches we had ever been to. The calm waters appear fluorescent and served as a backdrop for the distinct large cliff that form its border. The parking lot charged 1000 drachmas ($3) for each car, and was undoubtedly gathering lots of wealth for whoever owned this monopoly of raw land overlooking the beach. With no other place to park, we calculated that the landowner could be making upwards of $1000 daily and well on his way to catching up in wealth to the fellow homeboy billionaire Onassis, by just the minimal investment of a couple of plastic chairs that he and his wife sat on all day. Now if he only invested in buying a flushing toilet to charge an extra 500 drachmas a head (or rear) per use. On the windy road up was a long line of local people selling homemade wine, olive oil and honey. (Watch out for small kids handling slippery glass bottles; an unfortunate lesson we learned firsthand.)

Nearby in the village of Komilo was a brightly decorated cafe with exotic yet homey decor operated by two hip German ladies and surrounded by many exotic art objects.

Later in the week our attorney friend Nikos met us in Agios Ioanis in the morning and took us for a wonderful trip with his boat along the western shoreline of the island. We saw beautiful beaches where no cars could have reached and spent a few hours on one of the nicest spots. It wasn't too secluded however as we noticed a hairy "cave guy" that was our neighbor. We also successfully avoided eating Nikos' octopus picnic. Hopefully he wasn't too offended.

EPIROS

To compensate for our depression in not having enough money to send our children to the summer camp on Thasos island which we had planned for, we decided instead to detour a few days to explore the rugged mountainous region of Epiros-Zagarohoria even without having enough money for anything more than gas expense. In our challenged financial situation, the ferry boat car ticket from Acton to Preveza seemed quite expensive to us.

North of the town were some impressive Roman ruins which we kept saying that one day we will return to see. About two thirds of the way to Ioanina on the left is the a famous town because of its "many cold-water springs." The previous night had been their annual town festival "panigiri" and besides cleaning the dirty table and chairs, the usually crystal clear fresh water springs were full of wool rugs, heavy towels, etc. Perhaps this was a town ritual to clean these out the day after for good luck or purification.

In the mountains of Zagarohoria even at our high altitude, the heat was intense. Perhaps because we were closer to the scorching sun. Surprisingly all the springs were dry and the bathrooms reluctant to flush. Against the warning of a lady who owned a nearby café that we would suffer from sunstroke, we challenged this afternoon heat to take a short stroll to the Agia Paraskevi Monastery which perched over the dynamic scenery of the Vikos Gorge (a signpost explained that the Guinness Book of Records considers it the "world's deepest"). In the rear of the monastery we walked on a narrow path towards a cave but not any further than the spot "where early hermits used to creep along the cliff".

We circled back through the village of Tsepelova enjoying more beautiful scenery of the gorge but with equally dried up springs. The town itself had an expensive resort feeling, but we had to settle on enjoying simply staring at the specialty cuisine of zucchini quiches on peoples food plates.

Also impressive were the many ancient bridges across the trails built long before the age of roads. Being low on gas, we couldn't go further on the winding road to Vovosa (and its fabled river pools) and Samarina-not only the highest village in Greece, but also summer home to natives that emigrated returning from Texas and Georgia (according to our travel book). We must return some day to see if they indeed drive in long Cadillac convertibles, wear large cowboy hats, talk Greek with southern accents and eat specially flown in steaks, slaw, and hush puppies. We did enjoy a refreshing swim however at the fantastic natural pools at Makro Papingo. We'll return again to this area some day for the quiches and hikes on our future rain check list.

Our camping spot for the night was alongside the enchanting entrance to the National Park. Children played around at the crystal clear emerald colored beach below the river and were intermittently brave enough to jump into its very cold water. Afterwards we all took a sunset walk along the river trail which had a dreamy transcendental feel to it. Some people had pitched up tents along the way and a couple of older men were struggling to disentangle fishing line wire which their pole had thrown into a tree. I heard them blaming their problems on the bright moon which was spreading rays of its brilliance across the rushing waters and deep pools. I'm sure many of the rocky spots were positions of worship in earlier times. The night was refreshingly chilly, even though persistent flies and mosquitoes again manifested in our camp.

The next morning, lack of money again put me in a jam at the nearby town of Aristi. Our plan was to spend the last of our small change on a couple of coffees as long as the establishment's toilets flushed. The first candidate was the fancy coffee shop where on the previous morning we had seen the hippie that I wanted to talk to cleaning tables there. Since it was closed I walked across the street to the grocery store where the elderly proprietress sliced me up as if I were on trial in her courtroom. First mistake was in asking her what time the coffee shop across the street opened. She darted back "whenever they feel like it". Her not realizing my dilemma, I tried to put her off with "maybe I'll go get a plate of pitas there sometime". She quickly retorted that "Aha, I make the real home cooked kind, so how many of you are there and I'll have them ready by tonight." Again I stumbled so I mumbled a retreat about where can I find maps and postcards. Yes, she pulled those in front of me too. So with embarrassed reservation, I spent the last of my shrinking coins on one of her postcards. Probably the best hope is to come back some day, buy coffee from the hippie, then order a pita-quiche casserole from the little old lady in town.

RETURNING TO LEFKADA
Our return to Lefkada was a limbo of still waiting for money to be transferred from our US bank accounts into the Greek ATM

system. Living without much money meant in some sense freedom and empowerment. We had been doing fine eating just watermelon and drinking spring water for several days (even though I kept wishing for deep dish veggie pizza).

On August 6th we went to the famous homegrown lentil festival above the village of Eglovi at the church of Agios Donatos. It was nice to be able to eat lavishly for free as well as wonderful not having to deal with the oppression of looking at chopped goat heads though we did have to pull out a few sardines from our soup. We made sure we had saved lots of room in our tummies for the fine and generous portions of the blessed lentils. The live music was okay but short lived as most of the large crowd seemed eager to disperse and go down to the town below for more carnivorous style feasting. We felt quite royally in eating the "goods" and the only thing missing was the red wine which we observed being poured freely at the one and only table where, looking like plump pontiffs, sat the pampered and smiling local priests and police officers.

With the very refreshing winds blowing and the full moon illuminating the cave imaged structures where the village legumes used to be stored, we decided to camp here for the night. The landscape gazed down at the distant mountains and valleys below. The only objects that stood higher above us was the twin OTE telephone towers which have brought all the villages the same opportunity to gossip anywhere with anyone at anytime. Such miracles don't require a feast day but just simply paying the amount due by the due date or else the phone service dematerializes.

At some point in the night we were awoken by the piercing stare of flashing blue lights. Fearing the worse, the possible eviction from our newly found earthly paradise, I threw on my pants and stumbled out of the van to try talking to the soldiers outside. I was relieved to hear that there was no problem in our spending the night there as long as we didn't light any fires.

An observation made by Stephanie the next day while laying on Kathisma Beach watching brave teenage boys jumping off the rocks into the ocean surface below was their protective clutching of their penis areas right before impact. The same afternoon I made a penile observation of men holding on to their cellular phones on the beach as if clutching their penises as well. Swords. Power. Security.

Watching the bodies bustling through the busy platea square of Lefkada town on their evening stroll, I felt a blanket of protection which these changing faces of tourist flow provide. The plateas in non tourist resort villages are usually saturated with the same faces wearing the same judgmental stares which freeze you into the same anticipated responses. Fear induced tradition and neurosis. Summer in the islands offers an antidote to this psychological inbred poisoning. Paths among people to escape the narrow embalming that other people trap you into. Swimming into a wider ocean of humanity feels refreshing as does the cool water on the beach giving relief to your body being tired by the glaring eyes of the sun.

Returning to camp at Eklovi (site of the lentil festival) was again a pleasure in escaping the heat and crowds. Early in the morning we were awakened by the voices of a young couple that were camped near us as they were eating a delightful meal in front of the church and preparing to continue the luscious buffet in exploring each other's sensuality. They were interrupted in their affairs by an old man diverting their intentions into listening respectfully to a series of his life's tales. Patiently we stayed in bed waiting for his oratory to finish. After quite a while we slid quietly out of our van. The old man then focused his attention on us. Thinking we were German tourists he offered us the opportunity to take pictures of him and his donkey for 500 drachmas. I startled him by explaining I was Greek also and that I came from a village full of donkeys. Mostly ones that stand on two legs. I wished him well and he proudly explained he didn't need luck as he would be selling lots of photo shot opportunities to the Germans. Who then is the victim and who the victor of these shootings?

ZAKYNTHOS

Our trip to the island of Zakynthos was manifested in part by our providing a substitute family holiday since we were not being able to afford taking Nicolette to the Thasos camp. Also we still had fond remembrances of our previous visit to the island of our "funny friend" with the candy stick glasses giving away beach front land. There also was the mansion restaurant on top of a hill which could be the perfect setting for my upcoming birthday meal. Omens of what lied ahead beyond the horizon of nostalgia were felt as we landed at the ferry boat port of Killini. A huge line up of upper crusty yuppie sorts stood in a packed line were waiting to replace the equally packed large ferry boat leaving. Like an amusement park where people with tickets wait for the ride to finish before the new group gets on.

We landed around midnight, got somewhat map oriented, then set out to find a camping spot in what our tour books described as the "miles of undeveloped west side beaches." Obviously both the tour books and nostalgia need to be updated. Heading into the expected familiarity of where our friend had taken us to his forested domain once before was startling. Huge temple like discos now crowd the once quiet coastline ride. Beautiful young Greek nymphs lined up the entrances into the heavenly gates and circled each other all night long. And like any other Oz, temple or church, these discos appeared pathetically hollow, finite and vulnerable after the "service"- in this case the morning hour meltdown. But our own moment was the night, and we eventually crawled past the neon lights and zigzagged for a long time with never a sight of a beach to park our van and sleep. Eventually we did pull into Porto Roma and found our spot for the evening.

As the morning hours subsequently reaffirmed, the beach situation of Zakynthos is quite unlike what we were getting accustomed to in nearby Lefkada. First of all, except for part of the east side of the island, there are no beach roads and very few long stretches of beaches. Huge cliffs preponderate and when the road circling the island does lead down to a "paralia" (beach), it's usually to a very fancy well developed dead end serving as a parking lot for a taverna or ritzy hotel.

A less busy resort area where we spent a relaxing night's sleep along the beach was the village of Alikanas. Also while there we treated ourselves to a fine meal at an Indian restaurant. The waiter at first mistook us for being Indian, and when I realized he wasn't, we let go of the pressure to act "spiritual" or keep repeating "Namaste". Instead of Ravi's sitar records, we had to listen to awful "Rave" music. The food was especially hot and spicy and the long bread tasty.

Zakynthos is not a preferred island destination of mine. Unlike neighboring Cephalonia and Lefkada, the local people here are very much like cartoons desperately enslaved by tourism. And the general sort of tourists that come here are very arrogant and not at all appreciative of Greek culture or people. To them, they can't tell the difference between if they are in Zakynthos or the Bahamas. Beaches, except for the famous "Shipwreck", aren't very nice or plentiful and the prices very escalated. Possibly nice for singles pursuing the disco beat and, in that case, more pleasant to be at than the over hyped nightlife of Mikonos. An elegant version of Myrtle Beach. Still, the food is better and less expensive than burgers and corn dogs at Myrtle Beach with more exciting night life action than Waikiki (such as more churches to pray at if feeling guilty or victimized).

The boat ride we took around the island was fun and we were glad to have spent the last of our money in doing so or else we would have left Zakynthos without having experienced her true beauty. The highlight of the tour was swimming at "Shipwreck Beach" which is probably the most beautiful beach we had ever been to. The unique brilliant deep blue colors of the water gave our skin a radiant glow when swimming. The ship's captain was quite interesting too. When the boat landed near the beach area, he threw off his white ship officer's outfit and quickly put on his Speedo bikini swimming trunks. As the boat passengers packed up the exit aisles waiting for all 500 to fit into two small boats ferrying them the twenty yards to the shore, the captain pushed ahead with a charging command "to the beach... swim!!" which he yelled out briskly in three languages. Thereupon he invited everyone to jump off the side of the boat with him. He was an ideal captain in not wanting to "go down with the ship" when there was a chance to go swimming instead. The scene looked a bit like the Titanic movie. Another tale about our funny captain happened when the boat approached the dolphin caves and he ordered the fish to appear with the megaphone commanding "Barbara...this is your captain...come out..now!" (No, Barbara never did come out.)

In the evening, in the port town of Zakynthos, in front of the church housing the relics of Saint Dyonisius (not to be confused with the livelier pagan god of ecstasy), there was a lineup of merchants selling the famous homemade sesame, almond and honey candy "masteli". Twice I was offered samples of this tasty treat by a man cooking up pan after pan of this delicious dessert while making his sales pitch in an over exaggerated Italian accent. "Do I look Italian?" I thought. Should I snap back a Greek reply to leave me alone? Probably not as perhaps he himself was Italian and felt right at home trying to sell his candy in Italian because most of the tourist flocks on Zakynthos (or as it is called by its chic European name "Zante") are from Italy.

Food, entertainment, and hotels are cheaper on the Greek side of the Ionian Sea and the beaches much cleaner. Also, it allows some people to feel more powerful having a servant class of locals; tourist industry imperialism which the residents of Zante for the most part accommodate. Of 9000 permanent year round residents, during the summer months, a typical day has around 100,000 tourists on the island. Quite a lot of income to act silly over. What price dignity.

Another interesting incident occurred at a resort shop selling Italian cosmetics and various sundries including one of my favorite Greek magazines which has an excellent coverage of classic rock and roll music, Zoo, lying on a large rack of reading material. When Stephanie went to pay for it, the saleslady was shocked that a Greek magazine had slipped into her shelf. She was even more puzzled why we would want to buy such a product (like embarrassing filth on the counter) and even nervous selling it to us. For her, the only magazines to look at are about glamour and obviously Italian glamour is superior to the local pages. A scandal soaked expose about the Vatican would have felt more comfortable for her to offer us instead. Since she probably will never repeat her mistake of reordering Zoo again for her sales shelf, she might indeed replace it with a trashy copy of pornography instead. Italian chic of course.

Our personal new hide and go seek game of yuppie stress is called ATM (the bank cash machine) or, in other words, where does our money go after being deposited in US banks and how many days can we live on nothing while we wait for the transfer. Personally I found it a bit humiliating to be holding up a line of people who all seem to get instant cash while all our techniques and prayers to foreign bank gods only result in a rejecting "insufficient funds" statement from the smiling cartoon face on the machine. (Surprising why this logo didn't even stick its tongue out at us as well.) One four day stretch on Zakynthos from "deposit to access" was in some ways liberating though. Living on basically bread, rice and watermelons was reassuring as more energy was placed in our attention span in dreaming of the simple pleasures such as chocolate cake and some nice CDs, on my birthday. When money finally did manifest, we made up for some of our lost time by stuffing our stomachs with pizza and ice cream. An even more enjoyable result of our "money drought" was the delaying of our return to

Xirokambi by several days thus having more time for simple living on the beach.

August 15th is one of the biggest holidays in Greece, the feast of the Virgin Mary, "Panagea". We joined the several thousand Zakinthos town residents in a procession around town following the band, incense, and splendidly outfitted priests holding up the sacred icon of Mary. It is the tradition. For once on our visit to this island, we saw no crowds of tourists. Perhaps they were scared away by unfamiliar rituals or the possibility of actually participating in the experience of authentic Greek culture. They were instead pleasantly embalmed in a mirage of Greek Disneyland-safe, secure and brain dead. Tonight was the procession where there would be as many people marching as would fill just one of the large chic Argassi town discos (on a slow night of course). There would have been even more people in the procession if the children's amusement park wasn't so close to the church. A convenient excuse to lessen the stress of the parents and an opportunity to start a new tradition as it was more fun riding the ferris wheel than praying to the Virgin Mary. The procession thus is good business for the residents who can fill the amusement parks with thrilled children and after the long march, swell the ocean side tavernas which benefit from advertising their tasty delights on this holy promenade to the hungry and thirsty pilgrims. Tonight was Greek night. For once, more Greek voices than Italian accents were heard in town. But tomorrow?

The procession moved at a slow but steady pace. I held my youngest daughter Sophia on my shoulders so that she could see the many people. I noticed several old ladies living by themselves in deteriorating but still glimmering apartments along our route. They looked out of their windows with faces of loneliness, pride, hope and memories. Some had tables full of flowers and all of their rooms were a tonight showcase of being neat and clean. As the procession ended up back at the church, fireworks exploded above us. Ancient memories were triggered of perhaps Lakonian warriors from Sparta invading from their fleets to destroy cultures and steal women. Perhaps nothing changes much past appearances as the Greek culture of Zakinthos is disappearing like a passing prop on the stage of history as many of the island's beautiful ladies are being fondled by drunk Aryan tourists behind dark beach shadows. Would if only these ladies could honor Aphrodite before their love feast instead of selling themselves to the power of money, stupidity, and "demon rum" (or local ouzo). None of these are classical Greek values. The procession now ended and the still sizable crowd headed to Church for the festival, the Panegere which was a more important custom than even Christmas. We took a detour for pizza to avoid looking at the traditional meal of boiled goat heads but we did make plans to show up later for beer, ice cream and local dancing which in most Greek villages lasts all night. When we arrived a short hour later, all vestiges of the festival was gone except for some minimal garbage. No smoky stench of goat meat or any loud local music distorting through the speakers. Puzzled, I asked an old lady closing up her candy booth what happened to the Panegere. "My dear boy" she answers. "It's already over". Perhaps it really is over for Zakinthos. The lights have been turned off. "No need to chase away the tourists with our peculiar and outdated ritual performances. We had to prove to them that we are now part of the same contemporary European cultural mass. Closing up the town in the name of God is no longer acceptable. We can't perhaps show a bit of our religious faith to foreigners. That kind of stuff is reserved for the Roman Catholic, not Greek Orthodox missionaries. We aren't pushy like them. So let's go out, celebrate and make money." The lights go out and tomorrow is a new day.

MORE RAINBOWS

Learning that there was a Rainbow Gathering of Greek hippies in the northern part of the mainland, we instantly made plans to attend. The road to the gathering was at times long and windy but definitely worth the mileage. As afternoon darkened into evening, we decided to "camp" along the coast where the freeway touched the ocean at Karavomilos above Lamia (worth remembering this oasis of the road).

The next morning's slow start only brought us as far as Larisa by noon. An impressive and enjoyable small city with content looking inhabitants. On a side street adjacent the bank we feasted at the world's best gyro eatery (for the moment). Also in the area was a shoe store that John was interested in checking out. Searching for a map, John was asked where he was from and after answering Sparta, the proprietor in sincere seriousness told him he needed to move to Larisa which he adamantly stated was not just the "best city in Greece" but "the best place in the world". Although I am not quite ready to agree with his

175

obviously biased opinion, I would at least have liked to return and stay a few days sometime. Some of the live rock and roll groups playing in the local clubs would have been interesting to check out (with enticing names such as "Circle of Mushrooms"). As we drove through the city, it was nice to see public parks and green grassed playing fields. The local Communist political party, KKE, was sponsoring a street fair-demonstration at one of them which we had just missed.

Driving further north, the scenery changed into rolling green hills and picturesque villages which looked as if Bulgarian and Swiss influences blended. The town of Elasona was a pleasant stopover which I also promised to myself to return sometime and drink tsi-pouro (local moonshine) at the cafe whose owner treated us to tasty mezedes (appetizer plate) of oven roasted potatoes and zucchini balls. The proprietor and his buddies all had jolly drunken gazes and would have found it difficult to stand up.

After registering satisfying rain checks in our stomachs' memo-ry, we started the twenty five km long winding dirt road up the moun-tain towards the small village of Katafigio (which means watchtower). Along the way was a nice cold water spring next to a monastery that we didn't have a chance to visit. Surprisingly there was some life and beautiful scenery in Katafigio where we picked up Manos, a Greek hip-pie hitchhiking on the way to the gathering. Preoccupied in enjoying the mountain scenery, we at first missed the turnoff to the site we were heading and got confused with directions a couple horsemen gave us. We retraced our steps and soon were "home again at Rainbow."

The setting was dramatic. A plump yet comforting mountain with gentle slopes on one side; long expanses of pine forests dotted by small streams and bright red Amanita mushrooms on the other side of the panorama; and a large field in the center covered in yellow haired grass (of which I recalled Terence McKenna mentioning being a type rich in the psychedelic chemical DMT). Truly a sacred space.

A large tipi in the middle of the meadow was the expected fo-cal point of the gathering and several smaller tipis where the forest started served as meeting rooms and kitchen. The sun shone often during our three days there but the seasons turned dramatically from summer to winter when the heavy strong winds blew bitter cold air on us. Our most cozy resting area was our camper which well re-minded us of BC ("before children") days of excursions; a convenient

176

opportunity to lay in bed till early afternoon. John stayed in his separate tent which he put up quickly and which resisted the winds and occasional rain and lightning threats. The wind would be a dominant factor at the gathering and be the cause of many other tent structures being blown away. It also threw parades of clouds through the skies and shook my bones. I remembered my scorched nights in the village where I chocked because of the lack of air and oxygen. Perhaps the winds decided to stay in these kind fields instead of ever making it down to air stagnant Sparta.

Although there wasn't an official welcoming committee and not too many workshops, it definitely felt like "homecoming." We met a wonderful tribe of people which helped us connect again to many of our shared values. Quite a few familiar faces were happy to see us again. Ever smiling burly bearded Fontas reminded us of the caravan that he was with as it came through Sparta not too long before. On that occasion he had brought some color to our usual drab village where the only tones were various shades of black.

Ralph from Israel shared a hug but did not have his melodic violin with him. His partner Emmy came by to visit us in the camper and felt very enthusiastic over her recent "growth experiences" which she described as "ecstatic." Care-taking the "mushroom takers" was one of her responsibilities during the gathering. Very happy looking and also nurturing to be around was our tall, blond, German lady friend Tanja, whom we had also previously seen when the caravan to Sparta had dropped by our neighborhood. Another Spartan, Spiro was also briefly here. Our friend Thomas wasn't around when we were there but had been with the group earlier in the week.

Along with "old friends and family" we also connected with some very wonderful new people having deep souls and common ground. Kentauros (Stathis) grey bearded and intermittently in a vow of silence, shared heartfelt energy and helpful spirit. He offered us shelter in Athens if necessary and advice for John's musical development. He tried repeatedly to keep us at the Gathering longer and we were sure at the time that we would have been in touch over a community land project. He also enjoyed and encouraged my "vocal harmonics" of which I am unfortunately too self conscious and in need of appreciation so as I don't feel as if I am annoying anyone else in drum circles.

Another grey bearded hippie from Thessaloniki named Harris enjoyed my company and "stories of the old days" which we pleasantly exchanged and shared with the appreciative ears of the younger folks. It was his first gathering and he was annoyed at Rainbow "political agendas" feeling the gathering purpose being solely for personal growth and nurturance. His invitation to join his tribe and travel Macedonian mountains eating LSD was appealing in my parallel universe.

Happy to see us also was a Swiss lady living in Greece, Fabiana, who was eager to have children play with her young son Achileas (certainly my daughters took care of her concern). A wide eyed high energetic fellow Alexander ("Java Man") ran off with John up the mountain to pick blueberries and later nettles for the soup. His beaming face and dilated eye pupils could have been from the Amanitas. His adventures had brought him through northern Russia whereupon he had documented "hippie tribes" as well as police brutality in his very interesting and informative review which he had posted on the bulletin board. His residency was currently Java and was planning to move soon to the island of Bali.

Also high on a lot on mushrooms was Yuri who shared valuable information on how to dry and smoke them. Together with a slightly arrogant woman from Oregon was a nice northwestern guy named Jed Smith who encouraged us to visit the Oregon County Fair the third week in July sometime. In the women's circle, Stephanie enjoyed looking in Luna's artistic journal whose powerful personal drawings showed the brutal face of police oppression she had witnessed.

Quite a dynamic character at this Gathering was a white robed Sufi looking bearded guy who made great music as well as fine cooking and wood carving. A bit egoistic though. My strongest connection was with the German Ottmar Lattorf, who gave a very nice lecture on hemp and was editor of a hemp and rainbow journal. Before the lecture I attempted to translate his "hemp" talk announcement, but I was sure he was saying why "ham" is dangerous, so I confused quite a few people (including myself) in the mis-translation of "hemp". His opinion was that Greece is the most tolerant place in Europe for Rainbow Gatherings and was intrigued by the proposed Arkadian land base as possibly a center for Rainbow education.

During the afternoon women's circle, I went along with the children for a climb up the steep windy mountain. Somewhat of a strain but the top views were beautiful with mountains and lakes on one side and the windy face of Mt. Olympus on the other outlined by the ocean and a sketch of Thessaloniki. Coming down was even more of a strain and at one point we met some Albanian shepherds who pointed the best way down through the forest line. The girls enjoyed picking more of those beautifully colored mushrooms.

As with other Rainbow Gatherings, most of the people were on solo journeys through life instead of with wife and children. Perhaps my totem is a bird as I like to fly from scene to scene; but what kind of bird-to be a bird who also likes to fly far, free and high, while still taking its nest along wherever it goes.

Even after repeated requests for us to stay longer by Kentauros and Ottmar, we departed. Along with us came Manos to join our exploration of the back road to Katerina. Perhaps there was another road as well, but our route was abundant in awesome views, pine scented forests and a magical spring spot with a waterfall in the background. Two hours later we were in Katerina where we dropped off Manos at the train station then soon falling into the abrasively familiar family dissonance again.

A couple of hours drive south we tracked down the campground in Kifisia (the nearest one to Athens) which by now had become a useful reference point for us. We chose, however, to sleep parked on an adjacent street instead, making our weekend residency among the more affluent Athenian villas and their barking guard dogs (besides saving on the camping fee thus rationalizing plans to buy a few CD's from a cool record store we had discovered).

On this visit to Athens we discovered the usefulness of riding the train. We were able to park our vehicle in the safe neighborhood of the Kifisia train station next to the spiritual protectorate of the Athenian Archbishop's mansion (besides with so many Mercedes in the street, who would want to break into our tenement hall on wheels).

A few of our missed opportunities in Athens on this trip included not going to the Peace Institute, Kannabis Shop, buying the Jimi at the BBC cd, blood tests at the health food store naturopath's office, and travel books at bookstores. Some new discoveries included the train and getting treated to fine Cretan wine at the gyro tavern in Monostriaki. Also for future reference, a well supplied vitamin/

homeopathic supply store at Kifisia Street near the embassies and the gyro shop was at where we once ate lunch.

Besides a brief chance encounter with Panayiotis Konides "Toulis", a friend from the village now care-taking 35 abandoned dogs, we also had a coffee break with the young hippie couple that we had met previously on Skyros Island, Nikoletta and John, who lightly promised to visit us before we sealed up our car at the customs office. They both seemed to be developing their individual life paths while still affectionately bonded.

A fresh surprise was running into two different rainbow people on separate occasions who we had met at the recent gathering. Not only did we have the uplifting feeling that Athens is one more familiar (be it larger) village for us (not "familiar" enough that we have to hide from anyone yet), but we also reflected on how no one from our "Sparta friends list" would probably feel comfortable at a Rainbow Gathering where we ourselves had a very comforting time. So why do I put up with some kind of social expectation to go out and "perform" with these people. I actually have no real connection with outside of language. The pressure in my head to come up with the "right thing to say" as well as losing valuable time from other priorities is truly exhausting, irreplaceable and depressing. Truly I would like to seek my tribe and follow my trail over the Rainbow. In the meantime...

IKARIA

Feeling a fresh familiarity of social networking and meeting people that we could have a more interesting and pleasant connection with, we made plans to go to as many other Rainbow Gatherings in the region that time and convenience would allow. Also, any chance to get out of Xirokambi and enjoy more pleasant natural and social scenery was always welcomed.

Desiring to visit the island of Ikaria, we were happy to be making plans again for another Rainbow Gathering taking place there a few months later. Being located in the far southeastern corner of the Aegean Sea, the ferry boat ride getting to the island was a grueling fourteen hours across the rocking and a rolling water. On first look once we disembarked off the boat, we were not very impressed with what looked liked desolate and arid scenery. The port town itself also appeared like a deserted relic, so we were eager enough to buy what few supplies we would need for the next few days and drive on to the other side of the island where the gathering was mapped out as being held.

Ikaria was the island where in the late 1920's and 30's the Greek right wing government exiled communists, free thinkers and other "degenerates". Several generations later, it still proudly had a very individualistic and libertarian presence politically and socially. We heard the story of how the electric company had tried to put up a power pole across one part of the island and the traditionally minded neighbors stopped the grid from being laid. The electric company then sent another work crew along with two policemen from the nearby island of Samos to make sure that the pole was erected. This time the community, along with a local priest came and cut down the pole, tied up the cops in their police car and sent them back on the next ferry boat to where they came from. At the moment, there was still no electricity. And by the looks of the port town not having the usual summer greeting of people wanting to rent rooms to arriving visitors, there was no big push on bending over to sell the need of unnecessary tourism either.

In the days ahead as well as on subsequent other trips to Ikaria, we discovered a number of other social, traditional and scenic pleasures. On the far edge of the island, in the village of Nas, a lush trail started at the statue of Aphrodite and meandered along an enchanting stream with one small waterfall and pool after another. On both sides of the island there were several undeveloped hot springs to soak in and one very developed bathhouse and adjoining hotel which looked like an old age retirement resort.

On the feast day of the local saint Dionysius, the pagan aspects of the same personage are celebrated with lots of homemade wine which is believed to be traced to a vine from ancient times. The spiral dancing that goes on with the festival can sometimes last three days and the old timers bring bedding to take rest breaks to be able to stay through the whole epic celebration.

Many of the village shops work on the honor system and have open doors any time of day or night with customers simply leaving the correct amount for the purchase in a money box. One time John and I wanted to drink a recently imported specialty soda we found in one of the convenience markets and as the owner did not know how much to charge us for it, he simply told us that we didn't have to pay anything and just treated it to us for free.

On another visit with the family, when we needed to rent a car, we were directed to go talk to an older man sitting in the town square who operated the tourist office and also rented vehicles. Stephanie started showing him her credit card and drivers license, but he laughed as if it was a nuisance to interrupt his afternoon with such silly paper work. He simply gave us a set of car keys and told us to drive carefully, have fun and pay him when we were ready to leave. With such unexpected comforting experiences, we were not only delighted to be visiting but also felt here was a place we could consider living long term.

The Rainbow Gathering was fairly easy to find. Right past one of the mountain villages was a long windy road that went down to a beach that also was adjacent a stream that came down from the river. About 200 people had come together from various parts of Europe to enjoy the week as well as deal with the usual and unusual challenges.

Even with the midst of challenging social dynamics and health issues, we had a lovely time in a beautiful location. We met some very sweet people of which we are good friends with today. Stephanie was excited to notice a young lady named Aubrey wearing a brand of sandals called Locals. These shoes are only available in Hawaii, so it was quite a happy connection. She and her friend Michael became instant friends that were traveling around Greece and would soon be coming for a pleasant visit with us in the village. Many years later, Aubrey would surprise us with a fun time visit to Hawaii.

When Nicolette and I walked up the road to the village for a chance to use a flush toilet and eat an order of fried potatoes, there was quite a commotion from a crowd of locals that had gathered and were talking about the "groovies", their nickname for the Rainbow crowd. Passing around binoculars, they were thinking that they were watching satanic rituals on the beach with lots of naked people. One lady said she was going to tell the village priest to lead a mob of residents to throw out the heathens. I'm sure if the priest heard there were naked women fornicating on the beach, his lustful eyes and pontificating rhetoric would lead a cross carrying lynch crowd to burn the camp and kick out anyone they could. Not being too shy to seize the moment, we surprised the folks in the cafe by assuring them in perfect Greek that there was no such activity going on. In fact, we impressed upon them a story that it was a wholesome family oriented gathering of artistic minded young people from all over Europe that had come to learn traditional Greek dancing and handicraft making. Assured that there was no naughty behavior going on, the crowd seemed pacified. Interestingly, several of the men at the cafe would come down to the camp over the next few days. But instead of looking pleased that there were no orgies happening, they were disappointed at not seeing any naked hippie girls to impress or even brag to the men in the cafe that they seduced (in their fantasy life).

Back at the gathering we observed that there weren't as many planned workshops nor enough help in the kitchen but the setting was pleasant and had lots of nice camping spots in the forest. Drinking water was piped to the camp with a strict warning not to pollute the top pools on the hill that were fed by the spring. Amazingly when Stephanie and I hiked up to it one day, we found a couple of young dread haired Israeli kids taking baths in the very same pool we were told not to pollute. To make matters worse they were using conventional non-biodegradable cleaning products and they were washing their dog in the water as well. When I politely brought it to their attention that we needed to protect the quality of the water, they ignored me with the reply that they were Rainbows and free to do whatever they wanted. Quite a stark, shocking, irresponsible wave of concern for a segment of the stereotypical hippies of my generation.

On the same subject of sanitation, a thin young man gave an impassioned message at the first night talking circle that he needed help in building more "shit pits". Halfway through his plea, a big muscular guy got up and shouted that if he mentioned the word "shit" again during dinner time, he was going to punch him. From that point I nicknamed this bully "Conan" while trying at the same time doubly hard not to stereotype Israeli hippies as bullies and jerks.

Later on the beach, I overheard a rather heated argument among a group of Greek Rainbows about the true nature of Love. One of the men was reciting ancient philosophical texts to prove his point while his girlfriend was expressing love not as mind based but from the heart. Not wanting to be witness to couples punching each other over the definition of Love, I chose to leave the circle and go snuggle with Stephanie and share loving feelings in action instead.

On about the third day, the word was spreading that many of the people in the camp were having to go to the island's hospital because of intense stomach cramps and food poisoning. Although I expected the cause of the health crisis to have been the contaminated water, it turned out that it was from the dinner the night before. The person that had brought supplies from the nearby village bought a large quantity of a bean used in the stew that needed to be soaked first before cooking. The un-soaked beans had a toxic coating that about thirty percent of the population has allergic reactions to, so even though no one preparing dinner had bad intentions, the consequence was the abandonment of the camp several days early and our taking the first boat back to Athens.

The topsy-turvy havoc at the end of the gathering persisted on the ferry boat ride which was on especially rough seas. Most of the time I was laid out in the bathroom barfing and telling myself I would never ride another boat in my life. Finally as we reached the port and were disembarking from our ordeal, we were amazed to see a lot of news cameras on the scene interviewing people as they wobbled down the planks. We figured that there must have been some famous movie star on the boat but it turned out that our turbulent ride had been monitored by the news as we were in more perilous straits than we had realized.

ROLLING STONES

The decision to buy Sophia a ticket to the Rolling Stones concert in Athens was a good one. The show was fun-tastic and besides the immediate satisfaction of being there, it may well last within all of our family's precious memories. John mingled with the Thessaloniki friends we had met at the recent Rainbow gathering while the rest of us waited for the gates to open. While standing in line we were interviewed and videoed by reporters from a couple of television channels which were surprisingly both aired (making us "hometown heroes" in Xirokambi, Sparta and beyond). Sorry I wasn't better prepared for the stage light so I could have mentioned something profound like the Stones would never leave Greece as they came here to "climb Mt. Olympus and join the rest of the rock gods." Earlier in a long line waiting to use the phone, John and I stood behind a psycho threatening to shoot people (assassinate Mick?) yet managing to be interviewed by Athens News saying "drugs, sex, rock and roll with me first!!" Our tickets though fairly far away, were looking directly at the center of the stage (our official "Rolling Stones binoculars" did bring in a closer view). Many rows of seats around us had cleared out by folks wanting to join the arena grass area for closer looks at the stage. Quite an athletic event developed of people leaping the moat separating the seats from the arena. Luckily no one got stuck in the middle. Always having the intention of a pretty girl or two sitting down next to me, I was typically disappointed instead to be sitting next to a group of about eight middle aged Athenians with cellular phones and loudly reminiscing about when they saw the Stones thirty years previously. Later in the show we politely moved a few seats away from their distracted egoism.

After an occasionally satisfying performance by the opening act, a rock group from Thessaloniki and then a pee break pause it was time for the main event. The full sound system clicked in, the wrappings of the magnificent stage came down, and through the stage smoke Keith Richards escorted us into the experience of "Satisfaction." All was in excellent form: Mick was dancing as silky as ever; the stage show incredible; the giant circular screen was as nicely produced as any MTV concert movie; and the backup of Cuban dressed trombone players, sax, percussion and spine tingling background singers was superb. Personally I found the music at this concert even better than the last Stones tour we attended several years beforehand. The gap from when Mick Taylor left the group has evolved to a new sound polishing from the current band personal, depth and chemistry. The song selection was superb in covering all the major albums and only a couple of tunes off the new album which actually sounded fine-thanks to a bit of extended jamming. Mick's showmanship was sharp and he often added a few Greek phrases between the tunes. Catering to the most requested song voted on a Greek internet request line, they added "She's A Rainbow" to the playlist. (Thanks Boys!) The giant statues on stage seemed to change attitude with every change of lighting. As the steamy debauchery of the setting livened up, the band disappeared only to reappear later walking across a bridge where both the stage and band became redefined. Gone were the stage props; gone were the newly added band members. Who remained and then walked across the "Bridges to Babylon" where the original Rolling Stones band members (almost) walking to a simple stage with black and white lighting and no light show. The song selection for this part of the performance was simple rock and roll. So what did it all mean? In their life's collage, the Stones are in a sense dwelling in Babylon, yet still have a path of choice to their honest and untainted roots. So does a portal exist for today's yuppies and lost generations looking for Soul (including the blabbermouths next to us)? After the abundant and satisfying show, the call for an encore brought us a great version of "Brown Sugar" complete with an awesome light and stage show finale (which Sophia slept through after dancing up till then). A fine night was had by all, and I hope to one day be near yet another Rolling Stones tour.

In the morning, after unsuccessful scavenging for memorabilia around the parking lot where we had "spent the night together" we drove the car back to Kifisia. Besides deciding not to eat at the expensive Mexican restaurant, we took the train into downtown to do our shopping. In the evening, upon our return, we sought out a suitable dinner place to celebrate St. Sophia Day. Our luck brought us to "Magic Dragon", a wonderful Chinese restaurant in Kifisia; intended to be a "Takee Outee" but flexible that night to accommodate our fine dining needs. Not much atmosphere (although there was a pleasant park across the street to take the food to and eat). But our meal which was prepared by the two Filipino chefs (who couldn't speak Greek but would "cook by numbers") was served fast, hot, cheap, nutritious and very tasty.

XIROKAMBI AND THE MONASTARY ARGUMENT

Later that night when the traffic went to sleep we slid out of Athens and set up our camp on the old highway right before crossing into Corinth. A strip surprisingly quiet as a resort with nice shoreline, parks and amenities. Nicolette however unfortunately injured her leg while at a playground and thus our drive continued in a tone of pain. Eventually we made it back to Xirokambi where throughout the area we were greeted as "home town heroes" for having been seen interviewed on the Greek news channels (all of them) at the Rolling Stones concert. Feeling important and elated, our bubble sorely burst after hearing my mother's inquisition as to why we were on the news. Her mind was set in thinking we were some sort of criminals that once again was a source of shame and pain to her.

But not giving her too much time to continue spewing curses on us we talked her into coming with us on another visit to a sacred place. Since her friend whom we considered also a devout "Church Lady" wanted my mother to visit the same monastery, it made the trip even easier to convince her to join us on. After turning west at Corinth and about halfway to Patra we crossed the channel with a short ferry boat ride from Rio to Nafpaktos. The vista on the north side of the mainland opened into a pretty seashore, historic sites, charming towns and forested mountains. We finally made it to the nearby monastery of Agios Seraphim to meet with the famous monk who would tell us of the "Antichrist and the foreboding terror of the number 666". Both the ladies were feeling pretty righteous when we started our ride back. Effie and my mom had a restless time with each other as one went to emulate piety (even though she felt the Jewish race must be extinguished) and the other was overrun with a vendetta against our upstairs tenants for not moving. Another instance of modern Christianity in action and a diversion for my mom to forget how bad we were.

DRAINBOWS AND KRISHNA

But as settled as we felt in the home and village dramas, unexpected visitations were soon to bring about more waves of confusion. The first bend came when a group of about eight young people that we had met at one of the Rainbow Gatherings knocked on our door and felt us to be part of the universal hospitality zone enough for an open ended stay. In some ways it was nice to have colorful hippies in our household, but their limited sensitivity and respect became an instant burden. Going through my rare book shelf and then dripping coffee and bending pages was a rude gesture on their part. Taking food that we had bought out of our refrigerator as well as not cleaning any of the dishes they were piling up next to the sink was also unpleasant. But when they also started smoking cigarettes with stinky tobacco, I finally became firm enough to tell them to leave. Using the excuse that my 98 year old mother needed more attention and a quiet environment, helped in the eviction notice.

Another challenging group visit came not too many days later when another of the Greek girls we had met at a Rainbow Gathering showed up with several orange robed Hare Krishna devotees from the Czech Republic. After playing their harmonium and uplifting us with their chants, they invited us to join them in the town square where they wanted to continue their musical ministry. With the local villagers already staring at us more than usual after the previous Rainbow visitors came through, we would never survive such perceived insanity. We then convinced our visitors that they would reach more people if they went to the bigger town of Sparta to chant on the street corners. Besides the many gypsy solicitors and several Jehovah's Witnesses already proselytizing on the streets of Sparta, I told them there would also be much more acceptance and tolerance to their presentations.

Later in the year, we again were visited by a group of travelers from England who came through our village on their quest to explore historic sites of where psychedelics, opium and hashish were grown, used and distributed. Much more interesting and pleasant company than our last group of visitors, we were happy to be hosting them all except for one of the ladies that had recently joined their expedition. Showing amazing lack of sensitivity to the traditional norms of the village, she started taking outside showers in the nude and not even trying to cover up to the passerbys who starred in shock and horror. And as dread head hair style was also unusual to their eyes, the word started spreading around town that a naked woman with snakes in her hair was staying in our household. Luckily this woman started arguing with one of the other group members and split thus leaving us in relative peace.

VILLAGE ELECTIONS

As elsewhere, election time in Greece has its own unique rituals, emotions and expectations. Voting is mandatory and for weeks before the election date, local political candidates visit even remote barely defined townships to make speeches and toss out promises. Villagers who for years never see any government works programs, let alone officials, are bombarded by these campaigners with convincing intentions to build roads, schools and bake pies in the sky once inside their prestigious government position. And yes, how powerful a position in the thick Greek bureaucracy they all say and how important it would be for every citizen to have friends in high places to get anything done. The neighbors line up. Those on one side of the platea (town square) believe their candidate will be hiring their sons to build the roads and zone their farm land as prime commercial property while the mob on the other side believes the favors will soon be flowing into their pockets instead.

Recently in our village, because the election for mayor was so tight, a runoff vote was necessary a week later. So the strategists and goat herder think tanks needed to come up with a successful maneuver; a surprise move as bold as the classical Greek victories of Trojan war and Marathon fame. The ace up the sleeve was indeed delivered in just such a superb and dramatic stroke. Three days before the new election, an unnervingly familiar voice, posture and face paraded down the street with smiles and obvious self importance. Vriseli who just a few short weeks ago was taken to the mental hospital was now free and back in town. Had his recovery taken so short a time? Will he no longer steal old lady's underwear hanging on clothes lines or grab other peoples chickens to eat? His whole family actually suffered from various degrees of psychotic disorders and perhaps these flare ups would occur whenever they would mix up each other's medications as their own. In any case, his constant mischief eventually led to Vriseli being taken away. However, it was now political mischief that had brought him back to the village. If the whole family would vote for the correct grateful candidate, their son Vriseli would be free to leave the mental hospital and run loosely in the village again. Therefore, the tight race for mayor was won. Perhaps in equally bold strategy sessions, both candidates would promise everyone else in town that soon after the election, by voting for either of the contenders, the crazy fellow would be locked up again and the fear of having him back in the village would be removed. Ahh, how wonderful to live in such an insightful culture which brought us logic and democracy and which even in this microcosm of village politics can provide a win-win situation for everyone. The evolution of modern political theater and tragedy beyond the stage of kissing babies for votes.

OLIVES

Having the first hand opportunity to do so, we took part a few times in the ancient art of olive picking. Especially in the rural villages which make up most of Greece and are the bastions and depositories of its traditions, this activity is one of the most important calendar events of the year. The word for olive in Greek is "Elia" which sounds close to the name for Greece "Elada". The sun "Elios" and the name of most mountaintop churches, Agios Elias, also sound familiar. Every family member, young and old join in the harvesting. Depending on the size of the orchard, this picking ranges from weeks to months. The gathering of the olives is so important that it ranks higher than "ecclesiastic pardon" if it interferes with other responsibilities at the time, in order to pick this noble fruit. For example, a car mechanic saying: "Sorry I didn't get to fix your car last week because I had to pick my olives" is far more acceptable (and commonly heard) than "God told me to stay home from the garage and pray." And the olive tree itself is unselfish in giving so much of itself in bounty. Its branches are pruned for firewood and the leaves fed to the goats. The olives are themselves picked up by the oil-press factories and after keeping a small percentage for themselves, return the remaining amount as wonderful cold pressed virgin olive oil for tasty, healthy eating. And for all its generosity, the olive tree can grow for hundreds of years bearing fruit while requiring only minimal care. In fact most old time farmers claim that it is best to not even water the trees-that God's rainfall during the year is the optimal amount needed. And as there are a variety of climates and rainfall patterns, each region in the country has its own unique superior tasting oil. Now if some smart Greek scientist could come up with a way to create a car engine which works with olive oil instead of petroleum.

OLIVE PICKING

Our first olive picking season was a success. In our field across from the house, along with Nitsa and her son-in-law Kosta's help, we picked eleven 50 kilo bags from nine trees making a total of 40 kilos of extra virgin thick olive oil. In the process, John was fairly agile climbing the trees. The leftover firewood was a bonus.

Stephanie and the girls also made slices on each black and some green olives to pickle in brine as well. In the northern region, they put the olives in salt to draw out the water to preserve them. Stephanie had to rinse the olives for 21 days and then made a brine with salt. They were delicious after 2 months.

Ironically on Stephanie's 47th birthday, December 29th, was a sad day spent at the funeral of our friend Theodoros Makris in Mousga who fell off an olive tree and broke his spine.

FUNERALS

Attending a lot of funerals was a common and regular occurrence. An activity which is a major preoccupation of village life. Besides the actual burial itself, the Greek Orthodox religion expects the family of the departed to plan a variety of church services in memory of the departed at prescribed number of days after the passing. This focus on the rituals of death seems to likewise extend into the psychic killing of the living-perhaps a residual trait left over from the alters of sacrifice to appease the ancient gods. Not only in the slaughter of sheep herds to celebrate the feast days in honor of what must be blood thirsty saints, but also in the emotional and mental vampirism within people's families, friends and neighbors. Vicious gossip, humiliation and shame based conversation and behavior permeate the local consciousness anchored on prayers based on fear, anger and judgment. Distrust and Pandorean nosiness pulse people into each other's lives. Usual ties include Death of the Spirit, Death of Harmony and Death of Individuality. Death also to the more ancient goddesses who danced and held hands in joy and ecstatic brilliant honesty long before the logic of temple looting and domesticating the Passions within; damning the rivers of life and diverting healthy relationships. Under the masquerade of "tradition" there is a restless pressure now to maintain this erosion of our divine birthright to happiness. Rather than jump and sink into this social quicksand, how easier it is for us to find glorious relief in hiking through the beautiful living countryside and pondering bygone temples of cultural achievements and fertile prayers. Reconnecting with this eternal life-spring. In the interim, it's okay to go to the funerals and subsequent feedings the deceased's family provides for at the local tavernas giving us a continuous cycle of fine meals to look forward to. Bon Appétit or as they say in Greek, Yiasou-"to your health."

A VILLAGE BURIAL

Evangelos Konides emigrated to Canada from Greece when he was a young man and lived a typical life of hard work and loyal citizenry to his new country. His dream was to return upon retirement to live among his family, friends and traditions back in the "homeland." Like many other returning emigrants with similar intentions, he became old and then sick and eventually died beforehand.

Thus his last wish before dying was that he be buried in his village of birth, Komosta. This present medieval ghost town lies perched high between a ravine and upland meadow within the heart of Mt. Taygetos in the southern tip of the same mountain range the Alps lie in. Although this beautifully haunting setting now has no one living in its stone fortress homes, the views are still majestic and the air is filled with the scents of sage and thyme. Although no children are now heard playing in the relics of the school grounds, the birds still chirp, the river roars and the town's spring fountains never stop pouring. This lively town of Komosta is where Mr. Konides expected to finally settle his bones and gave instructions to his devoted relatives in Canada and Greece to bury him there among his other departed ancestors. He expected to be covered in the cemetery by local wildflowers and memories.

The migration from the high country isolation of Komosta eventually helped and brought the birth and expansion of the new town Xirokambi, ten kilometers down the mountain path in a central agricultural valley that grows TV antennas on every rooftop and sprouts tractors in every yard. When Mr. Konides' relatives first heard of his death and that he was being brought back to his family in Xirokambi for burial, there were the expected tears, acknowledgments and respects offered and passed around of the return and final resting of a well loved man. At first the friends and relatives felt tenderness for Evangelos desire to be buried in his ancestral village. However during the course of the day of his burial announcement, along with the procedural conversations a couple of days before the actual arrival of the body for burial, Mr. Konides specific instructions to be buried in Komosta where being altered into more of a nice sentiment than a realistic request. Komosta now seemed far away from Xirokambi. There would be problems. The road up is too rocky; who would be able to go up each month for the memorial services; the half hour needed to drive there could be used more productively. Pretty soon convenience became more important than an honorable man's honorable desire, so he was buried along with his unfulfilled wishes among the living in Xirokambi. The only way to make sure where one gets buried is to dig your own hole and jump into it.

PET CEMETERY

Influenced by the ongoing ritual of funerals, Nicolette and Sophia followed the tradition in organizing their own burial ceremony for our cat which was killed by a car in front of the house. The girls were saddened and respectfully buried it in the orchard across the street. Besides attaching a cross to its resting spot they also painted a cross in the street next to our house where it had been hit. Just as they had finished their project with one more prayer for the departed, the very dogmatic church going lady from next door came running to scold them for their disrespect. To her they were mocking a sacred Orthodox ritual reserved only for humans and not for animals. To dispute whether all of God's creatures had a touch of divinity and soul would have been unproductive to such a closed mind as hers. At least my daughters did not have to spend any money on providing the traditional coffee and cookies to all the villagers in the town square in commemoration of the departed.

LYP-SYNC

The assimilation of Greece into the political fraternity of the European Union is well observed when one watches a local television program and still wonders what national boundary he is in. Just like most towns in the US have homogenized their appearance as one long strip of Kmarts, Kentucky Fried Chickens and McDonald's arches, TV commercials throughout Europe now look disorientingly the same. Gone are the ethnic distinctions and unmistakably emotional signatures of dark skinned southern Europeans sharing their national identity through local dialects, idiosyncrasies, and humor. When you watch a commercial on Greek TV (as I'm sure soon-if not yet-Iranian, Tunisian or Turkish broadcasts), you almost always see "blond, blue eyed products" but even the Greek stuff. What really cracks me up as I'm stuck watching the commercials between the movies is how everything these actors and jingles say is lip synced in Greek. Not only so, but lip-synced so badly that often words are heard coming through closed mouths and un-synchronized faces. My laughter at the surrealism of this humor is laced with fear as I notice the Greeks themselves not paying attention to the aberration. Does this mean that the mostly blue collar, rough looking agrarian men and traditionally garbed ladies with black shawls will soon believe that the distant actors they see on TV are the role models expected of contemporary Greeks? I wonder if I were to go to England or Belgium, rent a hotel room and while watching TV commercials between the movies, I would likewise see bearded peasants with dark facial hair and olive oil stained cotton clothes advertising Gouda cheese, Swiss chocolates, and Rolex watches with Greek actors speaking a lip-synced English, Belgium or Swiss script. And as our international community gets smaller, will we be eventually watching Japanese martial artists selling lip-synced insurance policies in America or those same blond blue eyed actors we see on Greek TV.

CHAPTER TEN: BEYOND GREECE

AMSTERDAM

Dealing as best as we could with the mental, emotional and social challenges of living in Xirokambi, Stephanie and I decided it was time for the two of us to take a vacation again to the much heralded center of civilized tolerance, Amsterdam. Our kids seemed well capable of handling themselves in our absence and we soon were studying all the budget travel books to the city such as where to stay, where to eat, what scenery to explore, how to get around and what cannabis cafes to visit. We only would be able to go for about two weeks, so we didn't plan an extensive itinerary as on our first maiden budget a few months earlier, but I still used my talents of color coding various maps to make our trip to Amsterdam as organized as possible.

Like a magical dream adventure, Stephanie and I were flying in a plane that soon transported out of the Balkans and took us up to the north country. We checked into an inexpensive hostel and immediately set out to explore the fabled haven of Dutch marijuana tolerance. That part of the quest was not too difficult to find as it seemed that every corner had at least one cannabis cafe. Stoning out at as many as our low tolerance could handle, our holiday felt even more exotic and depending on the quality of the herb, various degrees of surrealism.

With our carefully mapped walking trips, ease of bus transfers and well marked and lined streets and canals, even in our stoned haze, we were able to visit parks, museums, and many interesting shops. We didn't find ourselves standing in line to pay the big ticket price to visit Rembrandt's museum or to sample the expensive coffee cakes, but we did enjoy learning a lot of interesting information at the Cannabis and Hashish Museum as well as feasting on cheap pizza and falafels served at the inexpensive hole in the wall immigrant food stalls and many market places. And by the time we came back late to the hostel, our daily delights enhanced the great love making sessions we made sure we had time to embrace ourselves with in this very cosmopolitan city.

LONG DISTANCE ROUNDABOUT

Not too long after we returned to Greece, with our peak experiences from Amsterdam still exciting our spirits, we once again were all on the road to Holland so as to share the wonderful experience of the country with our family. Encouraged by our camper van's mechanical dependability, our expanding desires to explore more scenery and cultures and by the elimination of most border checks between countries in Europe, our intentions soon manifested in finding ourselves on a ferry boat sailing from the port city of Patra en route to Venice, Italy which would be the gateway entry into more northern European adventure.

BOAT TO VENICE

After a fine dinner at both our favorite eating places in Patra (just to make sure we took in enough nourishment for the travels ahead) we set out at midnight on the ferry boat ride to Venice. The boat itself was nice enough with lots of space and our own separate on board camping area parking deck. The family was somewhat disappointed not to find the swimming pools that the boat agency advertised on television, yet this time of year, posh fanfare had taken its autumn holidays elsewhere. Besides being able to sleep on board, the nicest extra surprise was the continuous grade B movies playing in the film lounge. For the most part, most of the audience besides us, consisted of men trying to find a quiet place to sleep and during the quiet parts of the films, our concentration disrupted by the sounds of snoring or putrid smells of stinky feet. The twenty four hour boat ride passed quickly along and soon enough we were looking at the beautiful scenery of Venice as we pulled into the harbor.

Truly Venice is a work of art. Besides its obvious signature canal setting, the buildings display elegance and craftsmanship which also extends into a genuine feeling of pride among the people that live there and respectively adhered to by the many visitors admiring the delightful displays of sight, sound and smells. Tangy aromas of home-made pizza and perfect cappuccinos while gondoliers crooned to the rhythm of the water and accordions. Even with our slim amount of pocket change, we were satisfied to simply walk through the pleasant maze of shops and squares where no motor vehicles could enter. The only major expense was in parking the car in the scalping lane and our only major disappointment was not being able to locate anyone to sell us auto insurance (as we had previously been directed by the Greek port authorities to do). Sadly we also missed a Jimi Hendrix tribute festival the weekend before. The only aggression that we had witnessed on our visit was the harassment of a group of Japanese passengers on the docks by the obnoxious tones of the Italian port authorities. From what I hear, the rest of Italy is far less pleasant to visit, but we were satisfied enough exploring Venice for the day.

Even with a little drizzle in the air, the scenery sparkled, yet the low lying streets flooded to the point where many of the tourists chose to walk barefoot through the puddles. But assuming that with the sewer backups, probably less than desirable elements were floating in the water, we decided to extend our stroll through detours. We splurged on buying our first Italian cappuccinos which were cheap enough as well as following our travel book's map to a place that made great yet inexpensive pizza which we ate on a bench next to a canal. And for souvenirs, before leaving Venice, we bought Nicolette a t-shirt and for the archives a rare Tim Buckley CD.

After our Italian gateway of Venice, we drove through lots of rain and circled the town of Lugano extensively before finding a suitable suburb to park for the evening. Luckily the heavy rains helped conceal our campsite from the confused neighbors. The following morning we hastily started with our first need being finding a private place to pee. Nearby we parked under a bridge adjacent a busy park to find a spot on this early morning to relieve ourselves.

Thus with better attitudes, we drove a few more hours to the historic city of Bergamo where once more we had to leave our car in an expensive parking lot. Our first enjoyable site in town was the lovely gardens full of labyrinth and strange statues. The view from the top of the hill was outstanding. Afterwards we followed the clear map that the parking lot attendant drew for us to get to the Roman Coliseum. The massive structure was impressive enough but not worth our buying expensive tickets to have a look inside. Since I spotted an opening in the fence around its perimeter, I directed the girls to sneak inside for a picture to enjoy later.

Our walk led us to the Juliette courtyard where we joined the tourist taking pictures of the Shakespearean setting for his famous play "Romeo and Juliet". The square and marketplace nearby where impressive and we bought the fixings for a nice picnic next to a fountain. After a long visit to an internet cafe to catch up on messages, we again ate a delicious wholesome pizza from the next door bakery. Well fed we found our way back to the car after a stopover at an Middle Eastern food market to purchase goodies for the next part of our trip.

From the enchanting welcome of Venice and then the artistry of Bergamo, the delicious transformation of scenery sailed us north to Lake Como and a preview of the Alps ahead. The natural beauty that reached out to us was similarly matched by the emotional evasiveness of the business district and limited expressions of the people. After playing around a bit in the park we strolled across the pier and drank our last Italian cappuccino before driving to the north countries.

Before darkness the border grabbed us, we pulled into a parking lot next to a soccer field for a quiet sleep away from car and city noise. There was some activity early on as a soccer game was being held that night. The next morning we used the field as well for some exercises and stretches as well.

SWISS ALPS

Without parades or fanfare, our entry into Switzerland was pleasantly unnoticed. No border guards or welcome signs. Instead, what met us was vibrant scenery and calmer highways. To orient ourselves we pulled off at the first shopping area for gas and groceries. Even without language skills, we found universal ease of commerce in purchasing a few delicacies and food basics. Prices for the most part seemed higher than we had been used to but even here, an abundance of bargains were waiting to be found.

Since Switzerland is a relatively small country, it didn't seem too long before we made significant progress in the map to our next destination, the beautiful lakeside town of Lucern. At this point the Alps and the related scenery were coming on strong. Healthy forests, incredible mountain angles, rivers, lakes and villages arranged as garnish to the panorama. Lucern, even though a large city, was a fine introduction to the Swiss pride of respecting natural rhythms with a calm approach to being alive. It was here that we actually had our first welcome gift. While sitting in our car to eat lunch and admire the lake, an artsy looking guy pulled up next to us and handed us each a crystal for healing and to play with. An appreciative and unexpected trinket.

Soon it was clear that in the palms of this beauty was also the reality of our having to be very frugal with our money; another noteworthy Swiss trait that could now be understood in its own cultural context. Even though affordable basics could be found through a little effort, far more common was seeing skyrocket prices instead. In walking around the lake and stopping at various cafes to buy a bottle of water, the usual price for a liter was over five euro. An ongoing awareness for us to plan well our budget. Stopping off at a nearby hotel, it was pleasant not to be treated rudely for a change but with respect. The desk clerk politely mapped out where the local internet cafe was, as well as dialed up and translated our whereabouts to Stephanie's cousin, Marie Ming, whom we arranged to visit in a few days. We also reconfirmed with our friend Apsara whom we had met while traveling in Bali that we would be on her doorstep in a few hours after first checking in on our emails.

Besides the opportunity to find out our messages, our walk through downtown to the cafe gave us a nice snapshot of the city at night. Tucked away in the alleys were expensive restaurants and trendy cafes. But even among the expensive window displays were thrift shops, used book and record stores and cheaper funky gathering spots. The cafe we went to seemed like a nice smokey college crowd scene of internet serving computers, long communal tables of people enjoying cappuccinos, ample portions of tasty looking food, dark beer with loud music and dancing in the back room. A couple of walls were posted full of announcements of upcoming concerts, stuff to buy, sell, rent and spiritual/healing classes. Another nice place in the world to consider living awhile.

How fine a week ahead with our friend Apsara. From the moment we met her smiley face in front of her house in the suburban forest location outside Basel, we felt right at home. Her hospitality nurtured us with healthy meals, access to lots of music tapes to enjoy, warm comfortable beds, videos and happiness. Apsara was organizing an upcoming festival for leper awareness which was a nice opportunity for us to offer some help, and even though we didn't actually meet any people with leprosy, make some new friends as well as explore the downtown section of town. It felt very much like a college town with its eclectic merchandise, cafes and a head shop where I bought some nice homegrown Swiss cannabis. The festival itself was lots of fun with ongoing music and a bench to lie on most of the sunny day.

On my excursions around the area I chanced upon an alternative energy festival with lots of solar powered vehicles driving around the square. The cathedrals were impressive and the river magnificent. Our ongoing activities led us to a banquet for everyone that had helped at the leprosy awareness festival. There we had the opportunity to converse with some new folks, especially with the members of the reggae band. But John remembers the pumpkin raviolis the most.

Walking across the park afterwards, I saw lots of excitement in the various music clubs and ethnic looking neighborhoods. Later that night, along with lots of kids, we watched gas balloons lit and flown across the river giving the impression of flying stars. I'm sure someone seeing them could have easily thought they were UFOs landing. Our activities with Apsara extended into the next day as we went to see a dance performance which was exceptional in skill and drama. When our time to leave could no longer be postponed, it was truly sad to leave our new home.

Our next destination Lungrin itself, though an extremely picturesque village lying around a lake in the lap of the Alps, felt extremely boring. Its few stores closed down by noon whereupon life forms withdraw in quiet meditation of the beautiful scenery. We initially felt awkward in visiting an elderly cousin but the excuses we were thinking to leave early were soon forgotten through the warm hospitality and never ending views of the mountains and lake.

Our obvious language difficulties were surpassed with a minimal of high school German and sign language. I immediately recognized Klaus from his earlier visit to San Francisco, and he was in turn very eager to return our hospitality which must have left a very favorable impression several decades before. Marie, even at 85, was quite alert and especially enjoyed serving us meals and looking at old family pictures. Walter, Klaus's father, also in his late 80's, liked as well making regular visits to share some insights as well as his homemade schnapps.

Very eager for us to enjoy our stay and delighted to find that we were not "people of glamour", Klaus organized an exciting day ahead.

The morning started with a refreshing ride across the lake in his boat to the cable trolley depot on the other side. As comfortable the hospitality and serene the magnificent scenery, my mind was quickly drawing in the terror of what lied ahead for me. The pleasant conversation during the first part of the ride up the 10,000 foot mountain inside the modern enclosed gondola couldn't deflect the realization that in a few minutes I would be sitting in a traditional open three seater going up into space. God how my heart pumped and my nerves clutched my internal organs. Even in closing my eyes from the ascending panorama, I felt the many peaks and rolling valley edges drawing me into their essence. For a support crutch, I held my breath, repeated prayers, and counted down the elapsed time between the poles to anticipate when we would reach the top. Yet time seemed to stand still and it felt that we would never reach our destination.

The end of the line did show up though and we were soon enjoying a fine lunch on the patio that was embraced by the snowy elegance of the Alps. The treat was on Klaus who was celebrating his birthday. The cold beers tasted smooth even without having to be chilled past room temperature. We stretched a bit afterwards on a skyline hike as we watched the outline of John fade into the rocky scenery in having chosen to take the long hike back along the trail. I followed his lead but not his footsteps in avoiding any embarrassment for my being frightened of the cable car return journey down by my walking along the trail which was parallel to the cable line. Klaus joined me on the splendid hour descent with a stopover in a picturesque village where no one lived anymore. Later in the afternoon we were all relieved when John made it back before dark and Klaus rejoined us again for another birthday celebration consisting of a picnic dinner with authentic Swiss cold cuts and of course his dad Walter brought over more of his homemade schnapps.

Unlike older folks anywhere else in the Western world, Swiss people, regardless of age, are always crisscrossing their country's endless mountain trails. Rather than sitting around gossiping or watching the latest disaster updates on the news, hiking into the beautiful mountains is the national pastime. It was a pleasure to see people who otherwise would be in wheelchairs, out in groups or by themselves with walking sticks instead of canes. The pride taken in hiking is evidenced in the well maintained trail system with clear signs, trash cans, benches and of course, wide angle panoramas. Even the public bathrooms in most towns and business districts are well equipped and heated. So rather than walking around plastic, artificial climate controlled shopping malls, as a tribute to geriatric consumerism, Switzerland's white hairs blend nicely as part of the magnificent scenery.

With many promises that we will be returning in the future after a pleasant picnic lunch with our new extended family on Marie's porch, we followed the road past a series of lakes till we came to the ritzy city of Interlaken. Even though it reflected a feeling of opulence, a fine combination of magnificent scenery still stretched into the heart of the town from all directions of the never ending Alps. The weather was a bit wet, but we managed to do some pleasant family hiking. Parking meters were expensive, but the super market offered many discounts and the nearby campground was very comfortable. The manager was an abrasive old man who had lived in Texas awhile, but he did not disturb our enjoying those local beers he sold in his well equipped kitchen. Our two most memorable souvenirs during our stay were the fine quality shoes and the tube of foot cream for our persistent vile smelling bodily disorders down under.

Around Interlaken were a variety of smaller charming villages to explore further up in the mountains. By parking alongside the road, we visited one ski center with an exceptionally picturesque graveyard full of flowers and springs.

Driving through the impressive Swiss tunnels was an experience it itself as the mighty Alps were no longer in the way of travelers who for centuries were stuck because of weather or flimsy roads across their valleys. The traditional independent villager was not able to be in the social flow as well as the lowlanders in other countries. Now, just like a story from Arabian Nights, an "open sesame" portal would allow the transfer of scenery smoothly from one side of the mountain to the other.

During our drive through one especially long highway tunnel with Stephanie at the wheel and the children asleep, we had a traumatic experience that shook our otherwise Swiss engineered calmness. Sophia awoke to a strange sensation near her ear that she asked someone to take a look at. As John happened to be awake and next to her decided to take a look. But when John looked inside her ear with a flashlight and then exclaimed, "Oh my God, Sophia, oh my God",

I knew that we were about to be dealing with a major problem. The rest of us in the car were on razor's edge asking him to tell us what he observed, but John kept saying "oh my God" and exclaimed that we shouldn't be asking but instead, be looking for immediate medical assistance. Our imaginations were already in a flurry over what the worse case scenarios might be while at the same time realizing the reality of having another twenty minutes left before coming out of the tunnel. A precarious position indeed. Lucky for all of us that Sophia could remain calm through this period of apprehension and even when John announced that an earwig worm was crawling inside her ear. Images of brain eating parasites fueled all of us to take emergency action once we came out of the tunnel. At the first exit point, I ran towards the gas station and flagged down a couple of truckers who I heard speaking Greek and found out from them where the nearest hospital was. I raced back to the car where John and Nicolette were equally in a panic mode but more importantly, Stephanie was calmly exploring Sophia's ear with tweezers and eventually was able to get the pest out while also scolding the rest of us for being so emotionally upset. Mom to the rescue again.

Once our equilibrium was restored, following Apasara's phone suggestion for a scenic experience, we went further up to the town of Grisalp and found our evening camp to be in the town's parking lot. Around us was a great little combination grocery/bakery, an open all night heated public bathroom and high tech exercise course in the woods. Best of all, we felt comfortable in being a part of this lovely picture. By morning we were pleasantly stunned by a truly magnificent view. The lush scenery and bright fields of snow danced together in the crisp forest that spread all around us. John immediately jumped into a hike up into the mountains which were pouring themselves on us. Although we didn't join him on the seven miler, we did enjoy a shorter walk through the healthy crispness of the woods.

John's report when he returned in the afternoon was reason enough to stay another night in our own private parking lot and drive up to the new land he had mapped out. Wow. Never ending streams, waterfalls (some pushing themselves back into mountain crevices), dollhouse chalets, a lake, and of course the living heart of the Alps. Afterwards we celebrated our day with a delicious pie from the local bakery. Before leaving, we dropped in at a holistic center that offered yoga, meditation, and other self-help classes.

One of the beauties of Switzerland is that irregardless of whether you are in a small village or big city, a spectacular presence of nature blending with an artistic and fine craftsmanship by its people gracefully intermingles with your heart and soul. The capital city of Bern where we went to visit our friend Pius whom we had also met in Bali also was no exception. Nice pedestrian lanes interlaced between proud buildings and monuments. Melodic clock towers, eclectic shops, farmers markets, and a river that runs outside of Parliament (which incidentally had just decriminalized cannabis). Our discovery walk took us past several parks to the zoo and later back across town. At one point we were stopped by a curious looking man who gave us each about ten small bags of souvenir peanuts. Soon afterwards, we did a second take of looking at a lady swimming vigorously in the chilly river. These Swiss are tough.

Points of interest lied in all directions, but as we had a dinner appointment, we made it back to Pius' house before sunset. Quite a few other interesting people joined us as well for homemade pizza and Italian risotto with the dessert and wine provided by us. As with our visit to Apsara, we had a very friendly stay and enjoyed Pius' help in what he called "organizing" for us. Before leaving we had a nice musical jam with the girls contributing percussion work on his two giant gongs. They also enjoyed doing gymnastics on the floor mattresses. Pius' wife Andrea was pregnant and going to several Lamaze classes at the time, so we didn't see too much of her, but we did find out that in a few days she was registered for a seminar at the holistic center we had visited in Grisalp.

One more adventure awaited us in Switzerland as we went in search of Stephanie's father's family tree. From all that Stephanie remembered including conversations as well as pictures at her parents' house, the name of the mountain village her father had come from was Arvigo near the county seat of the larger city of Chur. Directly from Bern we drove across the country and its many never ending tunnels to the northeast corner of the Alps. As it turned out, we had come several hours out of our way because in actuality, the mountain hamlet we were in search of was in the south bordering Italy. From Pius house we could have been there in one hour. Still, no matter how many hours you drive out of your way in Switzerland, it's not a matter of time wasted but of life being enhanced through the beautiful scenery experienced.

There was no loss of scenery at all as we crossed a scattering of snowfall before ascending up past streams and lush valleys to the picturesque village of Arvigo. With the exhilaration of the panorama mixing with pride of ancestry, we followed the twisting cobblestone path up through the village. Although some of the folks understood my German version of "my wife's father was from here," it was soon obvious that the name Holzeisen wasn't known and that most of the towns folk were Italian not Swiss. Unfortunately, the town clerk was on holiday where the family records were stored. Still we found it enjoyable and even the artistic graveyard was pleasant. In a later conversation, Stephanie's father himself doubted the authenticity of Arvigo being his birthplace. So instead of lost time, it gives us another adventure to look forward to.

Switzerland's excellent motorway system, made it convenient to once again go visit Apsara. She was happy to see us arrive and to be able to express her warm hospitality of showing us many delightful places in Basel. The city itself was on the border with France and our first excursion into France was on a Sunday drive with Apsara to an afternoon party at a local artist's home studio gallery. Even though his shadowy magical concepts were often intriguing, for the most part, the pretentious and gaudy people floating around us was reason enough to stack up on the fancy cold cuts and wines, find an out of the focus spot to sit and wait for our moment to leave. It was nice that the artist perceived his home as an art object itself and had consequently filled each corner with something interesting to look at, but when you've experienced the visionary art of Salvador Dali and Mati Klarwein as we have, most other artists can be categorized as a different sort of four letter word. Apsara was glad we brought her so as to pick up some of her personal belongings and before we left, we gladly ate some more leftovers of French cheese with spicy mustard.

Our second excursion into France was again short but full of impressions. On the freeway we had an abrupt image of reality's dark side in our quick glimpse of heavily armed police officers tossing around a few long haired hippie people while tearing apart their rainbow colored van. Our night's stay in a gas station parking lot was quite comfortable and, as in Switzerland, provided an all night restaurant with affordable prices and hot showers.

Wanting to at least explore one city in the country, we pulled off into the historic town of Metz. It took a few detours to get oriented, but once past the warehouse section, we found an impressive older part of downtown which was centered around a majestic Gothic cathedral. The most obvious characteristic we first noticed was the empty feeling of being in such a massive ambience. The grey stone walls felt more like a prison than a temple as the ever present gargoyles traumatically persuading the faithful to live fear based lives which supposedly the high priests can provide protection from. And as with so many confessionals around the building, the payback was in squeezing guilt into the minds, hearts and souls of the congregation. The very existence of feudalism and slave mentality was displayed in every corner of this fortress. It was in this sanctuary where I was approached by a beggar asking for spare change. Indicating to him in universal sign language that I too was impoverished, he left me alone-for awhile. After our finish of sightseeing the church, he approached me again, but this time not to ask but to share by giving me a few coins from the apparent handful of change someone else had given him. A simple miracle at a consecrated parameter.

Our Sunday walk took us past a large cobblestone square with the smells of Turkish fast food and a nicely landscaped park along the river. Across the way we noticed a hobo happily preparing his meal on a bench and makeshift shelter. People seemed the same as everywhere else, and as we proceeded out of France, it felt comforting to have dropped behind any ethnic generalizations of snobbery or arrogance. Neither of these traits were evidenced and that episode with a beggar's hospitality will be respectively remembered.

LUXEMBURG

One of the more bizarre experiences of our trip, while at the same time ironically displaying a civilized and proper appearance, was in the small and very interesting country of Luxemburg. Hills and forests stretched in all directions with picturesque streams and elegant castles with tall towers and plush banks dotting every town. Yet these apparent subdued and proper folks can get as wacko as anyone. Our first night camping in this country was in a parking lot of one of those perfect postcard rural villages. By nightfall we were awakened to the loud thunder of rain and Oktoberfest. Joined by hundreds of Germans crossing over the bordering bridge, this small town was crammed with people screaming to loud music and festivities. After locking up our children in the safety of the car, we went out into the battle zone to come back with a very tasty pizza. It didn't matter that we didn't speak the language because soon no one babbled in any sense either. Elderly drunks puking on elegant hotel chairs while teams of other pukers were dragging their barfing casualties down the unstable streets. Lots of aggressive gestures with skinheads beating up girlfriends and smashing car doors.

The next day we viewed the disaster zone. All was tidy and sparkling once more. What a benefit for the country to be able to afford a full crew of immigrant street cleaners on duty 24/7 for such occasions. Afterwards we went to a hydroelectric plant in whose basement had a Salvador Dali exhibit. The whole scene was quite surrealistic yet at the same time felt very sane in the way the great artist himself would have liked.

In the next few days we enjoyed visiting several more friends that we had either previously met or with whom we had been pen pals with. In Belgium even more delightful than its famous waffles and extraordinary local beer, it was a pleasure to finally meet a friend that I had been corresponding with for several years, George Kanakaris. Along with his wife Vivian, they offered us wonderful hospitality and we have remained corresponding friends ever since. George, at one point, even mailed me a six pack of Belgium cherry beer when we went back to Greece.

After our happy pause in Belgium, we went on to our next destination of a campground in north Amsterdam which would now be our base camp for the next few weeks. Perfectly located in a woodsy rural area it was only a few minutes' walk to the harbor where the ferry boats kept a regular pace in taking people over to the big city.

AMSTERDAM

Too large a subject to write as one entry or from a single point in time, we found Amsterdam an ongoing spring of impressions and memories which we hope to dip our thirsty souls into over and over again.

For starters, our first literal steps into Amsterdam begin at Central Station, the massive train station downtown connecting travelers all over the country and other parts of Europe. In cold weather it provides a comfort zone before jumping into the city. In summer, it offers a shady relief from sun struck tourists. Foot traffic moves smoothly and if you feel sickly even a homeopathic pharmacy is located among its many shops and services. Street musicians greet you in hopes of spare change and even more desperate looking characters close in on you at the side exit ramps seeking your daily exchange rate. A Burger King is housed inside an elegant round domed part of the complex hinting of bygone days and traveling styles. Unfortunately there isn't a simple toilet in the building which doesn't cost payment before use, yet the sinks are always sparkling clean and the tissue paper double-ply.

The scene awaiting the visitor outside is magnificent in charm and uniqueness. The huge dome of Saint Nikolas Church, Gothic towers and street cars define the landscape. Mountains are nowhere in sight but river canals planted with houseboats zigzag in all directions. Scents of delicious cuisines are everywhere-including cheap pizzas and falafels for budgets like ours. Even more exciting dining awaits at squat cafes where you can find delicious healthy food for inexpensive prices.

The tour books are full of sites, museums, parks, restaurants and other suggestions for a memorable stay, but for us another dimension of Amsterdam is present which makes it one of the most wonderful places in the world.

By combining a tolerant attitude towards diverse lifestyles, promoting a public exposure to the individual pursuit of pleasure and providing basic services of shelter and medical care to the poor and underprivileged, Amsterdam has developed a very firm social infrastructure. People enjoy living here and feel comfortable that their basic needs will be taken care of. Thus I was pleased when researching the information for squat houses providing cheap housing that in the downtown area there was also a clinic offering free medical aid to anyone both poor as well as people choosing not to show identification. Illegal aliens and drug "criminals" perhaps.

Finally we could take Nicolette to a doctor that we could afford to examine her eye problems. Not quite sure of the address we were looking for, the minutes turned into a long hour walk over the canals through the warehouse district of Amsterdam. Not to mention the cold wind blowing on our faces. Finally we found the doorway to a desolate looking building, which turned out to be the correct place. Taking seats in the waiting room among the many veiled Middle Eastern folks, we felt clearly our camaraderie as poor aliens in Holland. Although the main language was Arabic, a few of these people spoke Dutch well enough to be interpreters for each other when they went in to talk with the doctors, a skill beyond our meager mastery only of English. Yet our Greek complexion in this Northern country did feel handy for fitting in. As it turned out, the doctor could find nothing wrong with Nicolette whose touching dismissed as a minor concern to a clinic dealing usually with weird diseases, gunshot wounds or drug overdoses. Pleased with the diagnosis, we once more entered the outside chill feeling much better about being in a society that cares even for aliens like ourselves.

In a busy city of noise, traffic and ongoing activity, it's an expected occurrence to see the outstretched hands of the needy. With so little money and so many mouths to feed, it becomes necessary to filter out spare changers -especially the younger and more physically fit. But even with our armature in place, we were still startled when a young thin man of dark complexion walked straight towards me on a busy intersection and proclaimed "I am Muslim, I must eat before 5." Before darting off with the normal reflex of "Sorry I have no money", I couldn't help but reflect on the encounter. Could I as easily stop people on the street and because I am Greek, I must eat feta cheese before sunset and thus society would be obligated to take care of my needs? I suppose in a tolerant city like Amsterdam such expectations might not seem as ridiculous as elsewhere. Perhaps this hungry fellow gave us a lesson on how to express ourselves directly without the unnecessary conversational excess. How clear if all of us could utter basic statements like "I like music, I must have a CD", "I like women, be my girlfriend", etc.. Personally I do not have any prejudice towards anyone's religious beliefs, yet if I were hungry, Muslim or not, I would take myself to either a Salvation Army kitchen or Krishna temple as surely the God of my choice would want my body fed no matter what language the song of praise.

CULTURAL HERITAGE

One of the obvious main draws of coming to Amsterdam is to see the rich variety of sculpture and art up close. Museums from A to Z are located throughout the city: Rembrandt, Van Gough, historical, natural sciences, etc.. Most are housed in beautiful Gothic castles with landscaped parks and long lines of people with name tags standing in line to pay hefty admission charges and fill designer shopping bags with replicas and souvenirs. Ironic how Van Gough was laughed at and eventually killed himself from the depression and lack of appreciation to his art, while now tons of gilders fill the museums from people admiring his work simply because it is considered masterpieces by self proclaimed experts. Certainly we found some authentic emotional expressions to Vincent's work and his talent that surpassed Rembrandt and other so called masters. But for the most part, the time wasted looking at this boring stuff could have been better used in "people watching" at the nearby park or staring at the cover art of Zap comics which we earlier passed by at another interesting store.

Another remarkable set of displays was located in the basement level of a fine arts store leading to a large corridor and called "The Electric Ladyland Museum". Fittingly enough, Jimi Hendrix music would be playing throughout multiple speakers while visitors would be treated to clay figures and rocks painted with a fluorescent paint that would glow brilliantly under the black lights that were placed in appropriate spaces. Not being stoned when we entered, the high art that we experienced left us feeling very stoned when we once again reentered the outside world. And just to make sure, we took a pause to reflect and re-integrate to multiple realities at the nearest cannabis cafe down the street.

Away from the glamour and tour books, housed in more mundane looking buildings in poorer parts of town, Amsterdam does have other museums which we found of incredible interest. The Cannabis Museum offers a wealth of information and exhibits explaining the history and use of cannabis throughout the ages. Similarly the museums of sexuality and eroticism are of great interest which everyone could benefit from visiting and learning more about their birthright. In a place as culturally rich like Amsterdam, it would be a pity to lose an opportunity to visit these lesser known and probably even many more eclectic museums and art displays. Just in walking through the city, you can see very talented artists at work in their shops as well as high quality political posters and beautiful murals in the coffee-houses. A sad shame indeed that because of propaganda and media hypnosis, second rate artists like Rembrandt are perceived in such superficial appreciation and true genius remains closer to the gutter.

Perhaps in the long run it retains its freedom from being commercial-ized that way. On the next trip to Holland we will make an effort to find more of the beautiful treasures of true artists such as M.C. Escher and Hieronymus Bosch- two great Dutch masters whose work is not as easy to find as their more famous big brother counterparts.

Besides the need for museums to enrich and nurture the soul, every civilized community needs an affordable marketplace for people to purchase necessary goods. In Amsterdam, as in the US, there are ample specialty stores supplying objects from all over the world. The Dutch mercantile tradition extends to many daily block long street markets with fair and bargain prices on new and used merchandise as well as farmer market style food. Our favorites were the huge Albert Cuup and the Nordmarket which had organic food and exotic used and newer clothes from all over the world. Year round, rain or shine, these markets always operate to supply at least someone's needs.

For us, another storehouse of treasures was a place called Cash Convertors on the far end of Vondelpark-a large thrift store with lots of used bikes, stereos and other electronic devices. Our eyes bulged with delight when we found several name brand laptop computers available at an affordable price for us to finally plug into internet with. After some stress in handling the slow speed of the cheapest unit, we finally traded up for the much better Compaq unit which even though cost us $800, would cost $3000 new. We figured with the several months of use that we had gotten from it, the money saved from not having to remain as long on line at internet cafes paid for itself pretty soon. Dave, the manager, was extremely helpful in helping us select, set up, and learn how to use the computer. If we ever do move to Holland the best choice for electronics is definitely Cash Convertors. Our memo-ries will always cherish the moments of Sophia running up the aisles inventorying her own selections as well as the peculiarities of stepping out the wrong bathroom door into a confusing world outside the store.

THE HIPPIE HILTON

Although the Dutch are hesitant in expressing their hospitality, the fact of the matter is that their society seems to provide a bed for everyone. Even the airport is designed with large chairs for people to sleep on during long layovers. Over the years a sociopolitical climate has cultivated in Amsterdam a prideful tolerance towards subcultures of artists, revolutionaries, anarchists and other such folks cut off from the mainstream to move into deserted buildings and stay rent free. The "squat houses" are legitimate when an absentee owner uses these abandoned structures for income tax write offs or speculation and intentionally doesn't make improvements or use them for any activity. The resident squatters, in turn, fix up these usually decrepit warehouses in industrial neighborhoods in colorful ways and often operate low cost healthy cafes, restaurants, and educational forums.

One night we went to one called Zaal where we ate five great meals costing us about ten dollars and afterwards enjoyed listening to a jazz workshop down the hall. The most impressive of the squat houses was a six floor formerly condemned dormitory style apartment building a bit out of town called the Elf House. From the outside it appeared very metallic and mundane looking but inside was a colorfully festive multi dimensional portal of opportunity which we called the "Hippie Hilton". The halls were decorated with murals, spiritual and political as well as information advertising a wide variety of classes and links. Lots of happy Rainbow people running around and always room for more for a small fee. Social orientation and job placement assistance in Amsterdam was also provided. Drumming and exotic music riffs embrace the spirit on every floor. The first of our two visits to the Elf House was one evening with our friend June Cox who introduced us to several acquaintances of hers in the cafe. Our second visit was as guests of several members of the Friends of the Forest who allowed Stephanie and I to sleep in one of their rooms one night after an ayahuasca ceremony. Time permitting, I would have enjoyed connecting with Dr. Jon Levy who facilitated natural healing workshops being conducted regularly in psychotropic sessions (actually we did meet him a few years later on Maui where we became and still are good friends). Even if not a resident, the ELF house was a great location to come hang out, maybe smoke a joint in the comfortable cafe and certainly find pleasant vibes and conversation.

FRIENDS OF MAN AND FOREST

With deep anticipation as well as nervous jitters of apprehension over the unknown cosmic journey waiting for us ahead, Stephanie and I made contact with the Forest of Visions group that I had been in touch with for several months and who now were offering us an opportunity to partake in an ayahuasca ceremony here in Amsterdam. We had been reading as much information as we could find on the internet about this psychedelic plant brew and were happy to be nearing the moment of finally experiencing its portals to the beyond.

Ayahuasca is a blend of various powerful plants found in the rain forests of South America used by indigenous people and their shamans for restoring physical health and exploring spiritual realms. Held in awe for several decades of search, I was quite excited to be considering partaking in an ayahuasca ceremony far from the jungle but close to spiritual harmony nonetheless in Holland (or as many people add a "y" and call this country the "Holy-Land"). For about a year I had been collecting fascinating literature about these plants and their use from Forest of Visions-a group based in Amsterdam which conducted regular rituals and were donating most of their profits back to several impoverished villages in Brazil. I had also communicated my interest in joining a ritual which I looked forward to with much excitement. As the days drew closer, I was shocked to find out that this organization had been busted by the police and all activities of the group cancelled pending court hearings. Apparently with strong pressure from the U.S., there had been joint raids on the same day on all Sante Daime churches in Europe because of their sacramental use of ayahuasca claiming that the church officials were smuggling a dangerous drug DMT across several borders. Unfortunately the weekend of the raid I was looking forward to contacting the church itself, Dutch police actually arrested several people during the service well into its psychedelic threshold. After many unanswered phone messages and emails to the church, I was delighted to get an invitation one day from founding member Yantra to come partake in a clandestine ceremony in Amsterdam within the next few days.

After leaving the children well supplied and fed in the bungalow, Stephanie and I proceeded by train then ferry boat to our holy destination. What a perfectly spooky afternoon. Lots of rain and wind that we scampered through and finally came to the correct address of a large Gothic cathedral. We talked a bit with several of the other folks there and then managed to fit into some spare white clothes laying in the closet before joining the circle of about thirty people inside the small chapel. The atmosphere was very complimentary to an otherwise cold stone monastic retreat. Along with the crosses, statues of Jesus, alter and stained glass that were added by Yantra and her friends many colorful flowers, incense, several eastern sacred pictures and a beautiful painting of a young Central American maiden in a forest who turned out to be the patron saint of the church. We soon lined up to drink the first offering of the potion which was very bitter and as we could tell from the many buckets and towels on the side of the room, could well have us barfing all night. Since there were to be three official presentations of the brew, I was able to get a rough idea for the dosage necessary for a nice experience. For the first hour we sat in silent meditation with occasional visits by individuals to the barfing room. The second hour was a bit more active with singing of spiritual songs in Portuguese soon after the next round. By now many people were starting intense journey work-laughter as well as panicked crying. Although I didn't experience such intensity, I enjoyed the flowers appearing as if they transformed the chapel into a rain forest jungle with snake like movement on the floor and vines crawling on the walls. My barfing was fierce but passed over quickly. At one point I asked Stephanie to help me lie down on a mat in the back where I huddled up into a womb like position shivering. Eventually warmth did move into my sensations and I felt much love and harmony with the service, myself and with the people in the room. Because I didn't feel like throwing up anymore, I only had a little more ayahuasca, but I could tell that the extra doses were bringing into the circle more laughter and bliss even for those folks who previously were crying and had seemed very unsettled. As the night lightened, the service came to a close and Yantra set us up with some people who offered us a spare mattress to crash on back at the hippie squatters "Elf house". Everyone besides Stephanie and I left their white clothes on which made me feel a little auspicious dressed in blue jeans and black sweater, but no auric harm seemed to have been done. We also made contact with an especially friendly artist named Steve who, looking like a holy man, gave us a moral emphasis talk on the importance of positive thinking and humility. His travels had led him during the early 60's to many sacred places in the world and the lessons of the road were well exemplified by his grace and simple, quiet tone. Before we left he gave us a nice slice of handmade organic space cake. The drive then back with the group felt like lots of fun as we explored the wee hours of Amsterdam with a group of psychedelic sky-troupers. I enjoyed a remark one of the ladies made about her looking forward to going to Brazil and eating as many different ethno botanical plants as possible for a variety of deep experiences in life. Eventually we made it to the dormitory for a few hours of welcomed sleep before walking into the early morning city streets. I laughed in seeing people at the front desk of the Elf house watching on TV the conclusion of the zombie movie "Dusk to Dawn" and hoped John was watching it as well back at the bungalow.

STEPHANIE FAINTS WHEN SHE HEARS A FAMOUS ROCK STAR

Another feature of being in Amsterdam was the wide option of concerts to be able to attend at any given time. During our stay, Stephanie, John and I purchased tickets for the Robert Plant show at the Milkweg Club. For many decades, this club has been the venue for most of the best musicians and now it provided our chance to see Robert at a small intimate setting on a solo tour after his marvelous career with Led Zeppelin. The girls were pleasantly occupied with enough to do on their own and even welcomed the opportunity to stay at the cabin while the rest of us took the train to the city for the show. As expected the place was packed with hardly room for a toothpick to squeeze in. But along with the squeeze on space, there was also a limited amount of air to breath which by now was also being taken by the various types of smoke coming from the audience. The three of us had managed to be about twenty feet from the stage when half way through the first song, Stephanie passed out from the lack of oxygen. At the same time, sensing a problem which might lead to our having to leave, John moved about another twenty feet away from us so as to be able to keep watching the show unless it was a vital emergency to do so. In the loud noise and confusion, along with the help of two other people, I was able to take Stephanie out of the crowded hall where she was able to recuperate before going back to the show. Of course first we had to reassure the club manager who had rushed over fearing that Stephanie had been stricken by a drug overdose and to offer finding medical assistance that she was fine and air was all that she needed. Back inside the show we again were into the flow of the concert and even saw John up in the front having a fine time as well. I suppose in retrospect, Stephanie could have said that she had fainted from fan adoration in seeing Robert Plant much in the same way that teenage girls would pass out when they would see the Beatles or Elvis. The song remains the same.

With understandable reluctance to leave such a wonderland of cultural freedom we started exploring more of the picturesque Dutch countryside including the breezy fog-shrouded northern coastal area. Even with our thick coats and ski hats, our bones shook from the cold weather to which the locals seemed quite adjusted to as they were wearing far less clothes as we did and seemed to not be showing any signs of discomfort. For us it felt as if we were freezing in the town appropriately named Freisland, however. Before moving on to sunnier horizons, we stopped at one of the many chips stands and loaded up on lunch and very hot coffee.

BORDER CROSSING

The next country we visited was the Czech Republic. Not being a member of the EU yet, we had to deal with border crossing from Germany which wound up taking several frustrating and even scary hours. Upon being requested to show our car information, the German customs authorities were confused and suspicious of our documentation. Our van was originally registered in Germany, abandoned in Greece and then issued special license plates belonging to the Greek port authority mainly for tourists intending to stay in the country. Stephanie's international drivers license was even more peculiar having been issued by the Washitaw Tribal Indian commission which she had purchased from a sovereignty group in Hawaii. After her being questioned for over an hour in a warehouse looking bunker next to the highway while I was waiting in the van with our children, I started worrying about who we could contact if for some reason we were not only detained but arrested. Holding Sophia in my arms to draw perhaps sympathy from any officials to our plight, I slowly walked past the room Stephanie was sitting in and when she saw me, she motioned that I join her. It seemed that in their long investigation, the license plate and registration were okay but the Washitaw drivers license was nowhere in the system. Calling the toll free phone number on the back of her card only reached an out of order number so the mood was becoming more dismal as to our potential having broken the law and could wind up in police custody as suspected criminals or terrorists. Luckily when they examined my international drivers license which I had also obtained from the same sovereignty group as Stephanie's, it's being issued from Uruguay made it acceptable enough that we could now enter the country as long as I was the driver. With a big sigh of relief that we were not going to jail but rather into a new land of scenery and experiences, we were happily on the road again.

Up to now, traveling through Europe never had any challenges in communication for us. Besides most people we talked with also speaking English, my high school German was able to help in expressing the basics. However, our entry into the Czech Republic was a wakeup call that we weren't just traveling in proverbial Kansas anymore. Stopping for gas was okay as we were fine with hand motions on the type of fuel and in popping open the gas cap. However as the fading sunlight started reminding us to make dinner plans, we started looking for a sizable enough town along the rural terrain that we might be able to find a restaurant. The various stores didn't offer many signs that were comprehensible but around 8 pm we saw a place that actually had words resembling the spelling of "restaurant". We pulled into the parking place and after glancing through the window and seeing several tables of people eating food and what looked like a plump waitress standing in the front of the bland faded yellow room, we decided this would be our best bet for eating that night. Trying to make sense of what the menu we were presented with offered was difficult enough, but our attempts to explain to the waitress what we wanted to eat was even more of a problem. She made an effort to find out if anyone else in the restaurant spoke English but the only replies she received were helpless shrugs. Since my back-up of rudimentary German wasn't helping either, I reflected on the situation and decided to come up with a more creative attempt to order a meal. That night Sophia was wearing a bright red sweat shirt with an image of a rooster on the front. Trying not to make a total idiot of myself, I pointed to it and started making quiet sounds of a clucking chicken. The waitress paused a few moments and then spread a wide smile across her eyes and excitedly realized that we wanted to eat chicken. Being on a roll, I pointed to the beer and Sprite bottles behind the counter and was thus able to order our beverages. Not wanting to push my luck and make a mistake in trying to explain ice cream and wind up with something else too weird to digest, we remained content with the huge portions of food that came our way as well as with the very low cost of our comical dining experience. Feeling more and more comfortable in talking with sign language, I was able to ask and then receive affirmation that we could park the van in their parking lot to sleep for the night.

Waking up the next morning brought our eyes a refreshing view of the forest as well as the dotted farms and industrial factories along the scenery. Nature was impressive in its expression even though the towns along the way looked bare and at times bleak. What a disturbing observation to see women of all ages lined up on most edges of the towns waiting with their bags and suitcases for any man that would want to take them away from the obvious poverty of their circumstances and be able to promise them a better life elsewhere. Getting closer to our destination of Prague, our next stop was the town of Karlovy. Once a popular nineteenth century thermal bath spa resort, the town now was a long strip of dilapidated and mostly shut down shop fronts. The one nice hotel in town stood out in looking very decorative and right next door was an even more out of character casino. Hearing the prostitutes and shady looking customers in its lobby speaking Russian, it felt very probably to be a center of mafia activity and not the place we wanted to be looking for a public phone. Back on the strip we bought an attractively decorated set of porcelain bottles with which we could drink from the many flowing springs that kept pouring their fabled medicinal waters. Filling ourselves and our bottles with as much as we could, we got back on the main highway and drove about an hour before approaching the outskirts of Prague.

PRAGUE

Following our travel book's directions we found the private campground we would be staying at and even though it even lacked hot water, it was still satisfying because of its low price and having the bus stop not too far of a walk away.

The bus ride itself was not a very encouraging view of what to expect. Miles and miles of non descriptive businesses, factories and track homes. The sort of imagery that even the great existentialist writer

Franz Kafka would be depressed being a part of. But as we started getting closer to the downtown area, buildings looked more architecturally interesting, neighborhoods were accented with nice gardens and people expressed an extra spark of vitality. We got off at the stop leading to the "Castle" which was a huge and impressive gateway to the core of the magnificent city of Prague.

The castle itself was a towering structural figurehead that looked below to the city enclosed by its walls and was now a center of tourist information as well as having in its several levels many meeting rooms, auditorium and museum. During the week of our visit, literary scholars from all over the world were gathered for a discussion of the visionary writer and artist William Blake. I was unexpectedly surprised when a couple came up to talk to me and ask for an autograph as they thought I was a famous poet. I appreciated the perception of my beard and appearance resembling such an honorary personage, instead of the accustomed looks that I had to ordeal in the US and Greece of being a "dirty hippie bum". I already was starting to feel I belonged in this beard-friendly country.

Overlooking the city was an awe inspiring sight. The many pedestrian bridges crossing the river were themselves works of art, as were most of the buildings and squares sprawling in every direction. With the embellishment of gas lit streetlamps, the city's legitimate claim to being one of the world's most beautiful was apparent both in day and night personas. Cobblestone alleys led to many interesting shops, eateries and well maintained public parks and playgrounds. Among the many highlights we enjoyed were the Toy Museum that featured a massive collection of antique mechanical toys, most of which still worked centuries longer than the junk being bought today at WalMart. The doll museum likewise displayed dolls from various time periods and places around the world. But the most interesting building for us was grimly called the "Torture Museum". All the devices used by the Catholic Inquisition during the Middle Ages were on display which thus served as both a painful understanding of the horrible deaths inflicted unnecessarily and as a warning of the horrible potential for mankind to even consider doing so again. (Since the US expansion of ongoing torture in Guantanamo Bay, such hopes have again be crushed by the cold heart of "civilization".)

But as a more pleasant antithesis, The John Lennon Peace Wall was a beautiful spot for us to sit on the bench and read the many poems of love written on its walls over the years.

A proud example of old world craftsmanship was also experienced in walking across the Saint Charles Bridge which connects the castle with the rest of the town. The elegance of the bridge is further accented by the many musicians and other artisans that perform along its way. Besides the spontaneous displays of poets and mimes, we enjoyed a man who was playing a classical symphony on small glasses filled with water.

Besides sights and sounds, another vital aspect of local cultures for us are the sensual delights and affordability of eating. In this respect, Prague again scored well with great tasting food and beer and with prices on the comfortable edge of affordability. So with quite a gleam of satisfaction we looked back at our wonderful impressions of Prague, as well as looking ahead to a return trip one day in the future.

Before leaving the Czech Republic, one more peak experience awaited us about two hours south of Prague. Nestled in a setting of old growth forests and a gently flowing river, the town of Cesky Krumlov was another majestic presence of finding a castle perched over a picturesque town and farmland below. Before exploring the town, we caught up on our growing backlog of messages at a very fast internet cafe in one of the chambers of the castle decorated with swords and emblems of royalty on the walls.

When we then walked down to the town, we were immersed in a scene out of a fairy tale book. There along the river were a group of colorfully dressed gypsies playing enchanting music with passionate songs and twirling dances. The jovial mood was also expressed all through the cobblestones pathways around the town and through its squares. Our only challenge was in picking where to eat from the many fragrant cuisines that were tantalizing our noses. When we calculated that our meals would be costing under two dollars each, we made the decision to eat at one place, take a long walk along the river and come back to eat at the other restaurant. The specialty of both was vegetarian stroganoff garnished with hearty bread and thirst quenching locally brewed dark beer. Filled with smiles and memories, we parked near the gypsy camp and off to the next stop on our return journey to Greece.

AUSTRIA

As in Switzerland, Austria's dramatic scenery of the Alps and its verdant green forests was impressive. At times the highway felt as if we were driving through botanical gardens. On the famous pass where Hannibal brought his armies to conquer the Roman Empire, we drove through a tunnel with ancient writing along its walls.

Needing a rest pause for Doblemalz Beer, we pulled off into a cute little town with a cafe facing what looked like a well tended public park. Taking a walk through its footpaths after finishing our refreshments, we realized that besides the many colored flowers and appearance of a rainbow over the mountains, it was a very old cemetery. There was a building where we took a look inside to a spooky room of stacked skulls arranged according to family names and with writing on them explaining birth and death dates and at times a few personal words from surviving relatives.

Not sure if it was from the beers or optical illusion caused by too many hours of driving, but alongside the highway, we started noticing multi colored cows. On our first opportunity to pull over and have a closer look, these objects were actually statues that had been painted as a local art project throughout the countryside. Art and reality definitely blended well in such a scenic background.

The next place we stopped at was to the town of Salzburg host of the world famous Salzburg Festival and dominated by churches, castles and palaces. It is also the birthplace of the classical musical composer Wolfgang Amadeus Mozart. The day of our visit was very auspicious as it was the annual celebration day of his birthday. My associations of his music played and enjoyed by just old straight laced people of sedate and intellectual temperament was tossed aside. Throughout the town, ranging from the castles to the bars, there were large speakers playing his music throughout the day and late into the night. Festive laughing and dancing was more reminiscent of a rock and roll festival instead of a symphonic beatitude. Obviously Amadeus was a town hero and I hope his spirit enjoyed the gala festivities in his honor. The buzz we picked up from the celebration was tainted a bit later however. While taking a small sleeping break at a rest area an hour or so later, the Austrian police woke us up for an abrupt investigation of our passport papers with concern that we might be illegal aliens. With adrenalin pumping after the encounter, we got back on the freeway and kept moving on.

With time for one more visit in the area changing our direction southwards, we visited the sea front town of Trieste in the northeastern corner of Italy. Displaying its important Middle Ages history lots of castles and solid rock structures where frequently seen while at the same time Balkan refugees congregated in groups around the port and side streets. With just enough time to stuff our bellies with homemade ravioli, pizza, red wine and cappuccino, we continued our drive down the coast to Venice and then back to Greece.

CHAPTER ELEVEN: HOLLAND

WILL THE REAL HENNY PLEASE STAND UP

Pondering on a way to be able to afford travel to Amsterdam again with our family, a breakthrough plan materialized while surfing the internet one day. Home exchange was a concept that we never considered before as we felt who would want to come stay in our place or even Xirokambi for that matter. But with only a few dollars to lose if nothing manifested, we registered with a home exchange company and shortly afterwards received a message from a person, named Henny that wanted to exchange a month of staying at this person's house in Holland for a similar time in our house in Greece. So without wasting time and risking Henny replacing offer of destinations with an exchange for a more scenic holiday apartment on a lively Greek island, we made arrangements to take the offer and were soon all on a plane to Amsterdam.

Our choice of bargain airlines was a good one. Malev, the Hungarian carrier, was not only a comfortable flight, but also the seats were plush and the silverware real instead of plastic. Even more important the food tasted healthy with even extra servings and free refills on the red wine. A very civilized way to fly.

In contrast to the relative confusion of other airports, Amsterdam Schipol International was an impressive and well organized massive complex of most known airlines A-Z, with travelers trailing through exotic itineraries and with all the expected stores and services provided. Chairs that you could comfortably lay down on and even sleeping rooms with televisions. Clearly marked maps of which way to go and information booths actually staffed with smiling faces and audible microphone systems. Even a train station was located on the lower level connecting passengers to every major town in Holland. Yet, even within this well planned port of smoothly run activity, after an hour of waiting, we stood tired and helplessly lost in figuring where was Henny de Berg? The email pen pal Henny whose bungalow we were coming to stay in for a couple of months had told us to meet each other at this designated muster station. Did the instructions mean meeting at the upper stairs to the departing train terminal or the lower stairs to the arrivals? Was Henny actually a few minutes late or was the offer to us a cyberspace hoax which would eventually leave us penniless in a large city of expensive hotels? Was the Henny we were looking for wearing a tweed jacket and briefcase a man or a woman? Was there even really a Henny de Berg? All sorts of confusion raged through our heads at what was now no longer a comfortable port of entry, but turning quickly into a labyrinth of thought and fantasy. In our efforts to visualize possibilities, we constructed a visual image of the personality and appearance of the elusive Henny de Berg. Perhaps a retired college professor, partially bald sporting a thin beard, a bit on the plump side with a weathered leather attaché case whose gloss had shined in capital cities throughout the western world. Although some of these mental etch-a-sketches could possibly have filled the puzzle, the mystery was suddenly cleared up by the voice of the actual Henny introducing herself with a tap on the shoulder saying, "Are you the Douvris family?" Images of our first adventure in home exchange aside, our original grip of reality was that Henny was in fact a very nice lady, eager to help and orient.

In one's life the most common thoughts of home are of a place where one has grown up and is the focus of many fond memories. For us and our many nomadic manifestations, one of the first places that comes to mind is Maui and our many wonderful years living there. Yet over the next few years, Holland crafted an emotional tone for us whenever we looked back on our comfortable moments there. We would in the future have the opportunity to again be staying at Henny's bungalow in Hollandsche Rading. Warm feelings embraced us as soon as we walked in, sat in our familiar chairs facing the cow pasture and turned on the television in search of the Simpsons show to watch. Just like we never left. Our joy at being home continued on our morning as we organized our shopping trips to Martinsdijk. Yes, the coffee would still be free at the supermarket and on our future stay we would add the pleasure of eating those very tasty potatoes grilled up fresh and cheap in the food stall set up in the parking lot before taking the idyllic walking path back to the cottage.

NEIGHBORHOODS

One of the distinguishing features of a classic large city in comparison to modern suburban sprawl is the unique and changing character of its neighborhoods. Most of this inner city charm in the U.S. has deteriorated into ghettos of poverty, depression and anger where once was housed the life blood of proud ethnic building blocks of a progressive society. Such charm still continues in Amsterdam as every section of the city proudly displays its own sense of identity. Lively shops, accents and cuisine with bustling activity day and night. Whereas people in American cities board up their lives behind several dead bolt locks, the Dutch are quite proud to have people look into their meticulously displayed home environment. Instead of walls and closed shutters we observed street level picture windows, even on busy downtown streets, showcase Dutch families sitting on sofas watching television or enjoying their own window views while fine dining on crystal or silver place settings. Wondering what it would be like if other countries had similar "glass house" customs, I would imagine lots of embarrassing scenes shouting and gossiping in Greek villages, while in the U.S. a dramatic rise in burglaries. Since the Dutch seem incredibly calm as a society, their expressing of tolerance to others translates to having nothing to conceal or be ashamed of or showing their public either. Just remember when coming out of a Dutch bathroom to have your zipper up or else you might have more public exposure then you care for. In fact, the only times I noticed any actual staring into windows was in the several red-light neighborhoods where bed and beauties unblushingly advertise their charming wares (and flimsy lace underwear).

CIVILIZATION

One of the fundamental attributes of a civilized society is its processing and storage of information through the generations. Great libraries have existed in our culture since the time Alexander built the fabled grand repository of knowledge in the city named after him in Egypt. And even today, most towns across the planet have at least one public library. Amsterdam, being as progressive a place as any, has a fantastic library in the downtown Princengracht neighborhood which we often enjoyed visiting. Besides a nice selection of English language books, the music department was magnificent. Nice CD's and videos available for a small rental fee as well as music song books of many great artists of rock, jazz, blues and more. Sophia located some fine Bob Marley, Cream, Hendrix and Pink Floyd reference books while Nicolette found a nice beginner's piano instruction book to learn a few more tunes to practice playing back at the bungalow. Quite a few free internet terminals with very fast speed were available on several floors, including the children's section. Time was limited to only half an hour, though with always an army of immigrant kids waiting to play electronic games, opportunities to get online sooner were easier. The children's section also had a free bathroom which I enjoyed sneaking into and thus avoid paying the usual fifty cent toilet tax downstairs. Many nice books were on display in this section, especially on art, and one of Sophia's favorites, a colorful book on animal habitats. One of the classiest parts of the library was the cafeteria where you can pause and read a magazine or book while enjoying a coffee, dessert, or soup. Whatever weather patterns you're trying to avoid outside-rain, sleet or sunshine, the Amsterdam library is a great place to drop in.

THE COUNTRYSIDE-REAL ESTATE- BUNGALO PARKS AND HOLLANDSCHE RADING

Hollandsche Rading, what a tongue twister for our American tongues. Try saying that name ten times over and over. Even in our continual attempts to understand the accent of train conductors announcing each destination, nearly a month of daily practice passed before we actually could master these first words of Dutch, Hollandsche Rading. Even before approaching our new home, we were respectively amazed at the Dutch train system. Although the locals did have some nit-picking complaints about its "slow" service, after dealing with no transportation in Maui and the sporadic rudeness of the Greek approach to public transport, it was a joy relying on the precision of this inexpensive train system. Free newspapers which even included world headlines and local T.V. schedules, comfortable seats with no rips or undecipherable graffiti and a schedule so accurate that passengers would panic if their expected trains arrived even a few seconds past the clearly proud station clocks. You could even put a bicycle on board and plan outings throughout the beautiful countryside. And as we would find out one day when exploring the larger city of Utrecht, the train stations fried potatoes food stalls offer gourmet spuds at meager prices loaded with Indonesian peanut sauce, onions, spice, and of course, the local favorite condiment, mayonnaise.

But back to matters at hand, we carried our burden of books and suitcases down the country lane leading to the bungalow park cottage where we would be staying for the next six weeks. Except for those moments when the cold weather would reach through the walls to shake our bones, the setting was perfect. Lots of woods that we would be hiking into exploring the moss and magical tree faces, and well maintained bicycle trails that eventually lead everywhere in the country. The bungalow had lots of shelves full of tourist information, a bathroom whose toilet flushed well and most important, a door that would remain unlocked for the whole six weeks that we stayed there. No one would walk by peeping through the windows or come over to sell us magazines, insurance, borrow ice, push meat on us, ask us where we're from, what we "did" or why my kids "didn't go to school." Occasionally a few folks would walk by thus reassuring us that humanity still existed, but for the most part we could rest among ourselves with no intrusions in our nest for an unlimited future.

The bungalow park did have a cafe which we never visited because of its high price and unavailability of anything we wanted to eat, an office whose mail service never received our package from Greece and a small zoo that the girls especially enjoyed which consisted of a beautiful pig named John and a few chickens. Outside the back window we would enjoy watching birds migrating across the clouds over the adjacent green fields. This secluded setting, although never private enough for the freedom of an open range piss, did provide us with shelter for several explorations of psychedelic space. Even a piano was in the living room to add class and practice opportunities for Nicolette and John. Even when dealing with the perennial curse of flat tires, the family was able to find enjoyable use from the two bicycles in the shed whose fleet later included a used bike we bought Nicolette from the nearby town of Hilversum.

By far, the nicest discovery in the bungalow and certainly a treat which we gladly extended into a habit was having a television whose movies would always start on time and the commercials would only be a few and short. What a relief from the lackadaisical Greek programming where movies would sometimes start several hours late and would be interrupted relentlessly by even more hours of whiskey commercials and redundant news breaks with endings of theme music, credits and often the ending itself cut off. Now we could actually sit down as a family to watch a wide variety of interesting movies and still stay awake without having to shout excuses and blame on each other for having fallen asleep before the ending of the program. With a bit of ingenuity, John was also able to rig the channel selector to triple our selection of programs to chose from. We were quite happy catching up with the boob tube's cultural episode of presentations of Taxi, Simpsons, and our favorite new show, South Park. Bye and bye, we'll be remembering our six fine weeks at the Hollandsche Rading bungalow park with fond memories and even nostalgia for this comfortable home we stayed at in our movement across time.

MARTINSDIJK

The nearest community meriting a dot on our map was Martinsdijk. Also another tongue twister of mush mouth consonants but a lot easier to turn into a ribald approximation- Martin's dick nonetheless. Unfortunately, it's one museum had nothing to offer in the way of Martin's personal organ or even anybody else's body parts. The only moving parts of sorts in this relatively obscure tourist site was a display of antique clocks.

Our shortness of time notwithstanding, we never felt the point of walking way out of our way in the chilly weather to look at clocks (clocks which in fact quit giving the right time decades ago). Our main attraction of going to Martinsdijk was the more down to earth need of buying groceries and with three grocery stores in town (with pretty much nothing else except for some appliances and card store) it was always a satisfying mission. The only discomfort was the initial impact of realizing that even though we shared the same Caucasian morphology as the other shoppers, we really were a family of foreigners when it came time to communicate needs and pay for purchases. Unlike the larger cities such as Amsterdam where most people speak clearer English than even many Americans, the Dutch countryside is still comfortably provincial without need of a second language of commerce. Usually however, sign language worked quite well with hardly a need for long philosophical dialogue about the merits of particular hardy breads or cheeses of the day. Money seemed to slip quite well out of our hands with purchases that left us well satisfied at dinner time. Our most perilous adventure at the grocery came when we tried to pour a cup of coffee from what we hoped was a free complimentary vending machine, but we had to sneak around without getting spotted by the employees. What a shame if we were to make the national headlines as a family of undesirable aliens deported for stealing free coffee samples at a grocery store. Worse yet, besides the moral disgrace, what if such deplorable behavior in the community would be a severe enough outrage to merit having our fingers chopped off Muslim style to discourage other immigrants from daring similar crimes. Yet even with possible punishment and humiliation hanging over our heads, the risk was well worth the pursuit of that fine tasting hot cup of coffee before the hour of return trekking back to the bungalow. And that warm up in the belly would be necessary on the path where the winds would blow across the open plain and the darkened skies would hint of icy rain approaching. Yet the solemn quietude of the walking path, the setting sun painting strokes in the clouds, the postcard perfect older folks passing us with a smile on their bikes, the eye contacting gaze of the grazing cows and the vigorous stretch of our legs through this new environmental experience all combined to provide every time we walked to Martinsdijk a pleasure.

AMERSFOORT

The town of Amersfoort in the pouring rain might have a romantic appeal in postcards, but for us having to sight-see on foot, it felt more like Moses crashing the Red Sea on top of Pharaoh's troops. Yet we still were able to appreciate the Medieval village square feeling of downtown as we ran from shop to shop to get out of the rain. At one store we purchased a few candies and further down we ate some spicy lumpias from an Oriental grocery. The highlight was a very delicious inexpensive Turkish pizza. The town's coffeehouse, which took us awhile to find, also was Turkish and had a very grimy, uncomfortable atmosphere which for us meant a quick in and out visitation. Soon after we walked into a health food store with a nice café in the back. Since the day before we had eaten a very disappointing cake for Nicolette's name day, we made up by ordering a few gourmet desserts and coffee here. The day old sale prices helped us make our selections and as a bonus the bathrooms had healthy smelling liquid soap to clean our hands before continuing on to Henny's house.

At this point, the rain was even more fearsome as we ran from the train station trying to figure out Henny's address among the neighborhood of crisscrossing streets bearing famous jazz musicians' names. The map she had sent us fell apart from the rain, but soon enough we found her door and after squeezing out a puddle of water from our clothes, entered her warm atmosphere of hospitality. Earlier questions of whether there would be enough for us to eat were quickly answered as the endearing smells from the kitchen brought us the enjoyment of Dutch style hearty bread, cheese and soup. After this pleasant interval we joined Henny for another walk in the rain to explore her neighborhood and town. Again the downpour unleashed another flood and as the hour was darkening, we sped on back home before the inevitable chill set in. By the time we got home half the Simpson's episode was over but we nonetheless enjoyed the dry coziness.

TOLERANCE

What does it matter what another person eats, thinks or smokes? Why should I care if my neighbor chooses to enjoy drinking broccoli wine or washing his teeth with it for instance? Enough has been said of the oppression of living under the insane "war on consciousness" laws and mindset of the US and unfortunately most of the rest of the world. Holland, and especially Amsterdam, still stands like a beacon of hope and tolerance in the growing darkness.

With freedom of choice of lifestyle so fragile in the encroachment of the modern world, it was nice to note that for the time being, Amsterdam, as well as towns throughout Holland, practice the Golden Rule of tolerance and sanctuary through the happy bliss of coffee shop culture.

Like us, I'm sure many other freedom starved and oppressed Americans share similar reactions too when they go inside a Dutch cannabis cafe for the first time. Is this for real or just a dream? You mean I can sit down and smoke a joint in a public place without getting busted? Wow!! Probably it's a bit irritating for the local smokers in these places who take freedom for granted and who don't really see what all the excitement is about as they view these Americans almost jumping in delight and staring at everyone with intense perhaps tear eyed gratitude. Like children in a candy shop, we went to sample some or all the goodies on the menu and realizing that eventually the return flight dates meant so much leftover hash and so little time to smoke it.

It was nice to have heard about the freedom to smoke pot in Dutch cannabis cafes but to actually experience it was to taste and inhale the exhilarating breath of freedom. Every neighborhood and often every block in town has a coffee shop (not to be confused with mainstream cafes) where menus offer numerous selections of cannabis and hashish from exotic sources such as Moroccan family recipes, hand rolled Nepalese temple balls, and just nice domestic grown strains. Prices are relatively inexpensive (less to get stoned on pot than to buy a beer) and most establishments have water pipes to lend customers. Such a change from the loud, tobacco stenched aggressive bar scene with the usual stupid conversations. For the most part, a smoke-shop feels healthier with better music and chances for meaningful talk. True, there are many variations in ambiance, decor, music and people catered to. Some have beautiful spiritually influenced murals, healthy foods, drinks and intriguing sounds. Others emphasize techno music and electronic games. Also the mood changes according to the neighborhood with central city coffee-shops usually louder than the more laid back suburban places. A few like Barney's, Paradox and Yoyo's offer delicious dinners while none are allowed to sell alcohol thus further enhancing their comfortable environment.

How long such freedom will prevail and if the model of the Amsterdam coffee shop scene will be followed elsewhere in the world remains to be seen. Some localized trends in other parts of Europe are encouraging yet short lived. Draconian pressures from the US and their blind feudal allies destroy access for people to a global cultural birthright of thousands of years while at the same time encouraging death and disease through alcohol, tobacco and chemicals.

HILVERSUM

One train stop north of us lied the busy commercial town of Hilversum where we would go for a variety of shopping and service needs. Several times we followed the long walking path through the woodsy countryside between the city limits and our bungalow park, but as the weather would dip a little lower in temperature every day these physical excursions became more of a trudging ordeal instead of a vigorous endeavor. The train station itself had none of the gourmet potato appeal as Utrecht's, but once John and I did come close to a major score on a Hendrix box set of CD's for five dollars at the station's record store. Yet when we came back a few days later with enough money in hand, some other sharp eyed music aficionados had already scooped up the prize.

Directly in front of the train station stands a mid-sized sculptor of two hands clasped together dedicated to tolerance. This same picture is on the cover of the "Guide to Coffee shops in Holland" and again underlines the Dutch open policy to lifestyles including cannabis smoking. Within walking distance were three very nice cannabis coffee shops offering a comfortable atmosphere and good smoke for an inexpensive price. The lack of paranoia about it all was a free bonus well appreciated. Also of special interest to us was that we were allowed to bring our children in as well to drink hot chocolate while we indulged in a few bowls of higher spirits. We never did find another community in Holland with such a laid back policy where the local police would respect a family's right to be responsible for its own actions.

Our favorite cafe was across from the station and was nice to hear the music of Frank Zappa on the stereo system. They also had a nice Indonesian mask collection, colorful bathroom and a Furry Freak Brothers comic book selection. Also nearby was a tourist bureau complimentary map machine which would dispense actual directions to most businesses and all the streets in town. One evening Stephanie and I followed our date plans with the aid of one of these maps to a progressive cultural center of alternative music and artsy movies. Unfortunately for us, the night of our outing was more oriented to a yuppie sort of "guess that tune game" with artificial snowflakes falling on the dance floor.

Beyond the neighborhood of the train station, our activities were more mainstream revolving around computer shops, travel agencies, bakeries and post office. Several appealing though expensive restaurants were also in the area but we started up the mantra "wait until Bali and Thailand" which carried us by their windows with only a pause to study menus and catch a sample smell.

On its main drag, Hilversum did have an opening to a rather long, confusing indoor mall where I found myself lost and disoriented a couple of times. Yet I, as always, managed to stumble out and find my way home.

UTRECHT

The city of Utrecht to our south had a growing appeal with each visit. The train station (always our first point of orientation) was a huge maze of groceries, bakeries, food stalls, and the usual array of stores found in most western shopping centers. The same orderly ticketing and train departures as in every other station and scattering of homeless looking junkie types lurking at the exits and parking lots. On one side of the complex was a hotel/convention center/concert hall. The latter advertising upcoming performances by Sting and Black Sabbath to add to its memories of earlier shows like Led Zeppelin and other greats. The other side of the building hosted a large, crowded daily bazaar on the entrance to the main part of the town. Visually Utrecht was beautiful both day and night. Gothic towers in business districts dotted by yuppie bars, cafes and coffee/smoke shops. We walked by several Turkish restaurants serving very tasty Middle Eastern pizzas but the most attractive were the numerous Greek restaurants with their charming interiors even though with inflated menu prices. Not that we wouldn't have minded paying five dollars for a gyro on the right occasion, but I really didn't feel a need to get involved in the usual explanations of self, family and business. Time was just too limited if forced into making "get together" plans or being stuck with another expensive meal price.

The Utrecht canals which at one time were used for unloading goods from boats now form a lower level of romantic lamppost lit river walks alongside attractive cellars and concrete cave ambiance restaurants-Indian, Thai, Italian and Brazilian which advertised a specialty dish of homemade alligator stew (hopefully not from these canals though). Also along the walk was one of our favorite cannabis cafes. The entrance had a feeling of walking through a narrow cave with wall seats and pillows on the side while pleasant concert videos were playing on a big screen movie projector. The Moroccan hash was trippy but manageable and the free coffee added a smooth caffeine mix to the buzz.

Nearer the center of town behind the Acropolis bar that we never found open and the Middle Eastern coffee shop which looked like a brightly lit closet with just pale yellow paint for decor, was a smart shop operated by Conscious Dreams. The San Pedro in the window was too expensive although we never went looking for a cutting that might have been cheaper. We did buy some nice mushrooms, exchanged Salvia tales and bought a nice calendar of colorful mushroom art.

Of the three health food stores in town, we only frequented the larger which, even though a bit costly, it did fill up our bags with tasty treats including organic wine, concentrated fruit juices and season specials on Christmas cookies.

Utrecht also was the place we chose to attend a few Greek Orthodox church services. The Greek-Dutch here actually looked more evolved than their village counterparts. None of the morbid stares, chattering gossip, or lurking around after the service to be nosy and force feed us stale white sugar bread or goat body parts. In fact, these churchgoers would politely disperse and on to their lives within ten minutes after the priest's adios speech; as well organized as the train schedules. The clean bathrooms worked well without need of payment, and on one occasion, we were treated to several cups of wine from a little old lady standing next to the door.

Utrecht also had the only cinema we could find that was show-ing the movie we were interested in seeing the most while on this trip, the Matrix. The film was extremely satisfying and top notch "thinky" science fiction. The only unpleasantness came from a nerdy American who turned around from his seat in front of us to say in a friendly way that it was somehow strange and wrong for us to have brought our chil-dren to an "R-rated" movie and weren't we at all frightened in possibly having broken the law by doing so. It was a real challenge for me to politely shrug off throwing the book at him and the bogus, hypocriti-cal values he represented. Coming from the American society where people get gunned down just for fun, most of its citizens living lives of economic prosperity while its capitalist system starves the world and sucks up its resources, where most of its citizens are jailed to become corporate slave labor than anywhere else in the world and whose gov-ernment, with public approval, was at the moment dropping bombs on women and children in Serbia in the name of democracy. Yet, I looked at this smiley faced mannequin as typical product of the hu-man engineered assembly line and saw him under a brain control de-lusion similar to the movie we were watching. The only other possible transformation of my disgust and anger was in being thankful that we expatriated from the land of psychic vampires whose bald eagle sym-bol has turned into a blood thirsty vulture.

Full circle, our tour of Utrecht ended at the train station where we again took care of feeding our bellies. Besides the wonderful potatoes previously mentioned, along with Nicolette and Sophia, while stuck waiting for John and Stephanie from the Convention Center's computer show, we feasted on close out sale sandwiches from the supermarket deli. Also we passed the waiting time by exploring other floors of the convention center where we found a room full of tourist information on travels to faraway places. We hung around awhile in hopes of a free cup of coffee and interesting brochures, but our best find was the comfortable and well stocked bathrooms which did not require the usual quarter fee to use.

ROTTERDAM

Many years ago I remember first hearing mention of Rotterdam through the gritty poetry of folk musician David Van Ronk. As with famous other ports like San Francisco's Barbary Coast days, the historic landscape was a lively collage of drunken sailors, bawdy songs, merchandise being tossed ashore from all parts of the world, red lights on every light post and sweet laced debauchery. The contemporary version, except for its still very large harbor, shows little trace or similarity to those glory days outside of a few paintings hanging on the walls of the many museums the current city fathers take wholesome pride in. In fact one of these places, specifically the Museum of Modern Art, was one of the reasons we had come to this city and drenched us by the icy rain on our hour march across town in pursuit of higher art appreciation.

This greeting of unfriendly weather didn't leave much room for sightseeing pauses, so soon after arriving we ran from the train station to the heated and dry sanctuary of the city's tourist information office. Maps were on display showing us the quickest walking routes to nearby sites as well as a large assortment of good quality tourist trinkets. The section of travel books had some very nice guides to locations throughout the world including one on Greece with the kind of detailed hiking paths that even the Greeks don't have. They were a bit pricey though and being written in Dutch would not have been worth adding the extra weight to our already maxed out backpack capacity. I tried buying a couple of sweatshirts for my girls with attractive local motifs but since they didn't seem to be too interested, I added them to my future purchases wish list.

Our walk took us through lots of window shopping study, especially of restaurants. One pizza vendor had several very tasty looking pies on his shelf but a nearby sewer pipe leak wiped out any desirable smells by the acrid odor which propelled us to walk away even faster than the thickening rain and wind. We were surprised to see many Greek restaurants, markets and even a National Bank of Greece. Needing to actually ask them a question about transferring some money into my mother's bank account in Sparta, getting out of the rain, and using their bathroom, I decided to pay this bank a visit. Instead of finding the expected ethnic greeting of "patriotes" and "welcome homeboys", none of the bank personnel spoke Greek, English or even seem to be Dutch. Probably hired from the low end of barely qualified yet not much in salary job market, the employees had a Middle Eastern, African and Asian appearance. Eventually we were directed to a shady looking Greek man inside a glass booth who answered our question in an abrupt and mechanical manner thus our realizing we didn't have to hang around any longer here for hospitality, mezedes appetizer trays or coffee. Better service if we had walked into an Orthodox monastery with an ATM.

As most Dutch towns, a place as large as Rotterdam did not have any shortage of cannabis cafes either. The nicest was called Sinsemilla and was operated by the same people as the same one in Amsterdam. There used to be a second floor featuring live music, but the Dutch have a very peculiar law that live music can only be played in an establishment selling alcohol. Since coffee shops sell ganja but not alcohol, they cannot have any bands playing for which to enjoy the holy smoke even more. This perception seems even stranger than their ethnic custom of dumping mayonnaise on fried potatoes.

Finally we reached the Museum of Modern Art which all the tour books promote as a "must see" and where we happily prepared to finally visit up close our favorite Dutch master artist Hieronymus Bosche and quite probably see the work of the more contemporary and fascinating M.C. Escher. And even more, the pleasure of seeing authentic Salvador Dali paintings which the book said filled several rooms of the museum. Horror of horrors, we found instead, a world gone topsy-turvy-kukoo. Instead of art, we found glamorized garbage. After walking through hall after hall and putting up with wasted time and paint on the walls, we found nothing remotely for us to consider as art. The only Bosche piece was an insult-only a fragment of a mediocre wood carving. How I remember those tiny detailed nightmarish creatures on record album and science fiction book covers that featured his deep art that I had often enjoyed staring at. Finding absolutely no M.C. Escher at all-nor hint by the staff where I could find any of his work in his native Holland. And for the final pain stroke of madness, the many Dali paintings we were anticipating seeing had been "temporarily removed for a couple of years." They were replaced by about five rooms full of close up pictures taken by a photographer of villagers she had met on a trip to Central America. Perhaps I can understand a couple of these pictures in her own photo album book of nostalgia, but to have this stuff on the wall as replacements for the magic portals of one of the world's greatest artists is a pathetic and ludicrous statement of the compromised sanity of the custodians of art entrusted by this museum to offer their community the best they can. We had to laugh at the situation to keep from crying and replaced our disappointment with a jollier emotion. It didn't take long as in looking out the large plate glass window facing the courtyard outside, we had a panoramic view of a winter wonderland scene soon waiting for us. Big puffy snowballs were dropping everywhere as the white stuff was filling up the environment. Before joining this holiday landscape, Nicolette made an attempt to receive a wrapped Christmas gift which was being passed out to a group of school children in the cafeteria. The confused museum guide wouldn't let her have one but did give us all nice artsy book markers for our collection however.

Surprisingly, for a full day of activity and dealing with the elements, we had not stopped anywhere to eat yet. We had been saving the gourmet black bread from the bakery to be spread by the Dijon mustard and other fixins we were looking forward buying at the Utrecht train station on our way back to the bungalow for homemade TV dinner. One exception to the usual norm was in seeing a group of musicians from Peru playing a song with the same rift over and over at the same spot day and night. They were indeed colorful and in some ways very talented to be able to keep on keeping on. I wonder if 20 years from now they will still be playing the same song in the train station?

"MORE EATS"

Never listen to travel books, even the budget guides, when they tell you that eating, even in the big cities, has to be expensive. A source of grave concern for a frugal family like ours is how to survive a trip without our budget starving us. The information I had researched about the restaurant prices in Amsterdam was no relief as the "inexpensive one star designations" corresponded to "under $10 a meal". Meaning what: $50 for five orders of fried potatoes? But the alarm didn't hold out for long and we experienced delight not having to endure a long fast either. The bakeries were wholesome and cheap as were the cheese shops. Farmers market seemed abundant even in the winter and the communal cafes in cohousing buildings referred to as "squats" meant we could even afford to "eat out" on special occasions. However one of our memorable (and inexpensive) meals was at a place called Falafel Dan's. During the happy hours between 4-6 p.m. this Israeli managed restaurant offered their very tasty falafels, salad bar and sauces as an all you can eat special for just three dollars. I suppose the average customer might eat a bit more than a hefty platter, but our clever family quickly mastered the technique of not eating the pita till the end thus leaving plenty of opportunity to keep stuffing falafel balls and fixings into the bread. Of course it could get quite messy having no forks on the table-probably to discourage our type of eating habits. We soon figured a way around that problem too by using the little tiny spoons on the sauce bowls as utensils for our bottomless plates. Yes indeed it's a pleasure to feel content eating a royal platter with a pauper's budget. I wonder if they continued the special price after our family visit or perhaps they placed a picture of us on their entrance wall saying that we would not be allowed into their premises any more for beating the system.

THE MILLENIUM

An important question for most people to consider on the last day of the year was where to be at the moment of transition into the 21st century. Probably for most people, at least in the U.S., the fear perpetuated by mass media hypnosis was to look forward to the new year with suspicion and fear. Terrorists, hackers, communists, anarchists, and any other leftover mainstream scapegoats from the 60's were supposed to be uniting in some sinister plot to disrupt civilized life as we know it through Y2K computer viruses and random acts of violence. (Actually, I too was posed for some kind of computer mischief by major banking conglomerates themselves under the excuse of "missing funds mysteriously disappearing" from their banks.) The safest place for celebration therefore would be the sitting rooms where Hollywood promised a safe gala event to home viewers. In "New Age" corners, many self proclaimed psychic channels of esoteric truth promised fireworks in the way of volcanic eruptions, earth changes and UFO landings. In traditional societies, New Year's festivities centered around the usual church services and follow up feasting. Drunks worldwide used this opportunity for celebration to meet the stroke of a new era with their heads in the toilet.

Ever searching for our own brand of politically correct alternatives, we bypassed paying attention to all the usual party goings including the all night music, dance and entertainment in several possible Amsterdam neighborhood squares. Our Millennium plans were to spend the day and night at Ruingard, a famous 60's commune/artist/alternative culture scene about an hour east of Amsterdam by bus. Besides the positive feedback from several coffee-shops and friends about Ruingard, their website was full of an impressive history of activism, celebration and sanctuary. Therefore after scanning all the various options, we happily agreed to purchase the last remaining tickets to the Ruingard New Year's party promoted as the "Burning of the Tower of Babel".

Catching the train midday in Amsterdam, we could tell we were nearing the seashore location of the community by the growing number of well dressed people getting on at each stop. Finally we could smell the sand dunes through the fog as we bundled up and followed the crowd through the entrance gate.

The setting we found was quite odd. Lots of desolation and erosion all around; probably one of the reasons the community was pressured to disperse after thirty years to make way for some kind of petroleum or toxic waste project. A few people were crowded into some sort of bar/cafe at the entrance, but the main event was apparently a little further at the site of the "Tower of Babel" itself. It's quite difficult to describe the structure as so non-linear that only a picture could do it justice. Thousands of pallets had been piled up like giant crooked Popsicle sticks to create a multi-story circular dormitory with a hollow interior. Many of the community residents enjoyed the comfort of home as evidenced by their bedding, alters and posters hanging on the flimsy walls. The architecture was soon to become a part of past history soon as the building had recently been condemned by the government, so the residents themselves had decided to create a "happening" by pouring lots of gasoline and burning the building up at midnight. Luckily we all got to appreciate its chaotic craftsmanship before the anticipated burning by climbing the spiraled staircase to the top and then down the other side.

As the day darkened, the rain poured and the cold started biting even more thus necessitating our hanging around at the various bonfires. The main circus tent which was to be the musical focus was not yet ready and the scattered open field entertainment was boring. A small error in our judgment was in assuming a Rainbow/Pagan Gathering atmosphere with more outdoor activity. Having to bear the weather until the tent opened past midnight, we cuddled up around a particularly large fire waiting for the featured burning. As it got later, the crowds started swelling and the festivities finally started with the main event of the Tower of Babel burning in a huge long, sustained blaze. The strong wind currents did send a lot of burning wood flying, but no one was hurt.

An event such as this one with over 2000 tickets sold was bound to attract a variety of peculiar people as well. Unfortunately, we encountered a couple of especially unforgettable characters that we had to eventually hide from so as to not have to mingle with later. One young kid was totally deranged trying to throw himself in the burning building area and afterwards seemed to be staring at us with glassy gazes. Another hobo sort of fellow sat around a bonfire enjoying his feast of one canned delicacy after another. After several yoga burps he started sprawling over everybody with the mantra "Baby, baby, baby". While the big fire burned, the music simultaneously started pumping out from the circus tent where we found ourselves indoors warming up in a safe corner to enjoy what would turn out to be our first Rave Party.

I suppose in some ways I was at fault expecting the trance music promotion of the event to at least imply some sort of 60's musical/spiritual/cultural perspective. Actually the Ruingard community did have such a New Year's Eve party happening simultaneously across town in Amsterdam at the Paradisio Club called the Balloon Party where most of their community, friends and supporters were all taking part in a very psychedelic happening. But back at the ranch, the theme was incredibly loud techno music being programmed by idiots (also referred to as DJs) to an even more foolish audience. This combination of noise, crowds, and crappy drug/alcohol combinations created a frightful night for us of dodging drunks and insanity. We happily greeted the early dawn as the opportunity to escape the chaos and walk through the cold pouring rain to the designated bus stop out. Being New Year's, bus schedules were not running regular with the first departure that yesterday's driver promised for today never showed up.

Thus we ushered in our memory of the new millennium by being baptized in the chilly morning downpour waiting for the bus to Amsterdam which never came. An immigrant taxi driver offered us a ride to the nearby train station, but we refused his extortion prices. Several other party goers were able to flag down rides even while dealing with their projectile vomiting problems. Even more cars were heading to the party scene we had just left as the disco was turning into a multi day affair. Finally a nice lady in a van must have taken pity on us and did a U-turn to pick us up and drive us all the way to Amsterdam. Even though we felt we had been through a bit of an ordeal, our millennium party was definitely an event which we will long remember.

SALVIA

In the 1960's, millions of psychedelic journeys were launched by singer Grace Slick's chorus of "feed your head." At least with the familiar pills and plants available back then, we shared a vague continuity of knowing which head you were feeding. While in Amsterdam, besides the pot, hash, mushrooms and ayahuasca which were not at all legal to partake of anywhere else in the world, the local smart shops also supplied a variety of lesser known psychoactive substances which had no legal restrictions anywhere. For the most part, these various flowers, plants and weeds could be found in gardens as well as growing wild. They were not considered very important as their usage doesn't have a long history nor are they considered to have much of a potent chemistry. Several years before writers Terence McKenna and Jonathan Ott presented indications to the psychedelic community that there are large and dispersed numbers of these botanicals which are very rich in

DMT, very easy to find and still were legal to use. One of these plants that had been previously researched as well by Gordon Wasson but was then found to be unstable and weak, is Salvia Divanorum, a type of wild sage used in divination throughout Central America. Intrigued not only by the experience but also by the melodic sound and imagery of its name, I was pleased to find a variety of Salvia products readily available in Amsterdam. Before deciding on use and purchase, I researched various books and websites and learned about the traditional use of chewing the leaves and then waiting for visions in the darkness. Terence discusses how he has used this method and often experienced "elf like self generating machine entities". A more novel method suggested by psychonaut pioneer Daniel Siebert and others is the smoking of an extract soaked leaf whose experiences, though still related to DMT, sounded even more intense and intriguing. Since these experiences would not last more than 20 minutes anyway, we decided that it would be safe enough to buy some fresh salvia to chew but also the smokable extract as well.

Research notes studied, set and setting in place, music, art supplies, and all the usual temple ambiance organized, I filled the deep metal pipe bowl and said goodbye to the mundane and then followed the smoke to a bizarre new land.

The intensity of the experience ahead was in no way possible for someone to explain not having had also taken salvia. This was not a journey across a straight path but more like rushing over Niagara Falls in a bamboo crate. Whatever grace and enchantment mushrooms, woodrose seeds or any of the other known psychedelics have blended in my soul were nowhere to be clutched in this Salvia experience of crumbling bridges with no guardian angels to embrace my fall. The portals into an infinity of parallel realities so frighteningly familiar was sheer horror and panic. Glimpses of two dimensional slides squeezing out of some deep memory banks like express trains pulling me into their windows. Could the "mainstream reality" I had come from be nothing more than a law and order thought patterns while these others be the master copies that until now I had only been reacting to? How could I pick which extension to pull myself through. Infinity all within the moment of mirror images with emotional bonds compelling me to leave behind all other memory banks and merge. Potent images of departed relatives, perhaps parents and/or ancestors, reaching out to me. Which one to choose as I felt in relationship to all. Stephanie and all that I felt I was just a few moments ago were disintegrating quickly as well as my body, ego and room as I now started screaming for help before the portal back to where I had probably come from closed. My bed was not a secure womb or sanctuary to trail the puff through the burning bush towards Divinity.

I felt trapped in some sort of plasma of self generating ferris wheels. Ah yes, the elves McKenna was talking about. For me they were a kaleidoscope of thin men with white outfits, bow ties and cook hats as worn in diners. The feeling was very 1950's; bright, crisp and so very real. Could these portals be pathways moving souls through bodies. Reincarnations? But where was heaven? Where were the angels? God? Any answers? If this was the place where all religions were pointing to, where was the welcoming home and Saint Peter was nowhere to be found? I panicked at this idea of a mechanical factory of reality and soul processing. Such a place suggests no salvation. No sanctuary. Just one dead end after another.

Once not being enough, I got my nerve up to smoke Salvia Divanorum extract several weeks later. Again the slide was fast and dramatic with familiar images claiming me as their own and engulfed me with confusion and self dissolution. Deep programs were triggered as I found myself speaking Greek as a primary language for the first time since I was around five years old. The images again were intensely familiar and had such a clarity to thus submit the fear of parallel universes perhaps more real in magnitude than the one we consider our "real reality." Baffling Stephanie and the kids, in Greek I cried out to these images the most essential existential question "who am I?" But this particular question was not asked in a tone of detached philosophical inquiry but in a state of frantic desperation from a man fading fast in a death experience with this extremely important thought on his lips. Are these the bardo realms mentioned in the Tibetan Book of the Dead or a hostile god's idea of a terrible and cruel joke?

Curiously John's first few experiments in smoking salvia were inconsequential even with loading equivalent dosages as my own nightmare journeys. On his third attempt, he did cross the threshold like being beamed out in Star Trek to a peculiar and terrifying universe. So much activity with so little smoke is perplexing and worth bringing to the attention of humanity as a fundamental question of our existence and purpose. Has any society or shamans of the past been familiar with these other dimensions or in smoking salvia in itself sending explorers into far beyond areas than Columbus discovery of a new land? Another possibility is that the smoking of the concentrated extract also compresses the experience into frequency unimaginable by our human mental, physical and psychic receptors. On the other hand, as for chewing the leaves in a traditional manner, the experience was negligible in intensity or significance. For me the correct portal still waits to be found. Amsterdam is indeed a gateway city for travel anywhere in this world and beyond.

HIGH TIMES AND HIGHER ENTRANCE FEES

One of the reasons we chose to come to Amsterdam in November, eating hearty soup notwithstanding, was to attend the High Times Cannabis Cup Awards. This legendary event always reminded me of pride, freedom, and camaraderie, and with some study and research, I had enough of an idea what to expect. Also, hearing that we could take our children along was happy news in planning our day at this event. Ironically, walking past the police station that shared the same block as the conference hall for once did not blend paranoia with the expectation of soon possibly getting quite stoned just a few steps away.

The entrance ritual was a bit confusing not only because of the staff being deservingly stoned, but also because of the misunderstanding of the price High Times had advertised for the event and the much higher ticket price which was asked at the gate. This year the awards were being organized by a travel agency in the US which was trying to squeeze out a higher profit margin for their involvement. Anyway, we paid what was necessary and soon forgot about the hassle as it didn't take long to join the ranks of the "way stoned". Like many other craft exhibitions, each booth offered its own handmade paraphernalia, clothes, philosophy, but most of all, signature series cannabis. Sample after sample passed Stephanie and me, so soon we weren't quite sure which was the smoothest smoke or that it even mattered. I still can't understand how the judges would be able to do a fair job being in a similar state of out of mind. Before zoning out, I remember being very impressed by Indian Joe's vaporizer pipe which drew in a very healthy taste to the smoke. Although we had bought the cheaper tickets allowing us to only be in the exhibition hall, we did try to sweet talk our being allowed to enter the music lecture hall to hear some decent sounds and thought provoking discussions and video archives. Mostly too confusing and boring, so satisfied enough, we slid back out into the streets. American tourists, hippie or straight, still have some common characteristics as noted in a conversation by a couple of long haired tie-dyed guys leaving the hall in front of us who were in a hurry to deal with their munchies and trying to figure out whether to go to McDonalds or KFC. Meanwhile, they had scampered past a block full of cheap and tasty Middle Eastern falafel, Turk and Indonesian eateries to delight their senses.

HARE KRISHNA

If I had to chose my religion solely based on what kind of meal they feed me after their church service, without a second thought, you would find me dancing in front of airports with the orange robed and shaved head devotees chanting "Hare Krishna". Endorsement by George Harrison aside, the Krishna movement has gotten a distorted image through the media without once stopping to ask what their beliefs are or sample one of their delicious and healthy meals. If the way to a man's heart is through his stomach, can his soul be that far behind? Our family is eclectic enough to have dealt with coffee and donuts on Christian Sundays, brown rice and sprouts at Rainbow Gatherings, generic spiritual fasting, and slaughtered goats on Greek Easter. But for us a joy found around the world is the Sunday feast at Krishna temples. It was a delight to find out that just a few blocks nearby in Amsterdam, was indeed such a celebration. The settings are always different, ranging from the suburban temple in Makawao to our memorable feast in Haiku where we followed a torch lit jungle trail to a netted shack among wild animal roars and pouring rain. The one in Amsterdam was behind a regular flat door, but inside the arrangement was very familiar. A nice display of books near the entrance, with a group in the back part of the room listening to a lecture in Dutch while a confused group of other people sitting in between the rooms. For once we did not arrive too late to chant but early enough to feast. In fact, we had a very enjoyable hour of dance and chant and our daughters were taught a few Indian dance movements by a very pretty devotee that was standing next to them. Since this particular temple had asked for a small donation for three adult meals (the girls' food was free), we had of course some concern that we might still remain hungry afterwards. Our concerns were soon discarded though as the Krishna devotees brought us round after round of superb food, drink and dessert. Leaving smoothly before having to hear announcements of future classes and expectations, we strolled to Jane's apartment content of body and soul. Hare Krishna!

JUNE AND DAVID

Before our trip to Amsterdam I had developed an email pen pal relationship with several people including David Russell, editor of the wonderful magazine called "Coffee Shop Culture". We finally met as he and his girlfriend June Cox joined us for dinner at Yoyo's, a coffee shop very near Albert Cuup Market which served not only great inexpensive vegetarian meals but also allowed children to sit down with their parents on the premises. We were to meet together several more times and eventually June asked us to be caretakers of her apartment near the market for several weeks while she went to London to visit family. Except for the night the heater went out, we enjoyed a very nice stay at her house which was centrally located and convenient for us. The Buddha statue in the room gave the place a holy glow as we enjoyed the quietness as well as recording lots of great music from her tape and CD collection for our future road trips.

Besides our mutual interests revolving around psychedelics, culture and media, David was very helpful in explaining lap top computers to John as well as suggestions of what to look for when purchasing and hooking up to the internet. June wrote out several travel itineraries for us and joined us one day for pizza and visiting the ELF house.

OUR PSYCHEDELIC PICNIC IN THE PARK

As goes with the layout of any civilized city, Amsterdam connects its patchwork of neighborhoods not only with roads and canals but also with many beautiful parks. One of our favorites was the very large Vondelpark full of greenery, lakes and bicycles. Close to the main entrance was a large historic movie theater featuring classic, cult and art films. On this trip to the park, John was able to enjoy a couple of Fellini movies and the girls a pleasurable day of bike riding on the various paths. Nighttime there felt a little spooky as homeless junkies wander in to find shelter in the nesting grounds. On our first trip to

Amsterdam, Stephanie and I planned on actually sleeping in this spacious park as safe haven for a magic mushroom experience. We had brought candles, blanket and food to be comfortable in the secluded magical spot we had located where even tropical birds perched in the tree right above us. These birds turned out to not be a hallucination as we later saw them being fed and cared for daily by a lady that came by. Because of the evening chill however, we had decided to conclude our adventure at that time with the challenge of an enchanting walk back home. Vondelpark, as well as all the other nice parks in town, was one more resource of pleasure making Amsterdam a wonderful place to visit and live in.

INITIATION

Our friend June was taking a trip to England and so we accepted her invitation to stay in her apartment in one of Amsterdam's more interesting neighborhoods. Beside the markets, cafes, ethnic eateries and head shops, around the corner was a long line of brothels with scantily dressed women advertising their talents in the windows. Next to one such building was a Hare Krishna center where we went and enjoyed the chants but were surprised at having to pay for meals that otherwise were given free in other temples that we had been to in the world. But nowhere as pricey as the brothel I suppose. However since June's apartment was decorated as a temple, we felt it fitting for preparing it for our own ceremony as John was now ready for his first psychedelic initiation.

From the local neighborhood head shop, we bought enough psychedelic mushrooms for the three of us to journey while the girls were content to be going to bed early in another room of the apartment. The shrooms were activating their magic and just as the parading visuals were warping all our previously known dimensions of time, space and sound, I noticed a bit of confusion on our son's face. After a blank stare that lasted what seemed like an infinite wave of time, he asked in an untypically sharp tone: "Who are you people?". Not prepared for providing a suitable answer, we explained that we were his parents whereupon his concern was even more heightened leading us all into new pages of panic. His existential uncertainties now were navigating his feet towards the front door which triggered my own security rush to jump in front of the door with my hands outstretched and pleading with him of a dangerous and insane rush of activity outside that he should not even attempt to investigate. My defensiveness made him even more certain that we were somehow wanting to hold him prisoner and that we were trying to hypnotize him into believing we were his parents. This was a situation that in no way was I prepared for, so with prayer and inspiration I resorted to a new direction of trying to convince him of our mutual reality base. As I started telling him what our favorite movies and places we recently visited, it at least halted his push to escape into the chaos that would be raging on his senses outside. By telling him to ask us questions that only as real parents we would know the answers to, he slowly started having a recurrence of trust as to who we were. The basis of his test was in asking me what were some of our most memorable meals together. A questionnaire that I was surprisingly able to answer with gusto and thus stretching again the adage of "the way to a man's heart is through his stomach." Now we saw conclusive proof that delicious meals also extend to his mind and soul as well.

Coming down from our mushroom adventures, the time approached for our trip to Amsterdam to end and for us to study closely travel ideas for our upcoming journey to Thailand in a few days. Stephanie and I had yet to have had a "date night" on our own while here, so the night before we were to fly across the horizon, we made plans to fly into the inner space cakes of a very pleasant looking cannabis cafe right around the corner. The menu had a variety of intriguing entries and with the background jazz music, we were set for a night to remember. The night did turn out to become a special memory, but not exactly as we anticipated.

To make sure that there would be no mishaps, before we went out, all the suitcases for our early morning departure were packed and alarm clocks set. We dropped off the apartment key to the owner's friend several blocks away who would give it to June when she came back from her trip to England. We asked John to not pick on his sisters and not retaliate if they decided to bother him for any reason either. And for extra safety and our peace of mind while Stephanie and I were out, to lock the door from the inside until we came back in about two or three hours. Feeling assured that nothing could go wrong, out we went to enjoy the same high experiences that folks in Amsterdam took for granted as a normal benefit of freedom.

Following our promise to be back within a couple of hours, we returned to the apartment and gently knocked on the front door so as to not disturb any of the neighbors that went to bed early. After a few rounds of knocks, we gradually started pounding on the door and still no one came to open it. It turned out that even with loud rock and roll playing on the stereo inside, after John had smoked enough of the stash that we left him to entertain himself with, he had fallen asleep without remembering to be prepared for letting us in. Several suspicious and annoyed looks from people passing by on the street later, we knew that there would be no way to wake up John, so we had to go to the next option of having to call the lady we had given the key to and tell her that we were coming over to get the key again. At this point, coming down from our high was not a pleasure nor for the obviously disturbed attitude of the lady with the key. But at least we were able to get back in, scold our sleeping babysitter, return the key and get a few hours of sleep before leaving the continent.

The adventures of the transition were still not over yet. With our warm coats on and wearing our tropical outfits underneath so as to save space in our baggage, we went to the corner bus stop but peculiar to the otherwise Dutch organized punctiliousness, no bus showed up. We asked someone passing by what the deal was and were informed the news that a bus union strike was taking place and subsequently no buses would be running. With just a few hours before our flight, panic led to resolution and we were able to flag a taxi down. When the driver asked us where we were going, we knew we couldn't pay the fare of our destination being Thailand, but we did manage to afford a ride to the downtown Central Station and subsequent subway ride to the airport just in time to check in for our flight.

My mother Despino and Nitsa her friend in
Xirokambi, Greece, Fukus playing violin, Nicolette
and John on neighbors donkey

John's first electric guitar surprise at age 10

George, John, Jason and Dave on Maui jamming in nature

Family in Fiji Islands with chief and drinking kava at local market

Hill Tribes in Thailand and Bali, Indonesia

Family receiving blessing from Swami Satchidananda

Stephanie and the children

Stephanie's parents LaVerne and Steve, Family with Stephanie's brother, Byron

Meditation

Tolerance statue in Holland and friend Soma in Amsterdam market

Reflections from New Zealand to Montana

Stephanie with Timothy Leary

George with Terence Mc Kenna

Don Jose Campos preparing for shamanic ceremony

Jack Herer and George

Family in Greece with Robert Venosa and Martina Hoffmann

In Bern, Switzerland at Albert Hofmann's 100th Birthday with Alex Grey, Jah Levi and Sasha and Ann Shulgin,

Sophia, Stephanie, George and Nicolette in Greece

High in the Himalayas

High again in the Himalayas

Guru Das (Roger Siegal)

Chris Dyer and Anne Cohen

Dennis Mc Kenna

Jim Fadiman

Lunch with Ralph Metzner

Neil Pike environmental conscious musician, activist and good friend
in Australia

Thailand island and train ride in India
Michael Balderstone founder of Nimbin Australia
Hemp Embassy
Hemp activists in Australia Dr Andrew Katelaris
and Andrew Kavasilas
Robyn Francis award-winning international per-
maculture pioneer and founder of Permaculture
College Australia and Djanbung Gardens

Radio presenter on NimFM in Nimbin, NSW, Australia

Nimbin's Last Session courtesy of Mac Mc Mahon

Harvey Martin and Peter Terry   Dennis Peron in San Francisco

Family portrait

Our 35th Wedding Anniversary Party, Big Island of Hawaii

John and his wife Ariel

Scott Huckabay

Book reading of Crossing Karma Zones at Kona Stories Bookstore in Kona, Hawaii

Hawaii State Senator Russell Ruderman and Dina

Hemp activist and minister Roger Christi

Bennie Zable international political activist and performance artist

CHAPTER TWELVE: THAILAND AND BALI REVISITED

RETURN TO THAILAND

Our arrival in Thailand from Amsterdam was as drastic a contrast as we expected. Our winter freeze memories thawed out fast as the familiar equatorial sun quickly shed the clothes off of us to make room for our sticky sweat. Sedate, logical Holland's environment was now replaced by relentless noise, helter-skelter movements of vendors and thick clouds of black pollution on our taxi ride from the airport to the budget guesthouses in the Banglamphu district.

Bangkok is huge. Perhaps the largest city we have ever been in. Twenty million people crowded within only a 50 mile radius. Fancy new sky rises stretched to the sky yet just as many shacks and rickety houseboats filled the panorama as well. Even in all these stinky troubled waters an obvious inner calm radiated in the people we saw, probably because of its Buddhist cultural value. Traffic was almost at a gridlocked standstill along the way but within an hour we reached our destination. Here in the heart of the downtown and very near the Royal Palace, the Banglamphu district has the reputation of offering very cheap rooms and the familiar scene of backpackers, street vendors and cheap food. In many ways similar to the town of Ubud in Bali. Just the right orientation for our one week stay before exploring other parts of the country.

Between the deteriorating downtown shacks, polluted canals, opulent Royal Palace and modern high rises, Banglamphu is one of the most charming parts of Bangkok. Granted rats, roaches and rabid dogs roam the streets at night, yet for cheap, homey guesthouses, inexpensive food and bargain priced t-shirts and cassette tapes, it is one of those unique areas of the world for shopping opportunities. Across its many streets, street vendors peddled healthy bowls of food and fresh juices for well under a dollar. The shops are full of nice t-shirts, counterfeit cassette tapes and videos, as well as other interesting souvenirs.

277

Not too many "upper crust" tourists are brave enough to spend the night, but it's definitely a comfortable gathering place of backpackers from all over the world. Behind the dreadlocks, you feel that you will always find a vagabond friend from previous global journeys. Most of the country's budget tourist agencies are here as are the Thai massage studios where you can get an hour full body massage for five dollars. One of the most surprising delights for us was to be able to watch first run movies ahead of the regular video release schedule that we had seen advertised the week before in Amsterdam as current hits on the silver screen. We enjoyed this wonderful opportunity to catch up on new films though the street noise of motorcycles and loud stereos was quite a distraction. The price of admission in most places was not more than buying a bottle of water. Another of our needs that was taken care of at a budget price was the use of internet whose cost was as low as eighty cents an hour at most cafes. And besides the nice price, the machines were very fast.

One of our favorite spots in this district was the food stall a couple of blocks from the main street where a regular vendor, whom we started calling the "juice man" blended a multiple variety of fresh fruit juices for about twenty cents a glass. Always with a smile on his face that was reminiscent to me of Laurel, as in the famous comedy team Laurel and Hardy, he never seemed to regret pumping the blender all day long as each glass meant an increase in his income.

Banglamphu did have its downside though. Between the rats and roaches another street animal to be wary of is the sickly looking cat population. On the day we improved our accommodations and moved to a quieter and apparently cleaner guesthouse, Nicolette was attacked and bitten by a cat which had for some time been growling at us whenever we would walk by it in the hall. This time however, it actually came into our room and without provocation jumped on Nicolette. Not wanting to take any chances as rabies is a common problem here, we took her to a doctor who insisted that she take a series of five shots. Quite a dilemma for us as we have always shunned away from vaccinations for the children. Yet given the circumstances and possible outcomes, we decided to go for the shots. Over the next month, Nicolette would have to go to the nearest hospitals on our travels. The island of Ko Phanang had the nicest of the hospitals being open aired and with smiling personnel. If I had my choice of which hospital in the world to be sick at,

I would certainly pick that one. I wasn't sick when we walked in the lobby, but I did feel much better when I left. Quite a contrast to the morbid, desolate Sparta medical center back in Greece. Unfortunately though, Nicolette did have some awful side reactions whenever she was given the shots. One night, in fact, she had to be hospitalized at a very expensive private medical facility on the island of Ko Samui. Two hundred bucks a night without even a decent meal. The conclusion was a bit ironic. When we went to Bali, afterwards we were unable to get the fifth and final shot of the series because since Indonesia didn't have a rabies problem, they did not have this particular vaccine. We were nervous about what to do and we even tried having the vaccine mailed over from Thailand. No luck though, so we just waited until the time elapsed that she would have shown any symptoms. We were happy that Nicolette did not, which meant that she never had caught rabies and those painful shots she had been given where not even necessary. Tough choices but the happy outcome was a relief.

CANALS
   In the hustle and bustle of the congested high rises often hides one of the nicer sides of downtown Bangkok- the canals, where for a few coins you can find relief from the big city noise. As for many uninterrupted centuries, the boats slowly slide down the river where you can catch a glimpse of houseboats, temples and homes while dreaming of earlier times and cultures. The sounds of gentle waves splashing and the shade of the boat's canopy also were appreciated feelings for our senses. Local people use these boats as means of transportation but surprisingly, few tourists seemed to enjoy the pleasure of such an experience. In contrast to the snail pace of moving around in a taxi, the canal boats are a carefree and graceful way to travel on ancient routes throughout the city. Banglamphu is conveniently located close to a boat harbor where we got on these boats a couple of times. Simply swaying from one end of the route to another was a fine experience in itself. Even though the massive size of Bangkok swallows up these relatively few waterways, the emotional distancing from the main part of the city they provide is grand. In time it's inevitable that the trash and pollution will disturb the appealing character of the canals. Yet as filth buries Bangkok at an alarming rate, it will be a long time before these canals become anything less than pleasurable.

Another of life's delights inexpensively found in Bangkok as well as throughout Thailand and all of Southeast Asia are the wonderful varieties of therapeutic massage. For under five dollars you can enjoy an hour of traditional rubbing with oils and herbs to relieve pain, restore vitality and otherwise help you feel better. More sensuous X rated full body massages can also be found for a few dollars more, but none were experienced on this trip to write about. Even with some differences in strokes, stretches and point pressing, the massages in Thailand and Bali were both very similar and beneficial. Both systems use pressure points which release pain as bones are cracked along the way even in the cranial area. Thai massage practitioners also use their feet to stretch out areas of the neck and back. Man (and woman) does not live by exotic bread alone but also through the pleasures like traditional health enhancing massages.

Another desirable reason to go to Thailand is for the delicious and inexpensive food. At most restaurants, for under a dollar you could order a large royal size meal both colorful and healthy. The cuisine offered is uniquely Southeast Asian in taste and scents. Many times in the past we had walked past Thai restaurants in Hawaii that we could only afford to window shop at, but now it was our turn to feast without financial guilt. After dining on many a meal in Banglamphu restaurants and from the street vendors, our appetite led us one day up an alley where we found not only one but two Israeli restaurants right next to each other. And what an ambiance; each one full of Hebrew speaking tourists with the stereotypical nitpicky complaints addressed to the Thai workers while Jewish movies were playing on TV. It would be easy to be drawn into absorption by the peculiarities of the scene, however our goal was to eat hearty and cheap which indeed we did. Not just once, but after discovering the joy of eating delicious falafels, humus, red rice and more, we made it a daily pilgrimage to alternate eating between these two Israeli restaurants. And with a happy belly, we always found room for a streetwise Thai meal from the street vendors at night such as corn on the cob, spicy noodles, stuffed samosas and creamy crepes. And, all great food aside, our favorite refreshment stop was still the fresh fruit juice man around the corner who never tired squeezing another smile into our exotic combinations of liquid delights.

LOVING IN THE FLOW

In a city as large in size and history as Bangkok even its alleys and byways are full of stories and character. Behind our favorite juice warung, the Salvador Dali Bar displayed nice posters, friendly waitresses, cold Bitang Beer and live music on weekends. What a surprise when we walked in one night to hear some great songs, both classic 60's and originals performed by a group called The Flow that were touring the bar circuit throughout Southeast Asia. Songs by Neil Young, Van Morrison and an upbeat stage presence along with a couch and floor pillows gave the music room a homey atmosphere and provided a chance to talk directly to the band between songs. Besides the happy audience, The Flow had been traveling around Southeast Asia for several years enjoying the scenery as well as night life. John happened to join with them on a couple of occasions and perhaps will one day cross musical trails with them again. So whenever our day turns a bit awkward, we can always recall the smooth "Flow" memories.

A STEP BACK IN TIME

Several decades ago when Stephanie and I first set out on long distance traveling, we made sure our plans included researching the destinations we intended to visit with as many relevant tour books as we could find. Over the years we have still followed the same preparatory steps and among the most useful series of travel books for us budget travelers is Lonely Planet. Sure, a good guidebook is helpful, but what I have noticed over the years is a growing reliance for many in the backpacker set to be using Lonely Planet as some sort of Biblical text to be followed devoutly every step of the way. Thus the world becomes a predictable Disneyland with a specific schedule for the "travel by number" tourist. What restaurant to eat at, what meals to order, which hotel to stay at, what bathroom to use, etc., that is the scene to expect whenever traveling the global grid of desirable locations. Unable to pull their faces out of the guide books to "smell the roses", you notice the Lonely Planet devotees stuffed in the same hostel or cafe with satisfied smiles of achievement holding their books in front of them like a badge to each other. God, we don't need to wear stinky badges or ordained travel routes. Across the street from the recommendations are usually just as nice meals and inexpensive rooms with views that go unnoticed. Perhaps that is the secret; to go to where no Lonely

Planet seeker has gone before. Like many years before on our first trip to Greece when we lost our precious travel notebook on the island of Kos, it had taken me many months of research to put together in my intention to provide a comfortable quest of the unknown with exact itineraries, food selections, taxi drivers to chose, etc.. For a long moment we were in quite a panic. Yet sitting in a playground where we assumed that the little girl who ran off with our colorful little book that had apparently crippled our trip forever, had actually freed us to explore our own journey without following the predictable steps laid out for us in the guidebooks. Perhaps the tree of Hippocrates on the other side of the global playground had brought us a natural dose of healing from the wise old physician himself. So see the world past the Lonely Planet books where the only loneliness you'll experience will be your own map of discovery.

As interesting as the levels of discovery within and near the massive area of Bangkok were, it wasn't quite the perfect holiday destination for us. The food was tasty and cheap, great movie selections, amazing massages, superb shopping, and a pleasant culture to experience, yet we were still in a large city of noise, pollution and crowds. Under ideal circumstances with no time restraints, we would have slowly worked our way up north village by village, waterfall by enchanting jungle landscape to the exotic hill tribe border of the Golden Triangle. The image of stomping elephants, swinging monkeys and river huts seemed much more appealing than the rats, roaches and claustrophobia we were experiencing too much of in the big city. But with our scheduled departure to Bali getting closer, we decided to put off the trip to the north country for a future time when we could set aside enough weeks to fully enjoy the journey. We chose instead to allocate two weeks of traveling through the three east side islands of Ko Phanang, Ko Samui and Ko Tao.

Conveniently enough, many of the travel agencies in Banglamphu offered varieties of organized tours of these islands at very competitive prices as well as cheap tickets to go anywhere in Southeast Asia. For the price of about eight dollars each, we bought tickets for a twelve hour bus ride to our first stop, the island of Ko Phanang. The cost included the overnight express air conditioned luxury bus ride, ferry boat service and even dinner (though we chose to pass after we observed the many living insects in the serving pots). As comfortable as the bus ride was, leaving Bangkok seemed like a city that never wanted to end. Besides its sleazy notorious night life activity, every neighborhood that we glanced at out the window expressed areas of neon lit bars, street merchants and outdoor food stalls. Even in decrepit parts of the city, there would hatch newly erected skyscrapers, gorgeous mansions and modern shopping malls. And of course, there would always appear monuments to kings and Buddhas. Obviously the Thai people enjoy late night socializing and dining.

Expecting the lull of the evening to eventually put us to sleep, our bus driver had another bonus surprise once we eventually left the city limits. Throughout the night the TV screen in front of the bus was playing nonstop video movies-all of which were quite interesting enough to keep watching. One particular flick, the grade B should be classic. "River of Darkness", was an amazing Indiana Jones sort of adventure tale with none of the heroes or pretty girls left alive at the end. All in all, it was a great way to travel out of Bangkok in search of a nicer side of Thailand.

KO PHANANG

Finally we were able to enjoy a tropical side of Thailand. Strikingly beautiful, this island of Ko Phanang was foreshadowed to be a treat from our first watering hole upon arrival. Thereupon we made friends with a mellow older lady whose restaurant near the pier boat landing had some great looking sandwiches and provided us also with plenty of good orientation advice.

Being time for Nicolette to have another of her rabies shots, our friend called her driver associate to take us to the local medical center. And wow, what a scenic spot for a hospital. Unlike the gloom of Sparta's holding area for the sick getting sicker, this building was in a lush neighborhood of singing birds and dancing coconut trees. The nurses were smiling and all of us actually felt better even though Nicolette was the only one sick among us. Afterwards the driver took us to the other side of the island where we planned to stay near the setting of the full moon party at Haad Rin Beach. The up and down roadway was like a roller coaster ride at times opening up spectacular views in all directions from where we were sitting in the rear of an open back truck. Our only regret was that our video camera had just recently decided to stop working.

Scattered around our destination of Haad Rin Beach were a series of funky looking jungle guesthouses to chose accommodations from. Eventually we found a great spot near the ocean in a quiet setting that required walking over a path across a few boulders to get to. Our family size bungalow had just been built which was well timed as it was unusual for a family coming to a full moon party zone. Actually we were about a fifteen minute walk from the shops and cafes which were obviously planning for the structured and anticipated insanity these small businesses thrive on every full moon.

Full moon upon us, we could sense excitement in the air as we meandered our way past bungalows, cafes and tourist offices to map out the area. Besides our delight in finding a Mexican and several Indian restaurants to come back to later, the chic shanty style development spreading from the beach itself was a lively mix of eateries and bars with each playing a tantalizing assortment of first run movies for us to consider watching later. The heavy rain which was pouring did not seem to halt the crowds of hyper fun seekers waiting for the sun to set and the moon to rise. Huge speakers were lined up and down the beach in anticipation of the approaching click. And indeed it arrived with a bang as the techno pop disco screamed its repetitive beat to the thousands of gyrating ravers decked out in body piercing and pounding movements. The full moon party spirit which started several decades ago by gentle young hippie vagabonds humbly absorbed in celebrating lunar magic, had now turned into a party animal heaven for the alcohol and pill set. Not too much nature worship was seen besides purely decadent exhibitionism. The emotional and actual electricity in the air seemed frightening discordant. And the rain kept pouring and turned the various paths to mud. Several times till about 2 am we managed to slop our way through the elements and crowds to feel the excitement of the beach scene. Yet we were just as glad to pass through and find our way back to our quiet bungalow without stepping on broken whiskey bottle glass or sticky vomit. The stench of apocalyptic debauchery replacing the visions of a flowery world of peace and love. We did make note of a couple of nice music bars in town, which were playing fine enough songs for us to investigate later when the full moon set was gone and the sun cleared the air of residual stupidity.

On the way to town, Mama's family restaurant was an exceptional place to eat healthy and delicious Indian food. Besides "Mama" herself who was a multi-star chef, lots of help was provided from her family as well. Her daughter Oi, had just come back from staying at a Buddhist monastery and spoke English very well and had lots of interesting topics to talk about. Her son Nen, was also a cool person who was playing lots of Jimi Hendrix music through their high tech sound system the night before. Oi was able to find us a nearby source for magic mushrooms and Nen was very eager to hear John jam some Jimi tunes on guitar. The two of them tried downloading some Hendrix sheet music from the internet and later on Nen took John for an all day ride with his motorcycle. We were somewhat concerned as the two hours that John was to be gone and back by noon turned out to be a full day and night. When he didn't show up by 9 pm to see the movie he was earlier excited about watching "Bone Collector", we became even more worried. Yet all turned out well as Nen and John had visited a cliff side cafe on the other side of the island overlooking a beautiful bay. The place called "Mad Bar" had just recently opened and was owned by a young man and his beautiful wife who also made unique glass bongs. They had quite a nice time jamming together with some German tourists most of the evening. It has been our future plans to return and stay in that area some day as well.

Another exceptionally nice bar in Hadrin also had a high tech sound system that was refreshing the airwaves with sounds of Santana, Zappa and the likes. One night we hung out family style, Stephanie and I dancing to the beat while the girls painted on a long table with florescent paints. John was not with us as he got caught up with the familiar Maui personality Fonzi who had invited him to come jam on stage together at another nearby bar where he was playing that night. As it turned out whatever dwindling talent Fonzi has as a guitarist has been eclipsed by his desperate ego. Under such circumstances John was not allowed to play a lick but did waste his time waiting. Earlier Fonzi had returned our genuine warm greeting with a pushy reply that we had to buy a few cassette tapes from him. Nicer company at the bar was a stoned out older hippie who offered to buy us drinks and give us some of his homegrown Thaistick weed for conversing a bit together about the joys of cannabis. The hour was late for us though, so it became a dangling conversation till we soon left.

The next island on our itinerary was the small lush Ko Tao with a reputation of being still "unspoiled" and an excellent location for sea diving. The small port was reminiscent of a makeshift frontier town in the older US "wild west". It appeared as a prop having been patched up quickly into place so as to make a little income through tourist support services like internet cafes, bars and cheap restaurants. We decided to splurge in our choice of accommodations for our first couple of nights by staying at the relatively plush Sensi Resort whose address we were carrying since Amsterdam. Since the Dutch owner was also the proprietor of several famous cannabis coffee shops back in Holland, we felt it wouldn't be as intimidating asking him directly about the availability of local smoking herb. We were not disappointed at all in his suggesting several places on the island for us to inquire including at the reggae cafe in the middle of town. Sure enough by walking just a few minutes and asking the kitchen staff for some "Laus", we bought ourselves an inexpensive bag of high quality Thai weed. A couple of nights later we would be going back to the same cafe to buy a bag of magic mushrooms which they kept in a large container for "special omelets" and milk shakes. A mild treat which we plan to take more on a future return. However, the hillside setting of our classy bungalow under the starlight and within listening range of the ocean waves was magical enough.

The next day we decided to hike directly across the island and along the way we recognized our friend Alex whom we had first met a couple of years ago at a Rainbow Gathering in Greece. We discussed some travel ideas with him and then went on our pleasant ways. As remedy for the midday heat, we stopped off at a newly built bar along the way where the Australian owner had put together an interesting assortment of impressionistic wood carvings as well as providing ice cold beer.

On the following day we took an even nicer hike along the eastern shoreline of the island exploring beach coves and local scenery. Along the way we noticed many guesthouses in stunningly beautiful locations whose access appeared to be only by paddle boat. Again one more dreamy location that we definitely felt would be worth staying at in a possible future.

BALI

Since we had thoroughly toured Bali on our previous trip, we didn't go on many new explorations on this journey but focused mainly on short walks around the village and schoolwork. Most of our time in Ubud was at Karen's house where we were staying as part of our one month holiday home exchange with our home in Greece. Her business partner Made and her family were excellent hosts who also prepared wonderful meals for us. There was some pressure from her uncle to buy his paintings and part of his land and also hire his transport services, but these requests were casual and not as obnoxious as the typical harassment from vendors on the street in town. The setting of the house in the rice fields was exotic and picturesque. All night long we would be serenaded by the quacking ducks reminding me of the idle chatter and gossip sounds of the old ladies in our village in Greece. It would be interesting to watch them following each other as the farmers lead them from field to field to eat the bugs. Often in the water, we would see snakes swimming, so we were very careful not to step into the streams. A couple of times, Made took our girls with hers to go swimming in nearby pools, but no alligator bites resulted from the excursions. A human creature has an even more menacing snap though. A family from the US living nearby invited Nicolette and Sophia to come in and play with their children but Made's kids, being Balinese, had to wait outside. It's those moments when I would like to see my kids express the lesson of "if our friends are not good enough for you, we aren't welcome in your house either".

Not having the extra time to visit many more places but as we still wanted to find a reason to give our driver friend Nyoman a job driving us somewhere, we decided to organize our own "Magical Mystery Tour" of the island during Nicolette's birthday weekend. Joining us also were our good friends from Bondalem, Gede and Kadek. It was especially nice because too often Balinese and their "bosses" do not go out together. Also a great opportunity for Kadek as well, who was from Bali but had never even seen most of her home island. Of course, besides our pleasant company, she had a giggly time dealing with Nyoman's romantic gestures. (Which would eventually lead to his getting in trouble from his perceptive wife who grounded his driving

escapades for a week of staying at home and the subscribed punishment of cleaning the pigs and their filthy shed.) Kadek was thrilled
being part of our excursion and surprised us all with a beautiful (and
delicious) birthday cake that she had baked with "NICOLETTE" written colorfully on the frosting.

One of our first stops was to take a small ferry boat ride to the other side of the crater lake of Mount Batur. The ancient aboriginal tribe
living in the village was noted for its burial tradition of leaving their
dead on the ground next to a large tree. The oils of this particular tree
seem to do a good job with the decomposition process as no pungent
smells were noticed. However, even though the dead were not much of
a problem, not so with the living members of this village, who had a bad
reputation for their aggressive begging practices. Quickly we followed
our footsteps out on the trail back to the parking lot and avoided as
many of the circling hungry people who were sticking their hands out to
us. The walk was beautiful but eventually we came to a point where the
road had caved in thus necessitating paying a few coins for a local boat-
man to take us past this blockage to a point where we picked the trail up
again and then went on to the car where Gede, who had chosen to avoid
raising the pressure on his heart, was waiting for us to set off again.

Our next stop was the lakeside hot springs resort area where with
the help of our Balinese friends we were able to bargain down the
cost of rooms to accommodate us all for the evening. The hot springs
entrance fee was rather expensive but noticing the local flavor of our
group, the receptionist turned the other way in allowing all of us to
jump in for a minimal donation. Refreshed, we settled into our comfortable rooms where most of us planned to sleep until late the next
morning except for John and Nyoman who set out at 4 am to climb to
the top of the mountain for a sunrise panorama. Unfortunately the
weather turned very rainy and even though they fought through the
mud and clouds, the view was quite limited. On the top they met a
group of German hikers who had paid for some local kids to carry up
gourmet provisions for their enjoyment. Showing mutated egos, they
didn't even offer John or Nyoman a cup of tea or even much of a greeting. Afterwards, as on their ascent, they bypassed the feared village
trail toll collectors who had previously threatened to fine them for
not paying (or worse, hit them with sharp sticks as another European
couple told us happens) if caught.

Hiking, swimming, resting, and eating aside, our journey continued to the downwardly fading once upon a time busy resort of Candidasa. The difference in the town from our previous visit of four years ago was dramatic. Many of the restaurants had closed, hotel projects remained unfinished and the beach rapidly eroding. After investigating a few places which refused to bargain down their inflated room rates, we decided to rent the "no frills" simple rooms located at the same place that Nyoman had previously found us the fifty cent fresh fish barbecue and two dollar massage. This time around we were not prepared for the extra entertainment of dancing rats and creeping roaches parading around the rooms and dirty toilets that wouldn't flush. Gede understandingly found the situation intolerable so along with Nyoman went and rented a room elsewhere. Kadek, feeling more obligated to stay with us for the duration, kept her smile but her eyes bulged and would scream loudly whenever the rats jumped around the room. Morning eventually came and we were all delighted not to find rodent bites on our necks. We felt that the sooner we paid and split the better. Except for Stephanie who formulated a list of complaints to the obviously nervous manager who cracked down and wept apologizing for our misfortune and taking all the blame. The rest of us managed to pull her out of the loop while assuring the poor guy that it wasn't personal and next time we came back to town we would certainly come stay at his hotel again. I believe with these words he started kissing the ground we just stepped on in appreciation as it probably meant to him that we wouldn't pursue our complaints to the owners and risk him getting fired and thus having to tell his family that they could face starvation.

As time goes by, there are certain standout moments to look back and remember. Such was to become our ongoing weekend of weirdness. What we expected to be a relaxed evening eating out and enjoying watching a movie turned out instead to be as stormy as the weather. Gusts of wind and intermittent sprays of rain made for an unsettling ambiance for our dinner in the upstairs veranda of the downtown restaurant. The nylon windows provided no holding back of the growing tempest which glued us to our seats with its shouts of thunder and blasts of lightning. Just as with the lights and television, the kitchen's electricity must have been disrupted because our Gado Gado looked old. The candles on the tables were useless as a light source with the wind blowing them out as soon as they were lit. The evening's crescendo peaked when wind, rain, lightning and thunder all blended in their assault. An elderly woman ran up the stairs with a flashlight clutching a monkey in a cage and shouting frantically in Balinese. The other western couple in the room looked as nervous as us in supposing that we might be in some sort of jungle magic ritual. Was the monkey a god or a demon? In any case, I was ready to jump out of this mad and sinking ship when another panicked woman ran through the restaurant shaking her head and pleading "I'm sorry " over and over. Maybe she was related to the hotel manager where we had stayed the night before. With both our hotel and restaurant experiences, it's quite possible to accept the locals' feeling that Candidasa is experiencing or responding to circumstances as if the residents of that town really are cursed. Whether it will take some sort of monkey magic or sacrifice for them to reach a satisfactory remedy, I don't know; however at that point the only thing that mattered was jumping through the rain puddles into the safety of Nyoman's van.

One of our favorite forms of entertainment in culturally rich Bali besides the exquisite dining, exotic art and talented dancing, was our regular pursuit nightly of grade B movies in the many bars, cafes and restaurants of Ubud. Since this year tourism had taken a downward slide, many of these otherwise popular places now remained empty. As a way of encouraging business, they would offer us any film selection if we would drop in. For the small amount of money in took to buy perhaps a snack and drink, the cafe would be all ours-our own traveling cinema. Often the employees and our driver friend Made would join us in enjoying mostly vampire flicks. One night we went to an almost empty Greek restaurant and where we watched the X Files. This particular copy must have been recorded directly from a movie theater showing as we couldn't even follow the dialogue because of the background laughter on the tape. At several points, we even saw shadows of people walking across the actors faces from audience members located in that particular cinema. Between Thailand and Ubud, we have certainly watched more first run movies in cafes than in movie theaters.

Our trip to Bali this year also coincided with the local New Years/ Nyepi Festival. On that particular day all lights go out and every home remains totally quiet. The darkness is broken by a parade of demons throughout the island. Every village takes pride in outdoing each other in the creation of gruesome floats which are carried by teams of men while making and listening to much noise and emotion. By burning them at the end of the parade, the new year is off to a clean start, without the curses of the year before. We were able to watch the parade from a nice vantage point near the cremation grounds in Ubud. Afterwards, in walking home to our homestay in Penangan, it was an ordeal dodging the many fireworks still being tossed into the streets. I suppose we should be thankful for these "blessings" which "scared the hell out of us".

One of our friends from our last trip to Bali was the artist Gusti who was instantly delighted when he saw us. We were a little reluctant to visit him this time because he had previously offered us his house to stay in on our return which we ignored. In any case, we had a nice visit except of the obligation we seem to have gotten ourselves into of promising to buy one of his paintings for $1500. The matter became even more complicated as he asked and as he instructed us, joining him for a full moon blessing of the painting which still awaits us.

BACK TO THAILAND

To be able to afford our air flight back to Greece, it was necessary first to fly one more time to Bangkok and a follow up weekend in Banglamphu. By now the routine was familiar: cockroaches crawling around our sweat soaked room, cheap air conditioned internet places, video cafes, more cheap stuff to buy on the street including defective cassette tapes to avoid, and lots of food stalls to stuff ourselves with "just one more time". This weekend was also a celebration, honoring the gods whom the people expect to usher in the rain season. And yes, the skies did unplug as if by clockwork. Thunder, lightning and minor flooding excited the usual street frenzy. Laughing faces squirting each other with high intensity water cannons and instant mud puddles every step of the way. Our major concern, understandingly, was how to get ourselves and especially our suitcases to the airport without damage. I guess the umbrella gods felt pity as, miraculously, our stuff which was tied to the roof of the airport van made it intact enough to travel further on.

GREECE BY WAY OF AIR PAKISTAN

Along with the low prices on t-shirts, phony passports and merchandise of any sort, the Ko San road section of Bangkok is also noted for the lowest price airline tickets to anywhere. Having seen a newspaper advertisement that Pakistan Airlines offered the cheapest fares to Athens, I dropped into one of the more reputable looking ticket agencies and inquired about us purchasing five one way tickets back to Greece. At first the agent kept telling me that the best price was with certain airlines such as Malev and Air France which were quite low but he still kept ignoring my mention of Pakistan Air. But as we started walking out the door, he pleaded for us to come back and explained that though he did not want to encourage us to fly with such a sketchy company, he did agree that they indeed have the lowest price tickets from Bangkok to Greece. And once he finally informed us that the full fare price was only $100, we insisted that these were the tickets we wanted to buy and which he reluctantly issued us.

Of course on the day we arrived at the airport, we kept questioning ourselves that perhaps the ticket agent knew some problem with the airlines that we should have taken heed of his warning. We actually were very relieved in seeing the plane had all four of its engines in place and none of its windows broken. And as we also received bonus mileage points and were able to order vegetarian meals, we went ahead and boarded the plane with more confidence and less apprehension.

Once we were seated in the plane, it was interesting to see that there were no stewardesses but instead bearded men that would be providing our services. And when the pilot himself walked over to where we were seating to shake my hand and thank us for flying with Air Pakistan, I felt an even warmer glow of satisfaction with our choice. However, when I turned around to look behind us, I saw the desperate stares of all the Pakistani men who were probably thinking of ways to stay in Greece without work visas.

Once in the air, I did not mind that no alcoholic beverages were served on the flight, but enjoyed instead the wonderful Middle Eastern food that was served to us as well as the extra leftovers they brought us. We did not pay for first class privileges but were still given real silverware, packets of entertainment for our kids and a very interesting movie to watch after several funny Simpsons episodes.

One of the down sides to our cheap itinerary was the seven hour layover in the capital of Pakistan, Karachi. As we were not very confident in reference points to be able to have a quick tour of the city and with its desolate looking appearance from the large windows in the lobby, we decided to be more secure and not leave the airport. In contrast to the vapid ancient landscape outside, the airport looked newly built. Between the empty spaces of unfinished shops there were quite a few fur sales booths which added an even stranger look to the mix. Being the afternoon time for Muslim prayers, several men gathered together down the hall and started chanting the word "jihad" whose tones of "holy war" admittedly did make me a little nervous. But my urge to go pee was even more uncomfortable, so I left my seat and started walking up the stairs to the clearly marked men's bathroom. However, just before I went through the door, an elderly man passing by asked me with concern if I had read the Koran. Wanting to be pleasant I answered in the affirmative to which he gave me the stark warning that according to the laws specified in the holy book, it is not allowed for a man to look at a woman before he goes to make a bowel movement or urinate. This truly put me in a bind of all sorts of new fears including my having to be executed or have my penis cut off because my eyes happened to glance at a maid cleaning the bathroom for instance. Luckily at that time since I was young and in good health, I was able to quickly go back to my seat and keep my legs crossed for several hours to avoid having to go to the bathroom.

On a more pleasant note, we were surprised to be handed food vouchers which, because of the long delay, we could have a free meal at the cafeteria. We ignored the hamburgers advertised on the menu and settled for spicy rice and vegetable dishes which added a smile to us before boarding the plane. Again, it was nice to see that it had four engines and that I could enter the bathroom as soon as we climbed into the cabin without fear of looking at any woman along the way.

CHAPTER THIRTEEN: RETURNING TO GREECE

GREECE-BACK AGAIN

Travels to exotic ports of call along the silk road behind us, we once again returned to our homeland expecting of course a lot less than a hero's homecoming from family and friends. In any case, historic roots being what they may, Greece, where so much of contemporary western thought fruited and thrived would be the ideal place to finally enter the modern age of communication by finally connecting to our own internet service. How dazzled and confused my mother and the other old ladies that bemoaned computers for being the tools of Satan would be when we brought before them the screen sights and sounds of Mount Athos' monasteries, church chants and a whole new dimension of mind expansion. But alas, ours was not to be as the simple task of hooking up resulted in an aborted mission. Whether John wearing out the plug or our technical friend Filipa sticking in the wrong end, the result was a burned out CD ram and our being stuck back in the stone age of communication. Certainly a setback in expectations but we retained patience and optimism that we would eventually hook up to the web. Also we were motivated by its apparent usefulness as a learning tool; the highly promoted need to access cyberspace of important visionaries, revolutionaries and heroes; means to cut down on our communication costs such as phone and mail; and finally, as John was pioneering the territory for us, a delightful opportunity to print out sheet music as well as being able to download free tunes. Amazingly we could use the internet to fill up a CD full of many hours of wonderful songs provided by other people through their own data banks. So with such a motivation our excitement brought us back full circle to the days of cruising flea markets for used records as being now able to download rare Pink Floyd, Hendrix, Zeppelin, Grateful Dead and so much more.

Besides memories and pictures from a nice trip, it's always nice to actually bring out a material memento which you can actually touch and hopefully find use for. Alas, our recent trip to Southeast Asia had not much to show for it as our two big boxes of gifts that we had mailed ourselves from Bangkok had yet to show up even seven months later. Trying to save a few dollars in shipping fees, we had chosen the slower boat route of shipping and thus not realizing the heartaches that we had in store as part of the bargain. Just as pirates of other times would hide their loot in caves, the modern day equivalent is an evasive bureaucracy where both the sending post office and the receiving one can claim each other is responsible for finding the boxes. The Xirokambi post office was especially lax in showing any concern, so it was comical when we told them that we had talked to their superiors in Athens who expected them to fill out certain tracer papers as soon as possible. Immediately their attitude turned for a combination of fear and shock. Being able to thrive in Xirokambi through their incompetence, they were genuinely concerned in not knowing what papers to fill out. So with token satisfaction we instructed them to contact their supervisors in Athens who were waiting for the documents. All in all it was becoming less hopeful of recovering our treasures, but we could at least find satisfaction that for the moment in actually seeing our local post office actually acting as if they did care for once. Eventually, about a year later, all the boxes made it to Xirokambi intact. A feat matching the precious cargo that Marco Polo had brought from the Orient as well.

CIRCUS

Besides the occasional weddings and frequent funerals, soccer games and church feast days, the biggest entertainment event in the rural villages of Greece was when the circus would come to town. Thus when the word spread that the Romanian traveling circus was going to be in Xirokambi, a high pitch of excitement echoed through the usual stale air of the neighborhood. Even more interesting was that it would take place in the large field behind our house.

Watching the crowds lined up to buy tickets to see an old dancing bear, a middle aged tightrope walker who was supposed to look sexy but could barely keep her pads of makeup from rolling down her face, and a muscleman that could smash wooden blocks with his swift karate punches were not exactly appealing to our family tastes. But as the big circus tent was only a few minutes stroll past our front door, we took my mother out to enjoy what all her other neighbors were so amazed and animated in witnessing.

Even in drinking a strong shot of Greek coffee right before we left, the boring and ludicrous performances were hard to stay awake through. Yet as my mom and her friends were laughing in joy, we stayed through the end and went home eager to watch a DVD so as to not feel the night a total waste.

The next morning as the tent was going down and the circus caravan was about to be heading to bring cherished memories to other villages further down the road, we noticed that the muscleman who had thrilled the crowds the night before was making his way over to our house for a chat. While he was drinking the glass of water, coffee and cookies that we offered him, he explained with tears in his humble persona that his family was in dire need of financial assistance. His circus act was not able in itself to match their needs and he was trying to find a way to sell one of his kidneys as an option to send them more money. Wanting to at least help in any way we could, I promised to make calls to the Sparta hospital that might have directed him to where he could go. We also gave him a $100 donation to which he was so elated by our generosity that he promised to send it back one day and that we would be honored guests in his house if we ever came to Romania. Not that I would be upset in knowing that we should never expect for a return of the money, but I was quite depressed in that none of my calls to medical agents offered any contact help for the muscle man being able to sell his kidneys to. So even though the circus act was a shallow event, the real life dramas were a much deeper story.

SAM

Besides the gypsies, many African men from Nigeria would go from town to town selling a variety of household items and pop music CDs door to door. For the most part, they were a very friendly and unimposing group that smiled a lot and even spoke excellent Greek. One such man was Sam who was soon on first name basis with us. On one particular day Sam invited John and me to come to Athens some time and partake in one of the Sunday morning worship celebrations that he explained were very festive and special. So as John and I were planning to be going to Athens anyway in the near future to attend a John McLaughlin jazz concert we made sure to accept Sam's invitation.

The day we arrived in the big city, we gave Sam a call and followed the directions to his apartment. His wife and he were very hospitable and prepared a delicious traditional African vegetarian meal that included spicy chickpeas, aromatic rice and cracker bread. After having to deal with the typical Greek village racism, he was eager to express his appreciation for our fellowship. Likewise, we showed up to the central Athens address with joyful anticipation where he told us to join him in worship, song and a meal. But as we walked through the door to the meeting room, the image we had painted in assuming a room of black people singing tribal songs and feasting on black beans and other homemade dishes was quickly discarded. Instead of an African ceremony, the setting was a fundamentalist Christian missionary service conducted by two very white bow-tied Americans straight out of Kansas. The songs were all about the greatness of Jesus and the meal was traditional, but not in an African sense. Just like in many other tasteless Christian Sunday churches, the back table was set with white donuts and instant coffee.

After enough verbiage was splattered by the preacher of how everyone on the planet that is not a Christian is evil and on the way to burn in the fires of hell, John and I looked at each other and came up with some lame excuse to evacuate the drama and go buy a falafel at the nearby Iranian fast and tasty soul food restaurant around the corner. Our bummer was resolved but we still felt confused on what to say to Sam the next time we would see him in the village. It would have been liberating if we could have honestly explained to him that it would be better for his friends to have burned the missionaries and stayed with their own cultural roots. Both the songs and the food would have been much better as well.

DIFFERENT WATER

While sitting at an outdoor cafe near the main harbor on the island of Zakinthos one morning a few months later eating our spinach pies, John and I were approached by another strolling Nigerian CD vendor. With a routine presentation of his array of disposable

Greek pop musicians featuring big boobed women nightclub singers and well groomed manly counterparts, he slowly started walking away after our obvious lack of interest. But as he heard me say
that why sell such garbage instead of real music such as the African
drummer extraordinaire King Sunny Ade, he came rushing back
with a wide smile and excited eyes at the shock of someone even
knowing who such a beloved cultural icon of his country was. "You
know King Sunny Ade music?" his awed voice asked again. And as
I asserted the name of several of the King's CDs that I was fond of,
we immediately made a new friend from Africa. Agreeing that the
music he was selling was indeed garbage to feed the masses (and
his family), he went on to not only discuss music but to also invite
John and me to come to his village in Nigeria as his guests and be
shown wonderful hospitality. If for nothing else but to drink the
much better water that flowed in his regional springs which made
one healthier than the Greek water which he claimed was turning
him pale. Even though we didn't feel we could make such a trip,
the water he mentioned sounded like a true elixir worth pursuing
some day. Also it was a relief to see that not all Nigerian vendors had
their cultural heritage stolen by Protestant missionaries. Perhaps
our other Nigerian friend Sam needed to drink more of his village
water as well before turning totally white.

THASOS

Besides the very important goal of the children being able
to socialize with friends and activities again, the emerald green island of Thasos on the northeast corner of Greece a few hours past
Thessaloniki, provided a quiet setting for Stephanie and I to be
by ourselves for a month. In the several years we lived in Greece,
we would be coming here for three summer camp sessions which
gave our kids a chance to have fun without us around. After going
through our pre-camp ritual of evaluating our needs and setting,
we dropped off the youngsters and quickly set up our special camp
spot on the bottom of a windy road beneath an old Byzantine monastery whereupon we organized our intentions of simple activities with
simple provisions.

One particular day we were surprised by an Italian convoy of
motor homes that were following each other past our site. Over a

dozen of these automotive behemoths finally showed up and parked in a circle which created their own private courtyard within a "wagon train" configuration. In the weeks ahead we would see more fleets of Italians moving in around us. Possibly the Greek waters are cleaner and more scenic for their holidays, but also another factor would be the as yet free camping and cheaper prices for food on this side of the Mediterranean.

Besides having plenty of time to catch up on reading, yoga, beach tennis and swimming, we prided ourselves on not having to keep driving to other places for supplies. About twice a week we would make an internet and supply run to the nearby town of Potos to fill our inventory needs for under ten dollars. Not buying cheese helped extend our budget, but we couldn't resist splurging each time in purchasing a few boxes of "chocolate digestive cookies". We could always fill up fresh water at the monastery or take a small hike to the spring on the other side of the cove. With no one to bother us for days at a time, we relished this well appreciated opportunity to be happy lovers in Paradise on what we nicknamed a "15 million karat beach".

With no major rush to do so, whenever we felt motivated, we did make several excursions to places familiar from each previous visit as well as exploring new areas on the island. A very appealing such new place was located about halfway to the village of Panagia from our end of the highway. A picture perfect looking cove with calm waters, shady trees and only one other car seemingly camped in the area. On closer look, we recognized the vehicle as belonging to the Rainbow folks who had previously stayed in a tent near us below the monastery. So with one more reason to add a new possible camping option to our travel map, we proceeded to drive down the dirt road which turned out to be a major mistake. From the highway it looked like a smooth dirt road for any car, however on the way down we realized that key parts of the road had washed out and even in four wheel mode, the drive was quite nerve racking. Eventually we made it to the beach, enjoyed the swim, but then faced with uncertainty our return drive to the top. To make matters worse, we tried helping another car to similarly drive to the top of the road, but they suffered certain damage to their clutch in dealing with the boulders and crevices along the way. When it was our turn to try leaving on this road, knowing that Stephanie is a lot calmer in these situations, I stood back with my eyes closed as she patiently handled the rocking motion of the van all the way up, and pulled us out of another fine mess we had gotten ourselves into. A mystery we will never know is how the Rainbows were able to drive their much smaller car down and even weirder, how they got it back out afterwards.

One of our familiar camping spots from earlier visits was the pine tree somewhat secluded parking area near the port town and beach side disco. Except for the mosquitoes and the potential fear of being bothered by psychos, it provided a nice camping alternative; especially when needed to stay close to Thasos town. One particular afternoon, a steady flow of traffic filled the landscape with unrelated groups of Greeks looking for a place to have an afternoon siesta. It was ideal under the shade of the tall trees and facing the sea breeze. All around us, by mid afternoon the vista was full of snoozing and snoring folks enjoying a break from the summer heat. Thus I had to be self conscious about peeing anywhere in a campground as well.

Another familiar camping spot for us in this part of the island was the nice beach stretch at Pahis. Unable to find our Dutch friends Ab and Ricky earlier in the year, we were quickly absorbed into an alternative Greek village community of trailers. Especially since both the driftwood carver and another guy with the ex-Dutch wife recognized us from before, we were thus inflicted with their overbearing hospitality. Not the sort of peace and quiet I was looking for to support intimacy with my wife. At times I felt we could sneak away, and at least go swimming at the far end of the beach. But it was soon evident that we were not good role players by not remaining around our neighbors the whole week. Such being the case, we decided to craft our escape from this new problem. Wanting to give Ab and Ricky at least one more day to perhaps show up, before leaving we sneaked past our camping spot to the nearby taverna where loud musical entertainment blared across the valley for "Greek Night." We were able to capture on video lots of drunk Greeks and even drunker blond and sunburned tourists dancing and drinking to various versions of the theme song to the "Zorba the Greek" movie. The festivities though did encourage us to pursue our own happiness, so we went back and planned an early morning escape out of this zone and back to the camping area on the other side of the island where we had been happily by ourselves a few days earlier.

Besides the joy of peaceful hanging out together, Stephanie and I would occasionally be treated to our own circus atmosphere entertainment when the goat herd would drop by on their regular walk to their grazing grounds next to the sea. The most fun would be when they would climb on top of the parked cars to reach the olive branches thus setting off the car security alarms which caused the car owners to come running from the beach to chase away the animals. Most of the time they wouldn't even be aware of the problem until they reached the parking lot to leave and then finding parts of their vehicles bent in by the goats' hoofs. One particularly pissed off guy started throwing rocks at the goats and getting even more hysterical as his girlfriend started laughing at the silliness of the situation. It would have made a hilarious scene on film. Trying to mediate, I went over and talked to him awhile suggesting that he sue the goat herder for damages. If he couldn't locate him, perhaps he could take one of the goats with him as payment. This comment of mine drew a chuckle and thus calmed him down a bit and probably kept him from yelling later at his girlfriend. For the most part though, whenever car owners would see the goats' activities they would be more often inclined to take pictures of the goats climbing on top of their cars instead of throwing rocks at them.

Another funny occurrence at our camp was observing the different reactions of people as they came down the winding road to the beach. The motor home crowd was delighted because of the long stretch of free camping awaiting them. Folks like us looking for peace and quiet were equally pleased. But for most people it was a different story. The most typical situation would be when a Greek family packed in a small rental car would pull up into the parking lot with their kids eager to blow up beach balls, boats and other such equipment. Then the men or teenagers would do a ritual parade around the area with their cellular phones looking for a good connection signal. The women would be reluctant to follow, but would encourage their children to take a quick run to the beach. By then the adults would come up with reasons as to why it was better for the kids to go to another beach while ignoring their children's pleas to stay. In other words, the adults were trying to use their kids as excuse because they themselves were not interested so much in experiencing a fine family beach day as they were in being at a very developed crowded beach where they can gab on their cellular phones, drink beers and frappes from the taverna and stare at each other. For them not having a beach front taverna with phone reception was terrifying. All in all it worked out great for us to have seen more of these loudmouths leaving instead of crowding "our beach." One example which pretty much said it all was when one such typical family that took a pause as they were leaving to ask me if I knew of any "real beaches" nearby. How glad I was to point further down the road. Way further.

One of our more lively experiences was when attending the August 15th, Panagere Festival in the small village up the hill, where we often would go to fill our water from the cold springs next to the church. This year the water flow was considerably less and in overhearing some of the conversations, was becoming a concern. Having arrived towards the end of the church service, we still had time to position between the street merchants and the people starting to stand in line for the traditional feeding. After the priest's blessing, the food servers would fill everyone's bowl with beef stew, potatoes and rice. Not sure which side of the table to line up, there eventually became two separate lines developing their own dogmatic justification as to which group was correct. And to make matters even worse, both of the food servers insisted that people from each of the ends line up in their own serving corners. The long awaited appearance of the priest to the dining area wasn't much of a help to the confusion, as he advised the people to line up on one side after a few minutes earlier, they had been led to the other by the head cook. More chaos developed when the second cook walked off in protest while the priest sneaked out of this fracas with a large bowl of food to eat elsewhere. Soon afterwards, one of the old ladies tried to land a punch on another lady who told her she was in the wrong line and had to move. By now, the church festival seemed like a riot as the pushes led to more pushes, I decided to take the honorable path of leading us all out of the free kitchen to a more pleasant picnic setting down the road.

Of course, the main reason for going to Thasos was the time alone that Stephanie and I would enjoy and the lovely opportunity for the children to socialize again at Euro camp. It was a bittersweet pause when as soon as we arrived on the opening day, how quickly our kids tuned us out and wanted to get rid of us like we were dirty laundry. This attitude would reappear again over the next few weeks whenever we would call or drop by to visit. Although it took us a few moments longer to accept, Stephanie and I were just as excited about our new freedom away from our family restrictions. An important step for all of us. Sophia was able to create her own bonding relationships for the first time independent of older siblings. Nicolette cultivated some more depth than in previous friendships as well. But the most independent, as predicted, was John aka "Havana Club" as well as "Maui". This year, as part of a deal which gave us a discount on enrollment fees, John was a youth counselor and had to sleep in a cabin along with the ten boys he was responsible for. The first day must have been the roughest, as I kept hearing reports of his room having to "cover up" damage to broken doors and lamps. Obviously, the luck of the draw was such that John was stuck with some of the "bad boys". Eventually though, he received commendation from the director Pitsa, as well as a following of fans that enjoyed the music he played through all hours of the night entertaining the camp.

At the camp festival, of course, Sophia and Nicolette performed excellent dances whose choreography was a joy to watch and record on our video camera. The real performance though was after hours when the parents left and the kids kept partying. From our camp spot in the parking lot, we were able to catch a great view of "Maui John" dancing his Tom Jones style disco steps while a variety of girls followed him around the stage. Of course the next day when we asked him about it, he calmly wrote it off as it must have been his "other self" we were looking at.

Whatever the "self", on camp's closing day, our departure was delayed quite awhile by John "Maui" signing autographs, getting hugs and kisses, as well as writing down orders from his groupies for cassette tapes he promised to make them of his songs. Besides impressing the little girls, it was a nice surprise when the camp director Marienela gave us a nice discount in consideration of John's talents and his helping hands and guitar fingers at camp. And, as in every year, we held on to the sentiment that we'll be back again to Thasos and Euro camp.

A few days before the camp session ended, Stephanie and I situated ourselves in a forest setting not far from where the kid's camp was. Having checked out this place beforehand, we felt it to be just right for us to have an Ecstasy experience, so as to embrace each other and be likewise embraced by nature. Just as the love drug was having its effect, a couple of cars pulled up releasing a loud bunch of fat kids and even fatter parents with a generator and plans to have an afternoon party. Feeling as if we were in danger of having our heart and soul exposed to predators, we clutched each other for several hours moaning in pulses of ecstasy while still having access to adrenalin that might be necessary in case of an emergency need to interact with other people or even leave this site. As the evening approached, the family took notice of our vehicle and sent over one of their kids to investigate. Right behind them came the mother and some other nosey lady to invite us to come share remnants of meat and wine with them. With a sudden burst of inspiration I explained that we would otherwise do so, but the night before we had eaten at one of the restaurants in town and were now suffering from food poisoning. They offered to take us for medical help but we explained that we were actually recovering and just needed a quiet rest. When they then asked us what the name of the restaurant was, we remembered a fast food place that had previously refused to make us a vegetarian gyro and told them that was where we had eaten. I suppose in a funny sort of way, karma could well have brought notice to the rudeness of that restaurant for not serving us what we asked for. We made sure to express gratitude to the family for offering us food and medical help and after they left we were relieved to once again be in a magical space for enjoying the fascinating night.

Our final stop before leaving Thasos was in visiting our friend Kosta and his family up in the village of Maries. As the year before, we feasted on ample amounts of fine food and wine (which they gave us several bottles of the acquired taste home brew to take with us). The father in law was no longer in the picture, but his wife was there and explained her being involved in some eclectic life extension regiment beyond Silva mind expansion. Before leaving, John was able to join with Kosta on some loose blues/Greek fusion jam.

The evening after departing the island we camped on the Nestos River on the edge of a wildlife preserve. The quietness was enchanting even though we had a fear of either getting busted in the middle of the night by police for trespassing or robbed by Albanians whose border we were very close to. As it turned out, we had a very pleasant rest listening to bird calls and walking through an ancient forest. Next to the marshland we tiptoed up an observation tower to enjoy the scenery and watch the long necked birds arching across the skyline. The stars were plentiful that night in the crisp air and our restful sleep.

Further north we explored the wide and verdant mountain valleys along the Bulgarian border. We were still in Greece, yet we noticed noticeable differences in architecture and language pronunciation. Along the way we stopped at a fairly large supermarket whose parking area was full of cars with Bulgarian license plates. The mystery of why they were there was soon unveiled as we were pleasantly surprised when we went inside the store and saw how low the food prices were. Because of the many people crossing the border to shop in Greece, most of the villages in this area must have worked out access to these highly discounted items. We too quickly filled several bags full of goodies and discussed plans to someday take a long field trip to go shopping here again with the other aliens and refugees in this village now on our map, Siderokastro. And if we want to make it an even longer stay, prices in the cafes and tavernas were significantly lower too. As with this area of northern Greece in general, we felt a more "big sky" feeling -wider terrain landscapes and less people. Lots more greenery, rivers and cooler temperatures. The city of Drama was especially picturesque with a lush park with many spring fed pools in the middle of town.

On the way back, as the hour was getting late, we pulled off on a dirt road near Kilkis to camp for the night. Our restful sleep was shaken early the next morning by a herd of cows that came to drink from the nearby water trough. Leading the pack were two growling dogs which I feared would take a bite out of John who was sleeping behind the trees in his tent. We soon made friends with the herder, Paulos, whom we had a nice conversation with and was very delighted that we made him a cup of coffee; his first ever in the pasture. He invited us to come visit him on the next trip in his village of Kato Potamia.

Later in the day we had the good fortune of pulling into Kilkis; a fairly large and busy town with a rather long pedestrian strip of cafes and tavernas. With a backlog of internet activity necessary for us to catch up with, we found our way to a bar where for the price of a drink we could stay there all day free if need be on the internet. And even better, the computers were quite a bit faster than the ones in Sparta we had been used to.

For this, and every other excursion, to work out smoothly, it was necessary that at least three times a week, we called my mother to find out how she was feeling. By carrying a cellular phone with us, we were even more comfortable in knowing that Nitsa could give us a call whenever there was any need to do so. Yet, irregardless of from where or when we called, it was pretty much the same reaction. As quickly as she realized that it was us calling, my mother switched from a pleasant greeting voice to one of harshness and insult. Always the same line that she was "dying", "we don't care", and that we "dumped her." Occasionally Nitsa was drawn into the script by picking up the phone before her and then following my mother's instructions to never say that they were well but always to repeat that they were both "sick and dying". A few times the ridiculousness reached silly proportions as Nitsa would reply to my: "How is everybody", question with: "We're all sick here; real, real sick." Knowing the trick, I would ask her back: "Are you telling me the truth?", to which she would emphatically answer: "No, no." So finding out that they were just "sick and dying" translated to "well and happy", we would hang up relaxed till the next call and knowing equally well that my mom would be feeling even better in making sure we believed she was terribly sick.

THE RAVE

Samothrace is one of the most enchanting islands in Greece. Located in the far northwest corner of the Aegean, it is buffered from ruin by not too many tourist developments and is blessed with a wealth of natural beauty including thermal springs, fresh water springs, and waterfalls. It also is the hub of a very ancient culture of the Cabirian mystery worship that even preceded the Olympian gods and goddesses of ancient Greece. The local people are very hospitable and show a calmness and seem very much at peace with their environment. Bridging into contemporary times, the island was hosting a major international rave party which would be bringing over 3000 mostly young kids from other parts of Europe for a long weekend festival.

Not as interested in attending this event but still wanting to visit the island since we were traveling in the area anyway, we made plans to take the ferry boat from nearby Thessaloniki and find a place to camp. John was not with us at the time and would be coming with a ferry to join us on the day after. With the exaggerated concern of "drugs" being brought by foreigners, the Greek police was fully present at the docks upon arrival, complete with buses to fill with apprehended criminals and a fleet of dogs to smell the baggage. Except for a few elderly folks that definitely looked as if they had never smoked pot, just about every passenger getting off the boat was escorted a few yards down from the ramp where neurotic dogs and stiff faced police stood eager to bust as many "druggies" as possible. Obviously, their anticipation was to make headlines as having been the cops responsible for the biggest drug bust in Greek history and the TV news cameras were all set to capture it all in live "breaking news" fashion.

Having the same scenario in mind, we did not have any traces of suspicious matter in our possession and in fact, I was a little disappointed how Stephanie, Nicolette, Sophia and myself were not checked like most of the other hippies, kids and foreigners. Perhaps we were profiled as some sort of model family instead or else the Cabirian mysteries had effectively cloaked our identities.

Once past the police barricades, while the rest of the family went to find some cheap food to eat and a map of the island to locate the best places for us to camp, I called John to warn him of the police presence and to please not bring any contraband to the island as it would be a major nightmare for all of us. Message delivered and understood, we went on to take our stroll across the town square and enjoy the symphonic sounds of the Greek band that still greeted all passengers disembarking from the ferry boats.

After waking up to a beautiful vista of proud mountains and enticing forest scenery, we had a swim and went back to the port town to meet John. As on the day before, the authorities were doing their best to arrest people and were relentless in their persistent searching. We waved at John who beamed a smile while we also worried that perhaps there might be a remnant of some forgotten pleasure particle that would be found in his possession. But as both the dogs and cops couldn't find any problem in his backpack, we didn't have to hold our breath for too long as we embraced and set out for our island explorations. As we were walking to the car I thanked John for following our advice and not bringing any troublesome substance with him to which he laughed and verified that he hadn't. But in the same breath he explained that he had hidden his goodies in one of our backpacks since we would surely be calm enough in not expecting to be investigated. At a loss for what to say that wouldn't draw attention in my screaming every terrible insult I could at him, Stephanie and I were even more thankful that our arrival had indeed not been a nightmare of major proportions.

For the next few days we enjoyed many of the beautiful aspects that the island had to offer. We did cruise the rave party but being a scene that didn't interest any of us except for buying a t-shirt, we had our own full moon party near the hot springs with the right sort of music and backpack treats. We enjoyed a blissful meditation in looking at the beautiful full moon just like the island residents had surely done for many centuries.

Our final camping site on the island was a nice beach off the beaten path which we shared with only a few other people including an interesting Swiss family also staying in a van. Just like us they were traveling with their children and enjoyed living part of the year here in Samothrace and the rest of the time driving back to southern Morocco which had been their home base for many years.

Before departing the island we went back to an undeveloped thermal hot spring pool just a short hike from one of the mountain towns. Our anticipation of a relaxing soak was interrupted by an irate old man who showed up with his intimidating cane to tell us that this pool was only for foot soaking and not for the rest of the body. He gave some quasi medical reason about how the mineral composition of the water was such that could result in our getting sick. If he was honest he would have told us that he wanted us out so he can have the whole pool to himself and possibly his whole body.

XIROKAMBI REVISITED

By now, coming back to Xirokambi was never a pause but a motivated reason to get our loose ends finished before our next great exodus. With our handyman Minas still injured and never any progress in endearing relationship with my mother, we continued the never ending schoolwork story, visits to the internet, garden work and repacking. The chicken coup which lay blocking the entrance to the rear of the house, was finally finished so we carried it over to the orange grove. The chickens had an automatic homing instinct and jumped right in looking proud and proper to be sitting in their new roomy lodge. Nitsa instructed our final touches of closing off openings to predators so thus one less hassle to worry about.

In order to avoid entangling interactions with neighbors, one of my irritating yet sole solutions was to hide. One of the few exceptions that I did peek out to talk to was Petros Konides, the artist whom the rest of the village perceives as an oddball. From past conversations of his telling me that he astral projects regularly, I felt that it would be helpful for him to smoke the salvia I was saving for my further inner explorations and insights. Since his return from Athens, he was taking care of about thirty stray dogs that he had staying inside his mother's house which meant lots of barking and confrontation with neighbors and other family members. After my explaining to him that the heavy impact of the salvia transporting him to another dimension, perhaps to a portal where souls reincarnate, Petros was thrilled for the opportunity which might give him the "extra strength" to carry on. I gave him careful instructions and asked him to report back to me of his experiences within a day. Nervously I waited to hear back from him as I was worried that I might have been a cause of his cutting loose altogether over the deep end. On the third day, seeing him with head shaved, I feared asking him of his report. However, as it turned out, his reaction to the experience was of minimal relevance to him. He did seem to have experienced the swirling fractals of deeper reality, yet they were not of the ego consuming terror that had so disturbed me on my Amsterdam trip. Anyway, different strokes for different folks.

RETURN TO LEFKADA

Loose ends wrapped and anticipation high, we once more set out for a project on Lefkada. Although the scenery would be the same, our anxiety was twirling with how my brother-in-law Byron and his wife Danielle would perceive both the island as well as our land there. It was a major expense for us to go back so soon, yet with hopes of their building a rental unit on our property, the costs were incurred as part of the investment needs. It didn't take long for the pressure to be relieved once we saw their delighted faces at the plush Aliki Hotel where we had reserved them a nice ocean front room. Yes, the Lefkada charm had worked its magic on Byron and Danielle. Not only did they enjoy the scenery but also they were marveled by how wonderful every meal they ate tasted and thus agreeing with our philosophy that delicious and healthy food is important in any place you live at. They found our land to be beautiful and the village of Katouna great. Yet as hard as I tried, I could not find a simple solution to our problem with the forest service restrictions of building on it.

As expected, any resolution of being allowed to build on our property remains elusive. The forest service now claims it has become state property because we allowed it to get overrun with wild shrubs. Our attorney Nikos recommended patience in waiting for a law to pass which would okay our plans. With Byron wanting a quick building permit, I entered the arena of having to pursue any and all options. Suggestions ranged from fiery independence such as "Nick the Greek from Denmark" who both insisted that we "fuck em all-it's your land; go ahead and build your home on it" to bribing the forest director through "the godfather", to slowly clear the land out ourselves, etc.. In any case, nothing was really accomplished except for Byron getting tired of waiting and thus buying his own house in the village.

Of course the character of Greek island villages changes depending on each season as we sensed in observing that Katouna had a very different ambience than our previous visits. Instead of the morbid persona of winter, it had a delightful charm of happy faces, children playing in the small square and folks eating nice looking food in the taverna. One weekend even a busload of red faced tourists was brought up by a tourist agency for "Greek night"; goat on a spit and colorfully dressed Greek dancers. Besides the popular Takis Taverna, we found it enjoyable to eat a couple of times at our new friends place next door. George, who owned the taverna along with his wife Froso, besides building artfully crafted homes in town, cooked delicious, healthy and unique goodies with a musical background of blues and rock. In fact, when I saw Tim Buckley in his collection, we made instant friends with each other and shared some of our personal favorite cassette tapes with them. We visited their very cozy house a couple of times and had a great time eating and discussing politics. John performed a three hour guitar concert of 60's message music while afterwards we were glad to take a cutting from their psychotropic San Pedro cactus with us. We felt that our friendship would grow in the future when we hopefully would be more settled in the village and that George might also be someone that would build our home here for us someday. His own vision was to design and erect a village "cultural center" where live music, food and good company will come together.

Between all the overwhelming frustration over the land issue, Byron and Danielle did enjoy relaxing by the pool and bars. On one occasion Byron came running to the hotel with his face swollen like a balloon from a bee sting. While drinking a beer down the road, the insect leaped out of his glass and stung him. We raced to the hospital with Danielle to the emergency room where I insisted that the hospital staff find him a doctor as soon as possible. With him reclining on the table while I was translating the nurses instruction for him to be patient and that a doctor was on the way. Danielle came running into the room with a huge syringe in her hand and with her thickly French accented loud voice yelled, "Let's go!" Needless to say, the confused medical staff stood speechless with mouths open as the three of us ran out of the hospital and into the car. Thereupon, Danielle pulled down Byron's pants and with his confused pleads: "Danielle do you know what you're doing and have you ever done this before?" Danielle answered: "Of course, I am a doctor", and proceeded to give Byron a long shot up his ass. Even with his concern about spouse incurred medical malpractice, the swelling eventually settled down soon enough, and he was able to bounce back to the fast lane.

One of our favorite spots in the world is Galo Beach on the west side of Lefkada near Porto Katsiki where we once more camped under a full moon. Very few other cars camped in the parking lot, as the high cliff behind us shielded the sun in the morning with a fresh air wind blowing across the beautiful ocean. Besides the two cantinas which serviced our needs, this year a full on taverna had opened over the hill with flushing toilets, chilled beer glasses and reggae music playing. Our stay was a nice rest break to our otherwise hectic activity with our land issue. More fun was our ingenuity in developing a golf game with the girls using rocks, sticks and other markings.

XIROKAMBI PAUSE

Our never ending journeys brought us back again to Xirokambi for a momentary pause, a chance to do laundry, check mail and argue with my mother. Before departing off again, a busy weekend of activity ensued for all the children. Along with a couple of thousand other hikers, John finally climbed the peak that he had been waiting a long time, Mount Olympus. No gods or goddesses were sighted, but I am sure there had to be a few sweet beauties in the multitude he was part of. Lots of panoramic pictures including a special one of the Sparta group on top of the mountains. What was especially important was that John was several hours ahead of most climbers even with carrying his friend's Kosta's backpack as extra weight.

More down to earth but still high enough in Kosmas, both of our daughters performed extremely well in a bicycle race with lots of contestants. With neither race quality bikes nor fancy racing outfits on, both Nicolette and Sophia did very well and came very close to finishing among the winners. For me, they were both winners, and I doubt if I will ever get them involved with the hyper competitive atmosphere of another such race again.

Back in the village, we quickly finished our loose ends including putting up a new wall between bedrooms, listening to Dimitri's Christian proselytizing and pushing Nicolette to finish some more schoolwork while preparing for going to Thasos camp for the month of August.

OLYMPICS

For me, one of the more interesting aspects of the 2004 Olympics was observing the opening ceremonies. The representatives of the many countries entered the stadium carrying their national flags and supposedly wearing ethnic outfits. However, these flashy outfits looked completely foreign to true representation of their country's society. The idea was to promote an elegance through the make believe world of Hollywood that would paint a pretty picture to the global audience as one more pacifier to actually sensing reality and the consequent suffering of people. Third World countries where most of the people are starving and dying from designer diseases caused by international economics, were represented at the Olympics by a well fed and dressed elite aristocracy whose plastic smiles didn't appear to be considerate of the plight of their less fortunate neighbors back home. During the social maturation of the 60's, athletes had no blinders from representing their countries social crisis. Cassius Clay (Mohamed Ali) similar to Marlon Brando's refusal of a Grammy award in Hollywood until Native American Rights were presented, threw away his Olympic gold medal for boxing because of U.S. war politics in Vietnam.

A more honest representation in the Olympics might be counting as to see which country's people are starving fastest. I'm sure as many records as individual tears would be broken. Perhaps another contest would be between whose air or water quality is sinking faster as well as number of cases of AIDS are found. In a world supposedly coming closer as a global entity, it is a sad shock to see how alienated people still are from reality.

JOHN AND I TRAVEL TO IKARIA

Of all the many Greek islands that we had traveled to, Ikaria was one of the more fascinating. Far from the mainland, one can see the outline of Asia Minor in its horizon. In fact, residents from the island often go there to the large open aired markets on weekends for deals on Persian rugs and Oriental embroidery. During the 1930's, Ikaria was where political and cultural "undesirables" were exiled to. When one arrives in its boat harbor, no trace is seen of the usual onslaught of vendors pushing rooms and services. There does not seem to be much concern over the almighty tourist dollar and perhaps even discouraged by many of the local people as a symbol of oppression. The island's representatives in Parliament are always members of the communist party and its craggy appearance upon arrival at the port feels like a warning to stay away.

Yet within that façade, there is also the invitation to be part of the freedom expressed by its proud people who are eager to open its scenic and natural treasures to anyone that comes to explore further behind the veils. Our family had a taste of the island's unique beauty and style when we had come here for a Rainbow Gathering, but now John and I wanted to take a journey of our own to experience even more. Still feeling the nauseating turbulence of the long 14 hour ferry boat ride from the mainland on our family's visit, we decided to take a plane ride of less than an hour instead. The government subsidized the flights to this island because of its remoteness, so the cost was just a little more than what a boat ticket would have been.

Arriving in the late afternoon was a lonely feeling. The airport was located about thirty miles from town and by the time we grabbed our backpacks, the ticket and information office had closed and there was no one around. Just a curious goat stared at us from a rocky hillside. Content to walk about a mile to a hot thermal spring area that we had seen on the map, we started our brisk walk in its direction. But about ten minutes past the airport, a car with an elderly couple pulled up and offered to take us out of their way to the town where our friends Kristos and Maria lived. A wonderful preview of the special hospitality that the island was waiting to share with us.

Having friends on the island was an excellent social resource for John and I so as to be able to branch out into more social networking and subsequent adventures, Kristos and Maria provided us a place to stay for a few nights and were able to take us on excursions to many otherwise unknown natural sites and villages off the beaten track.

The general tone of the islanders was one of pride, individualism and distrust of government and industrial development. Many of the stores never locked their doors so if a customer came in after hours, they could leave the correct amount for the purchase in an "honesty box." Another village didn't have any shops or services available during the daytime so that people could attend to their farming needs during that time period. From 10 pm to 6 in the morning, all the stores, restaurants and even the post office and bank opened for business. Many of the cafes that we visited had no electricity by choice and preferred to cook with wood and relied on kerosene lamps for lights. John and I saw a ginseng soda in a mini market refrigerator but when the owner could not find the item on his order list, he just told us to enjoy it and pay him back some day in the future.

Up in the hills above the town where we were staying was the farm of our hippie friends Dimitri and George, whom we had met on our first visit to the island. They had remodeled a very old stone home into a work of art and off grid simple elegance. And as they were both musicians with ongoing gigs, John and I moved our base to hang out in their realm for our remaining days on the island. During this time we met many eclectic and interesting people including an assortment of aging political activists and even a hedonistic professor of existential philosophy, who when he wasn't teaching at a famous university in Germany was at home in Ikaria engaged in debauchery and orgies.

At one point several years beforehand, the electric company had wanted to put up poles so they could bring their services to someone who had requested it in the neighborhood. Determined to keep their neighborhood from being "contaminated" by modernization, several people went and cut all the poles down. A few months later, another work crew arrived from Athens to put up new poles. Along with them were two policemen dispatched from the nearby island of Samos who would not have any personal reason to not force the compliance of the project. This time around, not only did a large mob come from the village armed with pitchforks and axes to take down the poles, but they were being led by the local black robed white bearded priest to make sure the demons were removed. The cops were subsequently tied up, put in their police car which was then taken to the harbor and sent back on the next ferry boat to the island of Samos. Neither the electric company nor the policemen came back to enforce the installation of the grid in their neighborhood.

Kristos was a frequent visitor up to the farm but Maria was too concerned with what she considered lack of sanitation to want to come and risk getting dust on her newly washed clothes. One afternoon Dimitri, John and I went to their door to see if Kristos would like to join us for a musical night of jams and merriment. Maria answered the door and shouted that Kristos was asleep and quite protectively scolded us for not calling first before dropping by so unannounced. Not wanting to waste an opportunity to irritate her further, after she closed the front door, Dimitri pulled out his cellular phone and called their number to ask if we could come visit them. Confused and angry at our impertinence, Maria started her harangue at our immaturity but Dimitri artfully deflected her attention by pointing out some spots on her front porch that had not been removed in her morning house cleaning ritual. Right about then Kristos showed up from the other room ready to run off with us. Maria switched from arguing to asking if she could come along. Dimitri tried to persuade her not to do so by reminding her how dirty she found his house on her last visit. He then told her that there would be a black man there as well playing music. Fearful that she might have to interact with another race, she nervously asked "how black was he". With a straight face, his answer was that he was "very, very black". So black that you couldn't even see his face in the night. At this point, so worried about the black man, the dusty floor and her dirty porch, the poor lady decided to stay home and read a book while the rest of us went back to the farm for a wonderful evening under the stars. Perhaps the night was indeed so intense that we didn't even see a black man in the house. Instead we found lots of homemade bread, cheese, wine, some young hippies and lots of music playing through the night.

The rest of the week on Ikaria was also packed with never a dull moment. On the far end of the island in the village of Nas, we visited an ancient temple of Artimis situated at the base of a swift flowing stream as it met the sea. We walked up the trail leading from the site and found several nice pools to swim in not to mention several wonderful tasting fresh water springs. The trees along the way also provided shade from the hot sun as well as accenting the scenery with their beautiful lacey foliage.

On our return to the start of the trail we met a friendly man who was eager to start up a conversation on how he had expatriated from the US and was now pleased to be living on this very special island in the Aegean. He invited us to come with him to his comfortably furnished apartment with a view of the waterfalls as well as the sea, where after serving us some refreshments, he proceeded to play on his electric piano the first part of a symphony he had composed. In our conversation afterwards he confided in us that he was a retired CIA agent presently living incognito and in fear of his life. Stationed in Moscow for several years and fluent in Russian, he inadvertently learned more secrets than intended in his line of work. Thus he now was here in Ikaria hoping to remain off the radar.

After leaving his place we went to a nearby internet cafe to catch up on our emails. Just as we sat down to cyber surf, the owner of the cafe came over to tell us that since he saw us earlier with the American, we should be warned to stay away from him. Earlier that morning he had received a phone call from the local police saying that "certain higher authorities" had learned of our friend's location by identifying the IP address of the computer that he used regularly when he came to the cafe. Apparently he was under surveillance and his arrest imminent. Needless to say, we quickly left Nas and decided not to contact our new friend again, even if it meant not having the privilege to listen to his performing the second section of his symphony for us. Also we were relieved that he did not share any of the state secrets with us in his conversation.

It turned out that the next day we would once again have reason to be back to this same village. Our friend Dimitri was invited to play his festive violin rhythms for a wedding reception at the local taverna. Thus he encouraged us to join him and enjoy the bounty of food and merriment that would be provided. Not knowing any of the other people or even part of the band felt a little awkward for us at first. But we also realized we were on the special island of Ikaria so after a few rounds of wine were passed to us, we were feeling at home and part of the party. By three in the morning and the celebration was still in high gear, Dimitri took pity on our nodding out on the table, so he handed us his car keys to drive back to the farm while he kept on fiddling. He assured us not to worry about him as he would certainly find a ride by mid-morning when the party would start slowing down.

The stamina of these island folks could well be attributed to the local red wine which was explained to be from an original vine presented by the god of ecstatic intoxication, Dionysus over 2500 years ago. In honor of the gracious god (who now had a Christian Name day to keep in cool with the church authorities) once a year celebrated a feast day in his honor. Dimitri once again invited us to an epic event in which we were able to witness a traditional spiral dance which would last up to three days. The old timers even brought their sleeping mats to be able to keep on twirling like dervishes for as long as possible. Such movements and along with the sacred wine definitely felt like an altered state of consciousness had been reached by the several hundred local people that partook of the tribal alchemy.

Besides Dionysus, another famous legend of the island is the ancient story of Icarus, whose father invented him wings to fly through the sky. Our own travel wings were waiting at the airport to take us back to Athens, so even though with more to see on the island, it would have to wait for another future opportunity. But one loose end that we attended to was to go to the hot spring near the airport which we had originally planned to visit when we first arrived. Better late than never, we enjoyed a wonderful soak to refresh ourselves for journeys ahead.

Before leaving Ikaria, our exposure to the ways of the locals was well expressed with our outing to Socrates' Taverna. For several days Dimitri kept telling us of this mischievous proprietor whose mission it seemed to be in navigating people to states of dervishing bliss mixed with a slight dose of debauchery thrown in for fun. A true alchemist of the most interpersonal degree in the similar lineage of break on through artists such as Jim Morrison, the Native American coyote and the spiritual prankster Gurdjief. Right around sunset, we met Socrates in the town square where he was drinking coffee while discussing philosophy, politics and sexual liberation. When we asked him what time his place would be open, he simply smiled, passed us the keys to the restaurant while with the same motion continued making a point to his audience of comrades captivated by his precise juggling of facts and metaphors.

Following his cue, John and I joined Dimitri and a few other friends that were able to squeeze into his old rusty Chevrolet V8 cruiser that noisily zipped us to the taverna where we all took part in chopping up vegetables, frying potatoes and preparing appetizers. By the time the food started appearing on the long tables, the stereo was pumping out clarinet music and Socrates stash of homemade wine was filling our souls like thirsty sponges. Right around 11 pm Socrates showed up to what was by now quite a celebratory scene. The party clicked into even higher gear as under one arm he carried a 5 liter bottle of wine and in the other hand he held a rooster by the neck. Without much of a pause, he snapped the rooster's neck which was the main ingredient of the soup along with special herbs and spices which he claimed would fortify everyone in being able to add energy to their intoxication through the night ahead. John and I held up until about 3 am of eating, drinking and being part of the dance and musical jams until we realized we did not have the same stamina as the other taverna residents who had by now been transformed from mere humans into roaring expressions of passion and revelry. Perhaps our having chosen not to partake of rooster juice might have been cause for our wimpiness. Dimitri was kind enough to give us the keys to his car so we could escape the insistence of Socrates that we stay and keep on partying. But as festive as the night was, John and I knew that we had a ferry boat to catch the next day which would be taking us out of this unique island in the sun. It was amazing to learn the next morning how this was typical behavior at the taverna at least three or four nights of the week. Grown men would usually be crawling on their knees out the door by the time the sun rose and then pouring several cups of thick Greek coffee down their throats to start their work day. A mentor to some, while to others with a more straight laced approach to life, Socrates was a madman. One of the few remaining Zorba archetypes still left in the country.

CHAPTER FOURTEEN: HAWAII ONCE AGAIN

COLLEGE TOUR

John and I next continued our journeys by leaving Greece to go to the US on a college tour. For over a year I had been doing extensive research on over 3000 colleges of higher learning in the US from which to narrow down our top five for consideration of his enrollment. The criteria included the desire for a liberal and progressive curriculum, scenic setting and affordability. The final category being dictated by which school would provide enough of a scholarship that would reduce the amount we had to pay to a minimum.

By the time March came, we were prepared and were soon on the plane to upstate New York where we would be greeted by our friend Dave who was excited to see us and then drive us into Vermont for our first school visit. After about an hour of his not showing up at the airport we were a little concerned, but there through the sheets of falling snow, Dave pulled up with his old clunker and a big welcoming smile and even bigger hospitality joint for the ride back to his house in the working class neighborhood that he had grown up in. At one time Gloversville used to be an affluent community that gained its reputation for manufacturing well made hand garments. Over time, cheaper gloves from third world sweat shop factories became mass marketed which then turned this region into a grey looking economic ghost town. The highlight of driving around town was taking a stroll through the local Wal-Mart to provide us with a homeopathic immunization dose of reentry into America and then lunch at a pizzeria run by a family of Greeks that Dave enjoyed our ethnic conversation with. That evening, besides reminiscing our days on Maui, we listened to a lot of rare Grateful Dead music while Dave made us tapes of more goodies to take on our travels. Early the next morning he satisfied my quest for eating breakfast at an authentic diner by taking us to one of which Gloversville still held on to as a slice of Americana's better days before globalization descended like a pestilence all over the country.

Driving through the snow in Dave's old station wagon was classic. The heater was broken and only one of his windshield wipers worked, but his stereo still sang and helped us enjoy the drive into Vermont and the first school we visited, Bennington. Besides the impressive campus performing arts center and attractive landscaping, Dave and I remarked on the higher ratio of pretty girls to guys and reflected on how John would find it beneficial as well. As with all the schools on our itinerary, we were treated to cafeteria passes that would help us analyze the important factor in comparing what meals would taste like. Bennington again scored high in this category as we filled our plates with lots of pasta and organic vegetables and wholesome desserts. Filled with energy to make it to the next stop on our tour, Dave surprised us with his discovery of one more level to the cafeteria. Around the corner from the food bar was an area where we could make our own sandwiches. So without further ado, we each made about three hefty sized sandwiches and out the door we flew with the icy breeze.

We parted ways with Dave at the office of Oak Meadow School, which was the home schooling base that our kids studied all those years and finally at least a couple of us would get to see. No free meals here even though we discovered a nice bakery downstairs from the school that we snacked at. But nevertheless it felt nice to actually witness where our tests were being sent to. The impending storm meant that public transportation schedules were being minimized that day, but one of the teachers was kind enough to drive us a few miles down the road to make sure we caught the bus taking us to our next college visit.

Luckily, once we got off the bus near the Marlborough campus, we were able to hustle our way to the main office before its early closing. Civil defense warnings were already preparing for a powerful snow storm necessitating the shutting down of the school for the next few days. But not to leave us "out in the cold", the school had booked us a room for a couple of nights in a very historic old hotel in town, as well as a couple of free meal coupons to a downtown restaurant. As the blizzard pounded the city, John and I went for a walk around the block where we saw a Greek flag on a post on top of a movie theater. We also heard Greek spoken at a couple of restaurants we peeked in at as well.

Strange for Greeks to be immigrating to cold climate locations but it did give us a feeling of familiarity. On our early morning walk, we were able to offer service to a lady who could not get out of her house because of the snow buildup. For our helping shovel her a way out, she rewarded us with two loaves of bread. Fair enough. This unexpected divergence on our trip gave us a nice two day pause before heading back into the New England back roads.

As this part of the country was used to Winter storms, the snow plows soon had the highways cleared and the buses back on regular schedules. A short stop at Goddard and then not far away to the smallest college on our tour, Sterling. Since only eighty students attending the school, our appearance was a planned expectation. On both the entrance to the school grounds as well as the cafeteria, we were startled to see colorful signs announcing "Welcome John and George." With so many people treating us with open hearted greetings, it was obvious that the students and teachers shared a tight community bond. The outdoor wilderness skills curriculum was appealing to John but the small student body and remote rural setting felt a bit claustrophobic and potential drama infused for living over the next four years.

NORTHERN LIGHTS AHEAD

Our New England link of our college tour finished, we met up again with Dave and then an overnight visit to our dear friends Thea and Frans in Massachusetts for a well appreciated family meal. The next morning Dave dropped us off at the train station for a long endurance ride of 27 hours for what would normally be an eight hour car drive. Not knowing any better, we had mistakenly picked the local route instead of the ten hour express from New York City to Charlotte, North Carolina. If any consolation, we saved a full eight dollars on ticket prices and got to be entertained in watching a lot of strange fellow passengers on board with us.

In order to get to the next part of our collegiate investigation, Alaska Pacific located in Anchorage Alaska, we had to take a plane from Charlotte to travel to another corner space on the US map. Besides the appreciated extra mileage points, Charlotte was a fun opportunity to visit our friends James and Pam who took us out for a very tasty authentic Mexican meal where the food was zesty and home made with hardly any English speaking customers or employees.

With most of the colleges that we were interested in being in far corners of our life's experiences, it was ironic that on our final search list was Warren Wilson, a small private school in the Appalachian mountains of my home state of North Carolina. James and Pam were happy for a reason to take us on a few hours' drive west to Asheville. During our own college years, James and I would share many exciting adventures in that region and was now eager for the reason to visit once more.

What we originally considered as an afterthought on our search list turned out to be quite a surprise find for all of us. Even James, who like me, was very much into the notion of higher education, had never heard of this place which would wind up being not only the school John would enroll at but also in the years to come, so would Nicolette and Sophia.

The setting where Warren Wilson lay was spectacular. Rolling hills in every direction with no fences or other boundaries to stop trails leading directly into the Blue Ridge mountains and their natural treasure chest bounty of forests, streams, waterfalls and wildflowers. The student population was 5000 with an excellent teacher to student ratio. The curriculum was very progressive with such courses as Goddess History and Counter Culture Literature. All the buildings appeared like cute mountain cabins and most of the students looked as if they were on their way to a Rainbow Gathering. The health center offered meditation, naturopathic and Reiki services and the bulletin board was full of announcements for drumming and other fun get-togethers and concerts. Even the school president looked cool sitting on a rocking chair on the front porch of the administration building playing his banjo. As to other criteria, all the usual options of athletic and dramatic instruction were available, as was a variety of vegetarian options in the cafeteria and in smaller on-campus cafes. James and I were impressed enough by all the cute young girls and wondered why we never considered applying for work as teachers in this fine academic, social and cultural milieu. But getting down to the basics, as John was essentially given as close to a full a scholarship as possible. Warren Wilson would eventually turn out to be our final choice. But with our tickets already purchased for our trip to Alaska, we were excited about a visit to another part of the world we had never been to before.

Expectations of a smooth voyage did have a momentary panic though in an even different part of the country. In order to buy the least expensive tickets for our trip, we had to split it into two separate arrangements. First we had to fly to Houston and then a couple of hours later to catch our flight to Anchorage. But as our flight leaving Charlotte was delayed, we made it to Texas with almost no time to grab our baggage and literally run at a fast pace between terminals in order to catch up with our other flight which was announcing its final call. By swift feet and agility in running around slow people in our way (even if it meant getting nasty looks from the elderly and others we almost bumped into in our adrenalin fueled haste), we just did make it as the doors on the ramp were being closed. No way did we want to be stuck in Texas any longer than need be. All of our cross country drives always felt the same as well.

The memory still remaining in our taste buds of the extra hot salsa sauce of our Mexican fiesta the day before in Charlotte was necessary for John and I to remember as we soon stepped out into the crystal clear sunlight and bone chilling cold of Alaska in April. As with all the other schools we visited, the students that were responsible for showing us around the campus, were very cheerful and helpful. With the liberal reputation of the state in regards to pot, they were even more happy to take us to a few of the hemp shops in town and even took John to a late night party to try their own home grown green plant matter.

The school had an extensive system of underground chambers connecting each of the buildings and dormitories with each other so that winter conditions would not compromise comfort and easy access. Being April, we experienced not only ice on the sidewalks but also a visit from a wandering wild moose that stuck its inquisitive head through our dorm room window. Even though we considered many positive reasons for John to enroll here, the remembrance of more pleasant weather zones in Hawaii and elsewhere convinced him not to make a hasty decision yet.

Alaska did gift us a variety of memorable experiences however. For the first time in our lives we were able to behold the northern lights close up. For nearly an hour we stood on the campus lawn entranced by the motion of the spiraling colors in the night sky. And as we stood in quiet humility and contemplation, we could feel a soft energy in the air and even the subtle hum of mysterious sonic frequencies.

The city of Anchorage also had its intrigue. Wide streets with ample parking available anywhere. The downtown buildings looked quite modern and there even was the ubiquitous Greek pizzeria where John was offered a job if he wanted. Catching a bus back to the campus, we were treated to another aspect of the local subcultures. Because of the lure of high paying jobs in the oil industry as well as Alaska providing a sizable subsidy check to anyone that was a permanent resident, many workers with their families had at one time flocked to the state to take advantage of these and other social benefits. However once the jobs became scarce, many of these folks found themselves out on their luck and now living in insulated cardboard shanty towns. Conversations on the bus included tales of people robbing each other's blankets and alcohol at knife point in the middle of the night. We also learned of how the city had a late night van patrol to drive by the bars where often drunk Eskimos would have passed out only to risk waking up to frostbitten body parts. Adding the witnessing of Russian operated strip clubs and mention of their mafia connections, John and I agreed on it being a nice place to visit but maybe its own version of the wild west ambience not so nice for our family to live at.

The college tour successfully concluded, the two of us flew straight to Hawaii where we joined Stephanie and the girls in sunny Kihei back at our single bedroom condo. Once again we enjoyed the beaches but still actively searched for an opportunity to leave the tourist zone. We didn't have to wait too much longer as Makunda was happy for our return to our camping zone as once before.

JUNGLE LIFE

Our friend Dave was inspired one day to help us expand our comfort zone by building a couple of simple bamboo huts which only cost us about $100 each in parts. The bamboo we needed was harvested on the land, the pallets that they were laid on came from supermarket trash areas and the frameworks from used PVC pipes found tossed out at the sugar plantations. To deal with the muddy mess left by the daily rain showers, we laid out a series of concrete blocks between our huts to walk on and on part of the trail to the waterfall as well as the parking lot.

Being always eager to watch videos, we purchased a nice television for $30 from the thrift store and hooked up our speakers for an even more enhanced cinematic effect. In fact, we soon developed a regular weekly event called "Jungle Theater" in which people in our area would come by to socialize, take a swim in the pools, share pot luck meals then enjoy my eclectic stoney movie choices, while satisfying the munchies with Nicolette's fabulous popcorn.

Enjoying the freedom and natural life style that we had remembered from our last camp on the land, we continued our improvements to make it a happy, comfortable setting. Along with the bamboo huts, we also had put up a large tent that served as an office and even had fast speed internet.

Living practically next to a nice waterfall was also like a fairy tale of a dream come true. Every day we would be soaking in the pools and living the jungle dream. Mondays were a work day as over the weekend, the local rednecks would be leaving lots of garbage from their disrespectful partying at the pools. Mostly dirty diapers and broken beer bottles that we had to carry away to the dump. My impression of modern Hawaiians taking care of the "aina" (environment) took a downward opinion after these experiences.

SCHOOL

Home schooling had been an integral and enjoyable bonding experience in our travels through the Pacific, but because of more opportunities for peer socializing and our being close enough to walk to the road side bus stop, Nicolette started attending Kalama Intermidiate School. It was an affirmation of nature's beauty to start each morning with the hike to the road, as was the walk back and a refreshing afternoon swim in the waterfall pools.

Sophia also started her very first day of school. However, when she did not get off the bus at the corner after school, we became very worried. We were very relieved when she was brought home afterwards by a different bus because she had mistakenly boarded the wrong one.

Enrolling our kids in public school would also be a good test of better evaluating their home school programs. In all cases, they were far more advanced academically as well as in integrating information for decision making and creative thinking. Nicolette earned student of the month awards for the Kalama School as well as when she had gone to school before in Kihei. For the short time she attended Kalama, the social conditions were so challenging, that parents were being encouraged to take part in monitoring the school grounds to bust kids for doing drugs or beating up each other. Even going to the bathroom was a challenge because of aggressive gang behavior and broken facilities. Such feedback further reinforced our decision to eventually switch back to our correspondence school programs. Socializing in most circumstances was not such an ideal. We had learned that it was better to be part of teaching our kids at home and finding them specific extracurricular social activities and clubs that would socialize them with other kids with similar interests.

Even from an early age, Sophia was showing an expansive talent in unique art styles that she would continue to develop throughout her childhood and later on in life. Eventually she would also write beautiful songs that her voice would do enchanting justice to. But before she learned to play guitar, she was taught how to play ukulele at school. In late spring before the school semester was over, Stephanie, Nicolette, and I went to a Haiku School recital because Sophia's music class would be performing a few songs. Although her solo sounded pleasing, it didn't seem to have the extra touch that we had heard when she practiced at home. After the show, with tears in her eye and a flushed face of anger, she explained how some other kid in her class had borrowed her ukulele before the performance and had left it out of tune. Eventually the boy got in trouble for causing mischief and in the years to come, Sophia would go on to showcase her own music and art that would bring pleasure to lots of people throughout the world.

Even though at that time we all were living happily and free, Nicolette was a bit embarrassed to tell her friends about our living situation. Especially since many of her classmates lived in fancy houses with new cars. Even when we would drive her to school, she did not want to be seen associated with our rusted out jeep. To avoid embarrassment, she would want us to park a few blocks away from the school and then she would walk the rest of the way. Thus it was a moment of apprehensive tension when a couple of her new friends wanted to come stay a weekend with her. We stocked up our ice chest with delicacies, cleaned out the tents and hoped for the best. But what a relief for all of us when her friends were amazed at the natural wonderland of where and how we lived. Likewise, Nicolette's friends were also relieved not to have to spend the weekend in another stuffy house or with stuffy parents like they were stuck with. But even with her new found pride of exposing her life style to friends, Nicolette still would not let us drive the cruiser anywhere near her school.

SOPHIA AND THE MOUSE

With no cars or roads near our campsite, no awkward sounds interrupted the patter of the rain drops, bird chirps and the waterfall. Our landlady's two peacocks were an occasional and unannounced nuisance when they would start making their not at all pleasant high pitched cackling sounds.

In the tall trees above us was a nest of wild chickens. Unlike any other fowl, they would actually fly from tree to tree and swoop down at times to grab assorted food fragments when our kitchen was unattended. They also would attack field mice and horribly devour them with their beaks even before our cat could respond fast enough to enter the hunt.

Walking back to our camp from our morning waterfall swim, we saw that the cat had caught a small mouse before the chickens had targeted it. Dangling from its mouth, the rodent was barely alive and was soon to be several splattered body parts. Within a couple of seconds, Sophia snatched the mouse out of her bewildered cat's mouth and gave it an even more confusing nasty yell for trying to eat it. She then took the feeble mouse which was already in shock and bleeding from the cat's nibbles, down to the banana patch where she laid it on a leaf and comforted it with her voice and sending healing intentions through the palms of her hands before laying it back under the tree. Later that day when we were again on our way to the waterfall, the mouse leaped out from the spot she had left it, and started dancing circles around Sophia. All of us were amazed at the miracle and power of love we just witnessed. One more verification to respect all life forms. I wonder if we would have the same feelings though, if it were a sharp toothed rat instead of this cute little field mouse?

BUSTED AT THRIFT STORE

One afternoon as I was coming out of the Wailuku Salvation Army thrift store, I noticed one of the employees dropping a bundle of what looked like nice t shirts into the trash container located next to the parking lot. Being curious I took a look inside and found some very nice Quicksilver surf t-shirts that were relatively new and just the right size to give to John. But just as I was about to snag them out of the garbage, the little old Japanese lady that worked the cash register came running out in panic. She threatened to call the police for my action to which I mumbled that Jesus didn't mind my sharing the garbage with the underprivileged. But as she mumbled some nonsense about the store having no insurance coverage if I had hurt myself and she had already started calling the cops, I had to toss my beautiful fresh catch of the day back into the trash can and leave before I was arrested. All day I kept reflecting on how would an organization that was supposedly helping the poor, would not even let them share their garbage.

An even more disquieting event happened to our friend David a few weeks later. While taking a walk through Rainbow Park near Makawao, he found a backpack that looked as if it had been unattended for a long time. He took a look inside it in search of any possible information of the owner and found a library book with a name that might be able to be tracked down. So being the good hearted citizen that he was, he took the backpack to the local police station and explained how he found it and perhaps they could locate the owner. But instead of any appreciation for his good Samaritan effort, the cops looked at his disheveled appearance and started questioning him with suspicion that he was guilty of stealing the backpack. Quite a ludicrous notion, as why would he turn in the backpack if he had stolen it. Such was another frustrating and alarming example of society gone truly insane.

WAR

Starting in mid August, the next six months would be very eventful for us. John left for North Carolina to attend his first year of college at Warren Wilson in Asheville. Not only did he wind up getting all the interesting classes he had wanted but also cool was his work assignment being to help organize musical events for the students.

On September 11, we received a call of urgency from our friend Basil shouting that we were at war. Not sure what he meant, we poked our heads out of the tent and could see no parachutes or missiles.

Since we did not watch television we were not aware that the Twin Towers in New York and the Pentagon in Washington DC were supposedly attacked by Muslim extremists. Without questioning any facts, mass media and most of the people in the country were certain that this handful of basically illiterate young men were able to hijack two high tech airlines and fly them over two of the most high security air spaces in the country and then able to crash into both giant structures without being stopped. In years to come, the facts would show a very sinister alternative story of treason and an inside job linked directly to the highest levels of government in this country. But with the high emotion of the moment, America truly felt as if it was at war.

Wanting to get a glimpse of what was being shown on the mainstream news, we drove up to the nearby Haiku cannery where there were a couple of restaurants with televisions. Already in the parking lot, cars paraded around with big American flags flying and horns honking. Loud and angry conversations were inflamed with blood thirsty rhetoric of revenge and outrage. Even a "new age" midwife friend that we knew was shouting that we should be dropping nuclear bombs on every Muslim country in the world. Quite a frightening epidemic of hysteria was set loose on the land based on flimsy facts and assumptions. In our interpretation of the non-stop scenes being shown on the news, it looked as if the buildings that were supposedly crashed into actually crumbled down from bombs that were probably planted beforehand.

Riding the wave of fear and blood lust, President Bush swiftly changed the course and social landscape of America from what we remembered it being before that day. The Bill of Rights and other vestiges of freedom were trashed as torture, surveillance and suspicion became the dominant face of the country. When we went to our downtown storage unit, we now had to go through security checks and passwords. At Sophia's school, a bag of white powder that was found in the kitchen triggered the building to be evacuated and an emergency response team quickly examining the substance. The intimidating powder turned out to be an unmarked bag of white flour. Airports started intense security checks on all passengers who were now being treated as potential criminals. John called to tell us that what looked like young hippie students at his school were almost all waving flags and considering to join the military. The times they were -a-changing.

A couple of months later, along with all our kids, we attended a Sufi spiritual gathering at the Makawao Church community hall. For several years it served as a monthly venue for about 50-80 people in the community to come listen and dance to this very beautiful and uplifting music of divine love. Because of the ongoing fear of Muslim terrorists and consequent racist amplification, the familiar night janitor charged into the hall during the middle of a song of praise to God and demanded we all leave within five minutes or else he was calling the police to arrest us. I suppose if the police did show up they would find it somewhat confusing to arrest people in partaking in the Universal Dances of Peace, even with one of the names being chanted was "Allah". Associating anything Muslim with terrorism was becoming more and more epidemic in our supposedly free society. But even in our prompt group exodus to the outside lawn, we continued the dances under the stars and sang the words of peace, love and harmony.

COLLEGE

Otherwise, John was quite happy with college life at Warren Wilson and living in the Smoky Mountains region. Lots of nature to explore and enjoy as well as a liberal college with a progressive curriculum including Outdoor Wilderness Skills. For Christmas break, he was able to make plans for a group of students to pay him for an adventure tour to Hawaii. When he arrived at the Maui airport, Nicolette and I greeted him by putting a lei around his neck made out of toilet paper. He didn't appreciate our humor and tore it off immediately. At least we only used the one-ply kind so not much was wasted. It's the thought that counts!

In the next couple of days he was able to organize car rentals, planned an adventurous itinerary, bought the necessary provisions and set up several tents around our campsite. During the next two weeks, his friends had a delightful time hiking, swimming and sightseeing. They especially liked our alternative lifestyle that included an outdoor kitchen and staying next to an idyllic waterfall to swim in. John was happy enough that he made enough from being their guide to have paid for his trip to Hawaii as well. The following summer, he would again plan a similar trip in taking a number of students with him to Europe. Again he was able to make enough to pay for all his expenses. But he also was not sure if he wanted to "baby sit" college students any more that all had different priorities of what they wanted to do and with different energy levels of how to do it.

THE ORGAN RECITAL

During this time period, Stephanie was growing in concern over her parents health issues. Since both of their birthdays were in the month of July, she went back to San Francisco for a visit and left me with the pleasant responsibility of keeping the girls happy for a couple of weeks. During that time we organized several hikes, picnics, concerts and other pleasant ways to cope in not having mom around for a couple of weeks. Various discount coupons to many of the local eateries also gave us an uplifted attitude in dining well for less. But one of our most interesting experiences took place in a church located near the town of Makawao.

Wanting to broaden their cultural horizons, besides a couple of excellent rock and roll events, I was eager to take Nicolette and Sophia to a free organ performance of classical music. Following the directions to the recital venue from a bulletin board announcement, we pulled into the church parking lot on our map and because we were late, ran through an open door into a room full of people that we assumed were there for the show. Feeling a bit winded, it took me a few seconds of deep breaths to pay better attention to the setting. In the back of the room were a stack of bibles and next to it a coffee machine. That seeming understandable, I was next perplexed in smelling cigarette smoke. I couldn't spot the organ but I did realize that we were sitting in a circle of people who looked as if they were at a trailer park social rather than a stuffy piano recital. By now, the girls were also sensing something wasn't quite right thus requiring a quick trouble shooting as to what was wrong with this picture. The "aha" hit me like a hammer. The music venue was probably inside the church which must of had an organ and what we had wrongly walked into was the church's social room where an AA (Alcoholics Anonymous) meeting was taken place. In less than five seconds we were out the door and rushing to the church where indeed the music was taking place. The support group probably missed our sudden departure as I must have appeared like a single father with two daughters who was wanting to get rid of his alcoholic habit. An hour later as the three of us were falling asleep listening to boring classical music, we agreed that the AA meeting was probably much more livelier. But even better than these two options, we were happier listening to some good music on the car stereo and soon to be enjoying looking at the stars from our own beds in the rain forest.

TRAGEDY

Shortly after Stephanie returned from the mainland, while we were drifting off to a late night dream with a Grateful Dead tape providing the soundtrack, we heard a heavy thump in our daughters' hut. Wishing to avoid the inevitable reality for another moment, we took a long breath before rushing to see what the long screams were about. Worse than expected, we found Nicolette on her back after falling from the top bunk bed. At this point it seemed quite possible that our daughter had broken her back and the anguish was paralyzing me in tears and emotions of disbelief and anger at the universe as well as myself for letting them have such a dangerous bed.

Luckily we had phone reception and were able to call our friend Tina for advice. The 911 emergency help was called and in about twenty minutes we could see the headlights of cars and loud sounds of men rustling about on top of the hill who then following our directions down the trail to our camp through the pouring jungle rain. Nicolette was still lying motionless on the ground while gasping for air between soul wrenching screams. One of the police officers seemed preoccupied searching our premises with his flashlight while his partner was asking me a variety of questions as part of the profiles to bust us for pot and perhaps find cause of child abuse. My own will to insure their help was voiced through politely reminding them how very thankful we were for their coming so soon to help our daughter who was in severe pain from perhaps a broken back. Changing their perspective and role play, the cops actually became very focused on being helpful instead of predatorial. A few minutes later our friend Tina arrived and helped us take Nicolette to the hospital.

The initial conclusion after the X-rays and examination was that Nicolette had a broken shoulder and time would heal it. However her pain continued to be severe so we took her a few days later for a follow up examination by a specialist. His observation however was very different than the previous assessment and he directed us to make arrangements to take Nicolette by plane to a hospital in Honolulu

immediately as what she had was one of the worst shoulder disloca-
tions he had ever seen.

Luckily Nicolette's school insurance covered the medical expenses of the accident and, together with Stephanie, she was taken to
the big city hospital where after an operation of several hours, metal
pins were inserted in her bones to hold her shoulder together. I was
elated to know that her back was not broken but the dislocation would
mean that she could well be compromised in her life from athletics
and physical work. She had to drop out of the canoe club that she
enjoyed but over time, she has strengthened her muscles and is now
living a healthy and active life style. The bunk bed was tossed and I
encourage everyone that has small children to think twice before using one. And as for Sophia who was in the bottom bunk, she was amazingly able to stay asleep the night of the accident, even with Nicolette
screaming and the police and ambulance visit.

Coincidentally during the same month on March 1, 2002 my
mother-in-law LaVerne passed away in San Francisco. It was satisfying that Stephanie had visited her the previous Christmas when her
health was better and the bonding clearer.

SOVEREIGNTY

With rising interest in the local Hawaiian sovereignty movement,
we also became interested and attended several presentations from
various people discussing the idea of personal sovereignty as well.
Following their advice, we applied for an international drivers license
issued by the Washitaw Native Americans. Supposedly they were indigenous people exempt from the Louisiana Purchase, so when the US
bought that part of the country from France, this particular tribe was
allowed to remain sovereign while also be recognized as such by the
United Nations.

On our return to Greece, we would find no problem in using the
Washitaw drivers license. However on a road trip which we would take
into Northern Europe, as I previously mentioned, we were detained
at the Czech-German border because their computer would not recognize the validity of our document. Luckily at that time I also had
my own international drivers license issued from Nicaragua which did
register as being okay and possibly kept us from being arrested. When
we had access to a phone, we made a call to the phone number in

Louisiana which was on the back of our drivers license. Instead of the Washitaw embassy, it turned out to be an out of order phone number. Later we looked up Washitaw nation on the internet and when we called the contact number listed, it turned out to be a restaurant and bar. Perhaps the country had gone underground and their phone unlisted. Likewise, the sovereignty facilitators on Maui that had set us up in the first place where not to be found. Thus they weren't returning our phone calls requesting that they pay us a refund on their inadequate drivers license as well as some start up fees that we paid them for a project that we did not want to continue on. Even personal sovereignty should respect the common law of not ripping off people through bogus agreements.

JUNGLE CIVILIZATION

Our time in the Maui rain forest was a delightful period of my integration of social networking, cool people and events for us to connect with. The various community centers, churches, communities and even private homes constantly hosted free or low priced interesting workshops, lectures and concerts. The "Maui Family" was our hippie tribe and always held a familiar sense of community. The Twin Falls eco-village across the road was the scene of various gatherings including Peruvian and Native American spiritual ceremonies. On Sundays, the Temple of Peace, Sufi Center and Blue Mountain's home all offered places of spiritual activity as well. Our children would usually be with us but we also gave them the option to not feel they had to participate. Nicolette and Sophia would bring along art work and books to indulge in usually. All of us, however, would take part in any of the Krishna events besides the meditative experience, there was always a vegetarian feast that followed. My intention was for my children to at least have a "homeopathic" exposure to a variety of realities and thus in life feel comfortable either in downtown Philadelphia late at night, a Rainbow Gathering, a Greek Orthodox Church or Kmart. A social vaccine as well as a key of access if need be in their life's journey.

JUNGLE BREW

Terence McKenna had once told me that why did I think that going to the Amazon to visit an indigenous shaman would be the ideal way to partake of the legendary psychedelic brews that area was famous for. Considering the high cost of travel and the possible risk of catching exotic diseases and even getting ripped off, his advice was to be patient and wait for the opportunity to come to me instead. In due time, by living closer to our earthy roots, such access did come in our direction. A good friend of ours casually asked us one day if we would like to partake of the Ayahuasca tea in a group setting. Totally surprised by the invitation, Stephanie and I soon met with one of the facilitators that explained the does and don'ts as well as how regular meetings were taking place on Maui at a comfortable location.

As when we partook of the sacrament in Amsterdam, the ceremony was in Portuguese and was organized in accordance with the provisions of a Christian church group based in Brazil. All the participants wore white and the service took place at night but with all lights turned on. I wasn't sure if we should avoid eating food beforehand especially as one church member was emphatic that fasting was preferable but another explained that since it would be a "long evening" ahead, we needed to eat big meals during the day so as to have enough endurance.

The brew itself, as expected, tasted familiarly acrid and once consumed, I knew that at some point purging needs would have me barfing in the toilet. Each round of oscillating realities would take about 90 minutes whereupon members that wanted to drink more "medicine" could come up to the alter and do so. The men and women were separated from each other and visions were discouraged until the facilitators said it was okay to do so. Such emanations were considered temptations from the "dark side" which we needed to develop resistance and by doing so, increase the level of healing for our group. At some point there was a ritual dance which for me amounted to dragging my feet and giving secret winks to Stephanie's dilated sparkly eyes across the room. On another occasion I went to the bathroom where I became amazed at the visions I was seeing in the toilet bowl. Noticing my long absence, a couple of the church officials came inside to tell me to stop and to come join the group which I was "letting down" by my absence.

Being disoriented on many levels, once I came back to the group, I found a song book placed in my hands. As I looked over the shoulders of the other men singing, I noticed not only were they on different pages from each other, but one person had the book upside down and another sideways. I felt comfortable realizing that I wasn't alone in confusion.

Although the psychedelic experience was of high intensity, my personality was not well aligned with such an approach that felt too much like being back in an authoritative Catholic church. Church members wearing star badges would stand in back of the room to point out when we weren't paying attention to our song books or to prevent us from leaving the room. Perhaps such a style was helpful for people needing such a structure and we knew that we wouldn't be able to continue in what felt to be endless nights of listening to staccato music and feeling as if we were stuck in some sort of purgatory. Yet, because the medicine itself was good stuff, we still managed to go to several services and always more excited to be going home the next morning to turn on some Jimi Hendrix music and spend the rest of the weekend watching the trees and bird life.

As I mentioned earlier, we eventually were introduced to a Peruvian shaman who had come to Maui to conduct various ceremonies in which ayahuasca was treated in a different, more traditional approach. The visions were encouraged and with more melodic music without the guilt and shaming trappings of Catholicism. And even better, the several ceremonies he led took place only about a twenty minute walk from our camp in a delightful rain forest setting.

But also in due respect, we drank the brew with the church group at a later time and different setting which actually felt more pleasant than previous gatherings. A lesson for me as well to not be dogmatic and that also the ayahuasca is even more important than the rituals or outfits worn.

STEVE GOES TO SWITZERLAND

Being able to consolidate most of our air travel bonus mileage rewards through our several years of global travels, Stephanie and I had accumulated enough points for a free ticket from Hawaii to Europe. Even though it would have been nice for us to use it, we agreed that it would be a perfect gift to buy a ticket for Stephanie's father instead. Steve was only a small child when he had to leave Switzerland and now after nine decades, here was his opportunity to visit relatives and his birth-land. Also it might have been a pause from his grief in the recent passing of LaVerne whom he was with for over half a century. At first he was stubborn in not wanting to travel, but eventually he agreed as Stephanie mailed him the tickets and explained that they would be nonrefundable and thus worthless if he didn't go. Stephanie's brother Byron was staying in Paris at the time, so that is where he would land and stay a few days first. They rented a car for the drive to Switzerland and riding along with them was our son John who was still in Europe at the time after his leading a traveling group of students from Warren Wilson College. Though Steve's impressions of Europe weren't very exciting, it was a nice time of bonding for the three men to visit relatives and sights of family importance together. His active participation in Swiss-American activities around San Francisco were still the "real thing" for him instead of the country he never socialized in and was in reality only a "foreign place" with a familiar language.

OUR 25th WEDDING ANNIVERSARY

January 21, 2003 was the date of our 25th wedding anniversary. Stephanie and I were enthused at the possibility of having a ceremonial gathering of friends to join us in honoring such a landmark, so we started several months earlier in making and organizing plans for this special occasion.

By now, we had been active in enough social circles that there was a comforting support from many friends in helping co-create what promised to be a memorable event. Our goal was to have an all night party in the big starpod tent at nearby Twin Falls with at least 100 people. John kept trying to pop our bubble of anticipation by saying why would we expect that many people to come to our anniversary party and how would we find money for food, live music, etc. But the intent and enthusiasm were such that we knew that the alignment would be a good one.

In retrospect when looking back at our party, the only thing that we would have done different would have been to have made sure someone could have filmed all ten hours of it as every moment was a masterpiece never to have been forgotten. At the appointed starting time of 4:20 in the afternoon, Stephanie and I followed the gentle footsteps of our son John and his friend Chris who were the mistrals playing acoustic guitars leading us into the circus size tent. The structure was beautifully decorated by Nicolette and Sophia with colorful flowers and tapestries. Stephanie wore a radiant smile along with her white dress while I wore my very special Jimi Hendrix t shirt decorated with images of mushrooms, waterfalls and fairies.

The first part of the ceremony consisted of various prayers from the several "ministers" on the love alter. First our friend Kutira gave us a blessing and sang an exotic Hawaiian chant befitting her and her partner's Rafael's Tantric talents. Then Jah Levi shared his individuality as a Gnostic Bishop and Rastafarian. He was followed by the "Psychedelic Rabbi" who blessed us in his unique way of training through taking an LSD sacrament every Friday night for thirty years to honor the weekly Sabbath. The final blessings were from the Sufi tradition of Andy and Leilah Be.

As the afternoon unfolded into evening, the musical tempo picked up with the sounds of Jah Levi and many other guest friends. All of them being respected musicians in their own right, people kept asking us how did we manage to find such an all star line up of performances. Our reply was that they did it from the heart as their offering to the epic Love ceremony that it was.

In the middle corner of the tent was a regal couch that served as our place of honor for people to come pass greetings and gifts. Delicious pot luck food filled the serving tables and whenever we had a chance, Stephanie and I kept on dancing as long as our legs could stand. And even with the abundance of psychedelic substances and brews being passed around, we were able to stay in ecstasy with just the power of love and gratitude. During the night and afterwards, many friends kept telling us that they felt so much high energy in our celebration, that people felt incredibly high even without any trippy spices needed.

Along with the more recognizable musicians, John and the group he was rehearsing with for the event, took the sounds to an even higher level as they poured out fantastic cover songs of Led Zeppelin, Allman Brothers, Jimi Hendrix and much more. Right at midnight they played a dramatic version of the Beatles "Tomorrow Never Knows" which triggered a psychedelic response that carried its energetic field throughout the rest of the night.

By late night, the smiles were spread on everyone still dancing, sleeping or blissing out. We had many helpers to clean up trash, put the musical instruments into vans, return the generators and thank us for one of the best parties they had ever gone to. I suppose we'll have to plan another epic celebration for our 50th anniversary as well. And whichever direction our life would lead us, we felt we have definitely planted happy roots and respect on Maui.

But for now, it felt as if it was time for us to be on the move again. On the home front our opinion of the landlady was feeling strained. When we first moved to her land, she was charging us $100 a month rent for the camping site. After we improved our kitchen area and laid bricks so as to prevent stepping in the daily mud, she was so delighted that she explained we had done so well that she could now get $200 a month rent from most people but would let us stay for only $150. After we set up the internet and made our area look better, she again said she was so delighted that she might be able to collect $500 from someone but she would allow us to stay for $400 a month. Confused and angry at the situation, we decided it be best that we made no more such improvements and not feel our stay would be permanent. Also, we learned that because people such as herself meditate and wear clean Indian robes, they are not necessarily developing compassion as part of their spiritual path. Elitism masked behind dogma and chants. Leaving what we felt to be a corrupt situation was a relief in many ways.

Over the years we became close friends with many people on Maui who will always remain part of our extended family. Christine the dolphin goddess, angel of the sacred brew and forever soul sister. Will and Kalima who inspired us to sprout our dreams of a sustainable community. Bodhi and Leilah Be who shined their light of spiritual relationship into the depths of our soul. Doctor Roy, not only the finest chiropractor in the land, but an eternal beacon of positive thinking and ceremonial ascension with levity. Jason whose fingers extend from his heart of gold and express the guitar chords of magnificence and his wise humility echoes the vibrations of sacred sages. And our long time friend Ed who has provided healthy food to the community through his amazing health food store in Paia while always being a true representative of the Aloha spirit of honesty and grounded wisdom.

CHAPTER FIFTEEN: GREECE
FINAL CHAPTER

TAKING CARE OF MY MOTHER

With my mother's health declining and the soap operas on Maui expanding, time had come for us again to return to Greece. Not much had changed over the last couple of years. Not even our attitude of wanting to escape out of Xirokambi at every opportunity to do so. It did feel a little odd not having John with us on our travels, but nonetheless we now had more room in the van for the four of us to take on our field trips. As before, Nitsa was happy to take care of my mom when we took off, so they could read holy books together, gossip and probably rip off money from my mom's bank account as well.

BULGARIA

Being relatively close to the northern Greek border and knowing of a European Rainbow Gathering happening in southern Bulgaria, we navigated through the beautiful forest scenery in that direction. A few miles before the border we camped near a very unique hot spring. A dome Byzantine chapel had been built over the healing waters with the feeling that this had been a special chamber since ancient times.

About one mile before we reached Bulgaria we went into a large supermarket with amazingly low prices. Since many Greeks would make the drive into Bulgaria to buy cheaper supplies, this store was being as competitive as possible. Similarly when we crossed the border, several miles of shops were lined on the road catering to Greeks coming into the country to buy discounted food items to bring back to their village. An interesting irony was finding Greek alcoholic beverages such as the famous Metaxa brandy on sale for less than back home. Global economics have been getting more and more confusing ever since.

Crossing over into Bulgaria was not just a distance of a few miles but also a jump into a totally different society. People stared at us with blank looks and the buildings were concrete boxes without much personality. The many years of Soviet influence was evident. The grocery stores were very inexpensive but only carried basic food items without much choice which was evident in the lack of billboard advertisements. Yet in contrast to its drab cultural persona, nature was radiant with thick healthy forests, clear lakes and verdant mountains. As the country was preparing to enter the European Union I felt fear in that there would be eventual exploitation of these natural resources by global corporations.

Communication was a definite challenge for us. Neither English nor Greek was recognized and as none of us knew any Russian which was the second language for most of the local people, my rudimentary high school German was of some help for rudimentary needs. But we would still be getting lost because of another peculiarity in the culture. When someone means to say "Yes" they shake their heads back and forth but when they want to say "No" they nod up and down. Thus when we would show our maps to people, we would be getting even more lost because of the opposite understanding of directions.

Once outside the bigger towns, it seemed as if we were going through even more portals of time and space. Instead of cars or tractors, we mostly saw horse drawn carts driven with about eight women colorfully dressed in traditional clothes being taken to do the farm work for the day. The men would drop them off as they would head back to the villages to do building projects while the women would do the field work. As they thrashed the wheat which was prepared by the ox driven plows, they would be singing songs that felt as if they resonated across many centuries and from many ancestors. What a contrast to the cacophony of loud engines, weed whackers, lawn mowers, cars, tractors and pesticides in the world of modern agriculture in the USA.

But even though it took several extra hours of meandering through the scenery, we eventually found the usual colored ribbons indicating we were on the right way to a Rainbow Gathering. As usual, the scouts had done a superb job in finding a magnificent setting for the several hundred people that came not only from European countries but also from other continents including North and South

America and Asia. The trail from the parking area to the main field took us over an hour to walk but as we acclimated, every day it took a shorter time. Not only did our endurance level feel tuning up, but the fresh air and beautiful forest scenery were refreshing. Looking at the future however, we couldn't help but wonder if there would be some sort of service provided by the younger members to create a way to help elderly hippies and handicapped folks in general to be able to get to such areas easier as well as having their shelters prepared for them. That would be a nice gesture of respect and good karma.

Past the "welcome table" of blissed out smiles, we wandered around the colorful display of festive humanity attending and setting up their workshops and general kitchen and toilet structures along with making plans for which presentations to be attending. Strolling through the enchanting forest we felt happy to be among like minded and compassionate friends. And when we saw a children's mini village being constructed we released any worry of our kids' whereabouts who by now happily mingled with others their age.

Being near enough to the border of Greece, warning signs were posted by the government announcing terrible penalties for anyone wandering past the "no trespassing" signs. But on a sweeter note, we saw an elderly local couple at peace and smiling as they filled their handmade basket that they were carrying with freshly picked wild mushrooms. Salivating as I envisioned what these morsels would taste like if fried in olive oil and garlic, I asked him in my most polite gesture if we could purchase any of his gourmet stash. I offered the gentleman what I felt was a reasonable five euro note for a bag of the delectable looking fungi but as the old man shook his head, I felt that it might be more appropriate to offer him more. Without yet having learned the reversed way of indicating yes or no, I was thinking that I was insulting him by offering too small of a payment. When we reached the ten euro offer and he kept shaking his head more vigorously and with both of us totally confused in the transaction, a nice cut through the gridlock came when the old man's wife reached over and took the ten euro note I had offered and put the bag of mushrooms into my hands. Needless to say, we fully enjoyed our eventual meal and even more important, we were relieved when someone explained to us our confusion in not understanding when gestures of yes means no.

Much more organized than the regional gatherings we had gone to in Greece, we were able to enjoy several informative workshops. One of the more interesting ones was a presentation of psychedelics which included sampling of several designer drugs. The discussion ended abruptly when the facilitator took notice of a Bulgarian man that was standing in the back of the tent with a fancy camera whom he accused of being an undercover cop and was there to find evidence for busting people. Personally I did not find any validity to the accusation but the class was sadly terminated before I had a chance to try any of the aforementioned samples.

The same guy who organized the workshop did however succeed in a social experiment with a good ending. For several days, every time anyone walked by the Greek camp, the usual reaction was surprise at their loud and neurotic arguments and discussions. By giving them some "psychedelic candy" to try out, the whole group from the camp had transformed into the epitome of tranquil bliss later on at the nightly campfire.

One of the anticipated highlights of this particular gathering was the acceptance of the invitation by many residents of the local village to come join the Rainbow Gathering on the night of the full moon for a communal party. With excitement buzzing in the air, we prepared to see and hear the local Bulgarian chorus of song and dance. Stupidity and arrogance however were the unfortunate gate keepers, we witnessed the derailing of the epic moment of anticipated manifestation.

Around late afternoon a pickup truck of several men dressed in fine outfits drove down the road and parked at the entrance to the field. Seeing a young hippie trying to cut thick logs of firewood with just a hand saw, they quickly offered help by bringing out one of their chainsaws to finish the project. With loud shouts and tense emotions, the Israeli hippie yelled at the confused Bulgarians that the tree had a soul and one must not attack it with machines but rather sing to it with graceful strokes as he was doing. While this interplay of drama was going on, the Bulgarian men started bringing out cases of their homemade wine to share with all of us. Instantly, another dread headed hippie started shouting that alcohol was poison and not allowed at the gathering. With looks of confusion and feeling rejection, the local young men got into their trucks and went back to their village to make it clear that the Rainbow Gathering was a rude collection of elite foreign hippie kids which were the cause of the sad cancellation of the full moon celebration. With their idiotic display and lack of respect and sensitivity, I was made clearly aware that the hippie revolution had morphed into a pale reflection of the values that made the 1960's so radiant in my heart, soul and inspirational influence. In those days the circle was open to all as a sharing of love and light without distinction as to appearance or dietary practices. Only through kindness and empathy can awareness be transmitted and accepted.

As lovely as sharing a few days with friends and tribal familiarity was, the time arrived as in all gypsy camps to move on and spread seeds of consciousness in all directions of the world and multiple dimensions beyond. But the tentacles of bureaucracy did not allow movement to be free flowing or simple. During its Soviet institutionalizing of totalitarian control mechanisms, travel was restricted for only specific purposes. Visiting Bulgaria by foreigners, for instance, meant staying at a certified hotel and then having a paper signed by the proprietor that you had paid and thus given money to the country. To facilitate the "leaving process" properly, the local policeman showed up a few days before the Gathering was over to set up an office in a nearby farmhouse where everyone had to go and show their passports and visas before being issued an exit document. Since Rainbow Gatherings are all about freedom and not having to pay to sleep on our natural home-rights on Mother Earth, none of the hippies had any of the necessary receipts from hotels. Several people tried to explain to the police officer that the European laws had been updated and that the hotel stay idea was no longer valid, but being in a very rural and secluded part of the country, the officer had not heard any such news and still insisted that everyone had to come to show papers or else they would be arrested.

Realistically, I could not imagine where they could put 1000 young foreigners in a nearby jail and in all practicality, many of the hippies would not mind the opportunity of staying longer in this beautiful area. Long lines of people standing in line for exit visas were frustrating as people had come here to drum, dance and hug instead of waiting through many hours of boredom. The cry of "we are free people and do not want your stinking papers" was often heard but not everyone agreed that demanding our noble rights would be a productive way to influence the situation. At the last minute however, the police man figured out a way for a workable compromise. He again verified that if any foreigner stayed in Bulgaria without paying a room rental, they would be arrested as criminals. However after leaving the campground, if they would stay at a hotel for even one night and receive a receipt, they could show this proof of stay at the immigration office at the border and all would be fine.

Eager to comply with the law we looked forward to renting a room with hot showers, comfortable mattress and other such luxuries of accommodation. Being late at night when we started looking for a hotel in what looked like a reasonably large enough town on the map to do so, we found ourselves driving in circles and running low on fuel while not being able to find any signs for hotels or even gas stations. A police car that must have taken notice of our predicament came up to us and once he was able to understand our situation he promptly assured us that he would be able to help. His first question was what sort of class hotel we were looking for, so with some thought on the matter, we said Class B. Within a few minutes, we followed him to a gated building where he made a call on his cell phone to the proprietor and soon afterwards the electronic gate swung open. Although he was probably awoken by the late night call, the owner of the hotel was in a jolly enough mood as he showed us a suite of a two room fully furnished apartment with even cable television and a deck overlooking the city for the price of just $15 a night. Amazed at the low price, we wondered in retrospect what the price and difference in a class A room would have been.

The next morning we enjoyed our complimentary breakfast, filled up the car with gas and headed for a popular mountain resort town on the way to the Greek border. Soon, we drove through a rather large city where we stopped a passerby on the street to ask directions. In full daylight and with lots of other people walking on the sidewalk, this guy tried to swing open the side door to our van and pull himself in. As we surged ahead before he had a chance to do so, we sobered up to the fact that we were not at a Rainbow Gathering anymore and that we needed to pay closer attention to any red flags of economic desperation and frantic opportunism.

A resort town where we paused at was located in a gorgeous and lushly forested gateway area of ski resorts and other access to

346

appreciation of holidays in nature. Lots of happy people were walking along the sidewalks and the smell of home cooking enticed us from every side. While Stephanie and the girls went window shopping downtown, I made use of my nose to lead me to the best scents and my eyes to read the menus while paying close attention to the prices. Mission accomplished I caught up with my ladies and asked them to join me for lunch. As I proceeded to order not only large plates of food for all of us, a big bottle of wine (appropriately named Sophia Winery) and even banana splits for dessert, I could sense a feeling of horror in Stephanie's face as to the anticipated huge bill that the waiter would be bringing us for our excess. Not being able to hide my wide smile any longer, I started laughing when she did the currency exchange calculation and realized that the total cost was around twelve dollars for everything. As we were leaving the restaurant, we even felt happy to leave the waiter a three dollar tip which was possibly one of the largest ones he ever received and that he would be talking about for a long time to come.

NICOLETTE AND I IN PATRA

Because of the need to have our van taken out of the country to be re-registered, Stephanie along with Sophia took our vehicle on the ferry boat from the port of Patra to Italy. The trip there and back took about three days at which time Nicolette and I stayed in a budget hotel waiting for their return.

We eventually would hear that they had some interesting adventures in their few hours of stay in the port city of Brendisi including not being able to find any authentic Italian pizzerias and having to settle for one bought at a Chinese fast food restaurant. Also, Stephanie was given a guided walk around the city by a friendly man who eventually wanted to kiss and make out. A true self proclaimed Italian lover and not an Oriental facsimile. But his heart was broken nonetheless as he had to settle for just a simple flirt.

On our side of the Ionian Sea, Nicolette and I had an interesting time as well. Our walking tours transversed many sides of Patra including up to the high castle overlooking the city, as well as the many various levels of town squares. In many of the narrow alleys we discovered a wide variety of small shops, cafes and an interesting night club that I afterwards took Stephanie to enjoy Pink Floyd music on the sound system. In our walks around the city, Nicolette and I observed many interesting dramas including a loud, peculiar man that looked as if half his face was missing and carried a briefcase that we thought was accented with bird shit. We felt sorry for him but felt better seeing that he was very popular with many very nice looking women that he met on his stroll around a town square where we sat for a bit. Besides the nice picnics that Nicolette and I enjoyed, we also found some inexpensive taverna food as well in our explorations of where to later take the rest of the family.

We also had a very strange experience at the large Saint Andrew Orthodox Cathedral. On all our trips here before, it was always enchanting to look at the beautiful mural on the interior dome as well as it being a meditative experience to follow the long line of worshipers waiting to kiss the tomb of the departed saint. On this particular visit being the Holy Week before Easter, the church was full, so Nicolette and I had to go to the upstairs gallery overlooking the floor below. Wanting to be following the service and know what to chant and the appropriate moments, we kept looking over the shoulders of the lady next to us to see what page her hymn book was on. But after about twenty minutes of her page still on the same page and also noticing that she looked either asleep or perhaps dead, Nicolette and I made a quick exit so as to not be witnesses to any other weirdness that night. We bypassed waiting for the end of the church service and went instead to see a Robin Williams movie called Flubber that was very funny and had impressive 3D imagery as well.

SANTA

Probably because of my long white beard and sweet disposition, our friend Ioana asked me one late Autumn day to accept the role of Santa Claus in an updated children's Christmas play she would be presenting at a venue in Sparta. Although learning all the correct Greek pronunciation was a challenge for me, I accepted her request and set aside time each day to practice with my daughters who also would be in the play as reindeer.

Unlike the typical characterization, this Santa would be facing a lot of problems in bringing gifts to the kids. In this contemporary story line, I would find myself arrested for trespassing with my bag of goodies while going down someone's chimney. Subsequently standing in front of a courtroom, I would be also facing charges of parking my reindeer without paying the meter as well as having an animal rights group sue me for them carrying too much weight in the gift bags. I was even presented a tax bill and fine for my not showing receipts of purchase for the presents that I would be passing out.

With the suspense and moral anxiety of a classic Greek tragedy. I found myself standing handcuffed with my head down and emotionally deflated in front of the judge who was preparing to pass a harsh prison sentence on me after hearing my long list of crimes being emphatically announced by the prosecutor's shrill voice. The judge, staring at me with the piercing eyes of righteousness started his pronouncement when off from the side of the room came his own children to embrace me and tell the judge how wonderful I was and that they would leave home if he put me in jail. Then the rest of the kids of the village came running in to say pretty much the same announcement. With concern over this threatened children's exodus, the judge had no recourse other than setting me free. Hand in hand with the kids, the play ended with my giving a speech about how the true meaning of the spirit of Christmas is to share and give rather than expect to be given stuff. Ironically, afterwards however, some kids from the audience came briskly up to me and gave me a list of what presents they expected me to bring them. Nothing else to do, I shrugged and then joined the rest of the cast for a free meal and lots of delicious homemade wine.

PSYCHEDELIC SWITZERLAND

In January of 2006, John, Stephanie and I flew to Switzerland to attend the Albert Hofmann 100th birthday celebration and commemoration of his discovery of LSD. Our daughters were content to stay at home and the village seemed like it could survive without us. Besides being a once in a lifetime opportunity to meet some very interesting people, the weather was taking a sunny pause to make the ride into Alpine country even more accommodating. The conference itself was an epic three days. The convention center was filled with over 2000 psychonauts and interesting people, most of whom were white haired and in comparison, we looked like relatively youngsters. My "Links by George" newsletter was reaching several of the prominent attendees which made it more personal to finally meet many of them face to face. Multi media events, ongoing lectures, book and poster exhibits were just part of the thrill. In the evenings, Stephanie and I left John to mingle and enjoy the music and journey opportunities, while we had some nice interpersonal interaction with new friends such as Stanley Kripner, Nick Sand, Alex Grey and others. In fact we sat next to the visionary artists Alex and Allison Grey on the front row of the main lecture room for most of the time. I happened to write "reserved for George and Stephanie Douvris" on a paper which I kept leaving on our chairs after each lecture with no one questioning its authenticity or removing it.

The highlight of the convention was on the last day as Albert Hofmann entered the large auditorium. He put his walker aside and then made his way to the podium while being greeted to a standing ovation from everyone in the packed room. He was certainly a hero in the eyes of millions of people around the world and his impassioned one hour speech was incredibly inspiring and brought tears and applause. His emphasis was love for nature and for humanity through the expansion of consciousness and compassion on all levels. His last sentence was an expression of gratitude to everyone that attended the commemoration and for helping his LSD "problem child" to find maturity and purpose in the world.

After the convention was over, we rented a car and then took a detour to another mountainous region of Switzerland to visit an email friend Reverend D and his Church of the Sacred Mushrooms. In what was once a small ski resort, D and his family had created a spiritual temple and portal of psychedelic journeying. Truly inspired to be a conduit of the holy spirit, D's mission was manifesting an outreach to many people. There were several very comfortable guest rooms, meeting hall, music room and vegetarian kitchen providing delicious and healthy meals. The basement provided many trays of fungi and, as throughout all the building, psychedelic art and sculptures accenting the sacred visions. Outside were various trails, several tipis and an organic garden. D's care, well planned organization and dedication was an obvious extension of his guiding vision of heart and soul. On the legal end, he felt assured by the Swiss government that, as long as the magic mushrooms were for use as religious sacraments, he was not doing anything illegal. Although it was not possible for us to take him up on his invitation to take part in a mushroom ceremony that night, we were very appreciative of his kind offer and hospitality in letting us stay for no charge. And as a final bonus, he offered John a job as kitchen chef if he could return back to Switzerland within a few weeks.

Just as he had promised, Reverend D gave us a call as reminder that the offer of employment for John was still pending and that he needed his help in the kitchen very soon. So without much ado and lots of excitement, our son was packed up and flying back to the Swiss Alps.

Over the next few weeks, the reports from John were all glowing. He was meeting interesting people, enjoying the opportunities of nature's magnificence, eating healthy food, accessing spiritual sacraments, playing music and getting paid for the experience. So it was not a difficult decision for Nicolette to agree to when he invited her to come up as well as D's wife needed a nanny to take care of their two small children.

NICOLETTE AND SOPHIA MAKE A MOVIE

With Stephanie, John and myself in Switzerland, Nicolette and Sophia were given free rein of the house and the opportunity to create art without our interference. A few weeks earlier, Nitsa's older daughter closed down her dress store in Sparta and donated about eight manikins to the girls who put them in our basement for future use. With an actual plot better than most grade B movies and with only a simple video camera and no time for multiple takes or splicing the tape, they created two exceptional short films.

The story lines revolved around a couple of typical American spoiled young ladies who mistakenly make an internet reservation to come stay at our house in Xirokambi. Realizing it was not the luxury villa they expected was just part of the problem. After experiencing a number of confusing concerns with the house, the ambience becomes very surrealistic as out of our orchard appear a group of zombies thirsting for tourist blood. The black and white footage worked extremely well in providing the tension and the many tongue in cheek script lines were hilarious. In playing the part of the tourists, the girls had just the right look with makeup, outfit, accent and attitude. Likewise when they switched to playing the key zombies, they added even more talent into the changes of both set and mood. Having random passerbyers walking by the field and the house provided even more reality to their stellar production.

It never was clear if anyone had seen their strange goings on while making the film, but it remains for us an exciting, original and very good movie to watch again over the years.

I was personally so touched by the thematic expression of the movie that, both from inspiration as well as offering recognition to the filmmakers, under the cover of the night, I persuaded Nicolette and Sophia to walk with me down the road and write some appropriate graffiti on the welcome to Xirokambi sign suggesting that people stay away and to beware of the abundance of zombies in the village. The psychic vampirism which we had endured for so many years was now properly engraved. Similarly, many years later, John added even more character to the village in his naming it "Xiro-Zombie" which nicely summed it up.

Thus with his contribution, I can honestly say it was a Douvris sibling production.

FLOOD

When my mother's house was first built, the frontage road consisted only of dirt and the traffic was either by foot or donkey. As times changed with the need for accommodating cars the county paved the road but in the process created an angle that would overfill the drain gutters. Over time these gutters became clogged and along with more run off from eroded trees caused by the high country tree clear cutting, our fears of being flooded out finally manifested.

After a day of heavy rains, we were startled when we looked outside the front door and saw a splashing pool of water gathering in what was our garden space. And as the storm was not slowing in momentum, once the pool turned into a stream that was pouring into the cellar, we had to come up with some emergency plans of both protective as well as evacuation posturing. At full haste, we grabbed whatever of value that we could take upstairs and lifted the remaining objects on the ground floor on pallets. When the rushing water was now coming into the house from under the doors, it was time to tell my mother that we had to lift her out of bed and take her upstairs for her own safety.

Surrealistic madness now added a stroke of its own to the growing panic. My mother refused to understand the situation and started hitting us with her cane for disturbing her holy book reading session and trying to take her out of her bed. Outside Stephanie, John and I were trying to board up windows and plug up door bottoms in a feeble effort to hold back the flood. Meanwhile the fire department who was going around pumping water out of people's basements and helping folks that were trapped in their homes showed up. Besides my mother screaming at all of us to take her back to bed, the firemen were confused when they went to the cellar and found the manikins that the girls had used for their filming now floating and looking like a macabre scene of scrambled dead bodies. A few moments later a television news film crew came by to ask me what my storm experiences were. It must of looked quite peculiar for home audiences listening to my reply of blaming the county for clogging up the drains while watching an old lady screaming and hitting my kids in the background while firemen carried plastic bodies out of the basement.

About an hour later, the rains abated, damage was minimal, sand bags were bought to cover water passages the next time and my mother was still screaming at us. Life was normal again. In our emergency situation, it was great that John, who had finished a year in college, was once again with us to help and be part of the family zone.

MY MOTHER'S LAST YEAR IN ECSTASY

In her final year, my mother's health deteriorated rapidly. No longer could she walk without trembling nor do much in the way of independent action and thought. Yet her anger at us and the world in general continued to consume her passion. It was on such an evening of her cursing my existence that I reflected deeply on her situation. Under normal circumstances, I would find it unethical to give someone a drug without explaining to them the purpose and its possible side effects. But in this case of her being caught in such a web of emotional pain and negativity, I decided to give her the one dose of MDMA (or ecstasy) which I was saving for a special occasion. Not exactly the ceremony that I had intended for Stephanie and I, but now for a totally different love session need.

As she grabbed the little white pill that I gave her, my mother hissed the question of what was I giving her to which I replied that it was "heart medicine". Her retort was that I had been giving poison to her heart all my life with my existence and that here was one more intention of mine to kill her. I took a deep breath and felt the fear of a premonition that her experience could well be a very, very bad one. A decision that could well haunt me the rest of my life. Part of the feeling turned out to be true as that decision has indeed had a significant impact on my life, but in a far better outcome than even I intended. After giving her the "heart medicine" I said good night and left her alone. Checking in half an hour later, I found her sitting on her bed gazing at an icon of the Virgin Mary. The fact that I saw her smiling was hint of a profound event manifesting. But when I asked her how she felt, she softly said that "there were angels flying around the room." That was a trigger for me to run upstairs, wake up our son John and tell him to hurry back with me down the stairs with his guitar and that we had important work to do with his grandmother. For the next few hours we exchanged hugs with my mother and also witnessing her delight in listening to CD's of both Greek Orthodox religious hymns as well as her favorite Greek folk music. At times John would strum a few chords on his guitar with lyrics that we sang about how much we loved her. When Stephanie came downstairs to be part of the miracle, she asked my mother how she was doing. To which mom said in a very sweet tone, "the night will never end". A classic psychedelic experience of time extension beyond normal parameters of limitation. As profound an experience that the night's journey was, there was more amazement ahead. From that night on and for the next seven months of her life, my mother dropped her fear based masking and let her heart express itself in a very beautiful way. No longer would she judge or criticize anyone but instead say loving remarks. She would smile and ask to kiss us regularly every day. She no longer demanded I cut my beard but asked if she could stroke it with her fingers. Instead of not letting her granddaughters take her to the village in her wheelchair as before, she welcomed their brushing her hair, putting a flower in back of her ear and taking her out for ice cream. The young neighbor boy that she would always scream at for picking an orange from her orchard was in a state of shock as she now would smile and encourage him to fill a bag of fruit to take home to his family as well. That little white pill brought much joy in our lives and left us with heartwarming memories of my mother. It brought long lasting comfort in her remaining life and could well have helped her soul cross over more gently. No matter if the pill was gluten free or not, it is the finest example of a healthy drug interaction with long term benefits beyond just symptom relief.

DEATH TAKES MY MOTHER

The death of a parent is one of life's passages that eventually most of us have to be part of. We were present during my father's deterioration and held his hand during the transition and now the same for my mother. During her last few weeks she was having a hard time breathing and would experience periods of deep sleep and lethargy. Her heart palpitations and deep coughing episodes were becoming the focus of new concern which eventually meant taking her to the Sparta hospital for testing. At 100 years old we were not holding much expectation for a revitalization miracle and the doctor's prognosis of her having just a few days to live was not a shock. Yet my deep feelings of loss, abandonment and inability to change the inevitable flooded my eyes with tears.

Not wanting her to pass away in an institutional setting with tubes and high tech monitors strapped on her, we brought her back home where this moment would honor her dignity. John and Nicolette were working in Switzerland at that time while Sophia, Stephanie and I kept all day and night vigils as my mother's life force was quickly fading. She remained in a state of deep sleep and would not accept any food or water in her mouth. Not able to stay awake after an especially long session of telling her stories and images of family, memory and the great light beyond, I had to leave the room for a rest break. At some point during that time Stephanie came and woke me up and announced my mother had died as the sun was raising. My initial feelings were shock and upset that she left her body without my being with her. Yet on a higher reasoning, perhaps she chose to depart without pulling me through any pain in the loss. I held her hand and as her once tight signature grip was now just a limp body part, I understood that the journey had taken another turn in the cycle of life and death. Her power grip clutch had been a proud reminder of her Spartan heritage as warrior and of one who could live simply and sustainability.

Funerals were a common village ritual. Nitsa came over and together with Stephanie and Sophia, they washed her body in the prescribed manner with wine. My mother had anticipated this moment and had carefully gone through her wardrobe and picked the dress that she wanted to be buried in many months before. She even had the list prepared of who she wanted to come to the funeral and where she wanted them seated at the memorial. The custom of being to provide a coffee, cookie and shot of cognac at the village cafes for everyone was honored. Also family and friends were invited to a designated tavern for a dinner. She insisted that fish be served as was the tradition. But knowing that we were vegetarians, she was not too sure if she could trust us to do so. But as we promised, we did have fish available but also a pot of lentils for us and any others that did not want to eat animal flesh.

John and Nicolette flew down from Switzerland for the funeral and thus the circle was complete. As focused as we were on the solemn nature of this important moment of our life, there was unstable and disquieting surrealism as well. Stephanie noticed that my mother's wedding ring was not on her finger and when we asked Nitsa if she had perhaps taken it, her quick reply was that the "dirty gypsies" had snuck into the house and had pulled it off when no one was looking. And just like the death scene in the "Zorba the Greek" movie, even more of my mother's clothes and handmade blankets were vanishing from her room.

At the church, as expected, the old ladies wept while most of the men stood outside talking "business". The loudest and most sincere wailer, however, was Nicolette. Her tears were real and her loss deep. As I stood in the front row pew, on either side of me was Nitsa and my Aunt Hrisoula. My thoughts were somber and of my mother but they would both be interrupting me every few minutes to ask discreetly in my ear if my mother left them any money. But when I would say we didn't know yet, they would go back into their mock tears and hollow sorrow. Quite a display of reality and poor acting skills.

With prayers finished, the procession from the church was led by the priest to the graveyard and the final goodbyes. A few years earlier I had hoped to bring the bones of my father here to lie next to hers. But as it was not to be, my mother was set to rest in her family plot and one day her bones would be dug up and placed inside a box of bones of her ancestors. I still wonder if this will be my final resting place as well one day.

FATAL TOSS AT THE CEMETERY

Nicolette and Sophia would often go by the village cemetery to clean up the family grave site, keep the oil candle lit and put new flowers in the vase. After my mother's funeral their visits would be more frequent and they would both enjoy the time of sitting next to Yiayia's grave chatting to her spirit. On one occasion they even took the liberty to light all the candles in the cemetery which became a situation that caused a jolt of confusion in the village. At first they thought it was some sort of miracle or a wild party of the dead. But even when they realized it was my daughters act of honoring the collective village departed, there were words of praise being expressed for both of them and their consideration. On one of our visits to my mother's grave with the daughters and John, we were especially annoyed by a barking dog that growled at us when we had to walk past it's home. There was a fence which did protect us from it tearing its sharp teeth into our bodies, but nonetheless we still felt its desires to do so. On quick reflex of irritation, John picked up a rock and tossed it at this obnoxious dog which brought about an unexpected drama. Without meaning to do it any more harm than just a warning to shut up, John's toss startled the dog who then ran into a sharp branch which blinded its eye. As it yelped in pain, Nicolette and Sophia started pouncing nags and yells at John for his savagery. But it did keep the one eyed dog from barking at us anymore on our walks to the cemetery. Maybe some related meaning was connected to the phrase "A nod is as good as a wink to a blind horse".

FINAL REFLECTIONS ON MY PARENTS

Sometimes it takes a long passage of time and a deeper reflection of one's memories to have a clearer appreciation of bygone memories and family experiences. As I look back at my mother, besides the disagreements and frustrations, I can now sense other qualities about her that were not quite as obvious to me at the time. Her courage in maintaining what was right in her opinion was always firm and she didn't find excuses to limit her expressions. Life for her meant sacrifice if need be for the sake of taking care of the home nest. Perhaps she was overly concerned about my well being to the point of affecting my freedom, but her intentions were noble nonetheless.

Among her religious books and pamphlets was an old manual on natural health and healing. She shunned pharmaceutical drugs and rarely took even an aspirin while maintaining a philosophy involving fresh food and herbal teas instead of processed grocery store substances. My father and her would drink fresh dandelion juice, never ate canned food items and hardly ever drank alcohol. In my socialized American reality, I felt such behavior was "weird" as my food models included lots of hamburgers, greasy fries, sodas, candy bars and all the rest of a normal diet that I now consider poisons.

In retrospect I am proud of both my parents for retaining core values of truth, purity and sustainability even in adjusting to the realities of emigrating to a new country that promoted consumption as the norm. They never had a car and on many days would walk several miles for groceries, visiting relatives or going to work. We always had a garden where many of our fresh vegetables came from and even had enough surplus to share with neighbors. My mother would bake her own whole grain bread each week and with the left over flour make delicious cookies soaked in honey.

Besides my arguing with them that their natural food diet was un-American and my complaining about not having cars like everybody else, I couldn't understand why at night, they preferred reading or talking to relatives instead of laying on the couch and watching television like all the other neighbors. My father felt sports shows were for little children and when I would try to impress him with some high tech effects on the shows which he would dismiss as "all were lies", I would be always angry and frustrated. Now that we see the predatorial manipulation both conscious and subliminal in the media, his beliefs make sense. Likewise when my mother said Greece was being led into economic bondage by joining the European Union, and now we see how the country was tricked into permanent debt, her warning likewise are prophetic.

It is common for children to say that they wished they had a chance to have a conversation with their parents to express their love and appreciation. Now, many years after my father and mother have passed away, I too have come to that place of deeper love and respect as to who they were and even the lessons they laid seeds for in my own life. Their lives thus live through me as well even more than ever.

Because of the difference in age and cultural references, there was often a very wide gap of communication between my parents and me which agitated our relationship at times. Their realities had no comprehension of the changing lifestyles and mindset of a young man growing up in America. Whenever I would join friends on psychedelic expeditions, there was sadly no way to communicate my exciting experiences to them. Often I would say I was going out to a party of which their comments would be insults and terrible images of my taking part in aggressive debauchery with no redeeming value. Activities definitely not approved by the Church. And when I would return back home after a few days of high navigation, my mother's critical eye would carry judgments as if I had been out with fellow hippie psychopaths killing babies and burning crosses.

The same disparity in our culture led to stereotypes of which even I was perhaps guilty of. Just like they considered all hippies to be gangs of thugs and worshipers of Charlie Manson, I tended to profile my parents as victims of the plastic culture of the 50's which had no connection to their native or even spiritual roots. Often I would tell them their brightly polished new furniture was awful and my more enlightened preference was cardboard boxes with thrift store Arabesque mandala tapestry coverings. Now I am quite happy to have inherited their furniture which looks much better with the polish worn off to show the colors of the natural wood. Retrospect always leaves feelings of moments of love and acceptance gone with the winds of time. Hopefully a few residual messages have been gained as well in both honoring the relationships as well as learning how to perhaps be more accepting of our remaining loved ones. I will always know that my parents deeply loved me but their confusion with the world around them led to many fear based reactions in their intention of providing me with the security and comfort that they did not have in their youth. I love them very much and never a day goes by that they are not in my thoughts and heart.

CHURCH BUST

After the funeral, John and Nicolette returned back to the Sacred Mushroom Church in Switzerland. With Nicolette's updates from Switzerland sounding as delightful as her brother's, the next question was would Sophia like to come up for a few days and join her siblings for a dream holiday in one of the most beautiful places in the world.

Dreams can often turn to nightmares, however. After arriving at the lodge, Sophia was settling into the comforts of her own comfortable room with a view, she was startled to see a line of police cars pulling up into the parking lot. With a polite introduction, the head officer presented a warrant for Pastor D's arrest and explained that the buildings had to be searched for "evidence". The charges were obviously mushroom related as the cops ignored the many pot plants growing in various rooms but confiscated the several varieties of psychedelic mushrooms on the premises. They also, however, confiscated all the money they could find which included a box that had Nicolette's accumulated her one month salary.

Even though D had clearance from the Swiss government for the recognition of the Sacred Mushroom Church and allowance of the use of psychedelic sacraments by its members, the United States government had pressured the Swiss for his arrest. If he had just limited the presence of the church to the boundaries of the country, he probably would not have been busted. However by his registering members in the US and subsequently sending them mushrooms, the US considered it a major felony which they viewed as "drug smuggling."

D was subsequently handcuffed, shackled and taken away as a dangerous criminal. Not even his wife was allowed to see him for several months and even then without any chance for a private conversation. A terrible image for his children to have of their loving and gently spirited father. Not even murderers are treated in such a fashion.

Although our attempts to retrieve Nicolette's money never was successful because of its possibly being used in "drug trafficking", D's wife was able to send her a few payments as compensation. Irregardless of the money, Stephanie and I were happy that none of our children had been arrested. The scene of all three of them behind bars in a foreign country and with no legal access to their aid was a horrible possibility that we were ever so grateful to the higher powers of the universe for not allowing to happen.

ANOTHER RIDE NORTH

With the International University in cosmopolitan Lugano in the gorgeous Italian Alps a possible choice for Nicolette to go to college, a good enough excuse was fostered for our taking one more voyage with our van into northern Europe.

Since on our last trip in the area we did not have a chance to visit the yoga/spiritual retreat center that our friend Pius had been inviting us to come stay at, we decided now was our opportunity to take a short detour and pay him a visit for a few days. The center itself was situated in a lush area overlooking a beautiful lake and snow clad mountains. There were ongoing classes and special group workshops of which Pius allowed us to sit in on as well as have free use of the spring fed swimming pool and healthy food buffet. Even more exciting was his taking us on a scenic ride through the countryside where we were treated to creamy Italian Gelato ice cream and then to a steaming natural thermal hot spring.

Our visit afterwards to Lugano was not as impressive as the town had an elitist attitude and the students looked very arrogant. Even if they gave Nicolette a full scholarship, she decided not to pursue enrolling and getting stuck in this place for the next four years. At this point, none of us were in any rush to go back to Greece, so we set our navigation course for one more visit to Amsterdam.

THE DUTCH TEA PARTY

Not having John with us felt like something was missing from our new visit to Holland, but nevertheless it was still a journey with wonderful experiences. Having the van with us meant being able to not only travel around but to be able to stay in various campgrounds such as right across the bay a short distance by ferry boat from the downtown section of Amsterdam.

We visited our friend Soma who gave us a royal 4:20 treatment which started off with a stony ride through the downtown river canals on a hired boat he cheerfully organized. The flashing images along the way were surrealistic enough but the peak moment of the ride came when we pulled up to an Italian pizzeria right on the water that could only be accessed by boat. Soma generously treated our munchies to a delicious vegetarian pizza as we proceeded to continue sailing the waters into nighttime.

Having missed his once a month full moon mushroom party by a few days, before we left the city, Soma was happy to give us a bottle of his twelve mushroom tea mixture that he promised would open up visions and revitalize health. To fortify the opportunity, we also purchased a package of magic mushrooms from one of the local head shops to take along on our upcoming psychedelic picnic. Just as John had been initiated on our previous visit to the city, we were preparing for a psychedelic journey with Nicolette as well.

About a four hour drive east of Amsterdam was a wonderful national park where we set up our camp for the next few days. For the first time in years, I was brave enough to get on one of the many free bikes provided by the park to join Stephanie and our daughters in peddling through the scenery while having our own driving path safely away from the traffic lanes.

Having discovered a relatively private meadow, we decided that it would be the right setting for us to eat and drink our fungal refreshments. Within the comfort zone of the natural environment and the country's freedom to fly, we were soon laughing at the changing world views and started twirling around the forest. While the ladies were engaged in merriment, I found myself humbly laying in front of a large grandfather tree that was pouring love and telepathic messages to me. Our awareness was soon jarred by a van of Japanese tourists that pulled up near us and which passengers started pointing at us and taking nonstop pictures. The bus driver more than likely remarked that we were hippies on drugs, so the cameras were taking souvenir memories of their encounter. Prime for the occasion, Sophia continued dancing and making silly poses while Nicolette and Stephanie couldn't stop from laughing. My reflex was to go to my friend the tree and ask for protection from the menacing outside world. A fine time was had by all, including the lucky tourists with the photos they would be happily sharing them in Japan.

HOT SPRINGS ON THE BORDER

Besides mountains and waterfalls, another aspect of natural living we missed in this part of the world was having access to a thermal hot spring. Even though most people that we asked insisted that no such hot springs existed in Holland, perseverance and the internet located just such a spot close to the German border. And since we were fairly near there, we took a small detour in our quest for a healthy soak to follow up our memorable psychedelic picnic. Unlike the hot springs that we had been to in the US and also in Greece, this place was situated in a high end resort facility complete with fancy hotel rooms and dining hall. Even the parking lot was full of expensive, well polished cars in contrast to our road worn van. But even with the peculiar stares from the other guests did not compromise our pleasure in soaking in the relaxing waters which revived our bodies and added a smile to our spirit. Not wanting to get our purity contaminated by the silly glamour around us though, we soon were on the road heading back to Greece.

With the disappearance of European border checks, the freedom to travel between one country to another was a very appreciated relief. Finally. no more long lines of cars waiting to be inspected closely by tough looking snoops with guns and badges. Switzerland, by not being a member of the European Union was the one sore thumb exception on the crossroads. But not only did we find the customs booth closed when we entered the northern part of the country but also when we came out on the southern Italian border, the Swiss border guards waved us through with smiles instead of sniffer dogs. Greece had just won the prestigious European Cup soccer tournament, so our Greek license plates were a free pass. Not so happy a situation for us however, was when Stephanie explained how she had foolishly wiped out so many of our precious memories of experiencing Amsterdam off the computer.

SOPHIA AND DAD'S ROAD TRIP

With Stephanie escorting Nicolette to college, Sophia and I decided to take a trip to the island of Zakinthos where John was now working as a chef in a busy restaurant which catered mostly to summer tourists. The bus system took us by transfers to the western side of the Peloponnesus where we stopped to visit our friends Aris and Nikos. Even before we moved to Greece, Aris and I had become close pen pals and it was always a delightful oasis within the hectic big city to share some time and space with him. Our conversations were always refreshing as were our field trips to various power spots and temples of ancient times. And then as now, he has remained a very good friend. Before moving to Athens, Nikos and his parents had lived in this home near the ocean and came here often to get away from the big city.

Nikos' mother was delightfully hospitable and made sure that Sophia got the best portions of her delicious homemade food and always a sweet delight dessert as a bonus. Our not eating meat wasn't a problem and she made sure we were eating both healthy and tasty. The guys took us on some scenic excursions in the area that were likewise pleasant and we shared many interesting conversations of metaphors, sarcasms and exciting stories of their pagan belief system.

Leaving their house early to catch a bus to our next transfer point presented us with a minor setback as just when we pulled up to our next destination, the bus we needed to be on had just left and thus we needed to wait another three hours for the next one. But with nothing that we could do about it, we sat down and watched the clock until it was our turn to move on. On the bench across from us sat several local people that stared at us but could well have been permanent fixtures in the bus station which was probably the liveliest place in their village

Having been delayed by the bus schedule, our next fear was that we would arrive at the harbor too late to catch the last ferry boat to the island. We managed to get on the boat in time but when we arrived on Zakinthos it was already nighttime. Being left at the port after disembarking without any sign of John there to pick us up was disconcerting as our tired bodies and nerves were in need of rest. Besides carrying our own backpacks and tents, we were bringing John his guitar that he had asked for which made it even more difficult to travel past the point and time we now found ourselves at. Even more concerning, when I made a call to the restaurant phone number that he had given us, the person that answered the phone said no "Yianni" worked there.

Another hour of waiting at the port brought us to 10 pm and a need to decide what our next step should be. Buses were no longer running, so we hired a taxi to take us to the town located about fifteen miles away where John said he was working. Sophia sat with our stuff on a bench on the edge of the lively business strip while I went through all the restaurants trying to catch a glimpse of my son. Luckily, it didn't take too long to find him working hard in a big kitchen with only a quick moment to greet me and explain that the restaurant was very busy and he could not have taken off to meet us at the docks without knowing for sure which boat we were arriving on. And as to why they didn't know who he was when I called, he explained how he was being called by his English name John which came out sounding like "Tzon". I walked back to tell Sophia the news and to also explain that we were going to be staying on John's couch that night and would figure out camping plans in the morning.

Sharing the small apartment building with John was a group of friendly Nigerian street vendors with wide smiles and playing loud lousy music all day and night. His room was messy and smelled of rancid food and moldy laundry, however, we were happy to see each other and it made up for such minor concerns. After hanging out with him for a few days, Sophia and I took a bus to where we set up our base at a campground located near an even more touristy beach area about fifteen miles away.

Except for a few derelicts with no other place to call home, the campground itself was relatively empty. Thus it made it difficult for us to walk past the office where the nearly blind owner and his nearly deaf dog would want to flag us down and share their loneliness with us. However we managed to find an opening in the back fence which provided a portal of escape when the owner was taking his break from sitting on his porch sometimes during the day.

Our daily walk to town would take us about twenty minutes but it would be like travelling to a whole different universe. The endangered turtles which once had their birthing sites protected by the Greek government, were now totally exposed to the savagery of loud mouthed manic tourists. The white sand ocean strip in front of the bars and restaurants would be packed with hung-over northern Europeans on an early start to their daily drinking binge and working on their sun burned lobster look. A few words of Greek could be heard spoken between employees, but the native language was virtually unheard here. Sports bars featuring hundreds of channels of soccer spewed between the high techno beat coming from most of the other bars. Compared to authentic Greek cuisine, what was being served at the local restaurants looked tasteless, overpriced and customized for foreign tourists.

Zakinthos had now developed into a major destination spot for package tours catering to mostly young kids from the United Kingdom. The usual social pattern was for the guys to be cheering for their favorite teams at the sport bars around noon. By four in the afternoon, the more precocious of the girls would already be throwing their clothes off and table dancing in jerky alcohol drenched fashion. Night time would be aflame with all sorts of distorted passions. A couple of nights I left Sophia at the campground around midnight to take an exploratory stroll on my own. Making sure in being an incognito witness, it was fairly disquieting to see and hear the squeals of gang banging sex with lines of drunk boys waiting to have their jump on girls along the beach and in some of the back alleys. The scene after 2 am was even more apocalyptic. Young girls sprawled out in contorted postures swimming between sleep and remembering. Young men passed out as war victims at the mercy of gypsy kids slipping their wallets out their pants and then laughing while urinating on their faces. And in case they would be too disoriented when the sun shone again, many were wearing wrist bracelets with their names and what hotels they were staying at. In fact, part of the travel promotion insisted that bracelets would be mandatory so the parents would feel secure that their children would be properly chaperoned. Surely among the body count on the beach the chaperons were there as well in embrace of the night's pleasure and regrets.

Curious on how the conservative older Greeks that operated the occasional market in town felt about all this debauchery, the most fitting explanation they gave me was one of empathy and compassion. As one wise elder saw it, these young English kids were well aware that in a short few years they would settle into a very conventional, programmed life. This exciting summer in Zakinthos was their one chance to enjoy living and take a few epic memories with them into the rest of their boring lives.

For a change of scenery and ambience, Sophia and I would sometimes catch the bus and go visit the more subdued town that John was working at. Lots of tourists floated around but not the loud party animal zoo of where we were based.

With no one seeming to mind, Sophia and I slept a few nights on my son's couches. Across the alley lived a few teenage guys that John was working with, including the owner's son Alex. After work, John would hang out awhile with them and the few times that I went over, it felt as if they were eager to learn more about the wonderful 60's of which I was happy to tell them stories of.

Sophia and I also would take a long walk to the harbor town where we would enjoy walking around the squares and getting ideas of where we could plan to take John on his upcoming birthday which nicely coincided with his having two days off from work in a row. For starters, John came over to our campground where we had a nice lunch prepared that even included a bubbly two dollar bottle of champagne. Then with the car we had rented for the day, we took a scenic cruise around the island. One of our highly anticipated stops was at a church dedicated to Mary Magdalene. We made arrangements with one of the cafes in the village to contact the priest who proudly came over to not only give us a tour but took us out for coffee and desserts to honor John's birthday. After we left that friendly village, we drove to a private beach in a cove below a cliff which was the perfect place to enjoy the sunset.

Before spending the night with us at the campground, John joined us for a stroll through the land of the drunks that was a hilarious ending to a perfect day. But the elation was short lived as the next day had a whole different twist to it.

John was asked if he could come work later that night, so during the afternoon while he was away doing some shopping, Sophia worked hard to surprise him by cleaning his stinky room. But when he came home he looked at the changes as disorienting and even accused his sister of misplacing a 50 euro bill that he had in his drawer. Later he found it in the back reaches of his pants, but never apologized to his sister for his snappy response.

Sophia and I went to our couch beds early that night so as to catch the early bus the next morning back to our campground. But we didn't realize just how early and under what circumstance we would be leaving. Around one in the morning John rushed into the apartment with a manic feeling of concern. Apparently the owner thought that John was providing cannabis to his son and after kicking a few tables before firing him, shouted that he was going to make sure that he would have him in prison. Without any reason to waste time discussing details, we managed to pack up all our belongings and ran out of the room within fifteen minutes. Not wanting to be easily detected, we followed a zigzag pattern on the back streets until we got back on the main road and caught a late night taxi ride to our campground. And in the clarity of the morning, we all caught the first ferry boat off the island.

XIROKAMBI ROCKS

New Years Eve in the Xirokambi town square usually meant intermittent conversations of holiday menus, gossip and backgammon played by loners with nowhere else to go. With such a yearly tradition, it was quite a surprise to hear that one of John's musician friends had invited him to take part later that night in a rock and roll gig in one of the town's cafes. The possibility of customers throwing the band members out into the cold streets after probably insulting the village's attachment to listening to only traditional and very un-contemporary Greek music loomed as a dreaded possibility.

Stephanie and I decided to at least be a couple of supportive fans, so we made sure to show up early enough to be there from the beginning of the show. As expected, only a couple of old men where in the café watching a soccer game on television while on the outside table a few more men where slowly sipping their drinks while watching the card and backgammon players in their deep contemplation over their next moves. After setting up their instruments, we could tell that the band was also experiencing second thoughts as to their predicament and rushed quickly to the back alley to share some smokes and swigs of alcohol to build up confidence or numb themselves to a terrible situation if need be.

Then the holiday miracle happened. By the time John had finished singing Johnny B Good, the empty tables that were all around us were being filled. The younger crowd seemed enthused to finally be hearing rock and roll filling the stale air and even more surprising, older men and women were twisting their bodies and singing along to "Born to Be Wild", "Sunshine of Your Love", and "Foxy Lady". It was indeed a rare and ecstatic moment we were experiencing of free spirited elders shining again through the many decades of embalming fluid. Later on, a Greek clarinet player came up and started jamming away to an even more throbbing wave of people finding much more fun in enjoying New Years Eve in town instead of their boring and predictable night at home. By early in the morning when time came to shut down, the band was hugged and kissed by a village of new fans, treated to food and drinks and even paid a couple of hundred dollars for their performance. Town pride was accented as people witnessed themselves rocking out to a memory that would vibrate for many years to come.

With our own abundant family memories over the years of our stay in Greece, the time had finally reached for our travels to take us to other distant horizons. So we took one last visit to my mother's grave, packed away belongings that we could not take along with us, and started studying travel books on Southeast Asia and India.

CHAPTER SIXTEEN: CONTINENTAL DRIFT

Our friend Thea once told us that we changed continents more often than some people change shirts. Reflecting on our life style, we did indeed enjoy traveling to unique, interesting, beautiful and inexpensive places around the world, but also look forward to staying long enough in each place to get a nice feeling of the people, culture and environment. Thus our arrival in Thailand felt very familiar as if we were returning back to one more place we considered home. Our planned long term destination was India, but by flying to Bangkok first, the air tickets were less expensive for us to get there and also we would be able to go to the International Rainbow Gathering taking place in the southern part of the country.

Our stopover in Bangkok gave us a chance to get grounded again to being in Southeast Asia as well as visiting Kenny, an expatriate friend of ours from Maui who gave us a tour of some of the other more interesting off the tourist map sections of the big city. Besides the inexpensive backpacker neighborhoods that we were familiar with, he took us to one of the first colonial era hotels in the city which had many vintage photos including one of the king playing jazz saxophone with a surprising young George Bush senior standing behind him in the background. Afterwards we took a monorail train ride to explore several blocks of Middle Eastern fast food restaurants alongside a variety of strip and exotic dancing bars featuring prancing males, aerobic females and all sorts of gender confused humans in between. Kenny has remained a long time friend although chances of meeting again are slim since his life remains a free floating experience in Asia. Perhaps once I can grow travel wings again we might connect. At least on this trip we still had a delightful opportunity to have the chance to discuss music, arts and the changing "hippie-gypsy" culture.

Even though taking a long distance bus ride in Thailand is an exciting adventure in itself, this time we opted for a modern, comfortable, inexpensive and fast speed train for the three hour ride south. We then went on to visit several new outposts and a thermal hot springs before we managed to find the location of the Rainbow Gathering situated between a lush forest and a picture perfect pristine beach front.

In order to get to the setting, we had a choice of either a two hour hike in the hot sun or paying a few dollars to be driven down to it by some young Thai kids with motor cycles. Already a makeshift service area established by the local village with food stalls, t shirts, camping supplies and even a mobile internet cafe. On the bottom of the path, more food servers and even luxury tents were organized in case people wanted to get away from any otherwise primitive conditions at the gathering.

Not sure if we would have the opportunity of a good meal for awhile, we stayed a couple of hours at one of the cafes fine dining while waiting for low tide passage so as to hike the last half hour to our destination. Like stepping through the border of another country, we were greeted at the colorful "welcome home" booth and by all the smiling faces, windblown long hair and flowing sarongs and dancing spirits. We had missed the full moon finale by a couple of days, but there were still several hundred people from all over the country staying longer to keep experiencing the delightful opportunities of social networking in such a perfect dreamscape location.

But even dreams are sometimes shaken by unexpected changes. A few days before our arrival, there was a sad loss of a child being stillborn. Grief was being shared by the parents as well as the remaining hippie tribe which was then expressed in a funeral procession along the beach. Next to the crying parents was a basket of flowers which we assumed also had the body of the child which would be placed in the ocean in a traditional Thai ritual. Along our solemn walk of prayer, chants and tears, my attention drifted towards the horizon where I observed several fast moving motor boats heading in our direction. Evaluating the situation, my survival instinct was that the police were about to bust us for the death of the child and possible other unknown violations of laws and local customs. Especially after hearing murmurings of possible mass deportations because of how during the first week of the gathering, a group of young Israelis had purposely marched naked into a Muslim community to announce that "they were Rainbows and could freely do so". So with all these apprehensions running through my head, I told my kids to split as fast as they could and that if we were separated, to wait for each other at the top of the highway near the village.

With bureaucratic detail, the yellow t-shirted Thai officials that disembarked from the boats, walked around the Rainbow camp taking pictures and making notes before, without any explanation, got back on their boats and left us confused and in various states of anxiety over hypothetical scenarios. Explanations, however, were only two more days in coming when someone brought us an English copy of the local newspaper. A clarifying announcement was soon made that the king had sent a group of his environmental advisers to the Rainbow Gathering site to study and then evaluate what they found. Because of his interest in local sustainability, he was impressed by the hippie organizational skills in all aspects including the kitchen, toilet facilities and water system. His recommendation was that the tract of land that was the gathering site be designated as an experimental social model for Thai people to come and learn from the young Rainbow people as well. Even after we left, I would often check the website for this particular gathering and see that over the years, quite a few of those folks were still living and thriving on the site. An amazing turnaround from having to face the struggle of being visionary nomads in a cruel modernized matrix of the "other world".

After a short bus ride to Ranang, we then caught a ferry boat intending to stay at the lush island of Koh Lanta for a few days. On the boat we met a young man with a body covered with tattoos but also had a sweet disposition and who invited us to be his guest on a different island which he explained was more beautiful and relatively still untouched by tourist development. Feeling comfortable with this unexpected change of direction, we trusted fate and joined our new friend Tak when the ferry boat paused for us to transfer to the smaller row boat which then took us to the nearby shoreline of his island.

During the next couple of days, we enjoyed the freedom of not rushing through a scheduled itinerary as well as talking with Tak and his introducing us to many of his friends. The principal of the school even asked if we would like to be the island's English teachers. In a parallel universe, we probably would have been better as such for the indigenous people than trusting the present Western missionary education system. Tak seemed especially fond of us because we were traveling together as a family and he missed his own parents who were killed in an automobile wreck. As with all young Thai men his age, he had a choice to go into the military or become a monk in a Buddhist monastery for a couple of years. Tak chose the latter option and was living a peaceful life as a vegetarian who commuted to the mainland for a variety of work as an artist. Respecting our own dietary preferences, Tak and his friends would prepare wonderful vegetarian meals for us while not even allowing us to help wash any dishes or assist them in the kitchen. Our evening walks along the beach were rejuvenating as the spirit of the island was very healing for the body, mind and spirit. At the time of our visit, there were still no plans for hotels, harbor expansion or grid electricity. There weren't even any cars to be seen or heard. Hopefully that attitude is still the wish of the local people that did not seem concerned on acquiring more material comforts than what they needed.

Goodbyes were exchanged with our new friends and soon we were once again traveling by boat, bus and train to Bangkok and on to a new travel horizon, India.

CHAPTER SEVENTEEN: INDIA

WELCOME TO INDIA

Any obvious social or cultural similarity between Thailand, Bali, Fiji, and the countries in Europe that we were familiar with was totally alien to our initial impressions on arriving in India. The Calcutta airport was fairly functional except for a large number of employees on strike who had blocked the way to the only bathroom in the hall. Luckily we found a back way to the facilities which to my surprise were in good flushing order. But when we stepped out into the city, we were not at all prepared for the world that was waiting to be our home for the next few months as well as becoming a permanent experience in our mind, heart and soul.

One of the most noticeable sights at the airport was to see groups of Sikhs wearing turbans on their head and knives on their belts. Traditional rights of carrying such sharp weapons to protect the homeland superseded any other regulations in regards to contraband and what would be appropriate to carry on the plane.

Also in line were a group of Muslim women with scarves concealing their faces. As new airport security regulations required a photo I.D. to match their appearance, they were escorted to another section of the room where a woman security agent was allowed to examine their papers and faces.

The panorama that is India is not just confined to the Himalayas, ancient temples or tropical beaches. Every moment and inch of this vast country is dramatic and linked to ancient as well as modern manifestations. If I were to compare a visit to India as a movie, I would say it is a drama, thriller, romance, comedy, horror, scenic documentary and "all of the above" including "cult". Hinduism considers life to be full of illusions but makes no pretense to mask any of its expressions. In just taking a taxi ride to the train station we would witness millions of people living in the street while the chauffeurs of rich merchants driving high end limos would get out with sticks to push poor people out of the way. Emaciated looking living skeletons of people seeming as if they were in ecstasy would be seen chanting in front of temples behind and through clouds of incense and banging of gongs. A very long and well practiced dance of humanity. Long lines of traffic would be waiting patiently for slower moving cows to walk across the city streets. The sky was darkened by pollution but the smell of savory delights would bring smiles of anticipation to our hungry stomachs. By the looks of how difficult it would be to travel through such congested streets, we quickly realized that our many months of researching a travel itinerary that would navigate us around all corners of this country would not be very realistic. I suppose we were beginning to get grounded to the reality of being in a new and amazing country that could take us at least a few lifetimes to properly explore. So we agreed if our travel plans would have to make adjustments, we were fine and would be satisfied with wherever fate and karma would lead us on our journey.

Stepping into the Calcutta train station was an immersion into a crowd of thousands of travelers scrambling to catch their train as well as even more thousands of beggars that looked as if this huge building was their permanent home. Instead of the smiling dancing girls putting flower leis around a travelers neck when arriving in Hawaii, here in India it was the stretched out hands of people desperately hoping a coin or two will make their day a little more comfortable.

Once we squeezed past the multitudes in front of the station with our suitcases still intact and in our hands, we followed a dilapidated stairway up to a waiting room where fellow travelers were sitting until their time of departures. The remarkable look on their faces of contentment, even through the chaos we perceived all around us, was a necessary lesson for us to learn and practice on our travels. The rounds of vendors bringing hot chai to keep bodies refreshed was one more sign of civilization adapting itself to necessary changes.

Compared to the organized train systems of Thailand or Holland, the Indian rail transportation was confusing to say the least. The waiting platform was about half a mile long with endless lines of train tracks. None of the electric track signals were working while no official was around to ask where or when our particular train to Darjeeling would arrive. In a distant corner of the station was a small room with a sign that said "information" posted on the wall. As soon as I saw an apparent representative open its window, I made haste to go ask questions but a few hundred other people pushed their way in front of me which was a clear signal not to expect any help in return for my efforts. Besides, about ten minutes after it opened, the official closed the window leaving a growing mob of people shouting unpleasantries of anger at the building.

Back where I had left Stephanie, John and Sophia with our suitcases, I noticed several people hovering nearby and staring as if there might be a chance to snag one of our bags if they could find a chance to do so. Switching to a more defensive posture, John and I positioned ourselves on either side of the corner with a wall protecting us from behind. After about an hour of sitting, we saw a police man walking by and after we showed him our tickets, he told us that our train would be leaving in about twenty minutes from a track about one hundred yards away. Not wanting to be late, we gathered our stuff and walked briskly to where we needed to be but found over a hundred other people ahead of us pushing each other to get into the train. Since we had reserved seats for a class two cabin, we didn't think we had to worry much about getting seats but getting through this crowd and on the train before it departed seemed like a bigger challenge. An unexpected solution soon cleared the dilemma as several police men showed up with long sticks and started hitting people who didn't have reserved tickets so as to allow passengers like ourselves a chance to board. We realized later that many people without tickets were actively squeeze on top of the train as well.

Finding our way to the cabin door, we at first felt we had mistakenly walked into the wrong room as four men were already in it. One was in the top berth snoring while the others were airing out their feet from stinky socks. According to our tickets, our family had reserved the whole room, but being India and porters were nowhere to be seen, we were quickly learning the social norm of sharing even the tiniest of spaces. Our traveling companions were cheerfully smiling and asking us the usual questions of where were we from and how we liked India while making enough room for all of us to fit in. After exchanging small talk and then hooking our baggage to locks attached to the bottom of our seats, we settled in for the long overnight train ride ahead.

Between the endless miles of darkness, whenever the train would come to a stop, vendors selling chai and snacks would appear at our window trying to sell their array of refreshments. By peering deeper, I would sometimes notice night markets and the soft light of homes in the night scenery. Also the hands reaching in through the window rails were not always vendors but also random attempts to perhaps grab a backpack or even a hope for some spare change. Often these pursuits were not only from people outside the train but from the folks riding on the roof who had not yet been evicted by the station security cops. On one particular stopover point about an hour north after leaving Calcutta, our four roommates disembarked leaving us with room to rest easier and with no smell of feet or repetitive sounds of snoring. We once more expressed small talk and goodbyes with our previous roommates before making sure to lock our door from the inside so as to give ourselves a chance of a few sleep winks during the remaining long night ahead.

When we reached the end of the line, we were faced with fresh confusion. According to our travel book a daily train was listed that left for our remaining hillside destination of Darjeeling. But what we found out as we disembarked at the station was that the particular train which we looked forward to taking on a scenic ride through the mountains had been broken for several years. Thus the only remaining way up was to take a van which we had no trouble finding as we were soon flanked by several drivers eager to secure a customer.

The three hour ride was indeed scenic as it wound its way up the switchback mountain road but not at all comfortable. First of all, besides our family of four, the remaining space of two seats was filled by four more passengers as well as an extra teenage driver who would be changing gears while the even younger main driver would be responsible for handling the shaky steering wheel. The ride itself did present one beautiful vista after another but for me, because of the frantic speed we were being driven was so the van could race back to where it started in hopes of picking up another paying load of customers. It was mostly a blur and a literal pain in my gut. Eventually as we came to a ten minute pause for peeing in the bushes, my nausea finally could not be contained as I started puking out the food I had eaten on the train. The drivers were alarmed that I might be staining their rear seats. Stephanie at this point brought it to their attention that reckless driving was not expected as part of the trip whereupon after we started off again, the drivers did show better care in smoother driving. Again, more lessons and reasons to remember we were now in India.

DARJEELING

Being dropped off downtown was confusing. The travel books raved about Darjeeling's scenic mountainous backdrop as well as its cultural impact having once been a colonial British outpost and still a lush area of world famous tea plantations. Drained by the exhausting train and van rides, we now found ourselves standing on a busy sidewalk of rushing pedestrians, un-muffled screeching motorcycle noise, polluted air, heavy humidity and nonstop stares. I advised the family to go have a cool drink while I walked up the crooked streets in search of the hotel which we had researched to be suited for staying a few days.

Climbing higher and higher, I was feeling a shortage of breath as well as a reminder that our time in the Himalayas would necessitate both strong legs as well as deep and steady breathing. However I wasn't complaining as after a few minutes I realized that there was a nicer appearance to the city. Interesting shops, aromatic kitchen smells and peek a boo views were opening up to invite discovery. The sounds of mechanical rage were also quieting with the transforming and more pleasant surroundings. Following the path of other western backpackers, I eventually located our hotel and after announcing our arrival, dashed back downtown to bring the rest of the family up. None of our legs were able to consider another long walk uphill but as a taxi was hired for the ride, I could not fail but admire an old man with a long white beard who was able to take the same walk I did while carrying a refrigerator on his back. Another reminder that we were in India.

After the chaos of Calcutta, our compromised train ride and the morning's roller coaster van drive it was a relief to finally feel a better start to our excursion into this exciting country. The hotel was owned by a personable Tibetan family and provided comfortable rooms, delicious homemade food and lots of information on places to visit. In the downstairs floor we found a fast speed internet access which was usually not too busy except in late afternoon when the high school students would fill the room. During the expansion of the their colonization of the continent, the British set up Darjeeling as a colonial outpost and training ground for a managerial class of Indians. The kids using the internet were well dressed and polite which fit the image of the elite class that would one day be in high levels of the country's bureaucracy. Like teenagers all over the world, their prominent online interest was to play war games of mass destruction. But unlike the battle cries and yells we saw in other countries, these kids would be very calm and even sensitive in such exchanges such as "Sir, I am very sorry but I must blow up your house." And the reply, "Oh yes, I am very sorry you must blow up my house but sadly I now am having a bomb blow up your family too." When the time came for them to head home, they again very politely shook clean hands and went calmly on their way to do their studies.

The next few days were not only an immersion into the beautiful scenery and culture of this country of epic proportions, but also it became a literal feast for our bodies. For years we kept waiting for the opportunity to be able to afford the exquisite cuisine that we had in the past only window shopped the menus of Indian restaurants or sampled at the occasional Hare Krishna gatherings that we had attended. Now for about two dollars a meal (and oftentimes less) we splurged and kept on eating at every restaurant our nose and stomach would lead us to. And at no time during the next few months of our trip would we ever regret any of the memorable meals we experienced. The fear that many travelers had circulated about terrible diseases of the gut were not at all relevant to our reality. The thrill of seeing "pure vegetarian" signs on restaurants was an open ticket that no meat or lard was used in the cooking. Also by only drinking hot beverages that had been properly boiled, sealed bottles of water and adding enough hot sauce to our food that would almost bring tears to our eyes, encouraged our trust of not letting any germs or bugs ruin our gourmet dining excursions.

But besides investigating as many eating establishments as possible, we also took frequent strolls around the many parks and historic sights of the area. Our only scary moment came when we were stalked by a gang of aggressive monkeys while visiting a temple and had to carefully side step our way out of being attacked. I suppose in contrast to Indian visitors being ambushed by humans carrying weapons of fatal pain, we were relatively much safer.

SIKKIM

Over a period of several months we had been in touch with our Greek friends from the island of Ikaria, George and Dimitri, who had likewise planned a visit to the Indian continent. George and his girlfriend Maria were taking music and dance classes in the historic city of Varanasi and wanted to join us for a few days. Their desire was to visit the province of Sikkim which straddles the Himalayas and even though not technically a part of India, we still would have to obtain visas from a local office in Darjeeling to go there. Thus we agreed to travel with them into one more page of beauty as well as a much different culture crafted from Buddhism instead of Hinduism.

Hugs exchanged upon our friends arrival at the designated meeting location at the upper town square, we swiftly organized our plans to leave the next morning for the three hour van ride. So far, our expeditions of the last eight years had been solo family affairs. Now with our three friends as travel companions, our experiences were to be enhanced by their fun personalities as well as our being more conscious to cloak our sporadic family arguments.

Sikkim had considered itself a separate country until its recent history, so there was still the formality of a border check in crossing into its beautiful setting and warmly hospitable people. Our friends were somewhat frustrated by the unsanitary carelessness that they had been struggling with in India and were eager for a healthier turn of travel events.

Even though the taxi driver that our friends had hired was waiting at the designated spot to set off on the trip on time and eager to start the long drive, the rest of our group was nowhere to be seen. George and Maria had been looking for a drug store while Dimitri was picking a wild flower bouquet to add color and delightful fragrance to our trip. Our nervous taxi driver however was not able to hide his impatience and kept looking at his watch and asking us who was going to pay for his wasted time. Like most of the other taxi drivers, other people were waiting to be picked up after the five hour round trip that would be waiting in the afternoon to again drive the same route. Time meant money to him and we were certainly challenging his expectations of being on schedule. But after an hour of waiting, the rest of our crew showed up and off we went. Sort of. When it became obvious that our driver had a few more passengers to pick up along the way,

Dimitri insisted that we had booked the van just for our group and we would not allow any more folks to cramp the already tight sitting space. In typical "no problem" India style approach to such problems, the driver quickly figured a workable solution on how to transport the other two passengers on his pick up schedule. The skinniest one would sit on the lap of the drivers assistant and the other one could hold on to the outside running board of the vehicle. Since neither of these two other riders were going far, that challenge seemed to have been solved. The other problem that brought a new rise to tensions came when our friends informed the driver that he had to slow down so we could enjoy the scenery as well as not having our stomachs tossed around too much by nausea. If he wouldn't comply with the request, the threat was that we wouldn't pay him. Reluctantly but with unde-cipherable mumbling to our demand, we continued on the beautiful drive to enchanting Sikkim.

After a nice meal and a chance to get oriented, we made plans to leave the same day for a more remote village higher up in the foothills of the towering mountains that stretched all around us. The more we learned about Sikkim, the more impressed we became. The governor of the province had asked for the elimination of all plastic bags, the switch to total organic farming and the promotion of solar as the main energy modality. Truly civilized models that fit quite well with, for the most part, the unspoiled beauty of the landscape.

Our collective decision was to check into a hotel and then em-bark on a six day hike which would take us through forests, rivers, waterfalls, hot springs and bird songs. As we would learn to expect on every long trekking plans with our friends, their day needed to start with a "power breakfast". Although being a bit frustrating for us to have to wait several hours past our planned start time for the local home cooked meals to be prepared and then properly enjoyed, it did fit into a definite nice start to the day. Soon enough we would be hiking on ancient trails that would lead our navigation through homesteads and small villages that had no other road access than by foot or donkey. As we would approach such settlements we were always greeted with wide eyed smiles and offers of hospitality. Finding inexpensive places to sleep or eat was not a problem with no shortage of homes offering extra rooms and local style meals. At one village, John started playing an old guitar that was laying on a cafe table and within a few minutes about twelve young kids had crowded around him singing Bob Marley songs and treating him to many rounds of bitter tasting but pleasantly intoxicating home brewed beers and fermented barley wine.

The village homestays along the trails were also a well appreciated source of travel information. Following such directions, we hiked up to a hill overlooking a magnificent panorama of a deep river valley at the foothills of the towering Himalayas. A settlement of several buildings including a Tibetan monastery spread gracefully across a wide green meadow bordered by old growth trees that stretched to the puffy clouds flowing by in the breeze. Inside one of the buildings a group of young monks were playfully engaged in working while their older mentors seemed to be giggling from what we perceived to be more than just spiritual intimacy relations with the young boys. Even non-Catholic priests must have to deal with the celibate blues.

As word spread of the arrival of our group of travelers, several other teenagers appeared holding guitars and soon were singing and playing music with John, Dimitri, George and Maria. An out of the box mini Rainbow Gathering scene crossing division lines of time, space and culture. Meanwhile, Stephanie and I found an open back door to the oldest looking of the somewhat abandoned buildings and delighted in studying the various postures and posters of erotic Tantric wall paintings. The images from these paintings of hundreds if not thousands of years ago were all heterosexual couplings which could well have been a subject to compare in the probable homosexual activity of present day monks. But for whatever direction driven to deal with natural urges and their transformation, Tibetan Buddhists were definitely not in states of denial.

Because Stephanie and I were a little slower walkers than the rest of the group, we often would lag behind but there was no problem as we would catch up eventually. Perhaps it was the healthy climate and environment that helped us at times even walk twenty kilometers a day without feeling very tired. On our last night, we stayed in one of many bungalows that a village elder had set up near his house for long distance trekkers such as ourselves. The price of the lodging was inexpensive enough but when it came time to pay the next day, he would ask everyone in the camp to sit with him in a circle and for anyone that could sing a song of their own, the price for staying the night was free. My own version of "Row row row your boat" passed the audition.

Trekking up into high mountain villages had mostly rudimentary accommodations and comforts were the norm, we were quite surprised to find staying with us a middle aged Asian lady with high heels, lots of makeup and a designer suitcase. Past her superficial conversations, she gave notice that her plans were to investigate traditional handicrafts from which she would organize middle men to come and buy and then sell for astronomical prices in the "civilized world". Sadly the tentacles of exploitation had reached global dimensions even here in the high reaches of the Himalayas. Waving goodbye as we watched her descend the mountain trail, it seemed fitting surrealism that she had prearranged a shiny black taxi to pick her up and not risk tiring her feet or soiling her fancy suitcase. For the rest of us, nature was a blessing to embrace again as we continued the next leg of our hike through the trails that lay waiting to eagerly share their beautiful scenery, often accented with colorful prayer flags and smiling faces of curious children. Even without our having to wear expensive shoes for such pleasurable experiences.

The next few days we gave our legs a rest and enjoyed staying in several larger villages before we finally said good bye to our Greek friends. We went back to Gangtok for a couple of more days in the big city. Finding a budget priced centrally located hotel was the right choice. The two young kids that were working at the front desk of the hotel were efficient and courteous enough to at least let us know our room number but even as they were handing us the key, their eyes remained glued to a small black and white television which was broadcasting an American wrestling show with Indian subtitles. Sensing my cue, I entered into the enthusiasm of the moment and expressed how our hero was Hulk Hogan. Then after my naming all the same wrestlers that they liked and our favorites as well, they soon offered us a better room for a cheaper price. Such are the perks of being aware of all cross-cultural anomalies and similarities.

The city itself was a busy hub for commerce and government, but we did manage to explore several interesting temples and botanical gardens. The taxi driver we hired for these excursions noticed that we had an interest in spirituality, so he took the liberty to take us to a meditation center where we were greeted respectfully, offered a snack and then given a signed photo of the resident guru.

But the most memorable memory from our visit to Gangtok was the wonderful array of inexpensive vegetarian food available. Our nose for fine food smells never would steer us wrong as we ate several times at one of the more fancier restaurants in town. But besides the low prices, fancy white tablecloths, and very efficient waiters, the food was fantastic.

Although we still had many weeks ahead in India, we felt a little sad in leaving Sikkim and hoped one day to return. I even imagined it to be a suitable place to live long term, but unfortunately, a foreigner can only stay a maximum of two weeks in that lovely country. So off we were to continue our travels to another side of the majestic Himalayan mountains.

BACK TO INDIA

By now the reality had dawned on us that we might have to abridge our travel plans in India as it took much more time to get between one place or another on the crowded roads and buses than expected. To at least enjoy one base for the next few months, we chose to be in the Himalayas again but on the range facing the northwest corner. One of the legends of Hinduism was that the god Shiva had smoked hashish in Parvati Valley and would remain in a blissful dream for 25,000 years. We thus decided this area and the town of Manali, near Kashmir, which was a scenic mountain town in the valley mentioned as a favorable location for backpackers and being in the hub of many other places of interest to explore.

Not wanting to be stuck in a stuffed eighteen hour bus ride across the country, we chose taking an affordable air flight instead. The small plane was comfortable but the six hour delay before we took off was a minor inconvenience which we tolerated considering how miserable any other transportation system in the country would have been.

With not much interest in investigating the big city of New Delhi on this journey, upon landing we took a taxi from the train station as the next step in heading north. A couple of suspicious young men who claimed to be porters tried to take our luggage but as we insisted in asking a nearby police man which way the correct terminal was, they scampered away into another huge mass of humanity at the station. We did manage to get on the right train and even had a private room with no one else in it which thus gave us a chance to rest a bit on the twelve hour ride to our next destination.

The train did not go all the way to where we wanted but did leave us within a three hour bus ride which became the next step to take. At the half way point on our ride, we stopped for a rest break and when I went to the back side of the cafe to take a leak, it dawned on me that I was standing right next to a huge field of cannabis. Excited by my discovery, I went and grabbed the rest of the family which likewise were startled into happy laughter. Looking out the window once the bus started again, it seemed that the pot fields stretched for endless miles giving validity to the Shiva story of a sacred valley of marijuana.

MANALI

Being a commercial hub in the area, our arrival in Manali was an encounter with the expected tidal wave of buying, selling, bartering and begging in a dense eternity of humanity. The scents of delicacies mingled with motorcycles relentlessly blowing horns, shouts of arguments and the plea of the homeless for a few crumbs. And with every coin given, a pack of even more desperate figures would grasp us with hands pleading for help as well. Some of the gypsy girls would be holding on to dolls that were supposed to look like their babies while saying over and over that they were orphans themselves.

Flowing through the slow moving pedestrian traffic as best as we could, we eventually reached the bridge over the river that divided the main part of town from what would be considered the older section up on a high hill. Like walking into a different world, the crowds thinned and replaced by a profile of young backpackers from all over the world eating in cafes and catching up on messages at the internet. Realizing that the tourist lifeblood had to be filtered from uncomfortable pressures, the long meandering street of this tourist mecca was where one could find the tailor made hemp clothes to wear at Rainbow Gatherings, trippy art objects with spiritual imagery, techno music pumping, and the smell of cannabis drifting from all directions.

Walking past most of the shops we came to a two story guest house that looked far away from the street noise with nice verandas on the back side facing the panorama of the snow clad Himalayan mountains with the river flowing across their forested lap. The price of about ten dollars a room was fair enough so we rented a separate room for our kids as well. Down the hall was another suite that had been rented by two long bearded Americans who spent all their time being stoned and riding motorcycles. It turned out that they had been staying in the hotel for over three months and a few days after we moved in, they disappeared so as to not pay their overdue rent bill. A few weeks later we recognized them in a nearby town with a clean shaven look so as to be maintaining a new identity. At least they wouldn't be giving other bearded Americans such as myself a bad name for their future crimes. Men with beards that suddenly cut them off are a suspicious lot in general. In 1968 Senator Eugene McCarthy was running for US president as an anti-war candidate so lots of hippies decided to cut their hair and campaign for him. "Let's go clean for Gene" was the motto. McCarthy lost and politics did not change but most of those guys who cut their hair decided to return to being yuppies instead. But that's another time and place story.

Our tourist enclave also was filled with groups of long haired Israeli men wrapped with shawls that reinforced my perception of their being perhaps Rainbow kids seeking enlightenment. But after I would see their obnoxious and demanding behavior and petty complaining towards the locals, I began to have my doubts. Later someone explained to me that once an Israeli soldier is finished with his service, they are given a free trip to India to smoke a lot of hash and chill out. But from their military mannerisms and even having the audacity to fly Israeli flags from some of the guest houses, they were not heading for any spiritual pilgrimage or anger management workshops any time soon. It was quite an effort on my part to keep from intervening in defense of the humble Indians that had to listen to their bullshit such as wanting better prices on rooms that were already under five dollars or on internet prices that were affordably less than a dollar an hour. But not wanting to be caught in racial stereotyping, I was happy in meeting many other Israeli independent travelers over the next few weeks. One of our more frequented hangouts was a café that served delicious ice cream cakes and played lots of Bob Dylan and Grateful Dead music. And as in most places, there was always a water pipe or chillum being passed around.

No longer resolved to attempt seeing any more of the country than this particular province, we were quite satisfied in renting our two bedroom suite for a couple of months and having it as our home base for excursions to other villages and sights in the area. The river served as an excellent boundary from the high impact zone of the main part of town and the backpackers mountain retreat that we were staying at.

One of the most important aspects of our travels is always where and what to eat at an affordable price. The many restaurants around the hotel offered specialty meals for around two dollars each which was convenient enough but would take over an hour to prepare and seemed to be lacking in spice. But in venturing to town, we would be able to eat better tasting meals, quicker in preparation and cheaper in price at the places local people ate. Of course dealing with being bombarded by demands of beggars and fortune tellers was an obstacle, but the restaurants were always an oasis from the street circuses.

Our walk back to the hotel would take us through a beautiful park shaded by tall trees and alongside a very old temple. One of the kids that would be trying to sell me a shoe shine or artificial saffron ran away when with my best guru accent, I warned him that if he would rip me off, he would face bad karma and could well come back as a crippled cockroach. Perhaps after such a success at fooling the street merchants, I could move on to charging for imparting spiritual transmissions and guidance. Not too far from our hotel we actually saw an arrow pointing to a cave where a guru promised such teachings and even had an emblem from Visa on his sign indicating that one could pay with a credit card. The ancient heritage of India was adapting quiet well to contemporary tools of commerce.

Although it was obvious that the community's efforts to protect the "young westerners" from being bothered by peddlers and beggars resulted in less harassment in our neighborhood, we still had to dodge a few persistent folks that would always be trying to sell us jewelry and guided trips into nearby Kashmir. Finding back alleys and trails to get around such traps, I noticed a nondescript shack along a stream that always had a line of small taxis parked next to it. On closer inspection, we realized that this place was a restaurant that our taste buds, stomach and budget would be happy for our discovering. For the price of one dollar, we would be instantly served a large combination tali plate consisting of basmati rice, vegetables, dhal, chapattis and chai. Better yet, the friendly owner would come by to offer us even more rice, chapattis or chai if we so desired at no extra price. No wonder my mind drifted into one day retiring to this blessed country where I could eat and live happily ever after.

As absorbed as we were soaking in the majestic Indian culture, we also felt connected to the rest of our lives and world through very fast and inexpensive internet cafes such as one comfortable place just a five minute walk from our hotel. The owner, Raji, was a very pleasant, skilled and quick to be of service middle aged Indian man who in the next few weeks would turn us on to a treasure chest of delightful Indian music. It was from him that we first heard the inspirational Sufi songs of Nusrat Fateh Ali Khan who all of our family now frequently listens to. And besides all the fine music that we would be hearing Raji would make sure that all the computers in the room were always working. Whenever an interruption to inter-net service occurred, he would insist there was "no problem", then would quickly disappear and come back in a few moments with the service back on line. For weeks we thought that he must have had some sort of backup generator that would solve the problem. But one day we happened to be walking along the river behind his shop where we saw him hitting a monkey with a long stick that was jump-ing up and down the phone line. Again, ancient solutions for mod-ern problems.

Not content with just getting stoned at the cafes, being irritat-ed by the long haired Israeli army thugs and eating our way through India, we also were eager to visit as many places of wonder as possible. Behind our hotel was a path that would take us across a mountain trail where the big birds would fly, then through a road-less village where young girls would smile at us as they wove their cloth on old spinning wheels. From there we continued over a river and up another hill where after our two hour hike we would rest in a town full of exotic shops and a large but crowded thermal hot springs. From here we also took a couple of excursions that after an hour would lead to the mountain snow line. Crowds of Indians would come by buses from the southern part of the country for a once a year and often just one hour moment to play in the snow and then go back home. The wealthier folks would arrive in chauffeur driven Mercedes whose drivers would rudely force the lower economic classes off the road so they could pass. Along the way were many small hot chai stands and multi colored fur coat rent-als for people to find relief from suddenly entering the cold weather zone. Understandably lots of pictures were being taken, so as to show their friends in the big cities that were still dealing with 100 degree weather. Because of the hundreds of cars trying to maneuver going up as well as down on the same narrow one lane road, lots of angry yells and horns blowing made the ride even more uncomfortable. But the experiences that they took with them were well worth such familiar nuisances.

It was here as well where John rented a motorcycle and went off with Sophia to explore even more scenery than we could by foot and bus. Along one of their excursions they tried in vain to find someone described as "one eyed Willie" who was reputed to have exceptional hand rolled hashish. But considering the availability and affordability of the high quality smoke soon to be discovered, it was not much of a sad loss to have an empty pipe a few more days.

One of my hopes when we came to this part of the world was that we would have the opportunity to be able to visit holy sites such as the source of the Ganges River high in the mountains and from there perhaps enter Nepal. If we could have made it to Rishikesh, we would be able to visit the place where the Beatles studied meditation with the Maharishi and from there reach the western border of Nepal through Almora, a place where another of my cultural heroes, Timothy Leary stayed and wrote one of his transcendental books.

But with the shrinking reality of time and its quick evaporation when traveling through the country, we settled instead for a visit to the town of Dharamsala which was the home of the Dalai Lama as well as now being a major center of Tibetan Buddhist monks and refugees.

After several hours of changing buses and struggling to find poles to hold on to or even an occasional open seat, we reached our destination. As with the popularized sacred sights of Greece and I suppose other famous places, Dharamsala appeared as a busy commercial center for not only to provide shops and services for its residents but also as a tourist attraction that needed catering to the variety of whims foreigners were in need to spend their money on.

Downtown greeted us with narrow streets and the loud litany of motorcycles and street merchants. The Tibetan religion was a focal point of merchandising including music, massage, healers and amulet sales. Tibetan food was sold in all the restaurants and for the glamorous tourists that had only come to visit this area because of its popularity, there were exotic clothes and gaudy sunglasses shops as well. Dodging the crowds and motorcycles we walked enough blocks to finally find a hotel to stay at that was relatively quiet and of course, affordable. And with an internet cafe located across the street, convenient as well.

Even with all the hustle and bustle of tourists, souvenir hawkers and spiritual pilgrims, Dharamsala was a very worthwhile and healthy stopover. The Tibetan hospital allowed us to have an inexpensive traditional health examination and we also enjoyed the healing massage of many exceptional body work practitioners.

Ironically, as one of the main reasons foreigners came to Dharamsala was to experience the Dalai Lama conducting daily chanting and meditation in the impressively decorated Tibetan monastery. During the week of our stay, he was visiting Maui. Accepting the idea that we had exchanged locations for some karmic reason, we still were able to enjoy visiting the monastery on our own as well as on a guided walk from the owner of the hotel we were staying at who also happened to be from Tibet.

Not seeing the Dalai Lama was a bit of a loss but we did enjoy our stay in the town, had a wonderful massage, ate tasty food from another region, had my urine analyzed at a Tibetan hospital that said I would live several more lives and left without having bought any generic souvenirs blessed or not.

A few miles above Dharamsala was a very beautiful valley that amazingly had very few people staying at the ample number of homestays spread across the village. Being the start of many trails through the mountains, we took a hike of a couple hours with our destination being a spot of cascading waterfalls. Stephanie and I were quite content to relax into the perfection of nature, but John and Sophia ventured on their own to more spectacular settings beyond the refreshing pools. We arranged to meet them back at the hotel later that afternoon and when they joined us related impressions of the majestic views along their path. They also said at one of the crossroads stood a small makeshift chai stand where they met an interesting hiker from Australia. A few years later when we visited Australia, we also met him there and stayed on his land near Nimbin for a few weeks. One more of life's surprises.

NICOLETTE JOINS US

Traveling to exotic places with the family was always a full-count affair. With Nicolette away at college while we were traveling first through Thailand and now India, not having her with us felt as if we had a missing person in our transitions. As our fascinating experiences of India kept reaching Nicolette's ears, the more she kept expressing her frustrations with both not being with us as well as with school in general. Thus when she humbly asked us to consider her dropping out of college, coming to meet us in India and then finishing her degree work as an on-line student we gave her the green light to join us. After her agreeing to also read my educational "Links by George" newsletter carefully each month, Stephanie and I reflected on the situation and expressed our satisfaction of her plans and to come join us in our new home base of Manali. It was already May and she proposed leaving the day after the semester ended a couple of weeks later. Nicolette was thus in exclamatory joy at our invitation and made plans to take the long flight to Delhi as soon as possible.

Not being any direct flights from anywhere to Manali, the best option for Nicolette to get to where we were was to hire a taxi driver that was a friend of the hotel owners to go to pick her up at the Delhi airport and then drive her back to us. Going to help the greetings and transitions, John and Sophia would also go along on the ride. Having experienced some of the reckless actions of Indian driving, Stephanie insisted that the taxi driver not race over the speed limit or else we would not pay him. Taking her words literally, the usually three hour drive took about twelve hours for him to drive back to Manali. According to our kids, the driver kept both hands on the wheel and kept looking at the speedometer nervously so as not to be going at "excessive speeds". Even after our kids asked him to speed up a bit, he remained loyal to Stephanie's instruction and did not want any reason to be cited that would keep him from receiving his payment.

When they finally arrived at the hotel, we were uplifted to be reunited again. After nearly three days of limited sleep, Nicolette was obviously exhausted, but there was a spark in her eye assuring us that she was ready to absorb herself in the travel experiences ahead. And not to miss my chance to have some quality time with her, since she woke up earlier than the rest of the family, I convinced her to join me on a one hour quick walking tour of the area that included the temple, park and of course, one of the cafes where she was delighted by the mango smoothie I bought her. Life was good.

MANIKARAN

Leaving most of our baggage at the hotel, we took an excursion to another area of interest that required a few hours of patience and bus connections to reach. Manikaran was one of the holy places of the Sikh sect who are noted for their appearance of heads wrapped in turbans and men with full beards and large sabers under their belt. Because of their religious traditions, they can even bring these knives on board some airplanes without any scrutiny. The town itself is spread over a large and fast moving river where on one corner steam blows from its famous thermal hot springs. It is a place where few Westerners go to and especially no Israelis, who because of their reputation for complaining are not allowed to enter the holy grounds and act disrespectfully.

Walking across the river from the highway was a rush as the rapids below were swift and powerful. There had been historic moments when the river would rise and sweep away homes and people. As we crossed over, we noticed a fair amount of stares at us, but it wasn't because of our foreign appearance or my sacred beard but because of our two nice looking daughters. There were even several occasions where groups of young men would ask us if they had permission to have photos taken together with them. It was an interesting dilemma as even though Nicolette and Sophia were understandably uncomfortable with the notion, these guys were desperate to go back to the villages they had traveled from and would then be able to brag about all the cute chicks they met with pictures as proof. Even at our hotel restaurant, young boys kept coming in to sit at tables next to us and smile at our daughters.

As everywhere else we had been to in India, we were able to find inexpensive hotel rooms, great tasting food and crowds in every direction. Being one more holy site, there were lots of street merchants selling icons, temple jewelry, and crystals. But for us the main reason we stayed a couple of days was to soak in the wonderful hot springs. And unlike commercial baths elsewhere, in order to enter these waters, you needed to go into one of the large halls were you were expected to sit cross legged and chant. Being a beard friendly religion, I felt comfortable doing so, but the ladies had to put on scarves on their heads to not feel as self-conscious. In another room was a nice bonus of free food that was scooped out from big pots that were carried up and down the aisles. There were probably at least 300 people in the room and as this procedure went on seven days a week and twenty four hours a day, we figured tens of thousands of pilgrims get fed the traditional tali plate of rice, dhal and vegetables daily. Knowing that most of the places we visited in the country were vegetarian was a feature of our travels that we were appreciating every day. And as the main event, we enjoyed two days of such fine and free eating and soaking in the wonderful hot springs.

A short bus ride away where the road came to an end was our starting point for more adventures. Taking the advice of several locals, we hired a guide that would lead us up a very narrow and at times treacherous trail which after a couple hours of crossing streams and using our fingers to keep from sliding down narrow paths that led over sharp ravines. With the help of extra doses of adrenalin, we finally made it to what was a wonderful Shangri-La. Green meadows, high mountain views, fresh water springs and fast internet. Yes even here in what seemed like a remote dreamscape, tent like structures were set up to accommodate travelers with cheap places to stay, delicious food and a comfortable reward for seeking this sacred high ground off the beaten trail.

After enjoying the beingness of the first makeshift settlement, we hiked another hour to an even more majestic temple of nature. There on the base of a mountain was a wonderful hot spring that we gratefully jumped into. Soaking under the stars felt blissful but climbing back out to the high country chill was somewhat unpleasant. But the long haired sadhu that had been meditating in a nearby cave greeted us with a bowl of hashish which was a well appreciated welcome wagon which helped our mind stay clear of worries and our bodies comfortable again. His friendly gestures did not lead to any clinging dramas as he was quick to leave us when he saw a nice looking young lady ready to be impressed by his spiritual persona and lusty intentions.

The return back to civilization required the help of a guide again but our legs felt more limber after breathing the Himalayan air and revitalized by the healing waters. Sadly a few years later we read of a major landslide in the area that buried the hot springs and the access route to where we had been. Yet the dream memory remains vivid for all of our family. From this exotic gem of a secluded village, we then took a bus from Kosol and maneuvered getting off on the trail head to the fabled village of Malana.

MALANA SOUR CREAM

One of the more intriguing areas we visited was the village of Malana. Historically, the residents claim direct ancestry to Alexander the Great who supposedly visited the area several thousand years ago and which was to become the western tip of the colonial expansion of the Hellenic empire. The facial features of the people here are dark skinned but blond haired and blue eyed. They speak a language with a Macedonian root and their religion is not related to Hinduism but incorporates the ancient Greek gods and rituals. The people of the village do not allow anyone that is not of their same tribe to touch them as they are considered inferior and would bring contamination. And besides all these points of interests, the local Malana Cream hashish has long been considered one of the world's best. So with enough reasons to do so, we took a bus ride and settled into a local homestay for a couple of days in order to experience this village's history, scenery, culture and sacred smoke.

My idea of being accepted as a "home boy" because of our possible common Greek ancestry was not very realistic. After the strenuous two hour hike up to Malana, we encountered only suspicious stares from the few inbred looking people we saw in town. And after learning that we could be fined not only for touching people but their buildings as well, we made sure we kept our hands in our pockets and walked swiftly. Being definitely the most uninviting place we had seen in India, we were eager to get back to the world below. About ten minutes down the trail, we were met by a couple of teenage boys who sold us a gram of their fabled hash which was a nice buzz as well as a souvenir from a not totally wasted day.

Before we went back to Manali, we met a strange guy from Switzerland who was living in a shack in a lush meadow that was in an incoherent state of consciousness. From the bits and pieces of information we could understand, he had been living in this valley for several years and had been providing work-exchange for an elderly man who also was an exquisite hash maker. After a few puffs, we were becoming similarly incoherent, so even with the gracious invitation that we stay the night, we felt we should quickly propel ourselves out of the stupor and catch the bus. Perhaps if we had stayed, we too might still be there in a state of strange bliss.

With an opportunity to get off the bus and experience another special place, we stayed a couple of days at a lake respected by various traditions as having a profound spiritual presence. A side trip afterwards led to a cave found below an ancient Hindu temple. It might not have been magic, but there was definitely an energy field in the air as within a few minutes of arriving, the clouds turned dark and soon after there followed bolts of bright lightning and earth shaking thunder. Luckily we were able to scamper fast enough for shelter in the cave and when we reemerged outside about 15 minutes later, the skies were still and sunny again. In the meantime, the gods and goddesses must have worked out whatever they were arguing about and thus all was peaceful and harmonious.

THE DOCTOR

For several years I had been interested in experiencing the health benefits of the several thousand year old traditional system of healing called Ayurveda. But just as with Indian restaurants, therapeutic message and herbal supplements, the cost in the US was too prohibitive. Now, however, the one dollar meals also went well with our five massages that were no longer luxuries but had become much appreciated habits. Only the procedure where a practitioner poured a hot oil mixture in my eye did I consider having made a mistake but was glad that my vision was still intact afterwards.

Having asked many of the local people for a reputable Ayurvedic physician, we were directed to the home of one of the most recommended which was located very near to the hotel where we were staying. Looking through the door of his office we could see a long wall of what looked like herbal powders as well as an assortment of diagnostic tools, charts and massage table. We were motioned in by a man in his late 40's with a cheerful face and clear eyes who identified himself as the doctor but also explained that his English was limited and thus we needed to wait for his friend that would translate any details of my health examination. In the meantime he offered Stephanie and me a cup of bitter tea until we could proceed further.

During the one hour examination, I was given a pulse test followed by an aromatic oil rub massage and finally by muscle testing reflexology. The interpreter explained that some imbalances could be easily corrected by my taking various herbs that the doctor would give me. Also he suggested as well to using a special black hashish that when smoked right before going to bed, would bring me meditative dreams that also would accelerate the healing. Already very satisfied with all the therapies the good doctor had provided, a couple more bonus delights awaited us. First being that his bill for the hour treatment and all the herbs was only around fifteen dollars. Even the hash would have cost more elsewhere not to mention his excellent massage. He then asked the interpreter to invite all our family to his home later in the week for a vegetarian meal. No doctor that I had ever heard of in the US would offer their patients such personal service.

So pleased was I from meeting this amazing doctor that I arranged appointments for all of our family to also experience his treatments of which everyone felt benefit from. Up to now we had been satisfied from the various eateries in town that we had gone to, but the night of our visiting his household was truly a memorable feast which was prepared by his giggly young wife and several other ladies in the kitchen. We truly felt like royalty for the experience and after finishing the evening with group picture taking, we promised to one day return back and visit him. And as a final gift, he gave me an amulet to wear which would protect me from negative energies. Truly a holistic experience.

THE HOSPITAL

One of the advantages of needing medical assistance abroad is the realization that it won't cost an arm or a leg or even a gall bladder like in the US. While hiking on one of the nearby mountain trails, my foot slipped and after a couple of body tumbles, I had a severe enough pain in my chest to think that I might have broken a rib. With the help of my family and a passerby, I was placed in a taxi and taken to the local hospital in Manali. The building itself looked simple but not too foreboding and was at least built within the last few centuries. In the large room where about fifty other people waited for their turn to be examined. I was greeted by friendly looks but worse yet, I was escorted to the front of the line as if I were some sort of elite personage. Before being taken into the treatment room, I humbly sent out heartfelt messages of apology for not waiting the long hours that they must have camped in the same room. But no harsh looks were cast back; only smiles of people wishing for my speedy recovery.

I was then greeted by a friendly doctor who after a thorough examination, X ray evaluation and on the spot treatment of my painful bruises, wrapped me up in support bandages and gave me a prescription for pain pills. The charge for the pills was three dollars. The total bill for the hospital ten dollars. One more reason to consider becoming an expatriate out of the red, white and blue land of opportunity and opportunists.

THE BUS RIDE

As we would say for most places we had traveled to when it came time to leave, we were happy for our visit and would certainly come back. In the case of India, not only would we like to come back, but perhaps live long term. Houses were inexpensive to rent, hospital care was minimal, natural beauty was exquisite, food was delicious, the culture sacred and also very beard-friendly.

Leaving the country meant a ten hour bus ride to the airport in Delhi and as it would be during the night, we hoped there would be a chance of a few hours of intermittent sleep along the way. After packing our belongings we were still left with a few chunks of hash that we could either give or throw away. Being in a comfortable state of mind, I chose a third option which was to emulate many of the literary figures of the late nineteenth century and eat it instead. It certainly looked tasty enough like a piece of dark chocolate and the visions would be entertaining. In my case, however, the movie that would be created for my journey would be closer to a horror show than a romantic comedy.

The ride itself started out normal enough. A couple of hours after we departed Manali, I started having the first rushes of what would turn out to be an extended all night roller coaster multimedia production. A sudden storm complete with thunder and approaching lightning bolts was upon us and for our teenage driver to be able to see where we were going, it was necessary for his even younger co-driver to be wiping the front window with a rag. Just one small error of judgment and certainly the bus with all of us in it could well plunge off the curvy road and down the cliff where the rushing river could swallow us without so much as a burp. With such a set and setting, I started slipping from visions of the sacred to more like the panic psychosis of the scared. The bus started weaving more as we were descending down the zigzag highway, the lighting was cracking war zone sounds and its glow illuminating the bus while the driver's friend was frantically trying to keep the pools of pounding rain from the window where by now the wipers had become totally useless. My panic attack was turning into a nightmare, so I bent my head into my lap and hoped a fetal position would provide a comfortable oasis of hope. Not more than a few seconds into my posture, I felt a stream of liquid dripping on my head and I started imagining that a river of blood would soon drown me. A leak in the roof right above my head was just one more incident of the unexpected. But there in the darkest moment of fear, my tortured mind did see a light of hope. I had the sudden realization that yes, this bus was doomed and that we would all be dead very soon. But rather than be concerned, I gracefully lifted my head up and smiled knowing that since we were still in India, we would all be reincarnated again. And as my last wish before we left Manali was that we come back for a longer stay, my next reincarnation would indeed be here in India. After this realization, a wide smile of contentment came across my face, my breath was deeper and I broke out into uncontrollable laughter which brought a few curious looks in my directions from other passengers. I'm sure the local people have had enough experience with blissed out gurus or stoned out hippies to fit my expressions into their reality plate. Even with my eyes wide open, the rest of the bus ride was a pleasurable experience but of which I vowed never to eat such a big chunk of hashish again.

CHAPTER EIGHTEEN: NORTH THAILAND

BANGKOK

By now, Thailand had become a very familiar location for our travel paths. Its many budget airline ticket agents as well as the enchanting scenery, delicious cuisine, and Buddhist culture made it a comforting place for new expeditions of discovery or just relaxing in affordable luxury. Having spent time previously in Bangkok as well as having explored a few of the gorgeous islands in the south, on this trip we chose to head to the northern part of the country to visit the hill tribes and the infamous Golden Triangle area.

After barely sleeping a night in Bangkok's disco pounding noisy party zone and backpacker's ghetto of KoSang Road, our next step was to take the train the next day to Thailand's second largest city and gateway to the north, Chiang Mai. After the struggles of dealing with crowds and transportation gridlock of India, it felt like luxury to be riding in comfortable seats and clear directional information of Thailand's excellent train system.

Compared to Bangkok, Chiang Mai was less chaotic, better organized, more relaxed and no one wore masks to protect them from brown toned air pollution. The sky was clear enough to appreciate clouds and stars and the river that divided the city even had healthy looking fish living in it. Many parks, temples and fine smelling food were ample in every neighborhood as well. After settling into our comfortable hotel suite, we took a few walks of orientation and organized our maps of places to go and what to see over the next few days.

Besides traditional Thai cuisine, there was also a wonderful variety of other ethnic food and with no problem finding pure vegetarian restaurants. Several religious and vegetarian societies offered homemade delicacies for a small donation and we even found an Israeli outreach service which made delicious falafels. A nice surprise was eating at a Greek restaurant which afterwards we decided to avoid walking by again as all the owner wanted to talk about was how to make money while showing a contemptible attitude towards the local culture.

Even more inexpensive food was available at the city's world famous once a week night market. Considered the largest in the country and perhaps the world, on Sunday nights this market would extend for over two miles of streets in length with many other cross streets of vendors selling antiques, handmade art, musical instruments, clothes, herbs and of course much more. And besides the fifty cent meals, professional massages were available for under five dollars for a full hour of comfort, pleasure and health. While experiencing such strokes of release and bliss, I was startled when not only the massage practitioner but the rest of the several thousand people in the market stopped whatever they were doing to stand up and face in one direction with wide eyed smiles of devotion. At first I thought I had entered some sort of Twilight Zone. But with a little bit of thought process I remembered that a designated time during the day, everyone in the country stops what they are doing to show respect to their king whom they attribute almost divine qualities to. Being as he was also a fine jazz saxophone player, I did not mind the honoring but did wonder what someone using a bathroom would do if they could not stand at that auspicious moment. Hopefully it wouldn't be considered a crime. And from then on, as the king's posters were on display everywhere we went, I made sure to take an extra pause to show my respects.

Thai massage had always been a rare and expensive luxury in the US. Now, just like our eating fabulous Thai meals at restaurants daily, at least one of us each day enjoyed a very affordable massage as well. Across from the hotel was a massage school, clinic and spa that made it very convenient to have saunas before each massage with a total cost of under ten dollars.

Chiang Mail also had a very active music scene. We had heard about one club near the river which was owned by one of the country's best guitarists and was often compared to Jimi Hendrix whom he idealized as well as covered many of his songs. One night we all took a long walk to check out his performance which was okay but lacked enthusiasm. Probably playing the expected song selections every night for years had burned him out. But from the looks of all the empty beer bottles on stage, alcohol had taken a toll as well. Playing the blues while gulping the booze.

PAI

Our next trip was to book a van ride for the two hour excursion to the small but adorable village of Pai nestled in a truly gem of a setting located in a valley surrounded by mountains, forests, hot springs and a lazy river. And as many backpackers knew, it was also a gathering place for expatriates, hippies and traveling musicians. Just the right place for us to call home for the next few satisfying weeks.

From Pai's bus station and extending out in several directions we observed many small shops and market stalls of people selling all sorts of art objects, musical instruments, clothes and souvenirs. Plenty of food options were available in town and the character of tourism was reflected in the abundance of vegetarian options. Rock, jazz, blues, rainbow and even Thai music also filtered in from all the various cafes and art galleries. And as in all towns in Thailand, Buddhist temples and massage centers were accessible within short walks.

Making note of where we would explore later, we followed the footsteps of other traveling backpackers and budget travel books to the river which was a beautiful setting for accommodations. Crossing a rickety wooden bridge to the other side, we found a series of bamboo huts available for one dollar a night. Not caring that the doors were crooked or that there were some missing gaps in the walls and floors, we rented a couple of these very traditional structures to be our family villa during our stay. And as an extra bonus, an inexpensive cafe was located on the premise with internet access as well as being the starting point for trails through the nearby forest and hills.

Walking through such vibrant scenery was as if entering into a painting. From our porch we would wave at the old men with the wide bamboo hats that gently oared their rafts on the river. The town sparkled with a festive tone of constant celebration. Through our friend Albert from Maui who was now married to a woman in a nearby village, we were introduced to a delightful group of expats who had stories to tell filled with wonder and contentment. Many were staying in the nearby hills and living a life of art and spiritual expression. One such man invited us to his house which he had built as a multi dimensional temple and even had his own thermal hot spring facing the river.

With a little bit of explanation, John was able to talk me into renting him a motorcycle to expand his own parameters of discovery. It took much more convincing, but Nicolette, not wanting to feel excluded, likewise convinced me into renting her one as well. And even more surprising, as long as she followed her promise of only driving on certain safe country roads near town, she even was able to convince me to ride with her. My phobia from riding bikes had me on my wit's end of adrenalin panic at first, but after a few minutes, I felt like a veteran biker as she speeded up the time it would take me to go to certain places as well as now being able to go even further past the edge of town.

Five miles out of Pai was a small village with a predominance of Asian immigrants. Besides a very nice waterfall that we found to be a pleasure swimming in, the locals had a reputation for teenagers selling pot and opium. The idea sounded possibly worth consideration but we chose not to do so because of the other possibility of foreigners being set up by the local police whereby the villagers would get rewards for selling marijuana that would result in customers being busted.

With the predominance of young travelers in town, police busting kids for drugs was a very lucrative extortion business. The reputation for many years was that Pai was an easy place for accessing not only cannabis and hashish but for the opium that this region was famous for. But a new and ambitious police chief had declared a "war on drugs" which meant searching people that looked "suspicious" and even taking them without a warrant to the local hospital for urine testing. If illegal drugs were determined, the punishment would be many long years in a brutal prison. But in reality, if the person arrested could manage to get their family to send $10,000 within a few days, the prison term would supposedly be dropped and the penalty being simple deportment.

A few months after we left the country, we heard of a police sting operation that raided the house of one of our expat friends resulting in the arrest of its three long time residents. When they were taken to the hospital, another friend who did not smoke pot followed them and was cleverly able to sneak in a bottle of his urine showing no cannabis in their bodies and thus led to the dropping of the charges. James Bond couldn't have handled it any better.

As we gazed past the boundaries of the town, we felt the pull of even more sights to explore. Our first stop was a small village that was an example of the distortion of the cultural and social fabric by contemporary politics. For centuries, smoking opium was a traditional part of life. Now the government as part of pressures from the US had not only made it illegal but also had given orders to soldiers and police to shoot anyone caught growing or smoking it. Consequently many village elders had been executed and through its replacement by cheap whiskey, the men would be abusive as well as non-functional. The women seemed to be doing most of the work while the men would sit around helplessly drunk most of the time.

About an hour past the village we got off at the entrance to a Buddhist retreat center where we enjoyed the beautiful and peaceful setting as well as the meditations and vegetarian meals. The vow of silence made it a bit rough, especially when trying to argue with each other through hand gestures. But a few minutes after we left we were pleased to see that our voices still worked and were able to express our passions again.

Further north we visited more temples and expansions of scenery. We didn't notice any of the reputed armed drug smugglers in the Golden Triangle border area shared by Thailand, Laos and Myanmar. However, taking a short excursion with a taxi driver, he pointed out what looked like a giant concentration camp where thousands of refugees from Myanmar were barely surviving. Considering the millions of other refugees throughout the world living in such squalor and worse was a horrifying revelation on the nature of greed in a world of abundance.

Back in Pai we had no shortage of ways to enjoy life on a meager budget. Cheap food, cheap rooms, cheap massages and free music throughout the town was a heavenly rest stop in life. By now John had made friends with various musicians and was playing often in many of the cafes. At one point he was playing meditative world music in one place and by midnight he was lead guitarist in a rock and roll band on the other side of town. A delight for us to get high listening to Indian ragas and then hearing him rock out to Suzie Q and Jumping Jack Flash. The only troublesome moment came when we had to walk home from the music club at 2am and had to deal with wild, angry and aggressive packs of dogs that roamed the streets at night. They might not have been muggers with knives but they certainly scared us with their sharp teeth and mean growls.

Another memorable ritual in Pai for us was to indulge in the fresh fruit smoothies that would only cost fifty cents each. Besides helping us stay healthy for a minimal cost. Not too far from downtown was a video rental business that also had several rooms available to be rented for private showings of the films as well. I'm sure behind the closed doors all sorts of kinky celluloid was being experienced with the well sound-proofed walls insuring intimate privacy. For us it meant the pleasure of bringing in snacks to watch recent films and have the whole room complete with large screen and high definition stereo sound to ourselves. And of course, we always brought in about ten mango shakes conveniently purchased from the Muslim family stall around the corner.

As John was becoming more than just a transient guitar jammer in town, he was playing gigs on a regular level and was even asked to perform at a festival hosted by a Japanese collective of artists and musicians. Not only did the show go well, but also between the acts we missed noticing his budding relationship with Ariel, a beautiful young lady from the US who also was a fabulous musician as well as an excellent massage practitioner. Over the years after leaving Thailand, they kept in touch through emails and eventually married in Hawaii. But then again that's another story at another time.

For now, time had caught up for us to leave Pai. Nicolette had to deal with dental problems that were never quite resolved satisfactorily in several dental visits and now had to hope for better results in Bali. Another unexpected situation, Stephanie upon hearing that her father's health had taken a turn for the worse, had to leave us for a few weeks to go to San Francisco to visit him.

CHAPTER NINETEEN: THE BALI VILLA

By now our travels, as exotic as they were, were navigating us to a country where we felt we could move to and live happily ever after. India and Southeast Asia were funtastic to visit but the reality of a family move was minimal. New Zealand was our new permanent home plan so even though Bali was always a picturesque treat to enjoy, we only wanted to stay one month before leaving to get to Australia which was a major destination of our journey. But along the travel map, Bali was our next interlude.

THE VILLA

On our previous trip to Bali, we had set an intention to purchase a small beachfront lot next to the Pacific Yoga Center on the peaceful and as yet undeveloped north coast of the island. Our vision was to be able to eventually build an inexpensive structure which we could come stay and even "retire". Thus we would have a pleasurable setting in life where we could do yoga, attend workshops and stroll along the ocean to the center for a cup of tea, meal or socialize with the guests. From the money that we had left in savings, we did buy a home lot previously and now was our opportunity to visit its location. Stephanie's brother and his wife had also joined us in Bali to familiarize themselves with this part of the world as well.

Byron and Danielle were immensely impressed by the scenery and culture of the island and were happy enough to accept our offer to be land partners in which we would give them half ownership interest. Their idea of what to build on the property however was not a simple hut like we had expected but a more expensive three bedroom two story villa with a swimming pool and fancy furniture. The idea of being able to rent such a place on the internet and split the profits was suitable to us, so agreements were made and the building was constructed.

In the next few years we did make financial profit from rentals that we were grateful for, but somehow we felt our dream was compromised. The type of renters were not the backpackers and spiritual pilgrims that we would have felt akin to but were often wealthy arrogant tourists with more demanding needs. Our working staff was pleasant enough but even when the villa was vacant, we would be required to pay them a salary which kept escalating. All sorts of undefined local taxes and unexpected expenses kept growing as internet advertising was both unpredictable and barely enough to cover these costs. We even were extorted by the local mafia who demanding we pay them money every time we had guests or else they would organize loud cock fighting events next to our house.

Inevitably, we were forced into selling the villa for a low price. Both we and our new partner who had bought Byron's share were facing financial difficulties and needed money. But before we did so, since we had the opportunity to be in Bali, we came with our family to stay for a few days and enjoy a taste of luxury that we were still owners of. At first the idea seemed desirable enough, but the reality was much more awkward. The two maids that were part of the staff would follow us around expecting to be pampering our family with constant cleaning and offers of help. When we would come into the kitchen they would be sitting cross legged on the floor waiting for our commands and would be confused when not only did we want to do our own cleaning but also washing our own dishes. The gardener, like the maids, asked us to double his salary, buy a golf cart to patrol around the "estate" and also supply everyone with uniforms as the workers in the fancy hotels wore. Such elegance was definitely not our comfort and as we moved back to simpler homestay living, we reflected on how nicer it would have been if we had built a simple hut on the land as we initially intended instead of this high class villa.

ADVENTURES ON THE PLANE

When we had purchased our tickets in Bangkok for Australia, the travel agent had explained that the visa stay on Bali could only be for thirty days and not the two months as in the past. With such understanding, we asked for the maximum day option to stay and were at the airport and on time as directed on our ticket. But as we were going through Indonesian government customs for exiting the country, we learned that the first day of the limit was counted and that technically we had overstayed our visa and we were facing a $100 penalty. Our shock was cleared up when we saw many other Western travelers lined up to pay the same fine which seemed to be a sly extra extortion tax.

For some reason, we found ourselves being able to board the airplane without having been asked by the customs agents to pay any extra fees. We held our breath to make sure we weren't going to be busted and as the plane started going down the runway, a smile broke across our faces for having beat the system. But the plane suddenly stopped and an announcement came across the sound system for Mrs. Stephanie Douvris to present herself to the front. Yes, our fears became warranted as Stephanie was asked to follow an airplane agent to the customs office and pay the fine for our visa breach. Moving into emergency strategy mode, Nicolette went with her mother in case of need while I tried to find sympathy between the stewardesses and the pilots by pleading that it was my birthday and all of us needed to be together on this flight. There seemed to be some progress in stalling the flight crew but the rest of the passengers kept looking at their watches and not showing much signs of patience as the minutes of Stephanie's departure kept sliding away. Finally as the stewardess started telling me that they couldn't wait much longer, both Stephanie and Nicolette appeared through the door. It turned out that Nicolette saved the day for us as she took Stephanie's credit card and was able to run a far enough distance to the ATM machine to race back to the customs office with the cash necessary to pay our fines and insure our being able to all take off together. Finally we really all could take a deeper breath and smile.

CHAPTER TWENTY: AUSTRALIA AND NEW ZEALAND

DOWN UNDER

Here we were. All five of us, sitting on benches in front of the Gold Coast Australia airport waiting to be picked up by someone we had never met except through pen-palling on the internet. For the past several years we had been comfortable traveling through Southern Europe, Southeast Asia, India and Bali. Now, ironically, we were back in an English speaking country with familiar Western architecture and fast food logos, but felt like strangers in a country that we might be becoming residents of. No street corner spicy warung food stalls and no one telling us to rent their cheap rooms or taxi service. Just a cold afternoon in a vacuum wondering what next and where might we be years, months or even days from now. All wondering on what would our next steps be if the person that we were to meet didn't even show up.

Such were the thoughts that were in each of our silent moments as well as in our eyes as we shrugged and looked at each other. But any concerns of abandonment were dispelled as an old van with a friendly looking young guy honked, pulled up and introduced himself as Leo, brother to my pen pal. He managed to get us and all our belongings into his vehicle and off we went. We immediately felt better in his being Samoan instead of Caucasian and the warm hearted cultural attitude we had been familiar with over the last few years. It turned out that one of his sisters was having a birthday which was very auspicious as it was my birthday week as well. So when we reached their house, we were greeted as honored guests and part of the party at a very festive introduction to the continent down under. After hugs, fine dining, and feeling at home once more with this new extended family of the same sort of village life we too felt connected with, Stephanie, Nicolette and Sophia were shown comfy beds for the night, while John took a ride with the brother to check out a few of the music clubs in the tourist haven of Byron Bay and have a taste of the local bud.

Over the next few days, our new friend Jayne and her family were happy to drive us around to some of the places we needed to know about as well as getting oriented to the scenery while reacquainting with western culture and life styles. First stop was the Channon, a festive Sunday market of colorful people, music and alternative energetics. Close by we drove through the fabled town of Nimbin which was the wonderful hippie town that we knew we were destined to move to at some time. Our end point Byron Bay was the gateway which had a surfer town feeling to it that bridged our Maui memories to new potentials. Several months previously we had arranged for a home exchange with a family there which would be staying in our Bali Villa for two weeks and in return we had a free place to stay in Byron Bay. We were pampered in having a holiday home with fast internet, large screen television with big speakers, separate bedrooms for all of us, bicycles and even a hot tub. A car was also included for us to have use of, but only Stephanie had the nerves of steel necessary to be able to drive on the "other side" of the road. One of the quirks in modern civilization was how in some countries one drove on the right side of the road and in others the left. There might possibly have been a reasonable answer but for all practical purposes I was scared shitless to even try. But Byron was a small enough place that we could walk to most places including the beach and even town was only a nice half hour hike.

The resemblance to Hawaii was interesting in many ways besides surfing and the ocean. The area was very green and had distinct reminders of its hippie past that started out as a sleepy stoned out backpacker's hang out. Over time, big hotels sprung up and the town was now full of fast food restaurants, fancy homes, and disposable souvenirs. Many of the early hippies had invested their pot money into real estate and were now quite wealthy local land and business owners. But there were still tie-dyes and yoga classes advertised on all the bulletin boards which even though too high a price for us, were high enough for the glamour crowd to feel trendy enough to pay for.

NIMBIN TIME

The two weeks we stayed in Byron Bay had their comforts, but the main event was still getting to Nimbin. Orienting ourselves to

Australia, the beach walks, watching bikinis, internet cafes and video rental stores were fun, but now it was time to move on. With limited public bus connections, our next step was to rent a cheap car for a month which we did so from a private enterprise in Gold Coast. After connecting with our friend Damian whom John and Sophia had met on a hiking trail in India a few months earlier, we gratefully accepted his offer to camp on his land which turned out to be conveniently located only about ten miles from Nimbin.

With transportation and accommodation falling into place, our anticipation of the Nimbin experience was finally possible. In 1973 there was a major musical event called the Aquarius Festival which, similar to Woodstock in the US, brought tens of thousands of young people mostly from the cities to this rural area for this epic gathering. Afterwards, as nearby land was available for a low price and even the downtown shops in the relative ghost town of Nimbin were purchased for $200 each, many of the folks that came from the festival stayed. The town was bought and every shop painted with bright colors and hippie murals. Intentional communities were started and the dream was grounded. Some of the local "new age" rainbow hippies told us to avoid going to the town as it was a den of drugs and debauchery, so thus we were motivated even more to take the drive through the beautiful rain forest and check it out ourselves.

Once we crossed the final bridge over the stream that was adjacent the town, we instantly knew we were finally where I wanted to live. The town was only three blocks long but full of familiarity in both the colorful shops and the appearance of the people. Like a hippie retirement community, most people looked like us. The small businesses were very laid back looking and were places selling exotic clothing, drug paraphernalia, vegetarian food, two hippie museums, hemp embassy, bakery, herbal and homeopathic medicines and so on. There were also conventional places like a bar, post office, hardware store, hospital and real estate office. A large park with a free Olympic size pool was also present and was the perfect place to lay down and watch the clouds and have a picnic. And being in a spaced out state of mind didn't seem to be a problem as the shop owners were mostly stoned all the time anyway.

During the course of the next few weeks, our usual routine was to drive into Nimbin each day, walk around and get familiarized with the town and its opportunities and then have an early picnic style dinner at the park adjacent the swimming pool where we would also have a table and light to be continuing school work with our kids. It did not take long to connect with many new friends and feel not as strangers but as having returned to our home roots. Our vital signs for immigration possibility felt quite high at this point as did our plans to eventually find a nice house to rent while living here.

Of the many interesting places in town, we found special interest in meeting the folks working at the Hemp Embassy which was a major focal point in information and products relating to cannabis and hippie culture in general. The Environmental Center was another valuable host and hub of grass roots activism and social events that was of high interest to pad our schedule of what to do while staying in the area. Besides living the hippie dream we were glad to find another dimension to the community besides the stereotype of laid back space heads. Nimbin had a proud heritage of putting bodies on the line in face of loggers and police in political activism to stop the clear cutting of forests which eventually were to become national park land reserves. Volunteerism was a high standard of helping in various needy causes as well as donating to the building of a beautiful swimming pool and full time medical center.

The several cafes in town were all comfortable including the Oasis which was owned by a Greek and offered healthy food, conversation and usually full bongs. And besides all the many interesting Australians in the area, we also met quite a few American ex-pats who were comfortable in staying in Nimbin even with expired passports. A worst case scenario we contemplated if need be in case we found ourselves not able to qualify for Australian residency.

Besides high times and environmental activism, the town also offered an interesting portal of arts. The local community center often featured art displays as well as dramatic productions and concerts from local artists. Two museums in town were dedicated to the hippie roots of the culture and one that was also a cultural center for the Aboriginal community. Over time we realized that much of the country was very racist towards the Aboriginal people while Nimbin was proudly a supportive oasis. The neighborhood center was a volunteer organization that was very helpful finding access to social services for anyone needing help. Even the town derelicts could drop by its office and be given a bowl of soup and emotional support when needed. The homeless laying comfortably in the parks along with the blood thirsty leeches swarming in the swamps were valuable guardians of the gate in keeping most mainstream real estate development plans and frightened tourist hordes away.

A few days of the week, an occasional bus of tourists seeking "alternative adventures" would park downtown for an hour. Most of the passengers wouldn't venture too far off the bus and walk in confused packs so as not to be attacked by their fantasies of drug crazed hippies. Many of the younger ones would try to buy drugs and be happy to pay the inflated prices of the back street dealers. One day several pretty teenage girls asked me if they could take a picture together with me. No money or phone numbers were exchanged. Another young lady wanted to know where to find local "special" brownies. She gave me a perplexed look when I suggested she go across the street to the town bakery. I reckon it was a space brownie that she was looking for and would surely find the right cook before she had to get back on the bus.

Among the many friends we made in the area, two of our closest ones were from New Zealand and lived about two hours north of town and it was always a pleasure to visit with them often enough to have a hot shower and a comfortable bed to sleep in now and then. Peter and Lorraine had organized the Nambassa Festivals in New Zealand during the 1970's and early 80's, which were the equivalent to our Woodstock. It was inspiring to see them still active in political and cultural awareness as well as creating a sustainability of food where they were living. They were also gracious enough to give us the names of several of their hippie friends from the "old days" in New Zealand which was to be our next expedition of adventure and hope of residency. John was now working in hopes of such a visa at a restaurant in the town of Lismore located near Nimbin, so he stayed behind as our remaining band of four headed to New Zealand.

NEW ZEALAND: THE NORTH ISLAND

Unlike our arrival had been to Australia, we now had a relatively planned itinerary and were grounded again to western society. The spoken accent was somewhat different to Australian, but close enough to not need to carry a translation guide. We had prearranged the purchase of a camping van which was waiting for us near the Auckland airport and by now Stephanie was also comfortable in driving on the left side of the road. So with all the travel pieces smoothly in place, in just a couple of hours after getting off the airplane we were driving north on our planned two month exploration of a country that might well be our eventual new homeland.

With just enough time allocated between visiting the North and then the South Island, there was a significant slice of east coast scenery that we had to bypass. But we felt no remorse as we still were able to visit several interesting intentional communities and scattered friends of Peter's along the way. It was nice making new friends and sharing familiarity as they spoke delightfully of Peter and Lorraine, as well as for the nostalgic communal living at Nambassa both during and after the two festivals.

Before we left the country, one of these communities hosted a music festival which we attended and met up again with Peter and Lorraine who had come over from Australia as special guests of honor. A few heartfelt hugs and farewells with our new friends and we moved on.

In the northwest corner of the North Island we took a small hike to one of the last remaining groves of giant Kauri trees. Our reaction when we saw them was jaw-dropping and bitter sweet. Their majestic size and appearance stretching up to the universe as well as girdling a wide stance of pride was only matched by the utter stupidity and greed of the loggers who clear-cut this corner of ancient roots, so as to make train tracks around the world. With deep reverence and respect, we all stood in teary eyes for a few extra minutes before starting our drive south.

By now we were getting used to the many excellent rest stops along the highways located and managed by the indigenous Maori tribal councils. Unlike how the Aboriginal peoples of Australia were decimated and humiliated by aggressive racism, the Maori people were able to protect their lands well enough to agree on a peace treaty from the colonial thirsty English. Consequently, their position in New Zealand society was more comfortable and also the control of their land more extensive. Being closely connected to the land, they provided places at regular intervals for travelers to pull over for up to ten days at no cost with hot water, clean bathrooms and usually a beautiful forest with well managed trails. So even with the high prices of the cost of living in the country, by purchasing a low cost van and buying their groceries at the many farmers markets one could plan for an affordable holiday experience.

Even from when our eyes first focused on its epic landscape, we shared the unanimous consensus that New Zealand was one of the most visually stunning countries in the world. Verdant forests, hot springs, waterfalls, snow covered mountains and panoramic valleys that were straight out of the Lord of the Rings movie backdrop. It took a little while longer however to sadly realize that this beautiful dreamscape was also one of the world's most dangerously polluted. Because of fearing the fast growing possum population, both environmentalists and farmers were in agreement on using the terribly toxic 1080 poison on every forest to kill these critters. A chemical company in Texas had arranged a five year contract with the New Zealand government to keep buying and using this poison which was sprayed through every forest by low flying duster planes. Consequently we heard no animal sounds on the trails. No birds or butterflies to add their accents to nature's symphony which had now become a funeral dirge of mechanical sounds of airplanes. The scenery still looked magnificent but at every park we saw skull and bones signs warning that poison was lurking in every direction. Later we were to learn that human cancer rates had skyrocketed during this period. Only once on our trip did we notice a possum who gave us a pensive look of why and for which we could not answer as he looked much more easier to appreciate than the tons of poison being dropped daily in this otherwise beautiful country.

HOT SPRINGS

One of the most appealing areas of New Zealand for us was the thermal hot springs area in the central part of the North Island. Rotorua was organized mainly for high end tourists looking not only for the hot water but also for pampering and fancy services. A short walk from the downtown area was a nice public park bordered by a stream with several hot pools that were perfect for soaking in and with no need to spend any money. Perhaps the plan was to attract budget travelers like ourselves away from being noticed on the hotel strip and its elitist atmosphere.

Curious to see what a twenty five dollar dip was like, we left our car close enough to the tourist strip to take a family stroll to the more elegant part of town. Out of the corner of my eye I noticed a police car having taken notice of us enough to drive by us several times before parking about a block away. Not wanting to waste my energy with answering stupid questions as to our identity and reasons for existing, I decided to play mental aikido by going to the cops and asking them if they could direct us to a comfortable family thermal pool to spend the afternoon as well as some of our money. The gaze of suspicion was dropped and they were actually friendly enough to give us a nice description of all the town options for pools, restaurants and accommodations. They even shook hands with me before we walked on to take a quick look at the hotel lobbies before heading back to our traveling home on wheels.

On our way back to the downtown parking lot area, we were discussing a news headline about the dangerous rise of gang fighting in the community. It served as a topical and funny story that connected these tendencies with the warrior prone culture of indigenous Maori tribal roots. Getting into our car, we observed two groups of kids walking towards each other with a presence of fury in their stares and body language. Straight out of newspaper print and now manifestation, we were on the verge of watching an actual fight between the designated champion of each of the gangs. Not wearing stereotyped tattoos and body paint, these fifteen year old kids and their friends were actually stepping into the arena of the street to prove their manhood. Although precautionary common sense would have dictated that we drive away before risking collateral damage to our car from perhaps a broken windshield, our curiosity was too much too leave. At least we had our seat belts on, doors locked, windows rolled up and keys in the ignition to be safe and one step closer to an emergency departure. There in the safety of our cars and front row center, the five of us sat in quiet but nervous anticipation for the brawl to begin.

The warriors kept staring at each other with malice while making jerky finger pointing and hyper hissing sounds. Finally one of these boys grabbed and ripped his opponents t-shirt. Not able to hold back any longer, the other one was forced into the role of throwing the first punch. Wow, I thought, what a perfect moment to jump out of our car and offer to take pictures of the action so as they could

414

have real show and tell reminders to display their bravery around the school and even to show their grand kids one day. But as in most such circumstances, neither wanted to experience too much pain, so a few light punches later, they each backed off while still throwing insults at each other, as likewise the rest of the two groups of followers. And as to the cops that were interested in our family an hour earlier, none came by to stop this act of violence that lurked in the resort town city streets in the middle of the afternoon. Darn it, I've seen better action at Greek soccer game fights.

Taking the back road out of town towards Taupo we followed the directions that a friendly person we met told us to and in about half an hour came upon a magnificent hot spring located inside a national forest. There behind a grove of trees, two streams met and between them was a waterfall of hot thermal water. As we entered this heavenly body of water, we noticed a local guy looking in deep meditation in the pool as well. After about twenty minutes he finally came to life and went back to his friend who passed him another joint. Aha, the local weed obviously helped lubricate the stairway to heaven. A ride we were soon on as well after a hospitable offering to us of the magic fire stick to help us enjoy the fading afternoon hour.

Too stoned to want to drive further, our navigational alignment was sweet enough to lead us down a dirt road to a large lake that actually was warmed from underground thermal spring as well. Although it was too late to go for a swim here at this time, we finished the rest of the smoke while enjoying the enchantment of the full moon. Our dream rhapsodies were startled around midnight however as a moderate earthquake shook us all up with confusion as to what was going on. In the morning we had a swim before heading to the next town where we learned that a major earthquake in the area with lots of damaged buildings and several people badly hurt.

WELLINGTON

The last stop before catching the ferry boat to the South Island was New Zealand's lovely capital city of Wellington. The Victorian houses that dotted the hills overlooking the deep blue bay and the chilly breezes reminded us very much of San Francisco. Parking our van in a convenient area next to the docks and only a few blocks from downtown, we put on warm sweaters and ski hats as we took a walking tour through both the early and contemporary accents of the city. In comfortable juxtaposition, an old Victorian mansion which was now a formal tea room of fancy dressed patrons was on the same block as a bungee jump extreme adventure park of adventurers while down the street was a small club pumping out hip hop to its tattooed and body pierced customers. Eventually we even found a Greek restaurant that we considered as a possibility for John to apply for work towards his hoped for residency visa goal if he couldn't qualify for one in Australia. Not far from the restaurant was a Greek Orthodox Church where he could go pray towards obtaining the visa as well.

SOUTH ISLAND

Heading to an even more southerly direction "down under", a two hour ferry boat ride landed us on the top tip of the South Island. The hour was too late to get fully oriented so we decided to spend the night at the first out of town parking spot that we came to. But first we celebrated our arrival to this new island by eating a large order of a regional specialty of fried sweet potato chips which we purchased from an all night fast food cafe near the docks.

Having made an email connection with a lovely young lady in the nearby town of Nelson, the next morning we drove across the windy road between the deep blue ocean on one side and the lush mountain of thick green forests on the other and found our new friend's house where a nice dinner was prepared as well as a comfortable room for us to stay a couple of days. It was also a nice surprise that our friend and her roommates were planning to attend a music festival near the town of Takaka which happened to be the "hippie side" of the island. So with a new set of friends and familiarity, we made plans to check out the weekend festival. In the meantime, we enjoyed the upscale town of Nelson that was a nice blend of artistic as well as basic shops and services. And like just about all the towns of New Zealand that we visited, it was nestled in a scenic alchemy of ocean, mountains and forests.

On a high misty mountain meadow pass which separating the northwestern coastal tip of the south island from another extensive mountain range, we joined a couple of thousand other people for a joyful weekend of music. Not quite a Rainbow Gathering as vendors were selling food items and handmaid arts and clothes, but it was still very alternative and fun. The food was inexpensive and healthy with lots of interesting events happening through the day and night. There was a lack of live music as techno predominated, but the local grown smoke, colorful stage displays, glow sticks and fire dancers filled the ambience with excitement. People were very friendly and as in similar gatherings around the world, we felt very much at home.

As the festival was drawing to a Sunday afternoon closing ceremony, one of our new friends told us about the alternative community that she lived at and invited us to come stay for at least the night. Still in the flow, we accepted and followed her directions to a pleasant setting about an hour's drive away located less than a mile from the coast and far away from any major roads or towns. Finding a place to sleep on several couches on the back deck we could hear the adjacent creek flow by and be lulled to sleep by a clear sky of dazzling stars crowning the tall pine trees that were waving on the mountainous foot hills all around us. The house itself was an extensive series of funky rooms with spiraling decks and lots of space for the twenty or so folks that had found corners to nest for the night. Obviously it was going to be the start of a weeklong party with plenty of musical instruments, an upstairs dance/yoga studio and meditation niches.

The next morning started with an uplifting circle in the living room where we all shared smiles and loving intentions and blessings for the world and all its life forms. As the last prayers were finished and a healthy breakfast was about to be served, one of the wide smiled guys in the circle identified himself as the house owner and suggested we each put $20 in the donation box that he was passing around for our night's accommodation. Certainly by being in a new country, it is always an essential point to understand the local customs. In this case, it was obviously a sly example of new age capitalism. And when we learned that this guy was born in the US where he also owned many rental homes, we decided that instead of supporting further exploitation of vagabond hippies, it was time for us to leave the community and discover the beautiful world waiting for us to explore.

For the next few weeks we immersed ourselves in the magnificent wonderland scenery of the South Island visiting glaciers, lakes, and forests with many quaint towns along the way. This section of the country was much more rural so there was less industry and traffic but plenty of free rest areas to enjoy camping along the way. Besides the at times frigid winds such as in the far southern tip of the island where it faced Antarctica, the only other challenge along the trip was the swarms of aggressive sand flies which lived around streams and beaches and carried a sting that would last for hours.

The only metropolitan area which served as the island's commercial and business hub was Christchurch. Unlike most other cities its size, it was beautifully designed with old English as well as tasty contemporary architecture and plenty of green belts and parks. Even with its relatively large population, people seemed for the most part calm and enjoying a natural tempo of life. The main square downtown was situated next to a large Gothic cathedral where ongoing entertainment was provided by anyone that had a talent that they wished to share. Impressed by its urban charm as well as the vast beautiful landscape within a short drive away, we even considered finding John a job at a Greek restaurant for his aspirations of residency in either Australia or New Zealand. A plan that he would follow up in applying for after his job in Australia was not helpful in satisfying the needs for immigration to that country. Many years later, the city of Christchurch was devastated by a catastrophic earthquake which brought a collective tear to all our family but in no way took away the delightful impressions that we still remember.

The prime directive was for any of our family to qualify for permanent residency in either Australia or New Zealand. Once that was established, that member could sponsor the rest of the family and thus we all would be able to enjoy expatriating from the US to what seemed like a nicer place with more social services such as free health insurance. While John was working for his residency, Nicolette was trying to get a foothold into New Zealand by seeking employment at child care centers. Even though we talked the same English language and seemed decent enough people, the qualifications were not easy. For instance, Nicolette would have to be proficient in the indigenous Maori language to work at local child care centers. And as to retirement visas for Stephanie and myself, we would need to have a two million dollar bond deposited in a bank. Quite a bargain once we learned that the price was four million to do so in Australia. The idea of Nicolette getting married through a quick "business arrangement" of paying a local person to be her official husband for a short period had some appeal, but there would be the need for pictures showing "proof of intimacy" to the immigration voyeurs as well.

DEPARTURE

Having circumvented both islands and much of the interior of New Zealand, the time of our visa was about over and time to head back to Australia. Being infatuated with the beauty of the country and it's being located in the Southern Hemisphere far from radiation zones, we wanted to come back again in a few months and make our home base near Takaka. A new friend that we had met at our welcoming festival told us that a lady named Jane was living in an intentional community that was needing someone to rent her large house while she was going on a long term Buddhist retreat in a few months. As that part of the South Island was a focus of alternative communities near the upscale town of Nelson and lay nestled between the magnificent coastline and high mountains, we agreed it was the right place and promised Jane we would come back and rent her house when we returned to the country.

CHAPTER TWENTY-ONE:
AUSTRALIA, FIJI, NEW ZEALAND
AND AUSTRALIA AGAIN

CUSTOMS HASSLES

Back in the days before the great fear of international terrorism, airplane travel used to be a much easier way of traveling. Polite service agents would greet you at the ticket desk and afterwards getting aboard the plane was no different than catching a bus ride today. Stewardesses would display more respect as well as providing complimentary beverages, food and movies. And then the 9/11 era started where now it feels as if all passengers are looked upon as suspicious criminals and subjected to x-ray scans and even body searches.

On one of our early flights from Bali to the US, the customs authorities had taken Stephanie and me aside to inspect our small bag of incense which had been given to us by a temple priest for purification of negativity. It didn't seem to work too well in our case as some very negative and obese people with badges, uniforms, walkie-talkies and low IQ's were eager to put us in jail because they felt that the herbal substance in the bag was hashish. For over forty minutes one expert after another as well as a manic sniffer dog kept at it until they finally let us go on our way. Of course, they did not even have the decency to put our belongings back in our suitcases in the proper order that they found them. I wonder what kind of sloppy housekeepers they were in their domestic life after work. Perhaps being sloppy was one of the requirements for the job.

Leaving Thailand one time, the customs inspectors there told us that we could not take our unopened bottle of peanut butter aboard the airplane. They then handed us six small plastic baggies that they told us we could scoop out and divide the peanut butter into if we wanted to take it with us. It was such a messy and ridiculous effort that we soon gave up and decided we could eat other packaged snacks we were carrying with us instead. None of us could figure out what the difference between having one container of peanut butter and instead having it separated in six other containers.

Not showing any different level of compassion, the Australian and New Zealand customs officials were just as menacing. Every time we disembarked we were pulled aside and went through similar thorough investigations. Assuming that Stephanie and I were being signaled out, Nicolette and Sophia tried a few times to avoid such scrutiny by not walking through the inspection checks anywhere near us. Ironically whenever they tried being apart from us through the process, Stephanie and I went through without being searched while our daughters were still pulled aside and closely examined. Clearly us elderly hippies did not match the profile of who could be a terrorist as much as younger ladies. But in my closer observation of the situation, I did overhear one of the male inspectors tell his colleague that he was looking forward doing a body search of Sophia thus making plausible that these guys are more interested in grabbing "cheap feels" rather than looking for terrorists with bombs. I also wondered if war criminals and twin tower bombing suspects like George Bush and his gang ever were given such security checks? The most ridiculous question that was asked Sophia one time was "are you strapped?" Answering honestly that she did not know what that meant, only angered the inspector into doing an aggressive and suspicious examination.

RE-ENTRY

Our return to Australia was much more comfortable with a familiar mental road map of where to go and what to do. Our friend Neil in Nimbin was hospitable enough to allow us to stay in the loft of his rural mountain cabin while we organized a set of various steps necessary to achieve our long range plan of immigration to either Australia or New Zealand. John was still working as a chef in Lismore and was staying in the back room of his boss's office who happened to also be a psychiatrist besides being a restaurant owner. Nicolette had registered as a student at a Gold Coast trade school, so as to earn her degree of child care coordinator as part of her plan to qualify for residency in the country. And as soon as she had found an apartment close enough to her school to rent, Stephanie then made her own plans to go to San Francisco and visit her father again.

MOUNT NARDI

Sophia and I now became the remaining core family unit establishing our base at Neil's on the majestic slopes of Mount Nardi. Besides our daily walks up the road and into the high country forest, we felt very much at home in what might be construed as an authentic hippie household. No need to worry about many of the constructs of up-tight mainstream society, Sophia and I relished the music, interesting company, intriguing conversations, high times and the non-stop fancy coffee machine in the kitchen and tasty pies from the town bakery that sustained our energy levels. We also enjoyed Neil's simple compost system of throwing leftover food items out the window for the bush turkey to delight in eating. Simple elegance.

By now, the members of our family were each taking different steps. John was busy working in nearby Lismore, Stephanie was visiting her father and friends in San Francisco and Nicolette was living in a household near her school with three other young ladies. Academically she was doing great but the mainstream world of her roommates and the very consumptive straight tourist zone of the Gold Coast was a challenge that she was not too comfortable with. So she took great pleasure on Friday afternoons to catch the bus connections that would bring her to Nimbin three hours later where Sophia and I would be eagerly waiting at the downtown bus stop with provisions including plenty of bakery cakes to share at Neil's household until she would return back to her other world by late Sunday.

During that time period, Neil's band, Pagan Love Cult had been rehearsing a spectacular set of songs and multi-visual experience for an upcoming presentation in honor of the date Albert Hofmann discovered LSD. The Bush Factory located in downtown Nimbin was the perfect venue for the event with its historic wooden floors, stage and plush old movie style seats. Its location was a short walk from town and set in a forested area right next to a stream and outdoor patio where one could also hang out at during the performance.

High and excited, Nicolette, Sophia and I went early enough to the theater with Neil so we could help with the setting up and also finding three choice seats for ourselves in the middle row. The show was great but just as the last song was finishing a little past midnight, the noisy sound of rumbling motorcycles and loud mouthed people quickly manifested in the parking lot. Being a late Saturday night hour when the town bar was closing, a group of teenagers resembling Neanderthals showed up to keep on drinking more alcohol and pick fights with the hippies. Two of our friends who were in a psychedelic frame of mind tried to peacefully approach these goof-balls, but wound up getting punched in the face. Quite a bummer as one of our friends had to be taken to the hospital emergency room where he had to have his jaw rearranged. By this point, I was taking a protective posture with my daughters and had to face off a young punk who sneaked into the theater and started tearing up the classic old seats. Neil showed up with a stroke of energy and was able to get the kid out of the theater and then was able to lock all the doors and windows. The ambience was now changing from psychedelic playground to fortress under siege.

After awhile of banging on doors, punching a few more hippies and breaking some of the outdoor furniture, the thugs swallowed the last of their alcohol transfusion and then rode off into the night. The police finally showed up about an hour after they were called, but instead of offering any help to track down the town toughies, they were more intent to look around for marijuana joints to bust any peaceful remnants of audience and performers. Quite a dramatic reenactment of the "heaven and hell" differences between sacred plants and the amazingly legal terrorism of demon booze.

FIJI

Our momentum for jumping over continental divides still being in gear, once Stephanie returned to Australia, we made plans to fly once more to Fiji and check out the small lot we owned on the island of Koro. For years we had been discussing building a small house on the land and now seemed a good opportunity to consider costs and options. Our stay in the capital city of Suva was intended to be just long enough to verify our land title, buy some essential food provisions and then get on the ferry boat to Koro. But because of the stormy weather, we had to change our plans and stay an extra week in the city as Sofi, the ferry boat had cancelled its service until it was safe to make the trip.

Every day of our stay in Suva the rain kept falling and minor flooding was happening all over the island. On Sundays, most businesses stay closed and the city seems asleep. At the 24/7 internet cafe, time and the weather didn't matter. Except for my lone exception, the rest of the computers would be displaying action packed video games while kids screamed in delight from the cyber slaughter. Meanwhile, most of their parents would be at the Methodist churches wearing the bright outfits prescribed to them by the missionaries and singing sweetly devotionals about God and love. These same people where in the town park the day before for a revival where bombastic Christian converts with bibles in their hand and through loud amplifiers and animated gestures screamed out about God's punishment to sinners and why their Hindu neighbors should be hated for not being of the same religion. Here at the internet, God's justice was inspiring. Hindu and Fijian children were together on the same side in killing their enemies on the computer war games.

So far in our daily walks around downtown we only encountered just one pushy merchant I was avoiding. Because I didn't buy an awful shirt he showed me in his store and chose instead buying a better one from the store next door, he grabbed me to explain to him why. He also wanted me to come talk to him about buying his home island for "a cheap price". Maybe the price was low because it had already sunk under five meters of rising ocean water. Desperate times in the city. At least with all the extra time of waiting for the Koro ferry boat to be sea-worthy again, we learned all the main areas of the city. The local thrift store had the best deals and it was where Sophia bought me a beautiful Jimi Hendrix t-shirt for under a dollar. One of the best souvenirs of any of my South Pacific travels. And at one of the hole-in-the wall fast food Indian restaurants in the middle of town, we made friends with the very nice owner lady that would serve us delicious and very low priced vegetarian meals. And whenever we finished eating and were about to leave, she would wrap up an extra dessert for us to take home.

With the extra time we had to stay in Suva, Stephanie was also able to have much needed dental work done by an excellent Indian dentist who charged only a fraction of the cost of what it would have been if she had it done in Australia. The only peculiarity of the office visit was when I greeted him with the traditional Hindu "Namaste" and he politely replied that he was a converted Christian. "God bless you" works just as well.

Even with way more food and other supplies than what we expected to bring with us and with a thunderous storm along the way, we somehow made it okay on our seven hour boat ride to Koro. At one point during the rocking of the waves, there was an announcement of not to panic in an "emergency" and that the skilled crew would be there to help. Right. The Greek shipping agency that sold this boat named Sofi to Fiji didn't even have survivor boats to escape the sharky waters with. Later in the evening as I got out of our bed, I saw lots of little cockroaches running around the room and through all our stuff that worried me into staying even more awake. But eventually we reached Koro's harbor around two in the morning where we were greeted by someone who was sent to bring us to the cottage we had rented in Dere Bay.

In contrast to the agitations of the night, in the morning we found ourselves on a beautiful island where the other world seemed far far away while the birds went on singing their tropical daydreams and anthems to life. From our cottage we started a pleasant daily ritual of taking walks to the several closest villages. The local people were open eyed and open hearted with genuine smiles which were uplifting reminders of our mutual humanity. Their needs seemed basic and their extended family important while treating nature with respect.

During our one month stay on the island, we made many friends in the villages as well as with our neighbors that had built homes in the subdivision. On the special occasions that we were invited to come drink kava in village celebrations, young kids would gather around me and call me Ratu Mossesi which meant "Chief Moses". My long white beard resembled the images of the Biblical archetype they had seen in their church pictures. And for even more dramatic impact, they would bring me a long staff to walk regally around with. Even the older kids liked us and would be eager to show us some of the special sights of the island including a beautiful waterfall very near their village.

The majority of home owners in the community were foreigners mostly Australian, New Zealand and even a few others from the US. They were all friendly as well and we often were invited to join them on snorkeling excursions to various parts of the island as well as to yoga and exercises classes at their homes. Although we never did decide on building a cottage, we did enjoy our caretaker and his family clearing out our land and bonding with us through regular kava breaks after work. Although for Stephanie and I being on Koro was a very pleasant experience, it was an obviously boring concept for our kids to consider a long term stay here. But overall we were happy to know that we had bought a place on this beautiful and relatively pristine island that one day we might be able to live at if necessary. But we were also just as happy to be soon returning to our residency goals in Australia and New Zealand.

Before leaving Koro we reflected on some of the social challenges facing our local friends. Christian missionaries were relentless in telling the indigenous people that they had to give up many of their traditions, including their kava ceremonies and even their joyful dancing. Only church songs were now acceptable to the new converts.

As we had a few extra days to wait for our flight back to Australia, instead of staying in Suva, we decided to take a short plane ride to a small island called Ovalau. The plane was a small twelve seater and to make sure that it would fly correctly, all passengers had to be weighed, so as to keep it balanced. A much more protective process than the horrible security checks in the Western world. As the math worked out, next to me sat a very large Fijian man while on the other side of the aisle, sat Stephanie, Sophia and about five other people. The man must have weighed over 400 pounds but in conversing with him, he had a very soft spoken voice and was very polite and as most people in the country, very sweet in tone.

Ovalau was a very pleasant way to enjoy Fiji before departure from the country. Once it was the capital and now even though the downtown was only several blocks long it still had a number of nice cafes, groceries and parks. Our stay at a cottage a few miles down the coast was also very pleasant. By making friends with a few friendly teenagers, we were taken on several scenic hikes, as well as providing us a chance to finally enjoy the local very tasty weed. Sweet memories and feelings for our return to New Zealand.

KIWI LAND AGAIN

By now our son John was no longer working at the Lismore cafe and was eager to come join our family exploration of scenery and potential residency in New Zealand. The large house on the north end of the South Island in Marahau that we had stayed previously, was being offered for our stay. It had plenty of room for all of us, while at the same time living with an active community of people with mutual interests as our own. The house was also located next to a nice stream with several swimming spots and an important bonus of having internet. Jane, the landlady, allowed us to all stay in a room on the bottom floor for a few days as she showed us all the aspects of the house that we needed to be aware of for maintenance. Her lessons were also an important part of our learning how to live off-grid, including educating ourselves on proper use and care of the solar electric system and the compost toilet.

During the course of the next three months, we enjoyed life in the community, our hikes along the coastline, music festivals, meeting interesting people and exploring more scenic and dramatic beauty of the South Island. Although none of the deadly crocodiles, snakes or blood thirsty leeches roamed the land as in Australia, there was a vicious life form called sand flies. These varmints flew in swarms and once they smelled body heat would descend and be relentless in their bites which caused burning and itching for hours. Thus the beaches were always quick hit and run activities to avoid these pests. Soaking in the hot spring pools would also mean having half your body immersed in enrapturing thermal waters while the facial area would be breathing clouds of these ravaging skin biters.

Other fun time activity included John's growing popularity of playing music. His talents were appreciated not only at several festivals and open mike nights, but he was also paid a substantial amount of money and free beers for playing old rock and roll classic songs to an older crowd at a campground cafe. And with the large garden of psychoactive San Pedro cacti growing in the community, we partook of several smooth sailing and enjoyable extra dimensional journeys as well.

But even with our continuity of living in the pleasure zone, we never lost sight of our priority in seeking long term residency in New Zealand. Our visits to immigration consultants held some promise but nothing fully convincing. The two paths that seemed accessible for our kids were either in working in childcare centers or as restaurant workers. As in Australia, one of the first prerequisites for an applicant was to find a specific job on the "necessary jobs" list that the government posted monthly as well as the need of it having been advertised for several months and not filled by anyone already a New Zealand resident. Childcare workers was an easier option in previous years, but recent new requirements included having a four year university degree as well as proficiency in the indigenous Maori language. And as for restaurant work, the only avenue open was in specialty cooking which again could not be filled locally.

Our landlady Jane and a few other ladies at the community kept complimenting our family for all the fine food that was always being shared out of our kitchen. Thus they suggested that John could apply for the job of head chef at the vegetarian restaurant section of the upscale spa center in the nearby resort town where our friends also worked as massage therapists. Along with our friends recommendation and John preparing a worthy five course audition feast, the owners of the complex were happy to not only hire him but also pull their strings of influence in helping him secure his eventual residency visa. Learning that the owners were Swiss, the proverbial icing on the cake was in making sure that he poured lots of homemade cream on the desserts to charm their ethnic taste buds.

The celebration of John's new job was just cause of being a family affair. It meant he was on the way to residency which potentially could bring the rest of us into the country through his sponsorship upon eventually qualifying for citizenship. The salary was adequate, the meals he prepared were healthy and delicious and he also was able to use the spa facilities including taking relaxing and rejuvenating daily sauna baths. And as a bonus, he would bring home to the rest of us leftover gourmet meals and desserts. Also he made friends with a lady that needed a few more flying hours training to get her helicopter job credentials which subsequently meant an opportunity for Nicolette and Sophia to be volunteers as passengers and enjoy a wonderful aerial tour of the beautiful scenery of the area not easily accessed otherwise. So it was with a satisfied attitude that Stephanie, our daughters and I returned to Australia once our travel visas expired..

TUNTABLE

One of the oldest and largest intentional communities that was founded in the early 1970's in the aftermath of the Aquarius Festival was Tuntable. Situated a few miles up the road from the town of

Nimbin on Mount Nardi, over 200 people still live in the community which stretches across 2000 acres of high country rainforest land. The waiting list for applying for membership was over three years long and even renting a place there was not too easy. However, with the help of many of the associations Sophia and I had made when we were staying at Neil's house as well as our having taken a walk down the hill to introduce ourselves at the community's office, we were on friendly enough terms to be soon connected with a lady named Gloria. This long term resident of the community had been living there for several decades and presently had a small cabin for rent. I suppose our appearance of being a family of hippies was helpful in finally securing our own place to stay at.

Along with Stephanie, Sophia and Nicolette, we met with Gloria who impressed us right away in not offering us fresh baked cookies as a conventional welcome gesture but rather her own home grown organic bag of weed instead. We were delighted in having found the sweetest landlady we ever had and long term friend.

Gloria was also editor of the Nimbin Times, one of the longest running alternative newspapers in Australia. Its articles provided excellent news to the community with far ranging information about health, politics, arts, and regional as well as international news stories. Her delightful editorials were all gems which were engaging to read and accented with intelligent humor.

The cabin itself was quite small but we managed to fit in very well. Stephanie and I would sleep in the loft right above the kitchen, Sophia in the small room next door and whenever Nicolette would come visit, she could sleep on the fold out couch downstairs. Living in the forest meant not seeing the sun too often, so our moldy clothes became an issue requiring weekly visits to the expensive and usually broken town laundromat.

The cabin's electrical system was a bit of a challenge also because of the lack of enough sunlight to support a very efficient solar system. But just as with the basic compost toilet we used, our family managed to be happy living in simplicity. We even managed to have fast internet reception to stay in touch with the world.

By now we were learning why Australia was considered a dangerous place. Here in the "bush", slithered eight of the world's most poisonous snakes. There were ticks whose bite could mean total paralysis if the victim was not taken to the hospital within half an hour. (A typical Aussie reply would be "no worries mate, it only takes about twenty minutes to get there so she'll be right.") Wallabies would frolic in the back yard as would the very large and intimidating looking five foot long Goana lizards that resembled prehistoric dragons. Gloria told us of the notorious jumping ants of which like many other people she was allergic to and had to carry the anecdote for such a bite in a hypodermic needle. If she didn't have an injection, she could slide easily into a coma. At least in the creek right behind our house there were no crocodiles as I heard were common in some other parts of the country.

In time, we became used to meeting large carpet snakes along our walking path home and even on our door step. But it was the tiny leeches that were the most problematic critter to contend with. Reviving from deep earth slumbering after a rain fall, these little wormy creatures would smell human blood and like vampires they would find their way to our bodies and suck it up until their own bodies would expand to the size of tiny balloons. Every time I would go outside for a bathroom visit, usually I would find a line of blood tracking behind me from the unnoticed bites on my legs. Our most severe experience with leeches came when Stephanie had one find its way to her eye. Thinking she just had an itch, she asked Sophia to have a look and see if there were any dust particles in her eye needing removal. However when her close observation revealed that it was actually a leech, I went into a state of panic on what to do. Sophia, with gentle focus, took a cotton swab, dipped it in warm salty water and then proceeded patiently to encourage the beast to slowly dislodge its clutches from her mother's aching eye. But even with its removal and subsequent okay of no infection from the Nimbin hospital, her eye felt painful and looked swollen for over a week. A reason to stay at home so not to have anyone thinking she had a "black eye" as a result of some domestic violence incident. With perhaps millions of leeches in the forest and with a very low probability of people or animals ever walking along their same path, I often reflected on how they survived if no one ever would come along. The existential fate of all vampires.

One of our unforgettable experiences was when a winter storm lifted the raging creek near the cabin to our front door and kept rising. We moved as many valuable belongings as we could to the top of our bunk beds as we weathered the onslaught of the aspiring flood. What was once a gentle stream near our cabin transformed into a roaring river which even had the power to carry big boulders down its path. Even remnants of household objects grabbed from neighbors homes on higher grounds and slivering snakes enjoying a free ride moved swiftly by. Eventually the storm faded and the water didn't reach a point of causing too much harm but it did take down the small foot bridge between our cabin area and the road where we parked our car. Until we managed to replace it with a new construction, John along with expertise guidance from Gloria built a sturdy rope support across the creek for us to hold on to as we had to walk through the still powerful current for a few more days. Another thrilling adventure of surviving in the "bush".

But even besides the challenges of wildlife and mold, the Tuntable Community soon felt very much like home to us. We enjoyed our new friendships, scenery and lifestyle which gave us one more reason to want to be allowed to remain as permanent residents of the country. As a show of faith in our intention, we attended all the monthly membership meetings and eventually were allowed to purchase a share in the community as well.

All members were expected to attend monthly meetings, pay a small amount for road works and other improvements and also volunteer a prescribed number of hours of work each month for community maintenance projects. As our concerns over getting sucked by leeches did not seem to appeal to us very much, we were not looking forward to the idea of community service which for most members meant working "in the bush." What a joy when the work proposal we submitted of our operating a cafe once a month was accepted by a majority vote at the next meeting.

CAFE

With the many fine cooks in our family and along with my own social zeal and organizing skills, we soon were able to fix up the old community store and prepare our grand opening. In the early 1970's, this building was a busy center of entertainment, cooked meals, bulk food purchasing and a main hub of socializing. Over the years however, it had fallen to minimal use and cobwebs. My intuition was right however in knowing that it would be a very successful venture into bringing back that same spring of activity, fun and of course, delightful dining.

The building itself was a large wooden shed with a remodeled and functional kitchen having a large walk in refrigerated storage room. For our restaurant needs we would first make a thorough cleaning, place colorful tablecloths on the assorted metal and long wooden tables, candles and various other visual ambience enhancements. The food was prepared by Nicolette, Sophia and Stephanie and was always wonderful, healthy, vegetarian and affordable. My job was to greet the customers and fill their cups with free complimentary chilled Sangria made with red wine and fruit juices. For people that could not afford a full meal, I would be providing plenty of samples and even successfully inviting and escorting extra help to the kitchen. (Which of course would mean they would also earn credit on their work dues without having to be out in the leech fields either.)

In time the monthly dinner nights started spreading in popularity and the need for the community to supply us with extra tables and chairs. Not only were just people from Tuntable coming, but from Nimbin town and beyond. What a delight to see that my intention to revive social interaction was a success as people that were neighbors and hadn't seen and talked to each other in years were now gabbing away as they had in younger times. By encouraging quality musicians from the area to come and play in exchange for a free meal also made it a delightful evening of dining and bridging various scattered groups and individuals. From our first grand opening night of serving about twelve customers, a few months later we peaked at nearly one hundred happy people. Even the mayor of the larger nearby city of Lismore came a few times to join in the renaissance of Tuntable's social outreach (which upset a few of the members who had preferred to live in a more "camouflaged off the radar" community).

Having grown past the maximum number of tables and customers that we could fit in the cafe, our next step was to try reviving the even larger community hall across the meadow. Occasional exercise classes and the once a month membership meeting were still taking place there, but it seemed that it was a building and opportunity waiting for even grander enterprises. So into the mix, we made friends with some very popular rock and roll bands in New South Wales that would sometimes charge regular venues up to $1000 to perform. But for us they agreed to come donate their time to the cause of helping our long standing hippie community in co-creating another page of history. And by our providing delicious snacks including what by now was Nicolette's famous cheesecakes and spicy popcorn, the hall was buzzing with delighted crowds. Wholesome entertainment for the masses that also pleased the bands that had brought their own families to join the fun in a tobacco free environment enhanced by open hearts, stoned minds, lots of Sangria and nature's own sacraments.

OASIS

With the wide spread community popularity of our dining expressions, Nicolette was soon approached and subsequently hired at the Nimbin Oasis Cafe downtown which was not only a pleasant working situation but also a chance for her to have more social outreach. The Oasis was more than just a cafe as it also served as an important community gathering niche. On a regular day between the table bongs and poetry readings, a variety of traveling philosophers, eclectic vagabonds, esoteric musicians and just plain happily stoned locals would hang out in a comfortable low pressured environment. It was also frequented by single older men who thrilled in trying to flirt with Nicolette which was an unavoidable challenge of the job. Whenever an unannounced police pot raid was sighted approaching the town, the community radio station would sound out the coded warning message sobering up all the patrons to quickly get out of the spaced out zone and cooperatively hide any traces of illegality from the sniffer dogs. When Nicolette had to quit working because of her eventual move to work at a childcare center job in Byron Bay, she passed on her position to Sophia who eventually passed it on to John when he returned to Nimbin because of the closure of where he worked in New Zealand for the Winter. It also became an excellent opportunity for John to socialize as well as sit down with other musicians for impromptu jam sessions. And with no older single women attempting to flirt with him, it was a more of a hassle free job than it had been for his sisters.

MUSIC

Besides being a pinnacle beacon for legalizing of cannabis use in Australia, a vivid resource of environmental activism, and a clear example of off grid community sustainability, Nimbin was also a focal point for excellent wide spread live music. Ranging from organic hippie to folk protest and experimental electronics, there was always enjoyable music at a variety of mostly free and laid back venues in town. Jam sessions could be heard at the cafes while the monthly outdoor market was always a festive opportunity to buy some healthy food, pass a pipe and hear nonstop musical expressions. New performers were always welcomed which was to turn into a regular gig opportunity for John to bring smiles and wake up people's dancing feet as well.

RADIO PRESENTER AGAIN

A typical resource of communication in most towns that have an active counterculture is an open access local public non commercial radio station which becomes not only a showcase of entertainment but also an integral part of social networking. Not restricted to corporate music of questionable artistic merit, listeners have the opportunity to be appreciating a wider panorama of music as well as hearing uncompromising news, documentaries, opinions and announcements that would not be possible in mainstream media.

Nimbin's radio station was a perfect fit to the eclectic cultural scene of the town and no matter what was being presented on the air, it was always a bubbling gem of anarchy and high consciousness. Having my own hippie roots blossom at a time when "underground radio" was feeding the heads of awakening during the 1960's, I was happy to dust off the untouched radio dials of our cabin's stereo, adjust the antenna for adequate signal reception, and spread NIM-FM's mind expanding soundtrack in our slice of the rain forest. Just as when I would sometimes strum imaginary air guitar chords on jamming rock and roll tunes, I would often make up radio song lists in my head as to what I would be playing if I too were a presenter on the station. One of my favorite jobs had been when I was a disc jockey on Maui but the pressures of dealing with commercials, precision soundboard settings, and senile judgmental station owners listening to my show had been a little too traumatic for me to attempt another incarnation on the air.

Besides the urging of Stephanie and several of the other radio presenters that I do a regular show again, it was an unexpected experience that suddenly triggered my change of mind. While driving home one day, one of the station's presenters kept mumbling incoherent rhetoric that sounded as if he was either a madman or someone on bad drugs. He then went on to say that he liked a new song that he had recently listened to so much that he was going to play it over and over for an hour. Like some example of North Korean brainwashing torture techniques, he went on to indeed play one of the worse pieces of dissonant noise excuse of music for over an hour. At that point, I had an epiphany that if that barely functional idiot could handle the dials, so could I. And as the station was totally volunteer, unless I was a major lunatic, there was little chance of screwing up or even risk being fired.

Early one Saturday morning I filled out my job application and was asked to sit in with one of my presenter friends to get a feeling for the soundboard. However it was a high anxiety moment when my friend handed me the microphone and told me he was walking outside to take a smoke break. Like a young kid thrown into a swimming pool as a fast track to learning how to swim, I was left alone to quickly assimilate the technical lessons I had just been shown how to do my stint on the air. Clearly focused and determined to fill the air with cool music, I expressed my desire to finish the whole shift on my own and to furthermore request a regular shift every week. Thus my show called Side Tracks was launched on Wednesday nights from 7 pm to whatever time I felt like going off the air and putting on the prerecorded music, which would cover the late night until the next presenter would come on the following morning.

Coming into the station a little early to prepare for my first show, one of my co-workers took me into the music library room where many of the presenters would organize what they would be playing. Also someone suggested that my program could be a Greek music show being as that was my ethnic ethos. As much as I appreciated everyone's helpful sentiments, I had a raging vision of providing a wide open presentation of "prancing, trancing and romancing." In other words, my artistic juices were intent to create the sort of musical environment for listeners to be able to find a comforting backdrop for being stoned, psychedelic, love-making, or just enjoying well laid out gems of creativity, imagination and/or political uprisings. The spirit of music was the path to healing and out of the box excursions which I was determined to help express as best I could.

In short time, I realized that the commercials were all funky and easy to stick on the tape deck. Some vocalizations were necessary from me once an hour, but no problem in what I muttered. Especially as most of my talk between thematic segments was either informative details about the music I played or stories of my experiences in having seen many of the great bands that I was playing the music of. My best discovery was that even though the soundboard was old and literally held together by thin strips of wood and duct tape, it also had a USB input. Thus I could download the music I wanted to play at home from the internet, place it on a small zip drive, and then have it all ready to be played in the order I had selected. I could then have a four hour radio show prepared before I walked into the studio. And with Stephanie being my technical assistant who knew how to stick the zip drive into the soundboard and be available for any on the air glitches, technology was good for me. So thus started our Wednesday night routine of driving down the hill early enough to stop off at the Oasis Cafe to talk to friends and promise to play their requests at some point before taking our hot cup of caffeine across the street to the station studio. We then would sit on the navigators seat for a few hours of fun. And besides the appreciative boost from listeners calling in to say how great the music sounded, it was also wonderful to finally have the opportunity to turn up the volume and not worry about bothering neighbors or using up a limited quota of solar electricity.

Sidetracks over the next few months became a high point in my life that I looked forward to every Wednesday night. The usual two hour format was just a tease for my long playlists and at times I would be on the air from 7 pm until 2 the next morning. Almost an eight hour work shift. And with NIM-FM also streaming on the internet, it was also a delight to have friends from all over the world listening in. On my last show before having to leave Australia, I made sure to "kick out the jams" all through the night. An epic presentation but sadly, it was also the night the internet had gone down and could not be heard through that medium. A conspiracy targeting my subversive music? Or perhaps just the universe intriguing me to make sure to return to Nimbin someday and continue my musical outreach. In either case, I set the intention that I would return sooner than later.

MARDI GRASS

The premier event that Nimbin was famous for both in Australia and around the world was the yearly Mardi Grass celebration held on the first weekend in May. For over two decades, tens of thousands of people would inflate the town's population for a three day festival honoring hemp in its many ways. Cannabis education included industrial, medicinal, and spiritual uses in workshops organized in various halls and parks around downtown. Films and live music were presented around the clock (which was another stage showcase for John), as well as occasional fire dancing and spontaneous street artistry. In the large field on the outskirts of town, the Hemp Olympics were an entertaining example of creative athleticism including such events as bong tossing and rolling joints in adverse conditions. By the mention of where each competitor was from, it was clear that there were representatives from most of the world's continents attending. The police stood in long lines behind the spectators and were often invited to come join a "tug of peace" game with Nimbin's own Hemp Embassy volunteers to which they turned a deaf ear to.

With all the focus on pot, Mardi Grass weekend was ironically also the time of year where few joints were smoked in public. Not only did the cops have an army of sniffer dogs, but every road leading to town was blocked by police vehicles thoroughly checking the cars and riders for cannabis. As a bit of grandstanding, on the first evening of the festival, a very long transport truck pulled up and as its rear door was opened, about twelve cops riding horses came marching out, as if they were proud Roman cavalry about to subservient the town's pride with their bright outfitted troops. In actuality, the Trojan Horse scene looked fairly ludicrous and was mostly a display of expensive ineptitude which did nothing to clean up the town's "drug use" but instead left a pile of horse shit for someone to clean up instead afterwards.

In my own observation of the police force, I noticed that they would walk around in teams of four and harass mostly elderly Aboriginal people with humiliating body searches and occasional pokes with their clubs. For these white racist cops, it was just an opportunity to use their badges as excuse to hurt others for no such reason. In response to these unnecessary acts of police brutality, Nimbin had organized a squad of about a dozen men and women dressed in blue facsimile police uniforms but instead of the logo "police" their outfits said "polite". Along with the aid of volunteer law students, the town's polite force would follow many of the cop teams around and document all instances of unlawful harassment and at times intervene to prevent people from being hurt by these gun toting thugs with badges.

To feed the masses that were moving in every direction, food stalls offered a wide selection for every taste including of course, for the "munchies". Because of our success with the Tuntable community cafe, the event organizers had asked us to be in charge of the main cafe which was located inside the town hall. After every lecture huge lines of people gathered for our fast, healthy and affordable plates of homemade food and desserts. And of course, I always had big bottles of chilled Sangria as complimentary refreshment for the town locals.

Like the culmination of many other grand festivals around the world, the Mardi Grass ended with a brilliant parade. Floats, musicians, outrageously dressed strollers and the ever radiant Ganja Fairies brought cheers and delight to the young and old. There was no fire engine, police van or Santa Claus at the end of the parade, but treats were still in store for some of us a few days later however.

While talking to friends in front of one of the town cafes, a car pulled up and suggested that Stephanie and I quickly follow. By a quirk of mistaken identity, we had just been invited to the infamous Nimbin Cannabis Cup Awards which take place in a clandestine location several days after the Mardi Grass. So not looking back or wondering if we should or not, we pulled up and joined about thirty other "dignitaries" ready to judge Nimbin's finest herb and hash entries. To make sure we were healthy enough for the competition, we filled our plates from a lavish free buffet consisting of all the sort of gourmet delicacies that we usually drool over as luxury items. Some munching on fine cheeses, dips, cakes and a few glasses of fancy wine later, we entered our names to be included in voting on the hash which only had a couple of choices to pick from. The pot competition, on the other hand, appeared to be much more intimidating to make proper choices of with about thirty samples of goodies spread out on six very long dining tables. And to make sure each entry had a fair chance of analyses, there was a large assortment of ingestion tools ranging from hemp rolling papers, water pipes, bongs and high tech vaporizers. A very professional and well organized event indeed.

For Stephanie and I, too deep puffs of the hashish was enough to make us extremely stoned, so we decided that to be fair to the growers, we each voted for either sample, and then faded into the lawn to watch clouds. How the rest of the judges could make clear decisions was beyond our logic, but felt honest procedures would merit acceptable awarding of the prized trophies. And as the judges deliberated, the rest of us were offered to go through the tables and pick from whatever leftover buds we wanted to partake in as well. A few more hits from the vaporizer and we both realized that we needed to focus on our drive back home where our daughters were waiting for our return with groceries. This memorable experience was an affirmation of how Nimbin was not a town of "drug dealing" as pot was never sold to each other but presented as gifts or a currency of exchange or barter.

PAST THE BORDER

Although Nimbin seemed like the epicenter of Australian counter-culture, we did learn in time that many pockets of similar activity were located throughout the country. The large cities of Melbourne and Sydney had a wide base of artistic, political and social activism and there were even off grid organic farm communities and pockets of free thinkers in most rural areas. There were sprinklings of spiritual groups such as the Hare Krishna movement as well as eclectic individuals living in remote settings and hermitages.

As we explored more of the region around Nimbin, we visited many of these areas of alternative activity to not only experience the beautiful scenery but also in case we found a more suitable place for our residency hopes. It was getting to be a funny cliché how some of the more "righteous" new-agers would tell us to keep away from Nimbin because of its "dark and druggy" persona. All things considered though, Nimbin with its funky outlaw town and true hippie roots was where we called and considered "home". Within short drives through the countryside we could still access a plethora of excellent music, beaches, and spiritual gatherings.

The neo-hippie Rainbow community was also well evidenced through its many regional weekend gatherings. With the opportunity to do so, we decided to take a ride and participate in one about a four hour drive from Nimbin and afterwards to then continue making a loop through the gorgeous mountainous interior of the region and then back up the coast. About fifty miles from the gathering site, our car broke down and thus we needed spending the day in a town along the way for a mechanic to fix the problem. Being in a picturesque location, we felt happy enough to be stuck here instead of somewhere more desolate. We also were content to take a family stroll along a park side area next to a crystal clear river and then to browse through some of the downtown stores. While Stephanie and the girls had gone off to find a public bathroom, I sat contently on a bench relaxing in a mid afternoon gaze. A rather plump faced man about thirty years old wearing a suit and a wide brim smile politely asked if he could sit down next to me. Assuming he was either a homosexual, a missionary of some sorts or just plain courteous, I guardedly told him to go ahead and do so. Then with a cheerful tone he asked me how I liked his town. I replied in proper pleasantries on how nice it was to which he took a pause and then stated in a direct tone, that if I were to stay longer in town, I needed to cut my hair and beard. In just as polite retort, I told him thank you for the advice to which he wished me a good day and off he went. Nope, we were no longer in Nimbin anymore but many miles closer to Kansas it seemed. Eager to get out of this redneck town, it was a great relief that our car was fixed before dark and we were soon among our kind at the Rainbow Gathering. A pleasure to see men with long hair and beards just as nature intended.

FLOOD

The topographical extreme contrasts of Australia's landscape were also evidenced in the climate and sudden weather changes. One day while sitting casually at an internet cafe in the town of Lismore, the sunny day turned pitch black within a ten minute period of time. The gusty wind and heavy downpour of rain was becoming even more intense. Street signs and a variety of rubbish whisked through the air which was soon followed by sheets of hail the size of golf balls hammering big dents on cars and possibly bouncing off unfortunate people's heads that happened to be caught in the crossfire. Nicolette was sheltered in her parked car but when a sharp burst of wind pushed her trunk open, she ran out to shut it back in place but in the process her wrist was hammered by hail so badly that we needed to take her to the hospital emergency room.

The scene at the usually calm and well organized Lismore hospital now resembled a frantic aftermath of a war zone. People were running in holding various parts of their bodies that were injured while at the same time trying to protect themselves from more intermittent barrages of hail or flying glass. Cars were pulling off onto sidewalks so as to find safety zones from the flooded streets. Electricity had shut down through the city so the hospital was using backup generators for the emergencies. And nearly hurricane force winds were blowing out windows all over town and even tore off much of the front roof and siding of the main entrance to the hospital from the over golf ball size hail. In retrospect, when we read how the river that flowed through Lismore was at one time red from the blood of the indigenous Aboriginal people that had been slaughtered by the white rulers, we wondered if it was the town's karma to be facing such weather related damage year after year.

EXIT FROM DOWN UNDER

Immigration being one of our main objectives in either New Zealand or Australia, we made the commitment to spend even more of my mother's inheritance in that pursuit. The cost for extra visas, vocational education and meetings with attorneys all ate up quite a hefty chunk of money. However with John qualifying for residency in New Zealand and Nicolette being promised a full time job in Australia, our investment was seeming well worth the expense.

Of all the childcare centers that Nicolette had applied to, she was excited to hear back from her favorite one that she was hired. It's location in fashionable Byron Bay was close enough to Nimbin, as well as in a focal point of entertainment, shopping, alternative culture and beautiful ocean scenery.

With all these signs of success, Nicolette bought her own car and rented an apartment not to far from work. Not being too interested in the nighttime bar life or daytime exposure to t shirt shops and fast food junk, she still enjoyed being able to take long hikes along the coast and through the town green belt parks. As wonderful as we all felt, we all were equally devastated when the Australian immigration office informed her that her hopes of a residency visa were cancelled. With only a few more weeks to have met the original qualification, the government had changed its expectations and wanted her to have a four year university degree. Although it could well have been coincidental, we felt tricked by the Australian government in not honoring their promises. Foreign students in the country comprise the third largest money making sector, so it was a good market to lead immigrants into the expensive university system in their quest for citizenship. For third world students whose family sell all their belongings in hopes that their kids can become residents in Australia, their failure to do so would be tantamount to total ruin as well as humiliation. It's at that point that a number of companies make money from setting up many of these young ladies with "nice, and wealthy older gentlemen" for marriage as one more option for being able to stay in the country.

In retrospect, we were of course sad that we couldn't stay in Australia, but at the same time started looking forward to a move back to Hawaii. As Bob Dylan put it: Don't Look Back. And with still owning a share in the Tuntable community and the Nimbin Mardi Grass as an event to come back to, we are looking forward to a return some day. And if the Oasis Cafe is still offering late night coffee, perhaps my Side Tracks radio show can find its way back on the air again too.

CHAPTER TWENTY-TWO: ENDINGS AND NEW BEGINNINGS

The sails of time and place eventually brought us back to familiar harbors in the Hawaiian Islands. The intentions of our odyssey to find a "new homeland" were never realized, but we did however eventually find our comfortable nest here on the Big Island. Spirals of life continue for each of the members of our family in the rhythm of personal needs and passages. As I sit looking over the rain forest from my room I take a deep breath and know that this journal remains as a testament to our journeys and as a reference point for our lives ahead. Besides writing my two autobiographical volumes, every day I continue researching articles for the "Links by George" newsletter which I have been sending out twice a month since 1998 through the internet as well as eventually through daily postings on Facebook. From the first issue of the satiric "Daily Erection" which I co-authored in 10th grade with my friend Carl Freedman to the time I was distributing underground newspapers in San Francisco in 1969, alternative newspapers in Montana in the early 90"s and even as a radio presenter in Hawaii and Australia, I take pride and devoted interest in sharing awareness of consciousness expansion through the arts as well as culture, politics and shamanism. The home schooling experience with my children has now expanded to a virtual classroom of several thousand friends and readers. I consider it as part of my social dharma as it helps networking people on varieties of issues that they otherwise would have only been confused about.

Our kids have now grown up and are continuing the family vision in their own way. Yet we are still closely bonded and are in the process of living on the same land together. I cherish the experiences of my life as vintage and vivid realities but I also am living in the present moment which is a slice of eternity and which also gives me the opportunity to be grateful and to never stop sharing love and light.

443

The importance of community roots was further reminded to us by the love expressed by our Hawaiian friend Uncle Robert Keli'iho'omalu whose family has lived in the village of Kalapana here on the Big Island for many generations and have been true representatives of the Aloha spirit of loving the land and all the people that live on it. Before his death, Uncle Robert even set aside a track of land as a peaceful sanctuary for extraterrestrials if they ever wanted to come and visit.

Integrating the concept of "unity" into the context of "community", in December of 2012 with Uncle Robert's permission, I helped organize the Flashback to Freedom Festival in Kalapana. Over a thousand people attended a full day of music, circus acrobatics, childrens' workshops, fire spinning, arts, crafts and food with the common denominator being that no matter how different we might appear, we all share the same breath and heartbeat. Speeches were presented by our State Senator Russell Ruderman, gay and cannabis activist from San Francisco Dennis Peron, representation of the cannabis ministry of Roger Christie, the sovereignty of the Kingdom of Hawaii, importance of organic foods, dangers of GMO foods, astrology and much more. It was quite a challenge for my keeping the schedule tight in allowing all these people and groups equal time between the music. Truly a memorable outpouring of love.

Love was also flowing in the breeze of our family land on Valentine's Day 2014 when our son and his lovely wife Ariel were married in a colorful ceremony that was accented by a variety of spiritual traditions.

And for even further expression of roots to the future, we now have our own family burial plot on the land we share with our family as well.

Over the years there were many places where we felt we needed a more permanent space of security or even "back door to escape to one day". But we learned an expensive lesson in that if you don't live permanently in such a place, there are unexpected taxes and pressures that will eventually swallow your investment. The land we had bought in Bali was lost because of such problems and now the small tracts we purchased on the Greek islands have been sliced into uselessness by encroachment by neighbors and taxes. Unexpected taxes are also threatening our inherited family home in Greece as well as the small lot on the island of Fiji. But rather than cry over our losses, we remind ourselves that we have found a place we are at that we call home and can feel our roots grow in.

I hope that my life's adventures have been at the least entertaining and an encouragement for everyone to honor and to express their own story. For someone to look back in retrospect and say if one could, they would make different decisions if given another chance does not give justice or trust to our deeper selves. We did what we felt was best at the time. Intentions are the vital link to how we can evaluate such experiences and then to let go of attachment to the consequences. Like clouds passing in the sky, there are down moments but soon afterwards the brilliant flashes appear of the sun's rays and the full moon's smiles. And as the thunder and lightning here in the rain forest shake, rattle and roll, I am always as happy to know that more rainbows are on the way.

Besides leaving this autobiography as a record of my experiences across time and space, it has also been a personal mirror for me to take a closer look to my reactions and perceptions in many situations. How I viewed my parents attitudes and responses to my beliefs and expressions now have a far different meaning. Thus in a more objective light, I can understand their reasoning as well as the plausibility of their reactions. Previously unresolved abrasive incidents in my relationships such as issues of abandonment now have a broader meaning in the wider scope of time. Perhaps now I can understand my insecurities of being left alone or not always being loved because of my parents threat to replace my position of receiving all their attention by adopting another child.

In a traditional sense, karma refers to the principle of causality where intent and actions of an individual influence the future of that individual. Non attachment to results is a prescribed way to avoid frustration as well as to not create negative karma. My journeys have led me to many situations across time and space. Each moment was very real and subsequently my passions were very real and formed an integral part of my ever changing landscape of interactions. Although I eventually had to leave these various stages of life, the scripts and dramas continue whereby even in my absence I still feel part of me always remains in those moments of time. Not as a frozen memory but as a very real and present person in the ongoing social scenery. Time and time again I would sincerely tell people that I would one day return.

Until such an opportunity arises, my eternal return continues in this autobiographical journey.

Our journeys were not just observations but real relationships with people and their different situations, needs, cultures and environments. These real world dramas continue and a part of us is still active in each of those stages even though we are located elsewhere in real time. As I learned in one of my psychedelic Salvia trips, it is too much to expect to be everywhere at the same time. Our identity is to be where we are but to still send rays of light and love to the people that still know and view us as part of their extended reality. These ego traps can be a source of prison for many but by crossing karma zones, we were able to transverse such totalities and be enhanced by the experiences. Ram Das reminds us to "Be here now" and fully present wherever we might be. Likewise another great role model of time and space, Buckaroo Bonzai adds, (also paraphrased by Ken Kesey) "Wherever you go, there you are". And as a final quote, in respect to the Grateful Dead I say, "What a long strange trip it continues to be."

> Thank you for reading my book and any support in sharing it with others. To all my friends along life's journey that I might not have mentioned in my story, please know that you are not forgotten and very present in my heart with honor and respect.
> Aloha, George

My friend Chuck Sanders added a final touch to his autobiography which I would like to end my book with as well: "Lastly, I have done my best to properly edit and correct any misspellings and should anyone find misspellings and they dwell on it then they have missed the entire reason for me writing my book!" (Col. Chuck Sanders disclaimer from his book: Life After Vietnam, When Chucky Comes Marching Home: Fighting with My Personal Demons)

PHILOSOPHIC MUSINGS

My lifelong search for spiritual meaning has taken me in and out of many portals of enquiry and experience both as a solitary mystical seeker as well as the path of tribal congregation. Comic books, science fiction movies and television shows such as "The Twilight

Zone" and "Outer Limits" lubricated my perspectives of out of the box and to wet my appetite for learning more. Strict Greek Orthodox family life and Roman Catholic high masses in my early schooling infused me with dogma, exotic hymns and enchanting incense. Books of mythology and the supernatural took me a step further. My maps of consciousness opened into studies such as Tarot, I Ching, astrology, Holotropic Breathing, Actualism, Reiki, psychic healing, channeling, Krishna, Edward Cayce, Santo Daime, Unity, Arica, Peyote Way, Urantia, Subud, Taoism, Mount Athas monastery retreat, Course in Miracles, Transcendental reflection, Eckankar, Buddhism, Hinduism, Sufi, Bahai, Gurdjief, Steiner, Krishnamurti, Rajneesh/ Osho, Sathchidananda, Carlos Casteneda, Neo-Paganism, Tantra and a variety of styles of meditation. I explored musical highs through Gregorian Chants, Byzantine hymns, New Age and more. My dimensional outreach expanded even more with psychedelic plants and drugs including cannabis, hashish, peyote, mushrooms, morning glories, Hawaiian baby woodrose, MDA, MDMA, LSD, San Pedro, DMT, Salvia and Ayahuasca. I have learned much from all these teachings but can never say one is any better than another or even has a monopoly on truth. Personal intention and integration of such experiences is a primary element in the equation.

After a spiritual teacher brings direct experience to people that gravitate to his or her teachings, a focus develops that eventually codifies certain procedures and expectations of the "members" that morphs into a religion. The direct experience of a higher power by a shaman is replaced by faith in a middle man called a priest. The next step becomes the belief that one's religion is the only true path and any other religion is wrong or even evil. "Holy" wars are fought as what then develops is a synthesis of power, religion and politics. Pure spirituality can indeed accent any political format. In the distribution of goods and services, a presence of love over gold can amplify the benefits of the political system. Unfortunately however quite the opposite is the record of hero as absolute power corrupts absolutely. The Holy Roman Church became the extension of the Holy Roman Empire. Even though I feel religions could offer a gateway for an aspirant to find his or her connection to the "sacred other," most members of a religion pay attention more to the dogma, outfits and images rather than the spiritual depth. I could never imagine in such cases an answer from Jesus, Buddha or other spiritual teachers to the question "who should we drone first?" Instead we would probably hear these advanced teachers say "Judge not that ye be not judged" and "By the grace of God go you or I." Tolerance is the antithesis to war as is the perspective of looking at what one has in common with their neighbor rather than the differences of separation. Our friend on Maui, Bodhi Be who follows a Sufi tradition would sum it up appropriately by saying "Be excellent to each other".

Organized religion can be a wonderful approach to spirituality, but it's essence is often corrupted by power and thus can only serve as a crutch. To connect to higher purpose of divinity, it might mean looking past the fancy robes, golden crowns and prescribed dogmas and thus be able to talk directly to the sacred.

As with my spiritual engagements, my political pursuits likewise covered a panoramic range over time. My early years were intrigued by local bias and so I investigated many fringe groups such as the Ku Klux Klan and John Birch Society. My first hand experiences helped me later understand the mind set of such extremes looking for simplistic answers. I became a member of the Young Republicans for a short while until I realized that I was more akin to the Young Democrats. Later I studied Ayn Rand and objectivism but moved on to the Students for a Democratic Society, and Libertarianism. Although I found some points of resonance with traditional Republicanism, I sensed that the Democratic party that seemed more humanistic and the Peace and Freedom party even more. Now I am totally disgusted at the betrayals most of these official parties have and are not to be trusted. The Bill of Rights would be closer to my eclectic views that would include freedom for all in the pursuit of pleasure and religion and to be safeguarded from all domestic tyranny such as a totalitarian police state. A good government should take care of the infrastructure that would make people's lives easier including free health insurance and guaranteed food and shelter for all. Our economy has the capability of doing it as long as it can be freed from the clutches of the one percenters.

The integration of my political, cultural and spiritual views come from my own personal experiences as a civil rights and also anti-war activist during the 1960's. At that time, much was also learned as well through my travels into psychedelic dimensions and integration of these profound experiences into my life. But besides my personal views, it is an issue that I wish to express to the wider community for reflection and commentary. Especially to those that were actually "there at the times". Except for the images capitalized by media dictates to the contrary, at least in the earlier years, there was a holistic blend of both perspectives in the movement. The materialistic separation of activism, heart and soul was a non-issue. Machiavellian pressures to distort both the hippie and the political movements led to the division bells which eventually challenged both. Hippies and activists became bulls eyes to be attacked and crippled by vested interests. Draconian drug laws, bogus health and insurance violations and a general disregard for the Bills of Rights did not differentiate. The FBI and CIA used undercover agents and lies to discredit both movements and to promote hostilities between them. Many people living a mainstream life were shown a deeper connection to their own selves and others through psychedelics and subsequently dropped out of previous negative attitudes such as racism and mass-consumption. The power structures were definitely alarmed. The integration of the psychedelic experience led to respect of nature and an awareness of injustices that had to be dealt with.

Subsequently, many of the political and activist groups eventually criticized the hippie movement as not using force to tear the system apart. Much of this fuel for the fire was again planned and orchestrated by government agents. When Timothy Leary escaped his 30 year prison term for possessing two joints, he joined Black Power leader Eldridge Cleaver in Algeria who in turn kicked him out for talking of spirituality as a root for total cultural change. Peace and Love as well as Justice. So which approach was right to me is as mute a point as in asking which arm is more useful, the right or left.

The hippie movement had an emphasis on leaving the corrupt mainstream system and creating a communal back to the earth lifestyle as an alternative which rejected traditional institutions such as school, commerce, banking and the rest of the corporate wheels that kept oppression in business. Was this not a political act? And even in the move out of the system, hippies still would be a part of anti-war marches as well as presenting a model of a way of life which likewise was definitely as much a political act as throwing rocks at cops who would respond with weapons of mass destruction and incarceration. I was there and still have my own scars and traumas from those moments.

As cannabis legalization is becoming a reality, I do hope that pot becomes the gateway drug that mainstream society was worried about.

A gateway not to addictions such as television and gossip, but as a true gateway to psychedelic plants that can lead us to a better connection with higher consciousness and interaction with all life forms.

Can psychedelics cause major changes in someone's psyche? Tons of books and workshops can make claim on all aspects of this proposition. My own opinion is that changes can only happen in a direction that an individual's soul and inner dynamics have a pre-disposition for. The CIA experimented with such substances as ways of spying, creating truth serums, and Manchurian candidates. Some people cracked while others rose to angelic levels of universal love. Likewise a country strangled from deep spiritual roots was given access to the liberation of experiencing spirituality as well as expanded humanism and consciousness.

So yes, possibly LSD was part of an agenda from higher elites to be used for another weapon of brainwashing and control. But in the hands of Kesey, Leary, and psychedelic music and art, the results were far different than what was expected. Most kids at that time had no interest in civil rights or stopping wars. But the wave of expanding consciousness brought a significant number to a breaking through those walls and becoming activists in many dimensions. The so called hippies that might be viewed as not being politically interested were quite possibly never going to be activists any way. But by the same token, their changes of perception and even lifestyle made a very positive difference in their lives and their relations to others.

For me music has had a profound and integral part to play in the psychedelic experience. Just like the sacred icaros chants of Amazonian ayahuasca sessions, Byzantine hymns of Christian monks, Sufi dervishing, Native American peyote songs, etc., the 1960's generation of psychedelic voyagers found a similar sacred resonance with the multi dimensional and mind expanding textures of the music of Jimi Hendrix, Led Zeppelin, Pink Floyd, Grateful Dead, King Crimson, Traffic, Beatles, Rolling Stones and many more groups typed as playing psychedelic music. These songs both help in a ceremonial way as well as trigger in me a full sensory taste of the divine as well. The Jimi Hendrix album "Electric Ladyland" for example still brings me to that high frontier no matter the set and setting as well as provides a safety net soundscape for deep inner and outer space traveling. If psychedelics were not so demonized by the legal system and the music industry not as co-opted by the priority of making money instead of high art, I am sure there would still be a vibrant and thriving influence of such music in society today.

In some respects, the psychedelic experience is a personal gateway which is not necessarily dependent on the psychoactive chemical combination. Over the centuries many sacred plants and psychedelic drugs have been identified. But just as sacred icons or gurus are not to be worshiped as one's personal spiritual experience, these plants are not the psychedelic experience itself but only the key that opens the partaker into entering a wider domain of consciousness than normal consensus reality. It is not the mailman, UPS deliverer, Skype or internet that is the experience but only the bringer of that experience to you.

Furthermore, the expansion of consciousness should not be viewed as the domain of specific utilization. If one takes a psychedelic drug for entertainment instead of a spiritual experience or psychological breakthrough, that can all be well and good and not any better or worse. Psychedelics represent freedom and not to be limited in such ways. Recently much more legal allowance has been provided for studies and usage in medical areas. But even if one is not "sick", healthy people can benefit from these experiences as well.

Psychedelics such as magic mushrooms have been used by spiritual seekers for thousands of years. In the Amazon, shamans who use ayahuasca are emphasizing that one of the messages of this psychedelic brew is that the world is being threatened, the corporations destroying nature, and that a political change is essential if we are to survive.

One of the mainstream media tags for the 1960's psychedelic culture was Timothy Leary's famous phrase "Turn On, Tune In and Drop Out". Mainstream media portrayed adherents of this philosophy and life style as being interested in not doing anything "worthwhile" for the status quo and essentially becoming "dirty, lazy bums". In actuality what the good doctor Tim was prescribing for an imbalanced culture was the opening up to wider levels of perception, be attentive to higher states of reality and to no longer be as attached to the materialistic rat race which corporate America had fixated as a vital value for established vested interests to perpetuating the "American Dream". In retrospect that sort of dream has morphed into a global nightmare of desperation, pollution, perpetual war and instability.

Another motto of the hippie subculture which also became a misinterpreted cliché was the praise of "Drugs, Sex and Rock and Roll." Again the foggy eyes of conventional reality were alarmed into feeling fear and disgust at the specter of unconscious sex orgies manifested by dangerous drugs which the sensationalizing media claimed damaged bodies and minds. Parents panicked that their kids were not as interested in listening to predictable pop songs but instead "strange sounds of ear popping electronic dissonance." Again another example of biased perception which failed to fathom the beauty of sacred plants, transportive layers of exotic sounds and deeper sensuality in general.

Having discussed the drugs and rock and roll aspects of the "hippie trinity", I would like to mention that sex was liberated as a sacred path. Unlike its enclosure in the mindset of the uptight mainstream culture which was fueled by neurotic repression and aggression which the psychotherapist William Reich had warned of as being unhealthy for mind, body and emotions, sex was brought out of the dark closet and now enjoyed as being beautiful. His work focused on the healing nature of the orgasm individually as well as for the collective health of society. I find that the ripples of energy and "body rushes" of a psychedelic experience are very similar to the feelings of orgasm as well. The return of some of the more archetypal pagan and naturalistic values of appreciating a fuller appreciation of natural living likewise freed sexuality from the selfishness, manipulation, lust and power trips of the "straight world". A refreshing beauty flowed into sexual relationships in which free love equaled free energy. Freedom was the undercurrent for the emerging psychedelic culture whose individual mandalas weaved into the bright patterns of the hippie lifestyle. Such experiences likewise integrated into my own world view as reference points for a healthier society beyond competition, greed and oppression.

To neglect the pleasure principle in political activity often breeds a fascist expression as William Reich eloquently wrote about. Fritz Lang in his 1927 movie Metropolis which eerily foreshadows the mechanized control enslavement of a world lacking spiritual roots and says ""The mediator between head and hands must be the heart!". And the social/political activist Emma Goldman said in 1923 and later paraphrased by 60's counterculture Yippie activist Abbie Hoffman, "If I can't dance,

I'm not coming to your revolution". Love is always the law for me as is compassion, empathy, and justice. Spirituality cannot just be a pie in the sky but grounded as well in our present relationships including our selves, other people, life forms and the planet we live on.

The Hopi Indian prophecy talks of a time when the world will be in chaos. Much of what we take for knowledge will be swept away as will many of our usual reference points. For anyone to survive this great upheaval, it will be important to know where one's food and water come from and who of like mind would be your tribe. I feel such a time might be well upon us. And even if not, these are still vital reference points to be always aware of.

My family and I are growing organic food and live in an area of many like minded off grid people who follow the way of the heart and live simply so others can live while leaving a soft footprint on the earth.

Karma is usually considered an individual journey. But it can also be perceived as a relationship of self and others. We come and leave this life alone but in another sense we are also part of what we call our family. That nuclear family unit is also a part of the "family of mankind" as well as with all life forms. That relationship then connects us across even wider branches of time and space as we connect to a universal consciousness which also includes our ancestors and our children's children's' children, we all are a part of Crossing Karma Zones.

ASSORTED POEMS AND REFLECTIONS

During our stay in Greece there were ongoing social challenges which at times swept a wave of depression on me as well as moments of self analysis in adjustment and integrating solutions. Being aware that many of the bleaker moments were only momentary shadows, here then is a sampling of that time period.

ASSORTED POEMS AND REFLECTIONS WRITTEN
WHILE LIVING IN GREECE

TWO STEPS OF SPIRITUAL GROWTH:

1) The exoteric religious practices of the masses
2) The more esoteric practices beyond external
   rituals and prescribed procedures of devotion).

Letting go of all standardized paths, rituals, etc., and blending directly with Spirit.

QUOTES:
"Everyone Backs a Winner Until He Loses"
"Dead Babies Don't Grow Up"
"They've Drained My Blood And Thrown Me In This Remote Tar Pit Barely Clinging"
Today is one day closer to the rest of your life.
A Fertile Mind is Full of Shit
Live your dreams or be starved pursuing your nightmares
"Life is a like a harbor, we land and get handed scripts of dramas to play temporarily and life goes on and after we leave, it still waits until we dock again in return".

Clutching onto a clear jar full of broken pieces of myself I am no longer the chameleon I used to be. Blending with so many hues of people's hopes, fears, and inflexible perspectives has bleached out one of my own colors and compromised myself expression.

Our lives are but a memory fading across time. Our future memories are carved in the permanent moment of now. Even as we interact in the reality of our activities, this substance will be nothing more than an image we can one day look back on (or decide to look past.) Be Here Now and Be Happy. Perhaps through Passion and ecstatic states of consciousness, we can cross over this veil of precious images into more intense Realities while learning to recycle our time beforehand.

There was a time when my life was breathing the vapor of inspiration and seeing beauty through vision. Today my life feels as if crafted by the chisel of pain. Faxes that never come, children that tell me to shut off the "lousy rock and roll music"; wife says only later we'll make love, mother who curses my birth and a variety of characters who somehow feel nurtured by sucking up my heart and soul without even a thank you.

BODYWORK
Always on the sweat and soil of our bodies drop remnants of memories, hopes and experiences. All the traumas of broken hands, broken hearts and broken homes. Castles are buried under shacks of

topsoil to be recycled in future dramas. Only our joys and intimate moments cast reflections off the wings of angels who can lift us past this deep sleep. When you touch someone's hand, your touch goes deeper than their heart to the far reaching temple of their soul. In the flicker of the two skins merging you can hear a lifetime of grasp and release; strokes and punches; pain and aspiration. A wise body worker can follow this journey with Love in acknowledging these creative processes of Life's manifestations while also, with humble dedication, weave and stretch the parameters to allow more Light to shine and penetrate through the clouds of the other's mirroring the face of God.

(a poem inspired at a memorial service for Theodoros. As my mind wandered between an angel icon and two pretty girls glancing over me as just one more feelingless redneck in the crowd):

If my heart were an angel
And your eyes said to come
We would fly together darling
Drawing rainbows past the sun

*

If my heart was a Love Song
And your ears quivered in its rhyme
We would dance lost in rapture
O Bliss lost beyond Time

*

If my heart was a porthole
For you to walk on through
In heaven our bodies would by lying
Bathing in refreshing morning dew

*

If my heart was a touch
And you its sweet embrace

We would flow into forever
And Love's Divine Communion always taste

❦

I never found the right time to take out
The garbage in my head; rusty oil spills
That hopes have slipped apart on
And sharp cracked glass thoughts
Which cut my dreams into painful pieces
Of memories.

❦

I took my life into the Shadowland
And was frightened by its familiarity
to the people who live there.
The Joy is promised to me later.
But does later ever have an expected
Time of Being.

❦

Whether I've killed myself through
Self-inflicted suicide from a lifetime
Of accumulated wrong choices and
Compromised behavior or died a quiet victim
In a tomb of random statistics.
I suffer nonetheless in this clock-less hell.
For is there not death in the rejection
Of one's expressions; the deflating
Of one's inner passions
Which have weathered the moments
And now were waiting to unfold?
Slipping by, no longer linked as manifestations
Of soul but as the fading, muffled cries
Of Pained Dissonance in a street choir dirge.

❦

Like a ship lost at sea
I look for shelter from the turmoil at times
In the deep harbors of sleep
Only to find my exhausted mind and body drifting help-
lessly into the next day.

Often I look at the old Christmas card picture of us on
the wall and fail to realize that those now looking strangers where once us; had different dreams and expectations.
Where, when and how did we lose each other. Surely the
faces in the picture wouldn't recognize us either.

BURNING BUSH
    The burning bush intrigues me as it did the Hebrews long ago.
Like Moses I thirst to go to it up the mountain and feel the radiance of
God up close. But unlike Moses I lack the courage to pass through its
portal of transformation. Not because of the fear of what my quest will
come across (some of which I've previously glimpsed) but in the even
more profound fear of what my search might not find. What if God is
not infallible after all and the infinite kingdom be only and endless
and hollow journey. My fear would be to find that even God searches
for the answers. Lucky perhaps were the Hebrews who knew of this
portal but found comfort instead in domesticated apples of faith rather
than biting from the Forbidden Tree of Pretentious Knowledge. Jesus
could thus be viewed as the Messiah after all. Perhaps he too saw the
abyss and proclaimed the ways of salvation as a loving trick to silence
our concerns. There is comfort in not being lost by oneself but together
with a group just as honestly lost as you. However when you find your
goal, the one you seek is just as lost, then begins the deep Fear.

Certainly people can learn to translate the worlds of any language.
However, translating the intentions of the Heart is a different story.

Even among those who speak the same tongue, similar sounding words can have different meanings. One can even experience the exact emotion that someone else tries to convey through language. Language is usually a mental key to the program, an access code, a cue for the heart to open its own ears that can reach out and touch the feelings of another. I have found that even with a limited vocabulary of another language, you can connect with deeper levels of communication in practicing this art of listening and responding from the heart.

HOPE

My head feels stoned like an ancient ruin
Carved from excavations of pain.
Being around most people for me feels like erosion.
Like waking up every day to a time card.
The only thing holding me up fits like a coffin.
I feel awkward. Like a suitcase left behind accidentally
By a passing bus tour.

PAPER TRAILS TO NOWHERE

The strong winter winds blow but our sails still remain down and we continue stuck-unable to move on. More vital than morning prayers, we inquire desperately about the faxes. The right ones never come through and the day sinks before it even starts. Growing stacks of useless paperwork write my own obituary. I'm tired of playing hide-and go seek with life. A scavenger in a day old Easter egg hunt. Without our wings I am no longer a family hero; not even Prometheus whose sacrifice at least was appreciated for the freedom spark he brought to the tribe. My sacrifice is generic bound. Yet I still cling to hope. The selling off of our property-our future- so we can live today. "In the land of money-without any, you might as well be dead instead." An awful rhyme whose missing stanza I need to find.

FINDING IDENTITY IN A CHANGING WORLD

One of the problems of identifying with tribal/national/historic identity is that one's ancestors and glorified cultural roots might not find today's society too agreeable-even though they occupied the same setting and identified themselves by similar nationalities. The past was appropriate for those who lived it as are the present footsteps of today's inhabitants who now live there. The Greeks of earlier time might find it more to their liking to being today's Turks or Albanians who today's Greeks perceive as enemies. Although different eras of people inherit a relatively similar environment, values can change dramatically from one generation to the other. Social change moves faster and faster and even within a lifetime these changes can be quite volatile. In my brief half a century of life, I have perceived the 50's to be a decade of innovation. Lots of gadgets were invented to dramatically change people's lifestyles. The 60's continued into exploration and experimentation. More radical ways of thinking accelerated these changing lifestyles-stretching even further the boundaries of what is possible. The 70's, 80's, and 90's solidified the discoveries through marketing and intimidation into a new order. Radical growth again became grounded in technology and consequently the need for money to consume the intoxication of its images. The explorers found it culturally unacceptable to follow unknown states of consciousness within anymore but rather become more socially interconnected in a new world order of growing global markets to sell the same products and ways of life to.

For me growing up as part of the 60's, my generational values seemed to be "peace, love and simple living" with an emphasis on "saving the planet." A few years later it seemed that young people discarded altruism and "dropping out of the system" in pursuit of high paying jobs and materialism. Thus I find it very awkward living in the same society I grew up into. Perhaps someone living in another time/place (Rome for instance?) would envy the "I, me, mine" oriented 90's whereas I might feel more at home in a Native American village or pagan tribe. So when honoring our nation's past and its ancestors in order to be honest, we need to be aware of cultural/social history as well in choosing to be proud or not.

While helping my daughter with her weekly Greek vocabulary class, I myself picked up an interesting lesson pertaining to language and how it defines culture and consciousness. The word for the main part of the altar a priest conducts his services in church is called the "Trapeza", and it probably has a long historic linguistic stem reaching back into pre-Christian temples as well. This word

"Trapeza" also is very popular in secular conversations and activity, but it has nothing to do with what goes on in church. Trapeza's most common usage nowadays means "bank" and probably generates more respect and devotion in contemporary Greek society (as throughout the "modern world") than the lesser used same word for spiritual activities. Such an obvious split might not be coincidence but a bold statement of modern society's worship of money on the new alters of man-the Bank. To believe otherwise is viewed as heresy and insanity. Consider if someone today would walk down the street burning a bundle of money. Rather than being viewed as a personal statement, his community would both be angry at such an act (why not give it to me!) and call the psychiatric board quickly to have him evaluated.

Have we really evolved as a culture past the medieval dogs of Feudalism. We still owe our allegiance to warlords, presidents and prime ministers who protect/expand their interests economically by promising us cheap consumer goods in exchange for loyalty and blinding ourselves from being concerned that our consumption is taking away the life of starving people in other parts of the world.

JULY 1999-IDENTITY QUESTIONS

We are like players in each other's karmic dramas. In order to grow, learn and evolve, we need to disentangle from all the roles and go off the stage.

As one's language changes, so does one's relationship with an experience. As different emotions develop in the relationship, so does a different vocabulary in the dialogue. Eventually what once perhaps seemed intimate now feels foreign and strange. It feels awkward to talk in the relationship or about it with the same words. Similarly new relationships can develop with what was once familiar with a fresh passion and exciting conversation.

As the shoreline of death approaches, the cry of ego is loudest.

The mind is a deadly serpent

What's the difference between a saint and a great artist like Jung, Hesse, Kafka, Dali, Hendrix - they all perform miracles.

We paint our rooms the way we see the world. The colors soak into the Heart as an offering from within to the God beyond.

People love an artist for expressing the magic in his soul. And the artist in turn feeds and grows his talent into filling even more love based art in the Universe. And for all people who can be as extensions of God creating a life full of love-everyone is an artist and the way they express love is their art.

The biggest money making drug of the decade might well be the legal by prescription "Viagra" which is advertised to the "sex drug panacea" to cure male impotency. Just as our technology can erect steady, tall buildings, this wonder drug guarantees even elderly men a penile erection. Quite an ego blast and certainly another step in removing the sex act from the wider scope of love making. No more need to worry about stroking, touch, tenderness and foreplay as men will transform themselves into the "dildos" they metaphorically want to be. The triggers will be pulled and the "game" conquered. The hypocrisy of this charade can be evidenced in comparing the issue of another drug which also was available by prescription awhile back, MDMA. With no harmful side effects, many psychiatrists and therapists were promoting it as a "love drug". Couples taking it together would share evenings in loving harmony, conversation, and emotional contact with each other. The sexual act was not the primary focus as the whole evening expanded into a sensual experience. Love making became an enriched and exquisite union and journey that included long lasting orgasms for both partners. Yet MDMA was attacked with vengeance and quickly made illegal by the peddlers of stress and frustration. For a couple using MDMA would rekindle or magnify their love for each other and radiate happy emotions for long periods of time. Having sex with Viagra however actually leads to prolonged sexual dissatisfaction. With no need for tenderness or foreplay, the male can "get his rocks off" but still feel at a loss for the missing ingredient- Love. The main issues are that we do not really want happily satisfied people walking around in love, but prefer instead stressed, frustrated people craving one more wonder drug. MDMA could with only two sessions open up a loving relationship while "V" at $10 a dose will be used over and over by emotional addicts who will never understand the ways of love and sexuality balanced by the gestures of tenderness.

It hurts not to be viewed as a hero in my sacrifice as Prometheus bringing fire to his tribe. I crucify myself to continual abuse to protect my family, but my efforts are never appreciated so I feel alienated-a stranger.

With so much mention of our approaching end of times and imminent Apocalypse, it is interesting to note how similar contemporary Western sense of time bends into a circular pattern like paganism rather than the linear "progress" of scientific materialism. God started from nothing and all roads lead back into that same nothing. Early Christian prophets would talk of future times as if they were "present-time" revelations. This same concept of being beyond the parameters of time could very well be the same link that psychics plug into. And again perceptions "beyond time" add another crack in the illusion of the linear time model and perhaps even exonerate Nietzsche's "myth of eternal return." Ultimately though, as the Christian time sequence fulfills the destiny of the "end of times," we do travel around in one very large circle back again.

Practicing Christian love is a very prevalent assertion with most local church goers around here to identify proudly with. But how far does it go and is it just one more cover up of quite different an attitude. Would a Christian love another human who is not a Christian so much as to look humbly past the Ego and be happy if his brother's road to God, even though quite different than his, would still be a "true path". Would Jesus Christ bless a Buddhist on the path and be happy that this person's belief lead to enlightenment. And one step further, would the Christian have enough love for the other persons to not relate the other person's salvation to his own? In other words, if the persons would say "Hey, I have found God realization and enlightenment", would the Christian break through his own biases and without even starting the usual mode of proselytizing "only through Jesus Christ can one be saved" be happy that this person found God. Must God always look like us or should we look like the much wider mirror of God.

If we are all children of God, for someone to be violent to another would be akin to committing suicide. We all are connected together to the same family tree. When our brother and sister are happy, we should be happy. If they feel pain, we too should feel their pain and moreover, as self conscious life forms, offer them food and satisfy their needs. For their needs are likewise our needs. By killing off even our own species, anytime we are responsible for the starvation or other forms of death of another, we are committing suicide. "I art Thou" and "Do unto others as you would have them do unto you" are two sides of the same Truth.

DARK DAYS AND DARKER BOMBS

In the closing year of the millennium, doomsayers are especially keen to point out how the "signs of the time" prove the end of humanity is soon upon us. It is just as easy to point out however that wars and pestilence have been a common part of our historic record-whether being swallowed regularly by dinosaurs or the mass deaths during the "dark ages" and the cause of alarm today is no greater or worse. But irregardless of the global and historic perspectives, when you are living near a situation of widespread death and horror, it is quite understandable and realistic to believe in these apocalyptic scenarios. During the period that I am writing this entry, such hell on Earth is manifesting in nearby Yugoslavia. Although I am sure some kind of political conflict has been occurring there for many years, the real time nightmare for these people started about a month ago (March '99) when the so called "civilized" European nations of NATO and their leader, the equally dignified United States, started mass bombings which have destroyed the whole country. Schools, homes, roads, churches, factories and people have been slaughtered. Even the refugees have been bombed as they were escaping in what many reporters describe as worse tactics than Hitler deployed. And as the economic indicators like Wall Street climb higher during this period, most Americans seem to support the "war is good business" philosophy and raise little protest. A far cry from the large anti-war demonstrations during the Vietnam invasion. The mask seems to have slipped off and the American eagle shows what a blood thirsty bird of prey it really is. And for a major country with such a relatively short history, how much of a culture beyond Mickey

Mouse and Dow Chemicals does it show the world - the genocide of the Native Americans, the enslavement of the Africans or dropping napalm on helpless Vietnamese. With no more cold war fears, the US empire has declared essentially that it can do anything, anywhere and at any time. Ah, but does it have the power to restore life to those it kills? Does its royal mandate of invincibility include the courage to exchange the bombs for hospitals, care packages and help for the oppressed? And what of the in-shock and in-pain refugees from the Balkan wars just a short way above the Greek border? People who one day had homes, jobs and personal belongings including family heirlooms from many centuries of living in the same ancestral home which now lies devastated and dust because of a young pimple faced pilot pushing a trigger of a "smart bomb" ordered by a brazen U.S. president trying to prove his own and America's potency through the dictum that "might makes right".

The Greek countryside which has been swelling from encampments of Albanians and Kurds now is preparing for the many thousands of Serbian homeless and hungry refugees moving into this direction. The usually hospitable Greeks are now suspicious and frightened of these outstretched hands lying in their olive fields. The bright colors of spring wildflowers are now shadowed by this grey shade of desperate humanity. Dark clouds of chemical residues also cross the borders and bring us closer to the horror. Today I have noticed several insects lying dead on their back perhaps from breathing now this air of death.

THE SUN COUNTRY

It is no coincidence that within the word ELADA, we see the word "ELIOS". The blessed land of the sun god. For Greece to look right, it definitely needs the sun shining on its landscape. Many other places such as the foggy US Northwest, misty London, and spooky Norwegian fjords carve their identity through shadowy veils. Greece, however, suffers from such concealment. Its passion and beauty need to shine with the sun as too the joyous attitude of its people. On cloudy, rainy days, Greeks are especially miserable, sick and angry. The horizon looks lifeless and the ocean without life. How different the feeling on sunny days when gods, nature and people dance together in celebration of a bright creation.

TWO FACES OF THE FLAG

Having come from the US of A, it is a righteous feeling indeed to represent a country way above primitive racial attitudes towards any one set of people. In the US all people and life forms (except for one's own) are equally hated, despised and to be manipulated.

Today is the feast day of St. Constantine and Helen in Greece and throughout the Orthodox Church global community. The importance of these saints was in the establishment by the not yet sanctified but otherwise warrior king of the Byzantine empire, Constantine, of Christianity as the state religion of the Empire, a deed quite a few hundred years in the making from the time Satan presented the same bridging opportunity of spiritual and secular to a worldly naive Jesus. The relatively easy going Jesus thus taught side by side with a variety of other spiritual perspectives at the time and some books even speculate that he followed a personal pilgrimage to Tibet- studying spiritual practices in a Himalayan monastery. Classical Greece had been a polytheistic society satisfying the variety of human experience, consciousness, preferences and needs with a pantheon providing numerous gods and goddesses. To a decaying Roman empire ravaged by relentless internal and external problems, its choice of Christianity as the official state religion answered many of its concerns over social cohesion, stability and control. By following a state religion in which present worldly needs/demands/attachments are secondary interests in deference to another worldly Paradise, a populace would be less likely to demand rights, revolt, or take the world and its problems serious. In fact, pain and oppression were favorably looked upon as positive Christian values to endure-quite a contrast to the more hedonistic pleasure pursuing peoples of ancient Greece and Rome.

Another social evolutionary materialization of Christian dominance at the expense of its polytheistic Greek background was in its contemporary view of death. When there are many faceted gods and points of view, all approaches have potential consideration and subsequent spiritual merit. Views of death, for example can be quite extensive and ultimately can provide a mortal human with insecurity because of the many possibilities. However with the Christian Messiah's "victory over death", a satisfying anthem was sounded which quickly spread in popularity. Equal in spreading popularity was the messianic fervor of the new state religion, Christianity, to wipe out all vestiges of other religions, cults and spiritual philosophies. By proclaiming the "only right way," there would no longer be insecurity or concern among its followers over the eternal question having to do with the meaning of life and fear of death. Future holy wars would have as their deeper motivation a crusade against this historic fundamental fear. The brotherhood of man under one God was actually a call for an anonymous elimination of the fear of death and choosing to no longer consider its inevitability. For such a grand charade to work, there had to be a anonymous consent. Emperor Constantine capitalized on delivering this state enforced religion to a deeply grateful people-perhaps even more popularly accepted than its founder Jesus who never perused a worldly kingdom and who thus had a more limited and persecuted number of followers than the new Byzantine Empire.

RELIGION

The basis of Christian belief is thus a hoax. For followers to be so insecure as to vanquish the opposition, their zeal stems from hypocrisy. Since they don't believe in an eternal life or in consequences/karma towards a future life, the door is open to oppress others as well as practice blatant greed and lust while still avowing to be "good Christians."

As the historic experience of Christianity drifts further away from its founders teaching of love, peace, forgiveness and harmony, the need for the Christian hoax to perpetuate and institutionalize evolves to even more desperate proportions. No longer sustained by aggressive assault on the world and its life forms through externalizing the individual's insecurities, the new Adam cultivates destructive tendencies into internal horizons. The contemporary Christian thus destroys the planet, then his social relationships, and finally his own self. Narcotic drugs, alcoholism and self abusing behavior are what distinguish a Christian (not necessarily a follower of Christ) from many other religious paths such as Buddhism which promotes a conscious awareness and non-destructive attitude in principle of compassion towards all life forms.

A PAUSE FOR AN ESSAY ON "IGNORANCE"

Amidst what seemed like a never ending merry go round of traveling for us, I occasionally savored moments of deep reflections such as on the idea of 'ignorance". We all are at some point "ignorant". Ignorance is simply what the unknown, that part of the universe which we don't have any awareness of. By acknowledging our ignorance, we are simultaneously lifting these restrictions and shedding some light into this previous darkness. There is freedom thus in acknowledging our ignorance. Ignorance in itself is not evil. A flock of sheep held in a coral are secure in "knowing" that they are protected from hungry wolves. However they could be ignorant of the fact that their owners will soon be slaughtering them for food. Another flock of free-grazing sheep dying from thirst would benefit from knowing that there exists a large water spring on the other side of the mountain. For them ignorance becomes an agony of life and death. A desperate human whose unpaid bills are about to throw him and his family "into the street" would benefit in his knowing which would be the winning race horse to bet on and thus restore comfort to his life. His ignorance is one of turmoil. These three examples of ignorance show a variety of perspectives. As people attach faith for answers outside of themselves, their fear or laziness gives governments and advertisers the ability to lie and manipulate them through such ignorance.

With such an expansive universe, it would be pompous and chaotic to suppose we could eliminate ignorance. There is always more to learn. Admitting ignorance is the first step to knowledge which then becomes the first step towards freedom. Ultimately as one keeps learning and becoming freer, we move closer to the Divine. God (or) supreme consciousness is perfect knowing and ultimate freedom. Since the universe is held together by forces of Love and Harmony, our life's purpose is to always be moving closer to the Divine Center of the universe- The Soul of God: god, love, freedom, harmony. As we keep expanding through this process of freedom, we let go of mistaken thoughts and emotions and filling these gaps with new knowledge of truth (God) thus becoming more god-like and dropping off decayed ego matter. If love is not part of our movement past ignorance then this error becomes not of letting go of ignorance but actually becomes more ignorance and restricted by less freedom. In practical terms you examine what has been learned and what you can do with this knowledge. Is it a movement with love as the navigator? What did the knowledge of building an atomic bomb create? What about Hitler's "undoubted knowledge" that the Aryan race had the right to kill millions of inferior Jewish people to fulfill destiny? What about knowledge that mass advertisers have of how to fabricate needs among people to sell them unhealthy products?

GREEK POSTCARD 1

I came to explore my family "roots" but instead have found settlements of New Growth. A New Age and a New World. Budding bloodlines growing under the shade of traditions.

GREEK POSTCARD 2

Although ancient and indigenous to the Greek identity, dwindling now are the sights which once filled the landscape of rugged donkeys and sprawling sheep which even recently were able to compete with the toys of Hephaestus the godly metal welder and Mercury, bringer of speed. New gods have now evolved. Powerful Toyota and Volvo compete with the relics fallen from the grace of ancient paths and march instead on road spaces freshly paved for the sirens to sing Greek accents of the American dream. Their death laments, mirologia, are drowned out as the dominant carvers of history sculpt new deeds, memories and icons.

I know nothing; I express only that which chooses to grace my moment of eternity with.

Man's creations eventually change roles and invent the man through the cultural environment he lives in. The medium of transformation sculpts society through these inventions. Computers become the goal of our human identity far beyond the a tool that we direct. The information age speeds up our inputs past the ability of our humanity to adjust or even completely process. We become a wrongly suited machine out of control without means or access to slowing this adjustment.

We are all memories waiting to be forgotten!

BITS AND PIECES:

People become for us a definition created by our own reaction to them. This reaction being a fluctuating ratio between their own independent essence and our own inner creations. So if I stay in a bad mood, otherwise inert people seem a bit abrasive. Egoism, reaction or energy exchange.

The world we live in today is very different than in the 1960's

Then it was a matter of choosing which perfect utopia to be.

Today it is simply a desperate escape from the ongoing collapse of the world as we know it.

Holding on to any secure stability is a utopia in itself.

Time eats up younger men's' dreams which get lost as if put off for a future of a wiser time which never becomes. An older man is only when he's loved such a life of lost and unfulfilled dreams. To float in the flow of eternity, always pursue your dream for, if not, we would never live the dream and thus not be alive but only one more lost or wasted dreams.

CONSCIOUSNESS IS A MEMORY FROZEN ACROSS THE STRETCHES OF TIME

TIME IS THE GRAVE DIGGER THAT WORKS OVERTIME

SOMETIMES IT'S HOW YOU'RE SEEN THAT'S MORE IMPORTANT THAN HOW YOU SEE (Sunglasses, etc)

Follow your dreams - sleep longer!

VARIOUS EDITORIALS I WROTE FOR MY NEWSLETTER:

COMPARING MUSIC OF THE 60's AND TODAY 8/13/12

During the golden time period of the late 60's and into the '70's, a wonderful crack occurred in the mainstream matrix and it felt as if the heavens opened and the angels and muses graced us with the sounds of transcendence, freedom, healing and happiness. Musicians were the shamans or at least conduits and channels in the experience. The vested interests were shaken as they were not prepared for such a lifting of the veils. Psychedelics were a key as was the baby boom feeling that we could change much. But the empire struck back. Radio stations were bought by conglomerates and ended the support which, even though was pop and trendy, the flow was still reaching the masses. Advertising promoted other stuff which was insipid in all ways including meaning, art or spirit. Embalming fluid for the sheeple. It no longer looks possible for a class or large group revolution of the arts. As with all such counterculture movements, it will only happen for individuals seeking a higher path or for small neighborhoods of like minded folks under the radar. For me it leaves a tear of sadness and anger in my soul when I see so many young "hippies" listening to so called trance or hip hop heart music which is dribble and empty calories. Hendrix, Beatles, Pink Floyd, Traffic, Miles Davis, and thousands of other known or more eclectic musical groups left maps of consciousness which can at least still be accessed by seekers of spiritual nutrition. Like Hesse's magic theater in Steppenwolf, the magic theater is not for everyone. During the 60's and 70's music looked like it was paving the way from everyone. Such is the irony and paradox as now that we need truth more than ever, people are not triggering to music for the transformative potential and holistic pleasure it can bring.

I don't want in any way to generalize as, in every generation, there are individuals and even small gatherings of clear eye and soul people that are sharing love and also in tune to not following the pack of fashion. But so many of the kids that try to look like some vestige of counter culturists are more in line of drain-bows instead of rainbows and who they follow show-men instead of shamans. Let the blind lead the blind and the fools invest in a lost future of nonsense. Trampled underfoot by media and glamour guides. Not wanting to be attached to their loss, I want to ignore them as they are nuisances and much better use for my time such as enjoying nature or music that has meaning, depth and is real instead of a coca cola machine next to an amplifier with some idiot called a dj with a fancy name and piercings playing so called trance trash. As Woody Harrelson once said in the movie White Men can't Dunk, "are you listening to Jimi or hearing Jimi?" But then again if what is happening today is basically a contemporary mating rite, then it might have validity as such. But please don't call that garbage music.

First of all, for anyone to respond, they would have to have some sort of depth to understand the substance of the issue we are discussing. Not a cliché like "all parents say their kids music isn't as good as what they listened to". That begs the question. I would be happy listening to lots of great music that independent artists are performing throughout the world. What we are concerned about is the actual lame, meaningless or new age masturbatory self elation garbage. I would be happy to listen to old time spirituals, or even cave men drumming in a cave than the stuff we are talking about being mass marketed. Like gmo non food, it's gmo non music. Frequencies that have been analyzed for limiting creativity, spirituality and health are being pushed on the masses as one more step towards an embalmed populace of the new world order.

During the late 60's and early 70's, music was experimenting with eclectic sounds and freedom of expression. There was also a merger of rock, blues and folk. Social issues such as racism, poverty, the Vietnam war, environmental desecration and spiritual pathways were all being sung about and the message clearly defined. Today besides the militaristic sounds of much of techno and the aggressive self adulation tone of popularized hip hop, the new age mantras of love seem to frequently regress to appointing each other as gods. goddesses and the crowning audacity to say we are the ones we have been waiting for. It's wonderful to be aware of such archetypes and influences but we need to also be aware that besides the organic food we grow there are children on the other side of the world starving and having their families blown up by drones that denialists are saying not to be aware of. Why don't "heart songs" talk about the suffering caused by the greed and war mentality of the power brokers as well?

⦿⟋⟍⦿

MY FACEBOOK RETORT ON PSYCHEDELICS AND THE HIPPIE CULTURE IN THE 60's 5/26/13

David, as you like to send critical remarks to many of my postings, I would look forward to your alternative suggestions. As I have also told Ray, even though I have a certain thread of beliefs that I circulate, it is just as important for me to see alternative postings because few issues are just black and white. Thus we learn from synthesis of opinions or at least to empathize with others that feel differently. Such is freedom of expression and the opportunity to keep learning. Please attach alternative points of view articles in the comments whenever you want.

My most active times of political and cultural expression was during the 1960's. I grew up in the embalmed Eisenhower 50's and lived in a small racist town in the south. My questioning the status quo and developing a core awareness of how aggression, greed and ignorance were toxic undertones of our society were clarifying my intentions and grounding my beliefs.

With the matrix of vested interests being as thick as what it was, I feel it was the spread of psychedelics through my generation that gave rise to the impetus of social change. Set, setting and intention were the key words in such usage and, as in all facets of humanity, stupid people misused these keys in stupid ways. But that does not mean we threw out the baby with the bath water. A new way of seeing past the illusions allowed a wider questioning of the social order that served to both see the world clearer as well as crafting portals to activate positive change.

Historical revisionists might be quick to discuss the shadows that fell over the psychedelic revolution but never should it be forgotten that we were just as victimized by not only or naive innocence but also by the empire striking by in full force. Harassment and imprisonment on all levels was the norm that led to an inquisition that still goes on today.

The youth movement of the 60's had two divergent forces: religion and politics. LSD, mushrooms, peyote brought a spiritual vision that was akin to the nature loving peoples of pagan times and of Gnostic revivalism of freedom. Love was spreading all around. The political factions claimed that the "stoners" were denying the very nature of the material game that led to poverty, war and oppression. Many of the hippies were heading for caves to work on their auras while others chose to go to smoky cafes to argue who was right: Marx, Trotsky or Mao. The common ground was thin but it was in that line of merging political awareness with psychedelic vision that evolution found a thread to grasp onto.

Again we are still sort of free to say what we believe and as you find fault for people taking acid, I would trust them more than guys in suits downing cocktails and figuring out how investing in drones and private prisons is a sensible reality.

MY DISCUSSION OF PSYCHEDELICS AND POLITICS DURING THE 1960's 12/30/13

In the interest of freedom of information and the opportunity for us to share a variety of points of view, I am thankful to all comments expressed in my postings, even the ones that I do not fully agree with. Several of my recent postings on regards to the positive benefits of psychedelics on our culture were meant by the criticism that the hippie movements and LSD destroyed the political revolution that was gaining momentum in the 1960's. My own beliefs on this issue come from my own personal experiences as a civil rights and anti-war activist during the 1960's as well as a traveler through the psychedelic dimensions. But besides my personal views, it is an issue that I wish to express to the wider community for reflection and commentary. Especially to those that were actually "there at the times". Except for the images capitalized by media dictates to the contrary, at least in the earlier years, there was a holistic blend of both perspectives in the movement. The materialistic separation of activism, heart and soul was a non-issue. Machiavellian pressures to distort both the hippie and the political movements led to the division bells which eventually challenged both. Hippies and activists became bulls eyes to be attacked and crippled by the vested interests. Draconian drug laws, bogus health and insurance violations and a general disregard for the Bills of Rights did not differentiate. The FBI and CIA used undercover agents and lies to discredit both movements and to promote hostilities between them. Many people living a mainstream life were shown a deeper connection to their own selves and others through psychedelics and subsequently dropped out of previous negative attitudes such as racism and mass-consumption. The power structures were definitely alarmed. The integration of the psychedelic experience led to respect of nature and an awareness of injustices that had to be dealt with.

Subsequently, many of the political and activist groups eventually criticized the hippie movement as not using force to tear the system apart. Much of this fuel for the fire was again planned and orchestrated by government agents. When Timothy Leary escaped his 30 year prison term for possessing two joints, he joined Black Power leader Eldridge Cleaver in Algeria who in turn kicked him out for talking of spirituality as a root for total cultural change. Peace and Love as well as Justice. So which approach was right to me is as mute a point as in asking which arm is more useful, the right or left.

The hippie movement had an emphasis on leaving the corrupt mainstream system and creating a communal back to the earth lifestyle as an alternative which rejected traditional institutions such as school, commerce, banking and the rest of the corporate wheels that kept oppression in business. Was this not a political act? And even in the move out of the system, hippies still would be a part of anti-war marches as well as presenting a model of a way of life which likewise was definitely as much a political act as throwing rocks at cops who would respond with weapons of mass destruction and incarceration. I was there and still have my own scars and traumas from those moments.

Can psychedelics cause major changes in someone's psyche? Tons of books and workshops can make claim on all aspects of this proposition. My own opinion is that changes can only happen in a direction that an individual's soul and inner dynamics have a predisposition for. The CIA experimented with such substances as ways of spying, creating truth serums and Manchurian candidates. Some people cracked while others rose to angelic levels of universal love. Likewise a country strangled from deep spiritual roots was given access to the liberation of experiencing spirituality as well as expanded humanism and consciousness. Martin Lee's excellent book Acid Dreams documents many of these instances.

So yes, possibly LSD was part of an agenda from higher elites to be used for another weapon of brainwashing and control. But in the hands of Kesey, Leary, and psychedelic music, the results were far different than what was expected. Most kids at that time had no interest in civil rights or stopping wars. But the wave of expanding consciousness brought a significant number to a breaking through those walls and becoming activists in many dimensions. The so called hippies that might be viewed as not being politically interested were quite possibly never going to demonstrations any way. But by the same token, their changes of perception and even lifestyle made a very positive difference in their lives and their relation to others.

I am very interested to hear more about the comment that LSD was manufactured by Nazi scientists. Even so, psychedelics such as magic mushrooms have been used by spiritual seekers for thousands of years. In the Amazon, shamans who use Ayahuasca are emphasizing that one of the messages of this psychedelic brew is that the world is being threatened by corporations destroying nature and that a political change is essential if we are to survive.

To neglect the pleasure principle in political activity is often breeds a fascist expression as William Reich eloquently wrote about. Fritz Lang in his 1927 movie Metropolis which eerily foreshadows the mechanized control enslavement of a world lacking spiritual roots and says "The mediator between head and hands must be the heart!"And the social/political activist Emma Goldman said in 1923 and later paraphrased by 60's counterculture Yippie activist Abbie Hoffman, "If I can't dance, I'm not coming to your revolution".

∞⸙⸚∞

"DRAINBOW SHAMANS" from a May 20, 2014
editorial in Links by George

One of the expectations of growing up in the middle class during the 1950's was that there would always be decent jobs available, adequate social services and an expected four day work week leaving plenty of leisure time. Looking at the situation today, such a projection seems like a flimsy mask of nonsense. The American dream and land of opportunity for all seems more like a nightmare within a matrix that leaves very few options for most of its citizens caught in its fly paper of vested interests. Most traditional societies had and some continue to have shamans whose duty was to enter a sacred space to connect with ancestors and to bring back messages of healing not just for sick individuals but also for sickness and challenges within a society. As such as pressing as ever in our own global village, it is heartening to see a revival of interest in shamanism. These important individuals are helping train more people in such healing work for the sake of planetary survival. In the process also lurk incidents of unethical practice and manipulation as well. Even more ridiculous are the urbanized westerners who go to exotic places to learn how to be a shaman but only to find a politically correct badge of glamour and personal "consciousness expansion". A true shaman would be one that would understand the need to help the community in every way possible. In psychedelic journeys, an intention leads to a vision which can well be an affirmation of helping the environment and all its people. A modern day shaman should thus also be a political, social and environmental activist on behalf of earth and all its life forms. How many people that come back from expensive workshops and Ayahuasca retreats that have "connected" with the energetic dimensions of the forest stay to defend that same forest from loggers? How many go back to their homes and join activists in ending fracking to the earth and the spraying of pesticides and destructive to all life and land GMO seeds? For those that actually fully integrate their experiences, life becomes more personally expanded and their vision of helping others becomes more than just creating a new age playhouse glossed in denial and ignorance. Often people on new-age retreats feel that once they have been" enlightened" they have succeeded their purpose. Important situations are marginalized as disposable news. Backs are turned on "negative issues" such as drones and starvation while prancing around with imported ethnic clothes, bird feathers, inspirational and impressive names of who they studied with as well as their own new name after their initiation. Facebook pages are filled with statements of "love" and pictures of flowers and cats. There are also people and traditional cultures in danger besides flowers and pets. It seems to be that the true purpose of their experiences is to now understand how all life is interconnected and must be respected and cared for. Sure being a hippie in the 1960's (and for some of us even now) included taking plenty of acid, reading tarot cards, living in homemade tipis and taking part in ecstatic tribal festivals. But at the same time, we marched against wars and put our bodies in front of logging trucks. Dividing definitions of people such as hippies, rednecks, yuppies, bikers, surfers, vegetarians, etc. is another line of separation that we need to heal. We are all humans. For instance a human who prefers to a vegetarian diet. A human who rides a bikes and likes to surf, etc.. We need to focus our egos not for personal glory and not wear so many "badges" or totems. We are one and let not one of us go to bed hungry or sleep with drones massacring their families or being thrown into private prisons of torture. A real human family does not segregate old from young, black from white, or wealthy from impoverished. "By the grace of God go you and I", and only when we quit looking at the lines of separation will we end our collective blindness that is bringing humanity and our planet to the brinks of self-destruct. And yes, it is vital to have holistic visionaries that include lovers, poets, healers, friends, smiles and even saints.

As a final word, George writes, "Our journeys took us through changing scenery and led us to many interesting people, experiences and situations. The karma zones we crossed were well integrated as you can see in this final photo of where the family odyssey led us to here in Hawaii."

ABOUT GEORGE DOUVRIS:

George Douvris was born in Raleigh, North Carolina, August of 1951. As an only child of first generation immigrants from Greece, he grew up in Raleigh and then continued his college education at the University of North Carolina with a double major of Psychology and Political Science. During the 60's he experienced firsthand the racial civil rights struggles in the South and then anti-war activism. The psychedelic cultural generation brought him to Woodstock and then a move across country to the San Francisco area where he met his wife Stephanie. Together, they have traveled over most of the US and extensively in Australia, New Zealand, Fiji, Thailand, India and Europe. They have also lived many years on the Hawaiian island of Maui, the Rocky Mountains of Montana and a small village in Greece. George has been a holistic health educator, home school teacher and radio station presenter. He also has been editing a newsletter called "Links by George" which reaches over 10,000 people and expresses his eclectic interests in shamanism, spirituality, political conspiracy, environmental concern, healthy living, visionary arts and music. He now resides along with his wife in a rain forest setting on the Big Island of Hawaii. Their son John is an excellent musician and along with his wife Ariel are living on the farm. Nicolette, a skilled landscaper and photographer likewise lives near them. Their youngest daughter Sophia is a licensed massage therapist also now lives on the farm.

George still writes and is a social media activist who can be contacted through Facebook.

OTHER BOOKS BY GEORGE DOUVRIS

CROSSING KARMA ZONES

CROSSING KARMA ZONES is a lively journey of growing up in a Greek-American family in the southern part of the US during the 1950's and then coming of age during a backdrop of civil rights unrest in the 60's. George found purpose in anti-Vietnam war activism and then followed the exciting hippie trail to the Woodstock festival and then a move to Haight Ashbury in San Francisco. "Sex, drugs and rock and roll" navigate into spiritual growth with an eclectic

integration of humor and reflection through the many exciting passages of experiences across space and time.

A FEW OF THE BOOK REVIEWS:

"A wonderful read for someone like myself, as I've pretty much been there and done all that but for a lot of the same reasons it would be a good read for practically everyone. It however, if you're not a Boomer you can find much truth about life in general and how this will relate to you and your experience. As in any good read it's funny and sad. It's full of love, hate, learning, exotic locations, the lies we're told by family, the church, the government and by friends, but mostly it's about the truth, and what that really means. Whether you are right, left, in the middle, man, women, straight or gay, whatever, this is a damn fine read and you should run, not walk, to Amazon and buy yourself a copy."

ERNEST STEWART. Philosopher, writer, musician and blog maestro of *ISSUES AND ALIBIS*

"Essentially a story of the clash of cultures between a post war immigrant Greek/American family, steeped in conservative European traditions and old fashioned family values, and their son George, an ever questioning hippie in pursuit of meaning. George's journey would ride the 60s 70s counterculture revolution that was sweeping across the U.S. and the rest of the world...Why this book is important, it offers a hands-on historical archival window into one of the most fundamentally inspiring cultural & spiritual renaissance of the 20th century. The hippie sub-culture broke onto the world stage in the sixties, intervening in a long held traditional war ravaged conservative pathway of western culture."

PETER TERRY. Activist, author and music festival promoter in New Zealand, *NAMBASSA*

"My friend George Douvris has lived a long and colorful life, growing up in Raleigh, NC, moving to San Francsico at the height of the hippy era, eventually settling in Hawaii but only after making many sojourns of length in other exotic locales. Along the way he threw himself into what the culture of the day was offering up, and there was plenty to sample from, drugs, sex, and rock & roll, and George pushed the limits of them all. Fortunately (for him, and us) he was borne Greek, and with his heritage seemed to come a certain level-headedness, so although immersing himself in numerous experiences and mad-cap adventures, he was able to maintain a certain bemused perspective about it all. As a result of that, I suspect, he managed to survive and even thrive through some turbulent but always interesting times. Those times were the same ones a lot of us lived through, and those who did will see much of themselves in George's stories. We all got through it, somehow, and here George shares his recollections, and his wisdom, the result of a life lived fully, not always easily, and not always cautiously, but always consciously. His distillation of his life lived is well worth the read."

DENNIS MCKENNA author of THE BROTHERHOOD OF THE SCREAMING ABYSS is an American ethnopharmacologist, research pharmacognosist, lecturer and author. He is the brother of well-known psychedelics proponent TERENCE MCKENNA and is a founding board member and the director of ethnopharmacology at the Heffter Research Institute, a non-profit organization concerned with the investigation of the potential therapeutic uses of psychedelic medicines.

"George Douvris remains a born-again hippie, despite an attempted exorcism by a Greek Orthodox cleric when Douvris was a long-haired, marijuana-toking adolescent. His ingested psychedelic alphabet soup consisted of LSD, DMT, MDA and STP, helping to fuel a spiritual revolution, while rock'n'roll became the soundtrack of his life. There was an evolutionary jump in consciousness, and the sense of community it created continues to survive. George's adventures and misadventures in this book provide the back story of his current calling. He serves as a diligent, online, ongoing archivist of the counterculture, as the seeds that were planted in the '60s are still blossoming now."

PAUL KRASSNER, is an American author, journalist, comedian, and the founder, editor and a frequent contributor to the free thought magazine THE REALIST, first published in 1958. Krassner became a key figure in the counterculture of the 1960s as a member of Ken Kesey's Merry Pranksters and a founding member of the Yippies.

⁘⁘⁘

"Early on, he became a gypsy soul who yearned for far-away places, exotic locales, and liberating points of view based on love, compassion, and deep respect for nature. With 60's music as his anthem and psychedelic experiences as his teachers, his watch-words became empathy, compassion, love, respect , and psycho-spiritual realization... His impressive travels throughout America and his equally impressive journeys through psychedelic inner worlds are told with wit, compassion, insight, and great love of many of the people he met in his travels. "

LEE UNDERWOOD : Lead guitarist with Tim Buckley (1966-1972); West Coast Editor of DOWN BEAT MAGAZINE (1975-1981); author of BLUE MELODY: TIM BUCKLEY REMEMBERED; poet, TIMEWINDS; pianist, PHANTOM LIGHT, GATHERING LIGHT.

⁘⁘⁘

SIGNED COPIES OF BOTH BOOKS AVAILABLE DIRECTLY FROM THE AUTHOR:
Email: gsrain@yahoo.com

Made in the USA
Columbia, SC
28 July 2022

64194844R00278